The Film Photography Handbook
3rd Edition

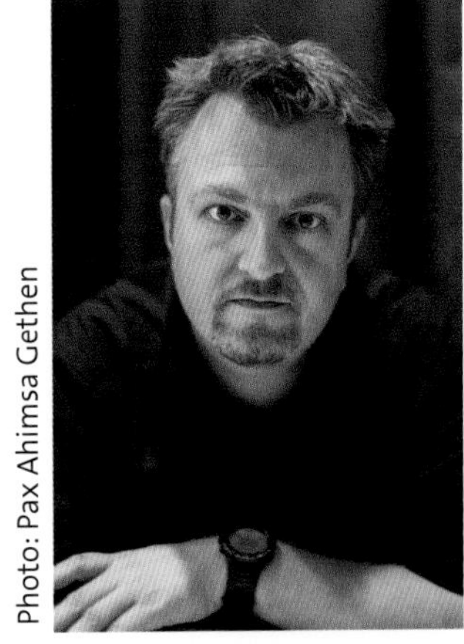

Chris Marquardt is a photographic mythbuster and the host of *Tips from the Top Floor,* the world's longest-running photography show. His photography podcasts have won multiple international awards. He has taught photography all over the planet, including Europe, Africa, North America, and Asia. He has often accompanied photographers to the world's highest photography workshop at the Mt. Everest base camp. Marquardt is a regular on Leo Laporte's *Tech Guy* radio show, which is syndicated across the United States and reaches an audience of millions.

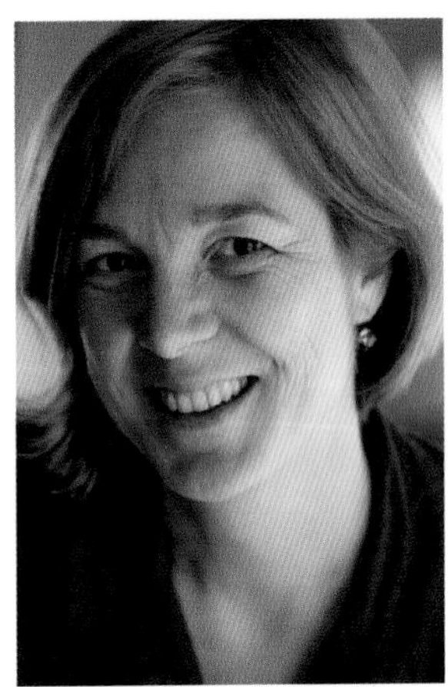

Monika Andrae is an award-winning online specialist. She is also on a mission: to make the increasingly technical photography world a little more creative. Andrae's podcast, *Monis Motivklingel,* has a large number of followers and her blog is a thrilling mix of everyday and creative topics. Together with Chris Marquardt, she co-hosts the Absolut Analog film photography workshops.

Chris Marquardt
Monika Andrae

The Film Photography Handbook
3rd Edition

Rediscovering Photography in 35mm, Medium, and Large Format

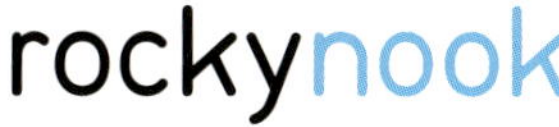

**The Film Photography Handbook, 3rd Edition:
Rediscovering Photography in 35mm, Medium, and Large Format**

Chris Marquardt, Monika Andrae

Editor: Maggie Yates
Project Manager: Lisa Brazieal
Marketing Coordinator: Katie Walker
Translation: Almut Dworak and Jeremy Cloot
Layout and type: WolfsonDesign
Cover design: Helmut Kraus, www.exclam.de
Graphics: Peter Marquardt

ISBN: 978-1-68198-941-9

3rd Edition (1st printing, May 2023)
© 2023 Chris Marquardt and Monika Andrae
All images © Chris Marquardt and Monika Andrae, unless otherwise noted

Copyright © 2022 by dpunkt.verlag GmbH, Heidelberg, Germany.
Title of the German original: Absolut analog, 3., erweiterte und aktualisierte Auflage
ISBN 978-3-86490-917-7
Translation Copyright © (2023) by Rocky Nook. All rights reserved.

Rocky Nook, Inc.
1010 B Street, Suite 350
San Rafael, CA 94901
USA

www.rockynook.com

Distributed in the UK and Europe by Publishers Group UK
Distributed in the U.S. and all other territories by Ingram Publisher Services

Library of Congress Control Number: 2022941891

Printed in China

Table of Contents

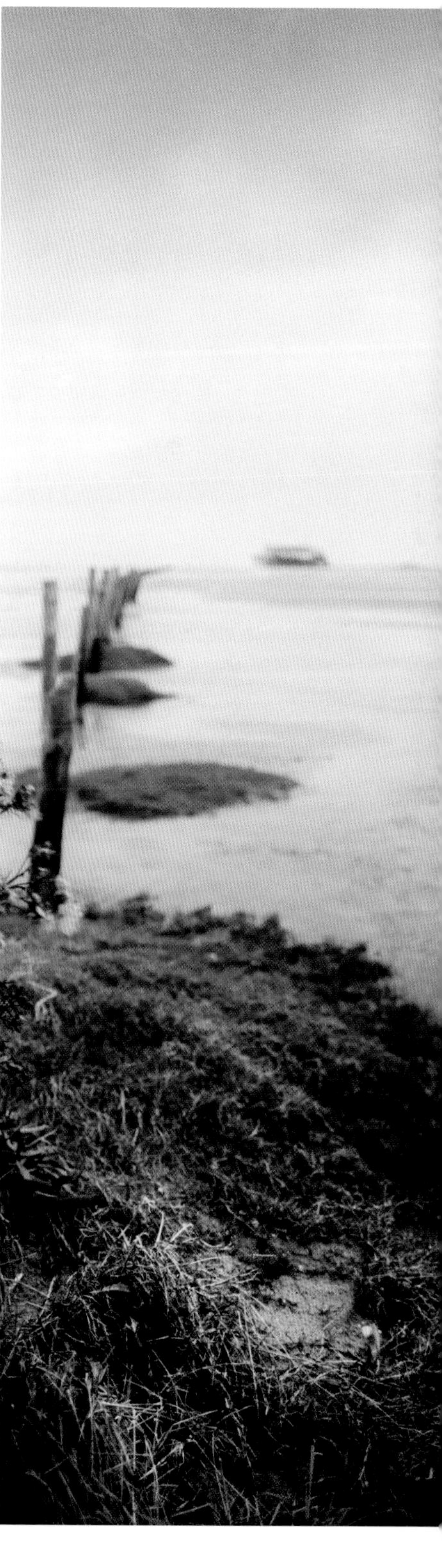

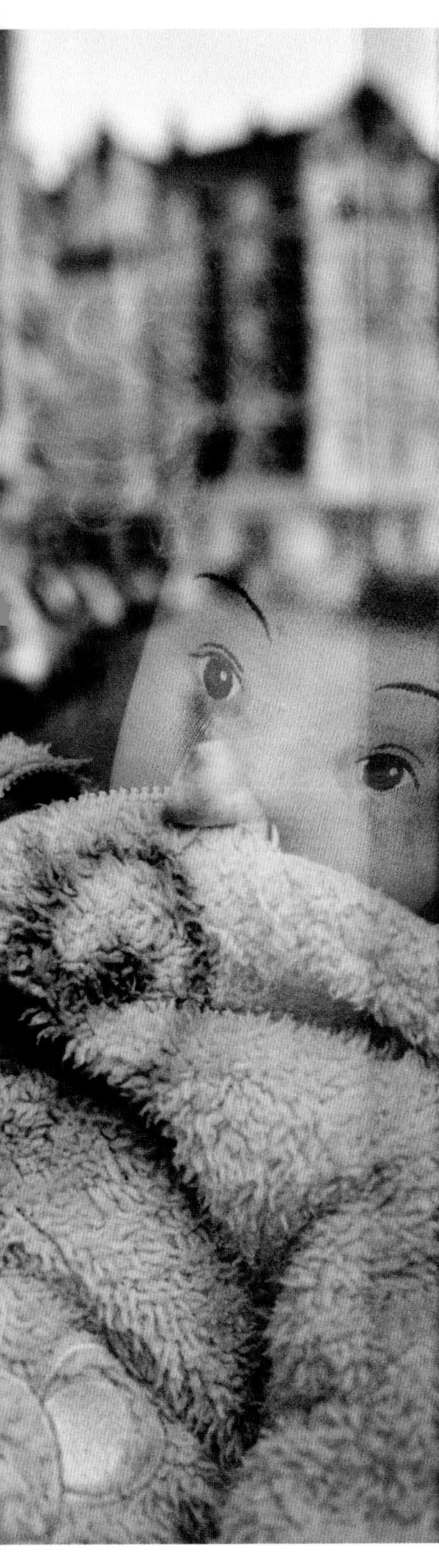

7   Post-Processing   191

8   Presentation   243

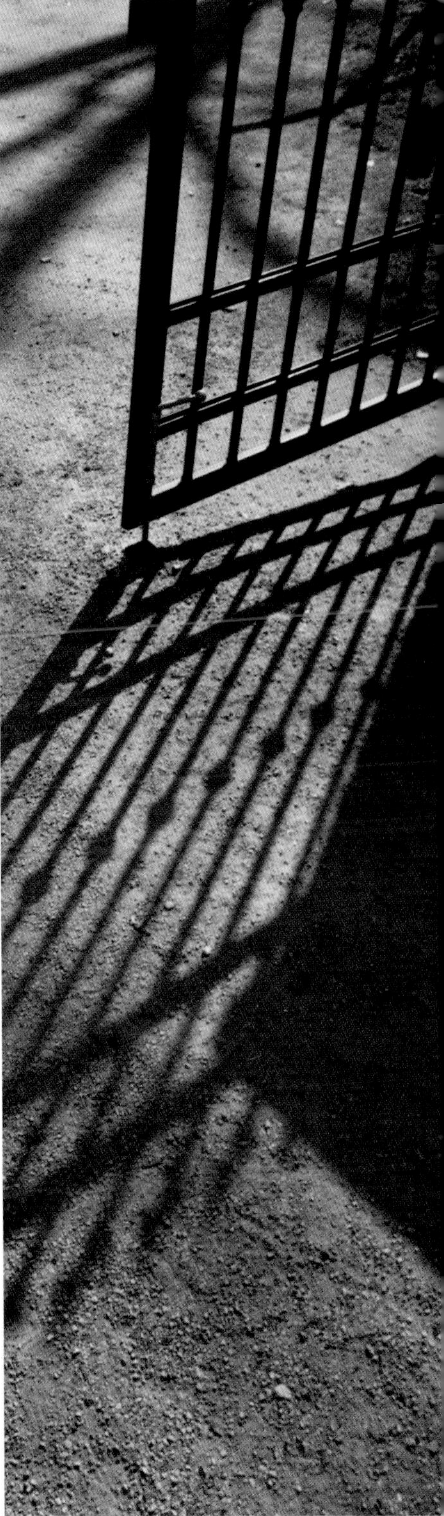

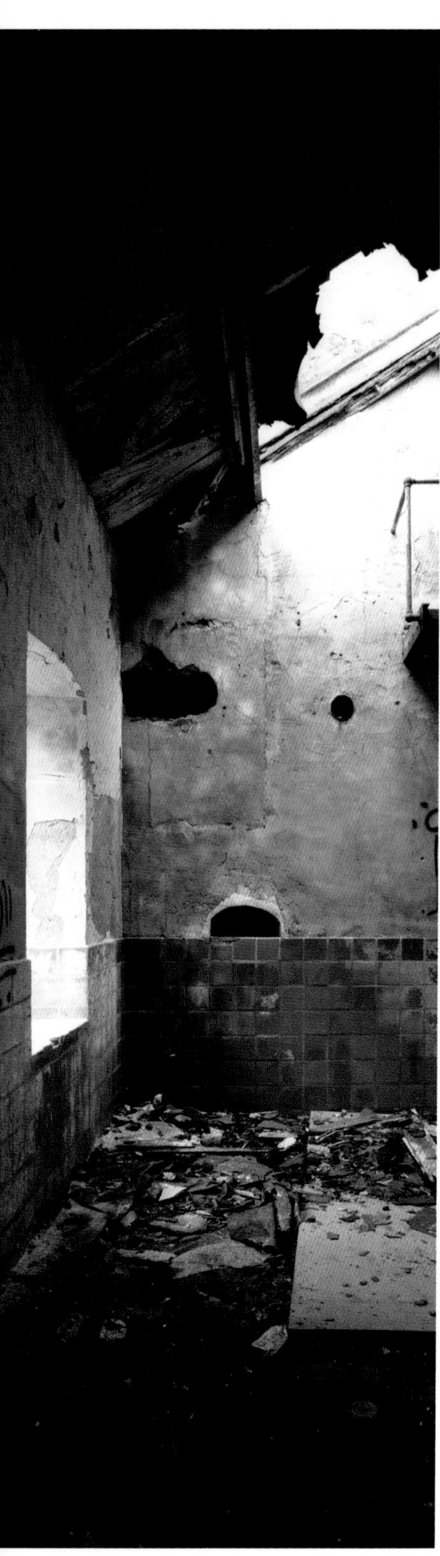

Welcome to *The Film Photography Handbook, 3rd Edition!*

In terms of photography, we are "analog natives." Our teachers were single-lens reflex film cameras. As digital photography began its triumphant conquest, we did what many others did: We stashed the analog film photography treasures in the cupboard and spent the next few years diving deep into the digital world. As hybrid beings, we are happy with the transition to digital, but still think back to consider our origins with film.

The Film Photography Handbook was born from our rediscovered passion for film photography. If you suspect our efforts are driven by nostalgia, you are only partially right; our motivation is more about greater closeness to the subject matter and the excitement of digging deeper into a different medium. The skills you'll learn for film photography will open new doors in many areas of the world of digital photography, as well. As an added bonus, working with the limitations of analog photography has shown us new, creative opportunities for shots that we hadn't thought about for years.

Podcasts

We produce various podcasts about photography, some in English and some in German. These cover topics ranging from film photography to visual creativity to an in-depth look at emerging technologies and trends. Our podcasts are all free-of-charge, and you can find them by typing our names, *Chris Marquardt* or *Monika Andrae,* in your podcast client's search box (or wherever you get your other podcasts). We are always thrilled to welcome new listeners.

Preface

Film photography is one of those art forms where an enormous multitude of different opinions, experiences, and beliefs thrive. Particularly in the age of blogs, social networks, and a huge number of online communities on this topic, it's unavoidable that some of these differing opinions will clash. Finding common ground is not always easy—in the digital world, we are working with discrete numbers and defined states. But in the analog realm, we generally tend to talk about continuous and fluid boundaries between states. This offers an ideal feeding ground for voodoo and self-styled shamans of all colors.

Correspondingly, along with the accurate knowledge and helpful information out there, you will also find a lot of half-knowledge or—even worse—pure nonsense. We have taken great care to avoid all the nonsense here. Our book is completely rooted in the knowledge we've gained through our years of experience. We don't claim to have all the answers to all the questions. But we are always curious to learn more, and we constantly ask "Why?" We give reasons and background knowledge about the topics in this book, and in those areas where this book cannot offer enough room for digging more deeply, we offer sources that can provide more information.

Does Film Still Exist?

Let's answer the big question right away, the one that we as film photographers hear the most: "Is film still around at all?"

The answer is a very loud *Yes*!

Yes, film is still around

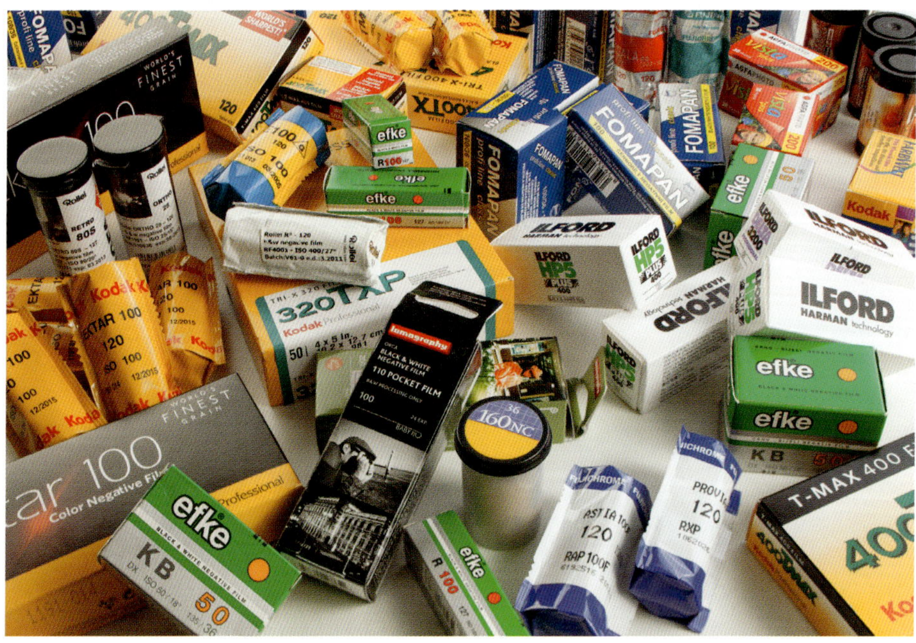

Sure, film has already seen its heyday. Around three billion films were sold in 1999 and 2000—more than ever before. Around 200 million of these were sold in Germany. Some markets followed slightly behind, with film sales in China and the USA reaching their peak in 2003. We will surely never see film reaching such popularity again, but there is a growing number of people who are (re)discovering this traditional medium and appreciate working with it.

News flashes about the decline of Kodak or popular film brands such as Kodachrome going out of production stick in our memories because the news media made a big story of it. You don't see film on supermarket shelves, any more. Most drugstores still carry a small selection of film cartridges, and they increasingly stock Fujifilm Instax instant picture film. Many drugstores and other specialized stores also offer color film, slide film, and black-and-white film development, as well as high-quality prints on genuine silver halide paper. But the boxes for the paper pouches with the developed film have shrunk, and have often been replaced by printing machines with memory card readers. The digital camera has definitely taken over; film has retreated into a smaller niche.

But in that niche, it's alive and kicking.

The advancement of digital technology has not made life easy for film enthusiasts. But more than just the big names, such as Kodak, Fuji, and Ilford, continue to produce film. Some smaller companies are also still on the market. Even an old traditional film company, the Italian Ferrania, managed to get a revival through a crowdfunding campaign in 2014.

The German film manufacturer ADOX is currently enjoying a renaissance. It is one of the oldest film manufacturers in the world but has managed to transform itself into a modern, innovative company. It manufactures photographic film, paper, and chemicals in two factories in Switzerland (now taken over by Ilford Imaging) and has even built a new factory in Bad Saarow, Germany. In addition its own line of products, ADOX also continues to manufacture a line of Agfa black-and-white photo products.

Today, film is mostly traded on the Internet. Various online retailers offer everything you need for ambitious analog photography—from film and photo chemicals to equipment for photo labs and darkrooms.

Many directors still use film for shooting movies. In February 2015, Kodak announced new contracts with some large Hollywood studios, which should ensure the production of material for analog movies for many years.

We shoot both analog and digital these days, and one thing we want to avoid in this book is to split the photography world into these two camps. Both methods have advantages and disadvantages, and they are both an integral part of our photographic life. Ultimately, this book is all about photography—regardless of which medium it involves. It's about the creative process, about creating pictures that the viewer takes another look at instead of just turning the page. The process with which the pictures in this book are created is important to us for many reasons. Mainly, we want to be advocates for film photography. In this book, you'll read about our reasoning, our inspiration, and about the photographic process.

Wondering if This Book Is for You?

If you are reading this text, you are expressing an interest in exploring film photography with the intent to learn more. That's wonderful. We wrote it for anyone who is curious about using film as a medium, and looking for an alternative—perhaps new—approach to their photography.

What draws us to film photography is the joy we get through experiencing a process that has given us a deep and lasting understanding of photography. Dealing with the topic in an intensive and, above all, playful way has changed how we look at the medium in general, and also how we look at subjects. We have learned to welcome the accidental and to learn from mistakes. Not everything we tried worked out in the end. Not everything that worked out was pretty. But we found beauty in places where we had never imagined it could be.

We cannot give you a recipe for great ideas and creativity, but we would like to provide you with fresh impetus to try something different with your photography and to expand your toolbox with new opportunities. If you enjoy doing things yourself and being a hands-on learner; and if you like experimenting and losing yourself in the step-by-step exploration of a process—this book is for you. Please use the suggestions in this book as a starting point for your own experiments. Pick out the ones you like, change things, dismiss others.

... Or Maybe It's Not for You?

With this book, we invite you to explore the process and spend time testing your new skills. We enjoy playing around and are convinced that it is a good way of developing new ideas.

What we describe on the following pages includes materials and cameras that might be considered faulty, inadequate, obsolete, or not state-of-the-art by today's standards. We firmly believe that technical precision isn't everything in terms of creating a good picture. In our eyes, it actually tends to get in the way.

Not everything you try will be a success. Even photos that succeed are not necessarily going to be museum quality. Our purpose is not to show you how to make great works of art; primarily, we want to show you how to have fun and to encourage you to think outside the box. We want you to ask "what if?" If you like the result, that's enough—whether or not others share your opinion should just be a side issue.

If you are one of those people who wants to get a standardized result as quickly and efficiently as possible, you may not find what you want in this book. If you appreciate maximum precision and absolute reproducibility in photography, you can certainly achieve these results with film photography, but this topic is not a priority in this book. Our main focus is on film photography and the creative possibilities of processing negatives. We will discuss both hybrid processing (digitization) of the pictures and their digital post-processing.

The main focus of this book is *not* on traditional darkroom work. That would probably fill more than one separate book.

Thanks

We want to thank Lothar Muth for the Berlin branch of our workshops and plenty of developments and prints; Frauke and Michael for rekindling our analog fire; Annik Traumann for inspiration, good talks, and contacts; Heinz Wille for enthusiasm and pictures; Allan Attridge for invisible cameras and visible chairs; Alexander Waschkau for helping us realize deep insights within ourselves; and @baumbaTz, @Hamateur, and @klein gedruckt for app tricks from the world of Android. Also, we are grateful to Lady Caraway and Lord Coriander for every hair they did *not* shed onto our negatives.

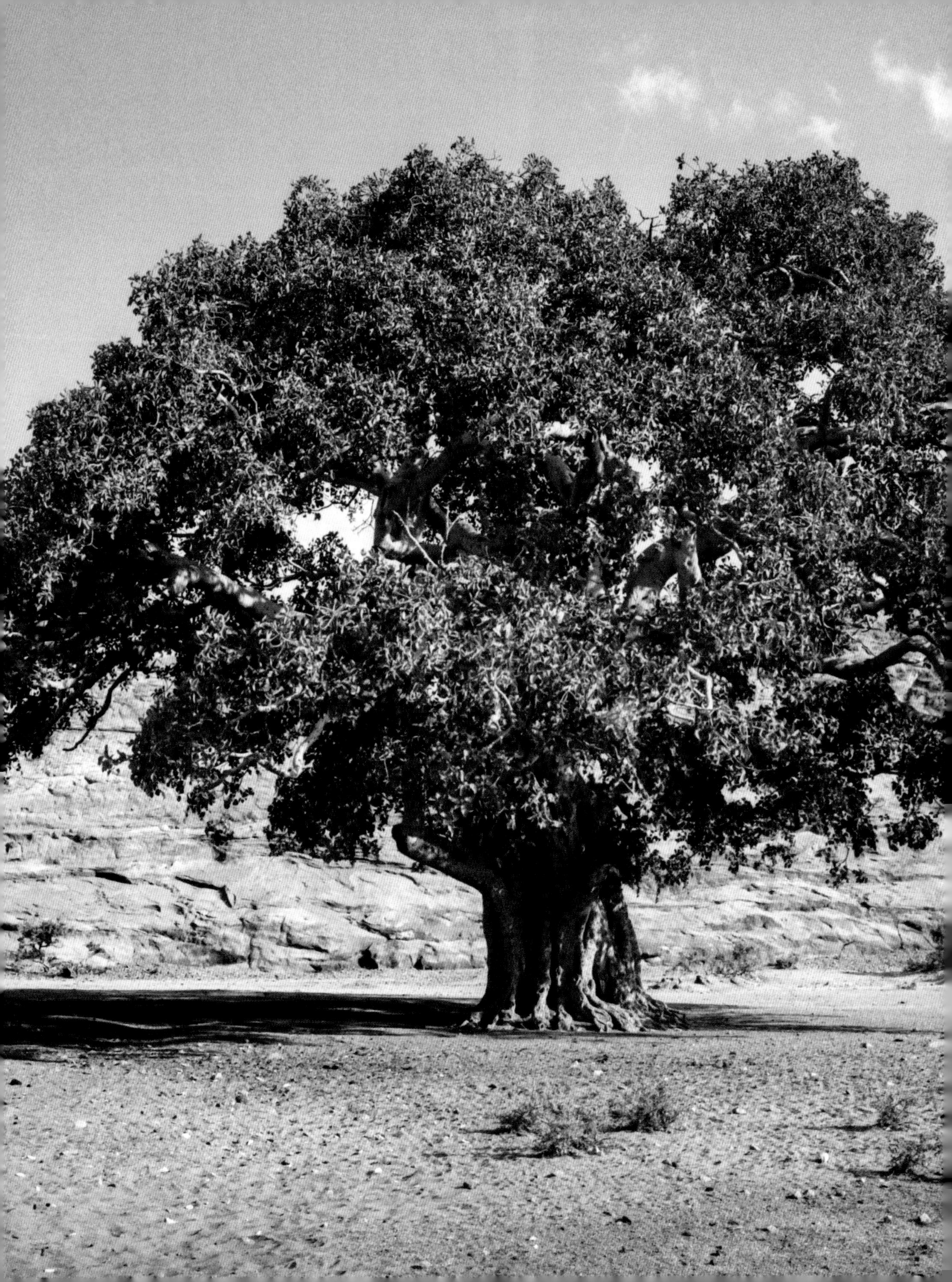

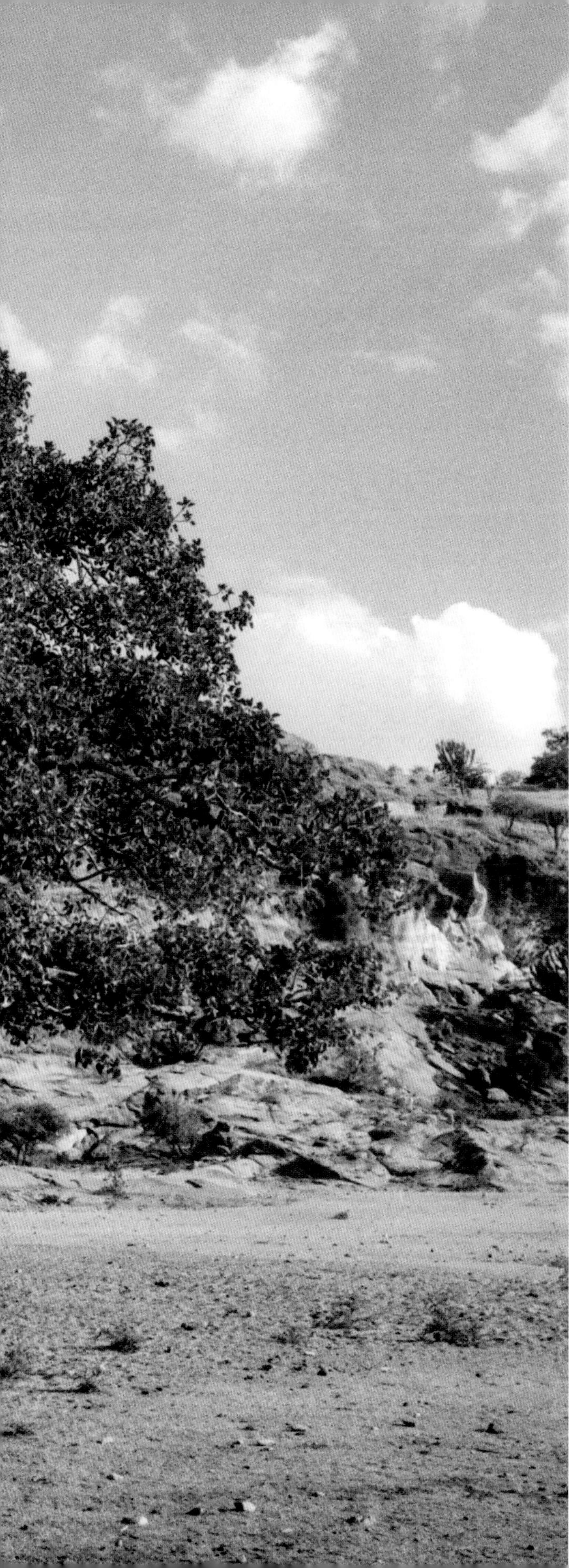

1
Why Film Photography?

With film photography in particular, people often question why we're using an "outdated" medium. Are we merely nostalgic? Or is it because being retro is currently trendy?

We like to say, "just try it out yourself, and you'll see." Indeed, there are many people who are curious about our workshops. They may not know exactly why they want to learn more on the topic, but they are always more convinced by the viability of film photography as a relevant art form after they take our workshops.

1.1   Enjoying the Process

Nowadays, if you decide to work with analog methods, despite the countless digital options, you sometimes need to explain yourself. The topic is much discussed, but still touches a nerve. Sometimes when you mention that you are taking photos on film, the statement is met with incredulity and triggers certain recurring questions.

"What can you do with an analog camera that I can't do with a digital one? Both just capture light—the only difference is, one does it with film, the other with a sensor."

"Why should I deal with the process of how the photo is taken any more than I have to? It's not relevant to the end result."

If you opt to use film and analog cameras, you do not just choose a different output medium or special aesthetics—you set the course for an entirely different process. What can you do with an analog camera that you cannot do just as well with a digital one? Both capture light, true, but the difference between film and sensor is significant. We are talking about a far greater difference than two differently colored buckets that hold water in the same way.

When working with film, you've made decisions (before any light even hits the film) that have a considerable impact on the end result of the photo. It starts with the choice of camera—its particular format, its features that might affect the picture, and its technical possibilities and limitations.

Then comes the decision about the film, depending on how much and what kind of light and contrast you can expect at the location where you are going to shoot, and how both can be used to create impact. The emulsion characteristics of the different brands of film can influence the resulting image just as much as the developer you are using. Ambitious film photographers like to have options, and before going out on a photo tour, they will decide on the combination of film and developer they will use that will best support the desired message of the picture or subject they are shooting.

You could expand this list because strictly speaking, it's not the end of the line yet: You can play around with developer temperature, tilt rhythm, and so on, without sliding into the esoteric—and that's just in terms of the development of the film and the assumption that you do hybrid post-processing. You haven't even been in the darkroom yet. This is an important and fascinating aspect of film photography: the enormous creative potential offered by the various combinations of camera, exposure, film, and developer—particularly with black-and-white film.

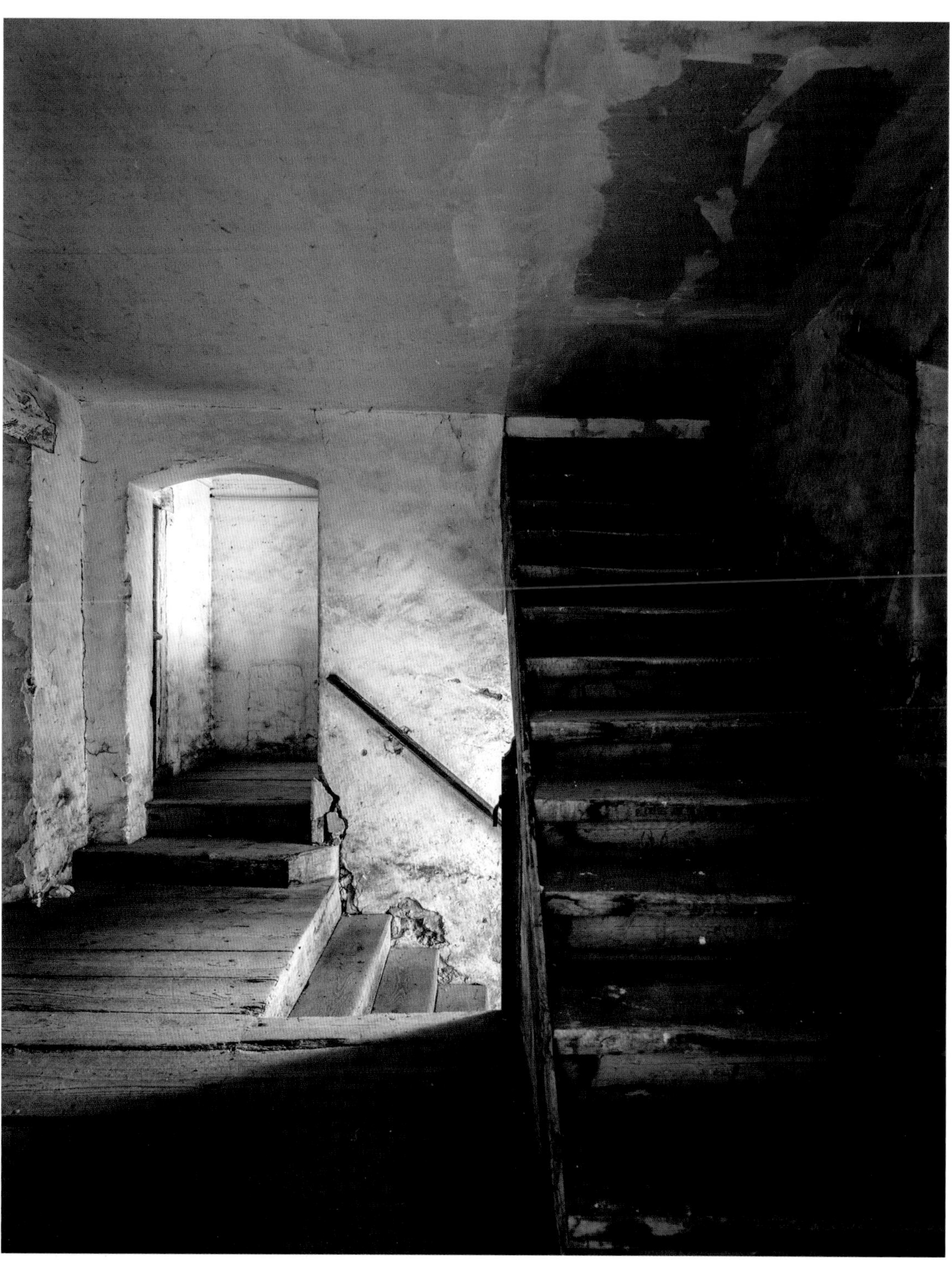

Inzigkofen Monastery, large format on Ilford Ortho Plus

If you have ever let films drown in light and then pulled during the develop stage or (vice versa) underexposed by three f-stops in the brightest midday light and then pushed during developing, you will remember that the differences are anything but negligible. If you do not consider in advance which film and corresponding exposure and developing you can use to implement your specific ideas, you either get only an average result or, in extreme cases, blank negatives. With digital photography, there are many decisions you can only make during post-processing. With film photography, you have to decide in advance. Otherwise, many creative ideas will never see the light of day. The key to working creatively lies in making the right decisions about processes concerning technical factors.

Of course, you can make it a rule only to expose films at their nominal film speed (the ISO sensitivity designated on the film) and then have them developed in a lab with any developer, in a standardized process. Then you can take the result as it is and simply enjoy what you get. But it is much more exciting to explore the deeper connections and possibilities, to find the settings and parameters that expand the photographer's options of expression to an almost unlimited extent.

The process of shooting, from manual light metering to focusing to manually winding the shutter, can be completely irrelevant to you depending on the camera type you use—but that means you miss a chance to learn more about this process. The example of the analog large format makes it impressively clear how many steps of the whole process any modern 35mm or medium-format camera does for you. Implicitly, any one of us probably knows that you have to cock a shutter before it can do its job—but you will only really grasp it if you have worked through your mental checklist before taking the first shot with a Graflex.

If you can manually focus instead of leaving it up to some autofocus function, you will be forced to think more about the subject and the elements that are really important to your picture. The same applies to the exposure: Where and at what angle do you measure the light if you don't have access to matrix or multi-zone metering with a connected in-camera database, but are brandishing an old light meter from the flea market?

Hands-on experience with the camera helps you gain a better understanding of photography, which will be reflected in the resulting photos. This deeper knowledge is certainly no guarantee for award-winning works, but the creative potential of analog processes is an area where you can dive into your hobby and leave the daily routine behind. That's precisely why the process is just as important as the end result.

1.2   Too Many Options Make You Unhappy

The digital world holds many temptations; not only do digital pictures appear on the camera display within fractions of a second, but affordable memory cards offer almost unlimited space for thousands of photos.

You can redesign pictures over and over again during post-processing. You can optimize them and even put off decisions about important factors, such as white balance and other details, until later. New camera technologies, such as light field photography, even make it possible to delay the choice of focus of a photo until post-processing.

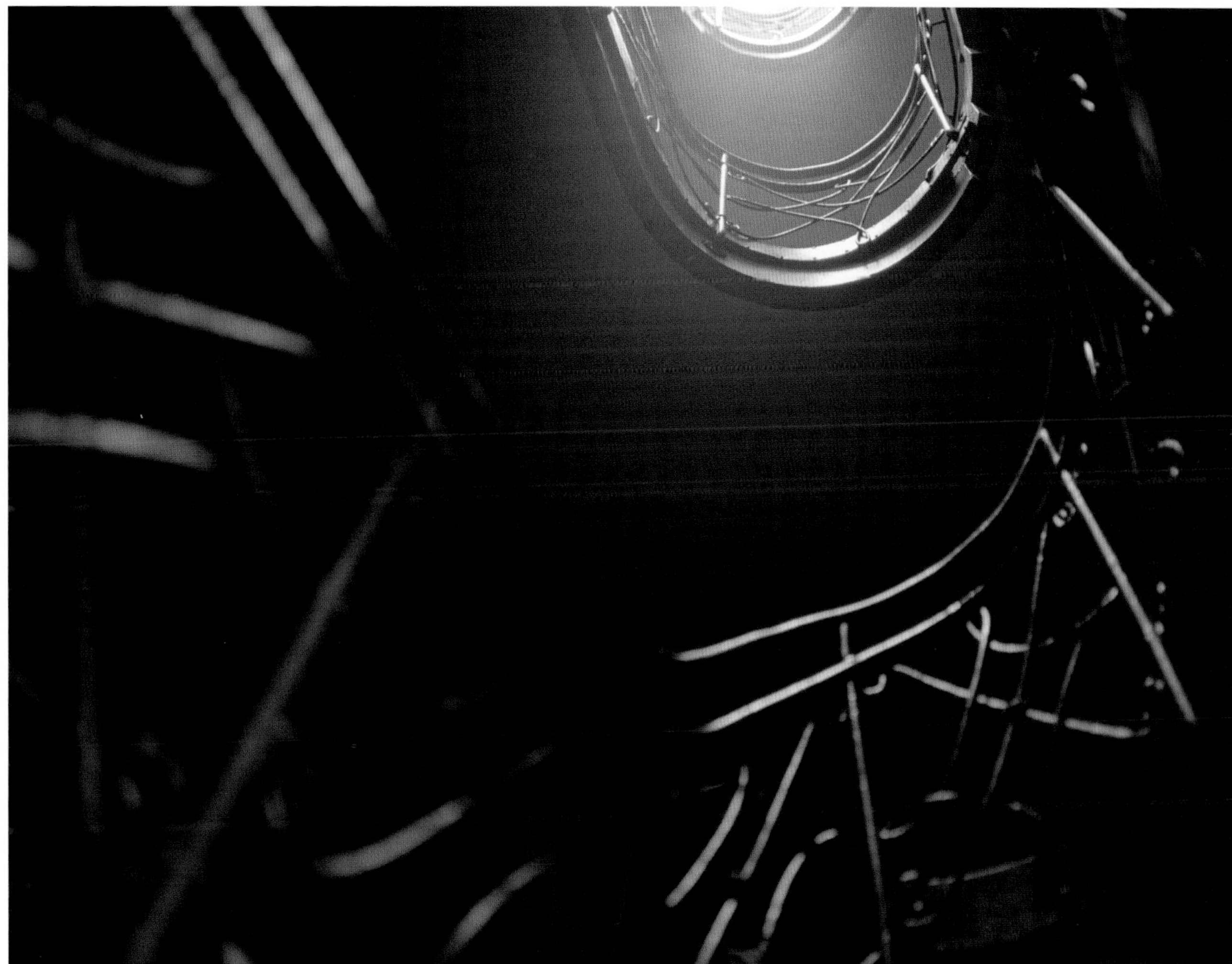

Staircase, Berlin, Kodak Tri-X in HC-110

At first glance, film photography cannot compete with the flexibility offered by digital equipment. Some things simply take longer in analog, and many decisions cannot be changed after you have made them. Once we insert black-and-white film into the camera, our world is black and white for the next 36 pictures. In film photography, we have to (re)learn to make decisions and stick with them. Many will see this as a disadvantage. Why should we limit ourselves? Isn't it true that more is better?

Not necessarily. Film photography forces you to concentrate on the essential. And that can also have advantages. The necessity to make decisions in advance not only has a photographic dimension, but also a psychological one. Numerous experiments and surveys have shown that our level of contentment initially increases with a greater number of options. But there is a point of diminishing returns: An unlimited number of choices does not necessarily make us incredibly happy.

"This paradoxical fact may surprise you at first. But many studies show this effect. The more options you have, the harder it becomes to make a rational choice. Buying a car is a good example. Today, there are countless equipment options, all of which the buyer wants to assess rationally. Studies have shown that people become unhappy if they are given more than about 10 options, and that people then feel overwhelmed. If you are asked to choose from a selection of 30 varieties of wine you will find it harder than choosing from only ten varieties. And the number of bottles purchased also decreases with the number of varieties available to choose from. This effect is constant through many studies. The desire for a purely rational decision is rather unrealistic in psychological terms as emotional factors also play a great role; for example, which make of car your father used to drive for decades or the brand of the first car you owned. People with brain damage in areas that are responsible for emotional decisions often have great difficulties in making decisions. This shows that decision-making is always a combination of rational and emotional factors... 'less is sometimes more!'" —Alexander Waschkau, psychologist

That explains why film photographers are often much happier with the results of their photography. This applies to us, too. Where we perhaps only like a handful out of 100 of our digital photos, this ratio is usually considerably higher for photos taken on film.

In this case, it also matters that film photographers often work with a very different level of care. Every photo on film costs a measurable amount of money. Unlike a memory card, film is not reusable. Although computers use electricity, the amount of developer used in analog processing is much more tangible to a person in terms of cost. For that reason alone, we almost always generate fewer rejects in analog photography than we do in digital.

Concentrating more on the process provides an important, positive side-effect: Dealing more deeply with the "how" and "why" of photography results in a learning process that is more immediate than it is with digital photography. So, the insights gained in learning to shoot with film can also be applied to digital photography. The circle is closed, and our contentment grows.

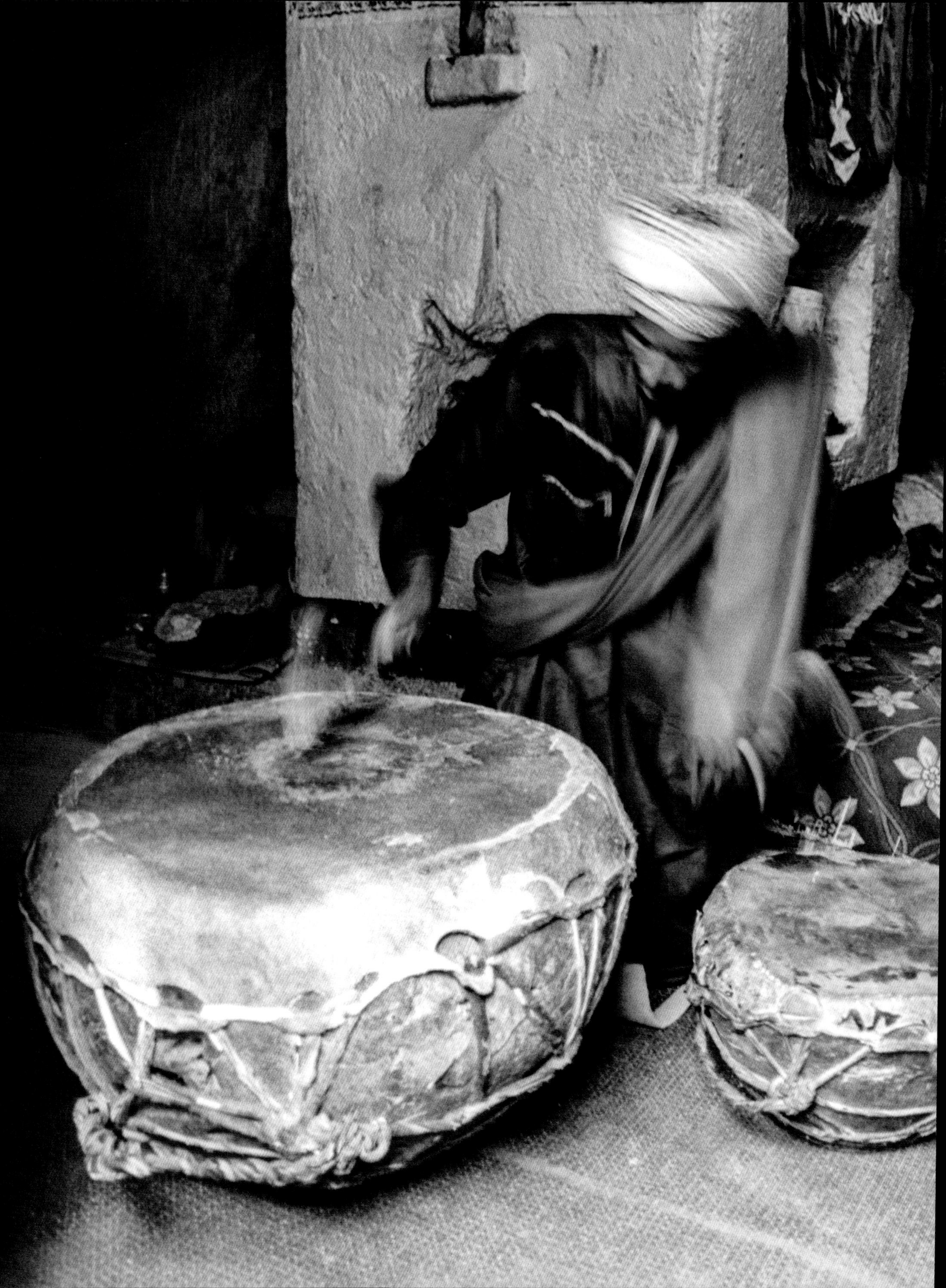

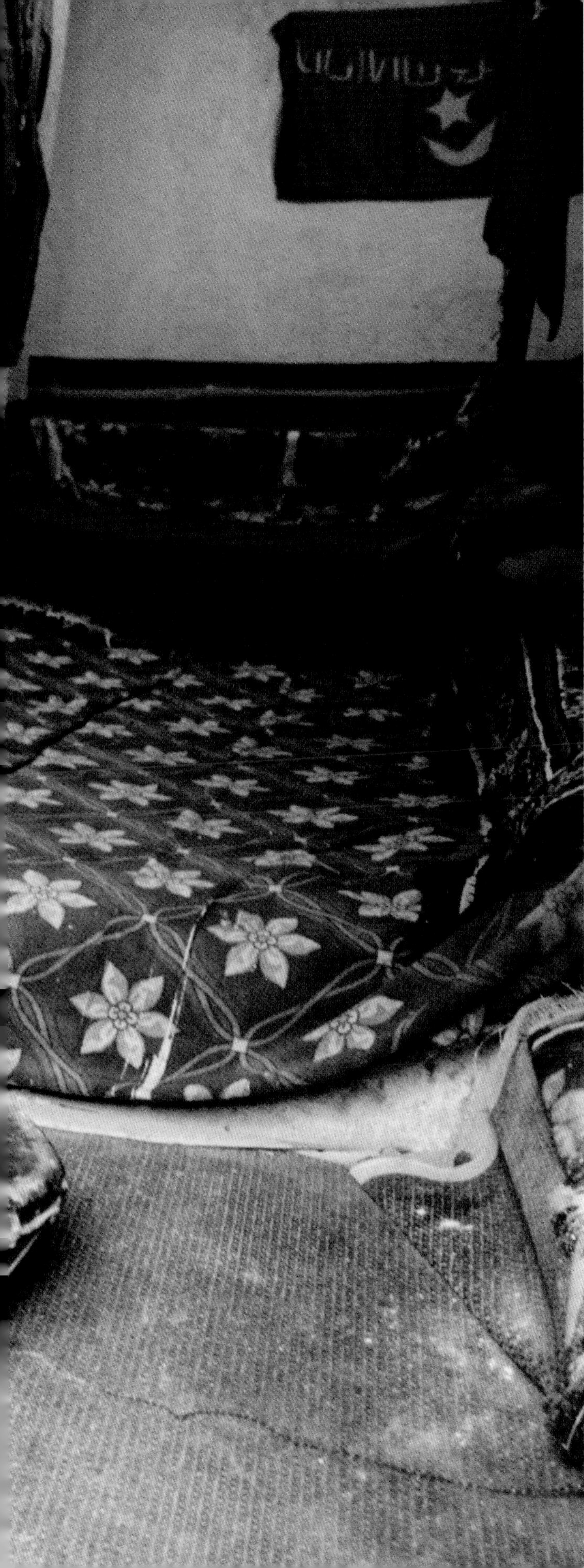

2
Analog or Digital?

People are always quick to make comparisons. In particular, the question, "How many megapixels does that camera have?" comes up a lot.

This question is not so easy to answer in regard to film photography. There is no straightforward conversion from film to digital sensor in terms of megapixels. There are simply too many differences between the two worlds. Even if we use the smallest light-sensitive units to make a comparison—the digital pixel and the light-sensitive grain of film—we won't get far. Should we perhaps talk about the individual silver halide particle, instead of a grain? Let's take a closer look at individual aspects of the different processes. Comparisons are not prohibited.

2.1 Film Grain

Let's first look at the shape of the film grain. It can be large or small, hard or soft, regular or irregular in its distribution. The grain structure of film can be completely different depending on the type of development used. Developing film (e.g,. in Rodinal) in a way that involves a lot of movement is going to highlight the film grain noticeably more than a 90-minute stand development where the film is left alone and still. Temperature, developing time, type of developer, and even the amount of movement when developing (the agitation) can turn the film into either a (crisp) grain beast or a silky-soft photo with a smooth finish.

The film sometimes shows a clear and rough grain; and other times, it shows hardly any grain at all. This is partly due to the structure of the film emulsion, which does not consist of one single layer of adjacent silver particles, as many people believe. Depending on the production process, it is usually a three-dimensional structure of several layers of differently sized and formed particles on top of one another. Kodak T-MAX is a good example. The original T-MAX had a layer of traditional pebble-shaped crystals with a layer of the new, flatter, T-shaped crystals on top (see the illustration below). The current version of the film uses exclusively T-shaped crystals.

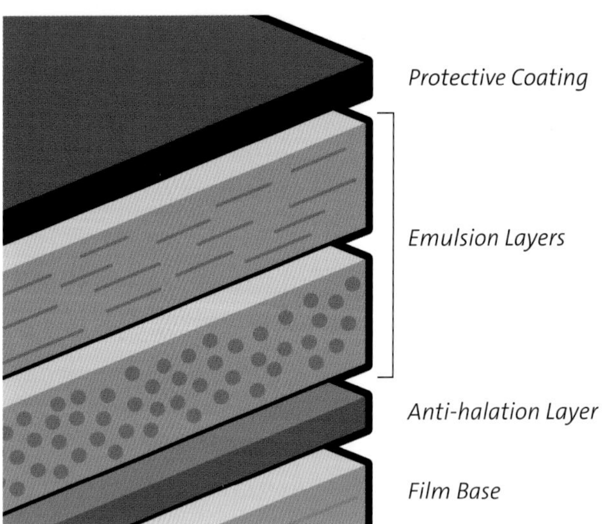

The multi-layered structure used in the original Kodak T-MAX film

If you look through this three-dimensional structure from above after developing, you'll see that what we refer to as "grain" is almost always a visual cluster composed of several particle layers.

2.2   Arrangement

If you place a digital sensor and film side by side under a microscope, you'll notice that the pixels are arranged regularly on the sensor. Each light-sensitive cell has its particular place in the grid. There are no irregularities. The grain of the analog film, on the other hand, is not regular at all. It is chaotically spread out over the entire surface of the film.

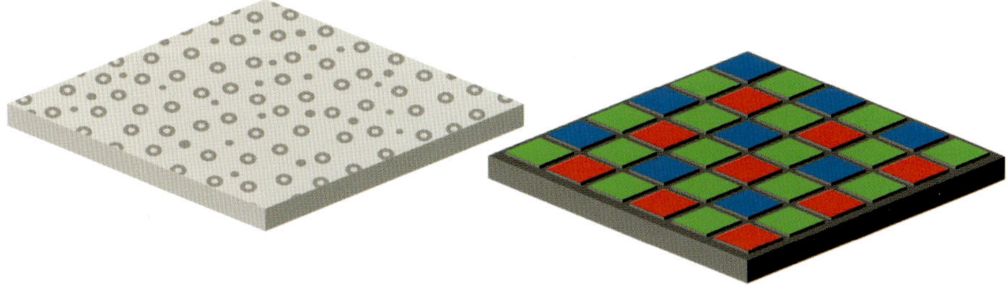

Grain or pixel?

The regular pattern of the sensor pixels results in lines on the image that run diagonally to the sensor structures, depicted as jagged little steps (aliasing). The more this angle approaches the arrangement on the sensor, the more prominent the aliasing. With the color sensor, this results in moiré patterns or local color distortions in the picture. Thanks to the organic grain distribution, film does not care at all about such regular patterns within the subject.

The manufacturers of digital cameras need to use tricks to ensure such structures are depicted cleanly: They add an *anti-aliasing filter* to their cameras, which makes the picture slightly unsharp during the shot. The formation of jagged steps is prevented at the expense of image sharpness. This explains why you should sharpen most digital pictures in the last step of post-processing. Film does not require this step.

2.3   Sharpness

The image sharpness can be measured in technical terms via the resolution capacity of pairs of lines. But for artistic work, the viewer's *perception* of sharpness is much more important. This perception depends on several factors.

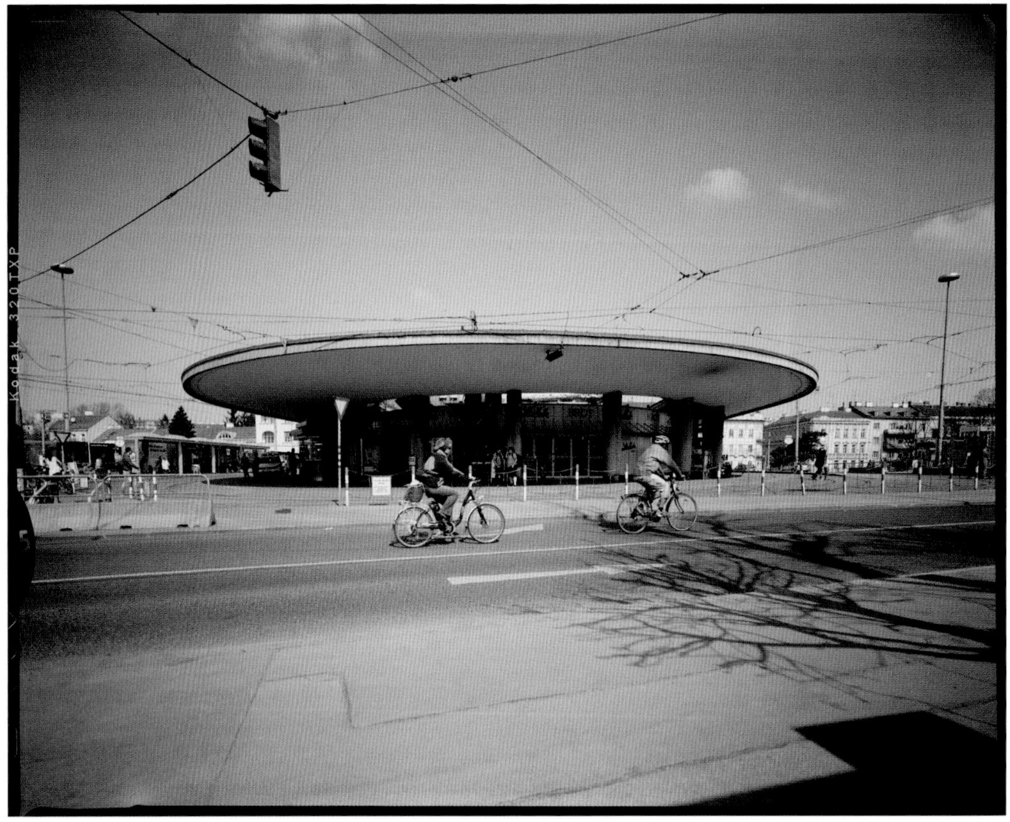

Vienna, large format, Kodak Tri-X 320. The high resolution of the large format manifests in a correspondingly high image sharpness.

The viewing distance and resolution of the picture play an important role in perceived image sharpness. The farther away you are from the picture, the less resolution is required to achieve an impression of sharpness.

The contrast in the picture also plays a role. The impression of sharpness is the same as the local contrast in the picture. If there are soft (low-contrast) transitions between adjacent areas, we interpret it as unsharpness. If the transitions are high in contrast, the viewer perceives it as sharp. To increase the perceived sharpness, you can use an unsharp mask, an old method from the darkroom days. This method involves increasing the contrast along the image edges. The dark sides of the contrast edges are darkened further, the bright sides are lightened. The viewer then perceives this increase in contrast as greater sharpness.

But the film grain also contributes to the perception of sharpness.

2.4   Area

In addition to the representation of fine structures, film and sensors also differ regarding how much of their area is light sensitive. With film, it's easy: The entire area of the film is light sensitive. With a sensor, it's a different story. The camera needs to get the exposure information from each individual pixel, so apart from the light-sensitive cells, there are also conductors on the surface of the sensor, which are not light sensitive. So, part of the sensor area is useless for light reception. Not so very long ago, the available utilization for light reception on the sensor area was well below 30%. Today, manufacturers are working on moving the wiring to the back of the sensor in order to increase this area, but we are still far from a 100% utilization of the theoretically available sensor area.

2.5   Contrast Range

Between the poles of deepest black and brightest white, every medium is able to represent only a certain differently sized area. This representable area is also referred to as contrast range or dynamic range. It is measured in f-stops. One f-stop corresponds to doubling or halving the amount of light represented.

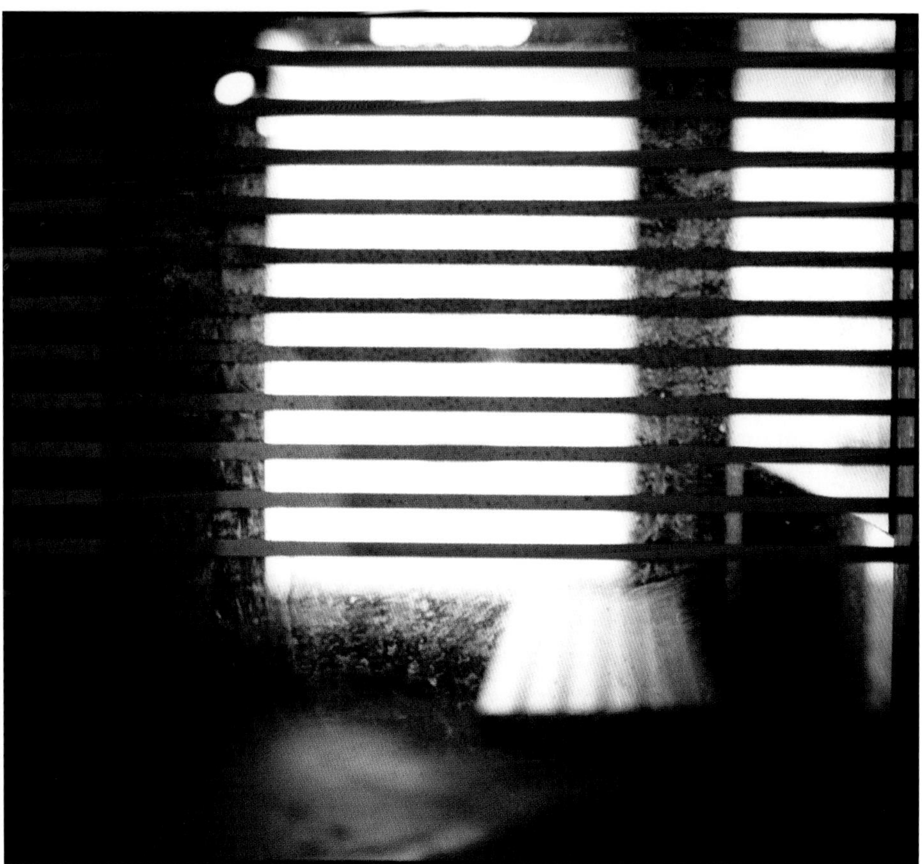

Bus stop, *Fomapan 100 in Rodinal 1+100. The stand development helps tame the particularly high contrast range of the picture.*

Whether we have a digital camera sensor or are using analog film, both options have one thing in common: They can best differentiate subtle nuances of brightness in the middle of their contrast range. If the exposure moves further away from this mid-range, fewer nuances (for example, fewer details in textures) will be represented.

One task of the camera's light meter is to direct the amount of incidental light for different light situations in such a way that the exposure is as far within this contrast range as possible. Otherwise, you are risking over- or under-exposure. Camera manufacturers like to boast with big numbers when advertising their flagships—this certainly applies to the dynamic range of the camera.

But how does film fare by comparison?

Color negative film and slides are largely standardized; the processing is fully automatic. So their respective contrast range is also fairly clear-cut. Black-and-white film is the real all-purpose medium in this respect. Every black-and-white film can be processed in any one of the countless developers, and variations in the dilution of the developer, the processing time, and the temperature also do their part in changing the amount of contrast in the final image, sometimes significantly. In particular, push and pull, two different methods of treating and developing the film that we will discuss in more detail in chapter 6, have an enormous influence on the contrast range of the processed film.

2.6   Angle of Light

The role of the angle of incidental light is another variable. Film captures light almost independently of its entrance angle; many digital sensors are much more angle-dependent based on how they are built. Although light generally falls onto a sensor and film from the front, the angles are different depending on the focal length, so different amounts of light are captured. For example, telephoto lenses tend to send more bundled rays of light into the camera, which hit the sensor or film at an angle of almost 90 degrees. If the light does not hit at right angles, less light reaches the individual pixels in the digital camera. The light beams of wide-angle lenses tend to come in at a rather shallow angle, especially towards the edges. When using wide-angle lenses, this leads to a noticeable darkening, especially in the edge regions of the sensor. To increase the light-sensitive area, sensors often contain micro lenses. These are little loupes that bundle the incidental light towards the pixels.

What makes it even trickier is that mirrorless cameras have a shorter flange focal distance, i.e., the distance between the lens mount and the film plane is correspondingly shorter. As a result, the angles are flatter and vignetting becomes more pronounced. If you are now asking yourself why the wide-angle lens on your digital camera does not show vignetting, the answer is digital trickery. If the camera knows which lens it is looking through, it can simply factor out the darkening in the image corners. Almost all of the camera manufacturers now apply this technology to their digital cameras—even Leica and Hasselblad.

2.7   The Bayer Pattern

Another reason for a slight unsharpness of the digital image is that sensors use the *Bayer pattern*. Most sensors divide the light up into blocks of four in the three basic colors: red, green, and blue. In each case, two pixels are sensitive to green, one to red, and one to blue. This means only a quarter of the sensor area can sense blue or red light, and only half the area is sensitive to green light.

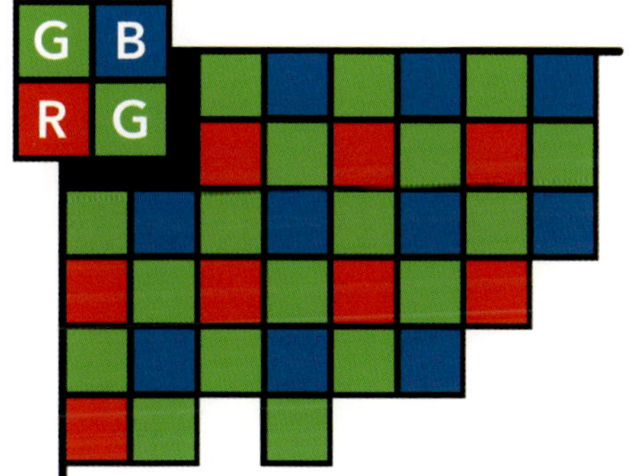

RGB sensor with Bayer pattern

While most digital sensors can see red and blue on only a quarter of the sensor area each, film can see all the colors in any place due to its layered structure.

These three color channels are then converted to 16 million colorful pixels inside the camera, and sharpness gets lost again during that process.

Instead of the widely-used Bayer pattern–type sensor, Fujifilm uses its own proprietary X-Trans sensors in many of its cameras. This design uses the same red, green, and blue micro filters, but they are arranged in a 6x6-pixel pattern that is reportedly less prone to moiré artifacts while delivering greater image resolution.

Sigma goes a different route with its Foveon X3 sensor. Instead of arranging the red-, green-, and blue-sensitive photosites adjacent to each other, Sigma places them on layers on top of one another. This design makes clever use of the way silicon absorbs different wavelengths of light. The layered design makes every pixel in a Foveon sensor sensitive to all three colors, thus making its behavior similar to that of color film, which "sees" all three colors over its entire surface.

2.8   Banding

Another area of the digital world that sometimes trips up people who switch over from film photography is the bit depth of digital pictures. The number of bits used to save the individual digital pixels determines the number of different grades of brightness this pixel can have. If we were to save with a bit depth of one, you could use this to represent exactly two states: black and white. Each additional bit doubles the number of possible gradations. With every additional bit, the potential number of represented shades of gray increases.

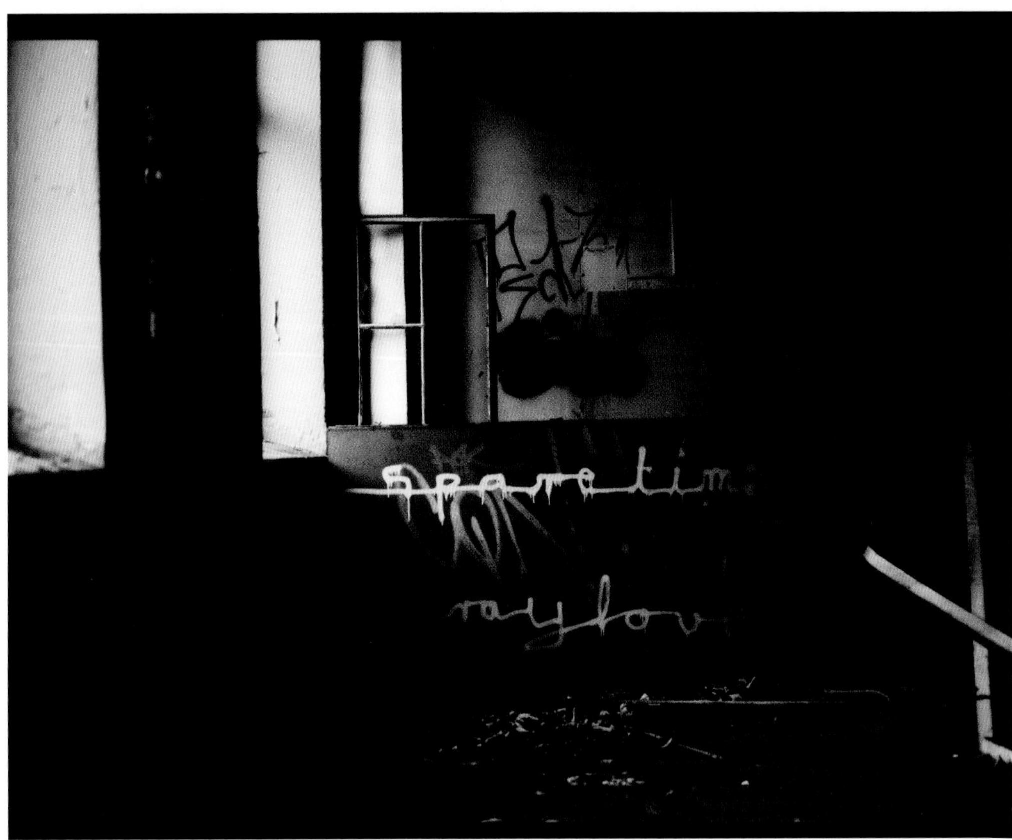

Factory,
Hannover,
Universal 200

In literature on digital image editing, you often read about bit depths of 8 or 16. Luckily, modern editing programs take the decision of what bit depth to use out of our hands and make the choice under the hood. They almost always work with very high bit depths. Only when switching between different programs does the question about the best setting come up from time to time. If you are not sure how many bits you should set for editing in another program, just remember that more can't hurt. In our case, the value for black-and-white pictures is usually set to 16-bit; for color channels it's set to 16 bits per color channel, i.e., 48-bit. You will come across this topic again in chapter 7.

If the bit depth is too low, it will be visible in the picture, particularly in areas with fine grading and color transitions. This includes sky areas where we like to see transitions from light blue to lighter blue over larger areas of the image. Without enough bits, these transitions disintegrate into discrete bands. Film only cares about all this for the transition to digital.

2.9   White Balance vs. Film Type

The term *white balance* originated with the appearance of the first (still analog) video cameras, in which the colored image was composed of the three different basic colors: red, green, and blue. Because this is still the case for most digital cameras, the term *white balance* is still used.

The human eye is amazingly flexible when it comes to perceiving different colors of light. We'll almost always see white as white, even though a candle has a much warmer coloring than a cold-white fluorescent tube, and golden sunset light has a completely different color than the cool atmosphere of a cloudy winter afternoon.

We are talking about the color temperature, measured in Kelvin (K). Somewhat counterintuitively, the light we perceive as warm has lower values (candle: 1200 K). The more blue content in the light, the higher the color temperature (cloudy sky in northern latitudes: 7000 K).

Unlike us, digital cameras cannot easily perceive the different light colors as neutral. Without white balance, a photo of a white sheet of paper taken by candlelight is going to look more yellow than white. Under a cloudy afternoon sky with its rather cool color components, everything in the photo will look blue.

To make these differences less severe, digital cameras try to control the mix of the three color channels (red, green, and blue) through automatic white balance. If the digital camera recognizes candlelight with its strong, warm (red) color components, it will ideally try to reduce the red channel and make the picture look more neutral.

With color film, we find something similar: The sensitivity of the different color layers is variably strong depending on the purpose of the film. The norm is usually daylight film, generally set to an average color temperature of about 5500 K. Under corresponding daylight, colors are represented as neutral as possible, i.e., neither too cool nor too warm. Depending on its type, artificial light can be quite cool (fluorescent lights) or warm (incandescent light bulbs), and to achieve neutral colors, the film type needs to be selected accordingly.

*Zeiss Ikon Tenax,
half-frame*

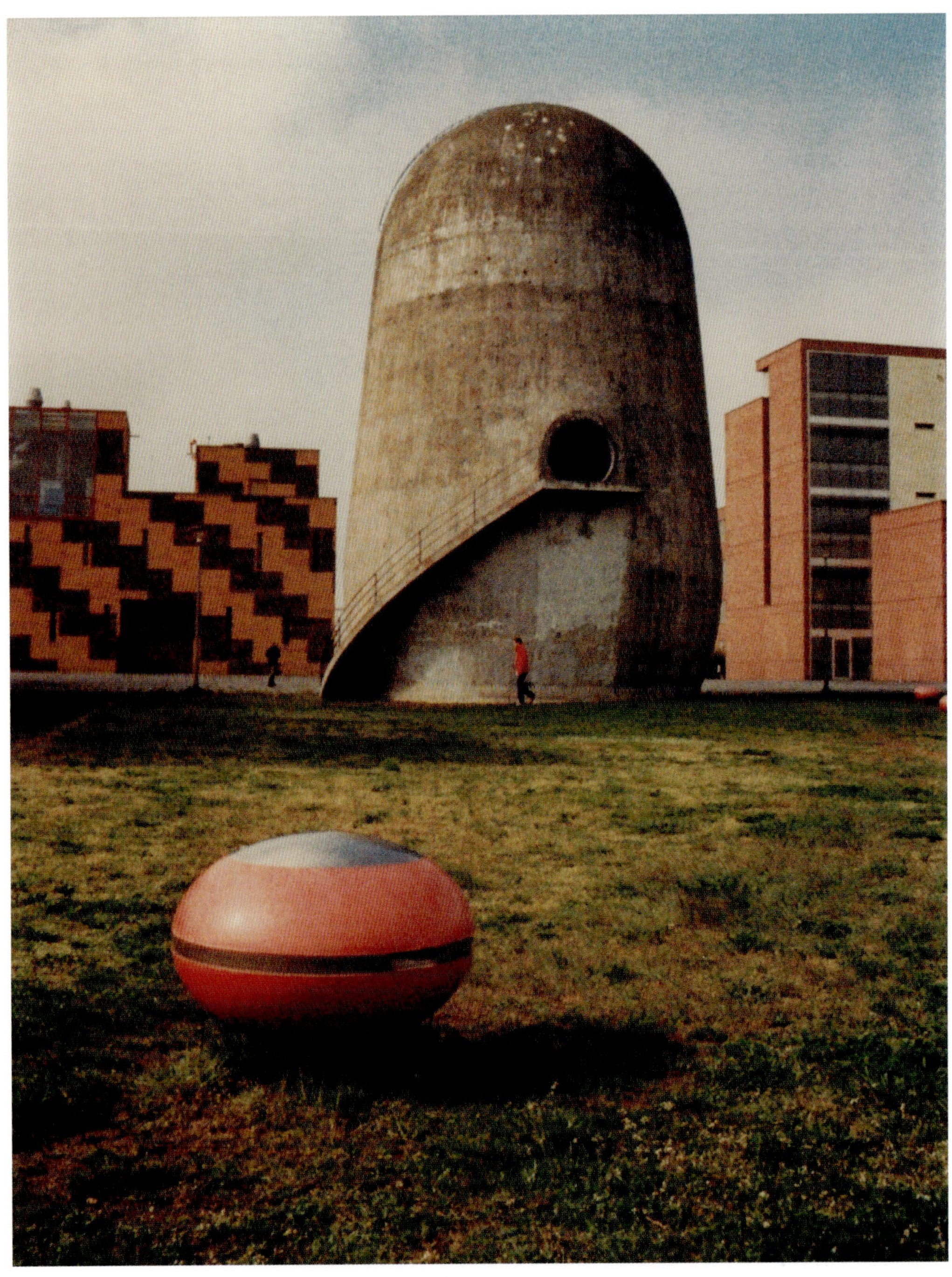

But today, there are only very few films that are optimized for artificial light. One example is the CineStill Xpro C-41 800Tungsten, used for warm incandescent light bulbs. To be able to use daylight film in artificial light, you can use filters in front of the lens to adapt the color spectrum to the film.

A 100% adaptation for completely neutral colors is generally neither possible nor desirable for film. Every color film has its very special characteristics of colors and contrasts. Often it's precisely these characteristics that make that film desirable, and they determine which type of film you choose for individual purposes.

2.10   Further Processing

To be really able to compare film photography and digital photography, we need to digitize the image after processing. There are two main methods for this: We can either scan the image or take a digital photo of it. The range begins at affordable flatbed scanners and camera-based scanning systems, and continues up the price scale to exorbitantly expensive drum scanners. The huge number of technologies and variable possibilities we have at our disposal in this area shows that a direct comparison between any absolute version of a film image and a digital image is virtually impossible.

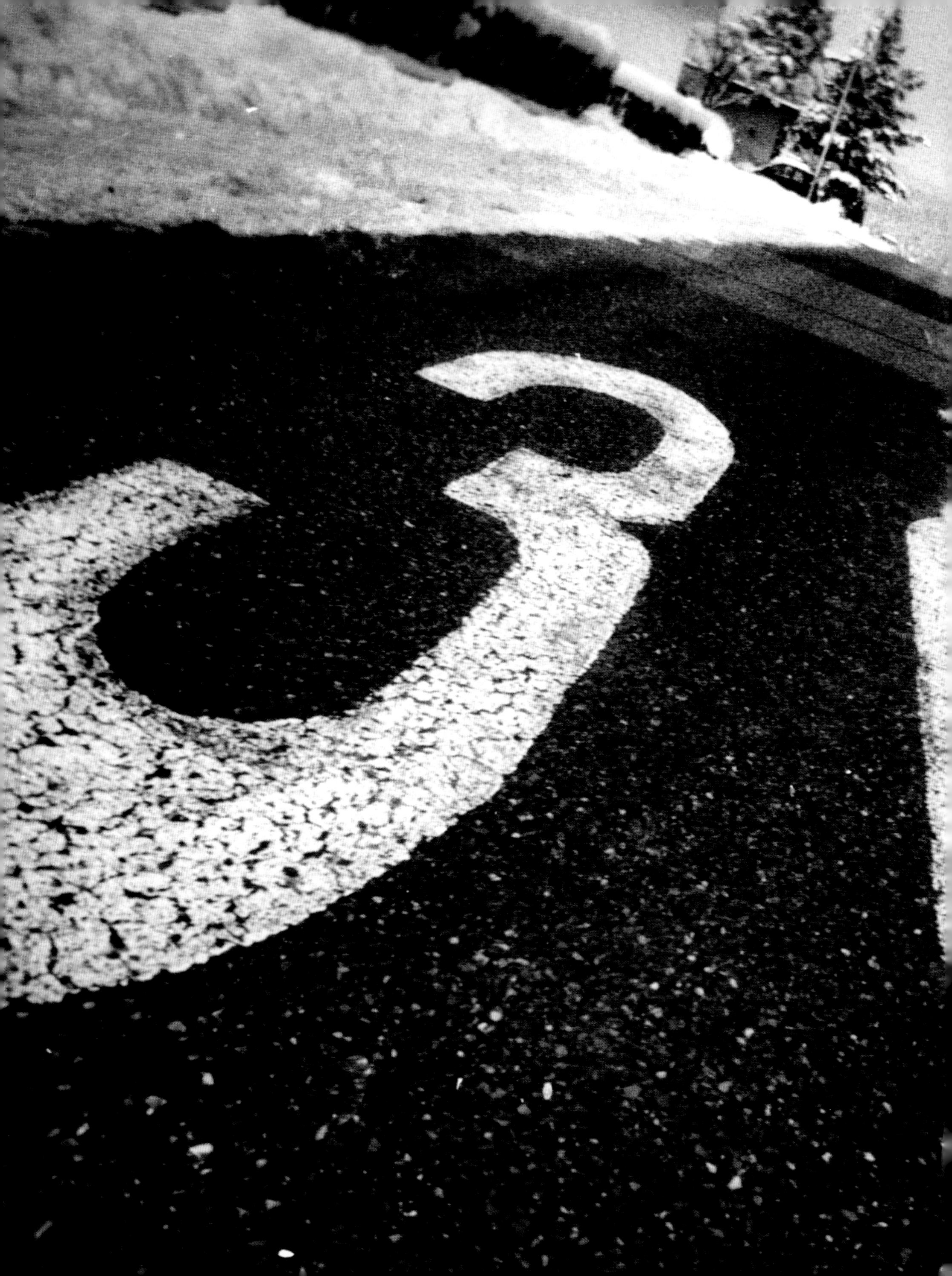

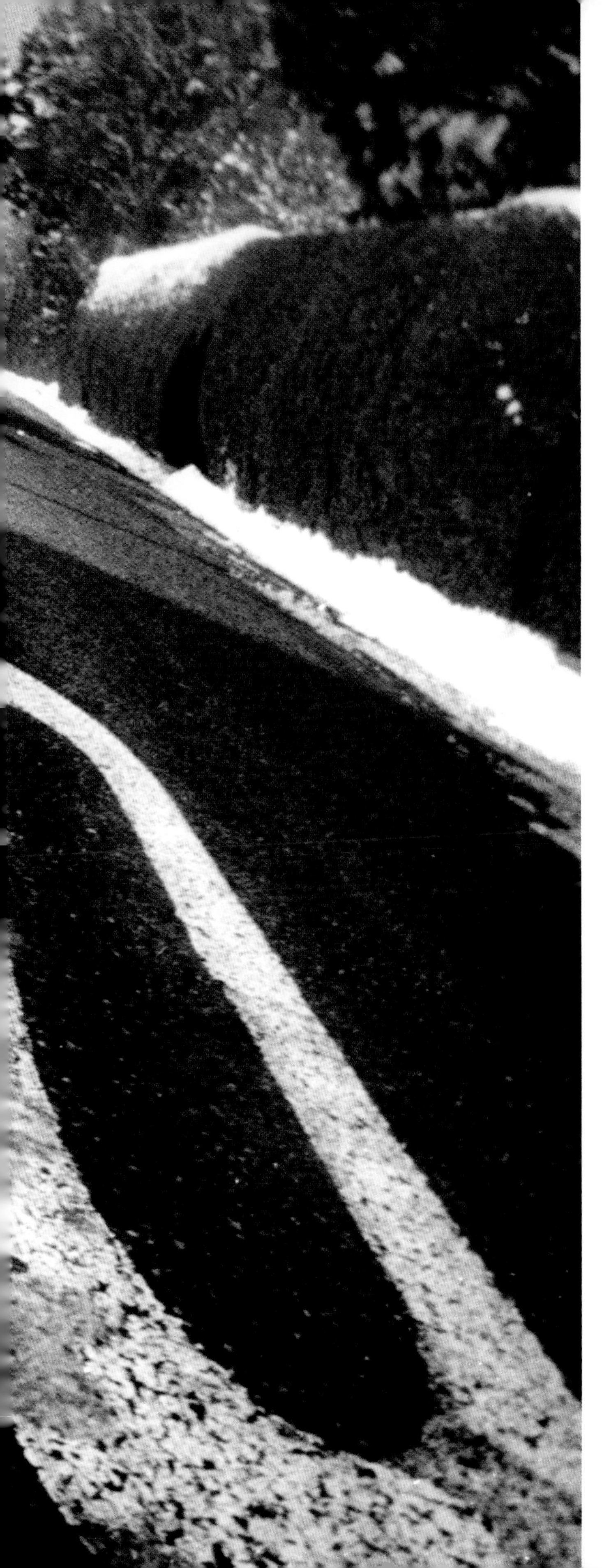

3
Cameras and Film Formats

Still cameras are not just distinguished by the way they are built, but also by the film size they use.

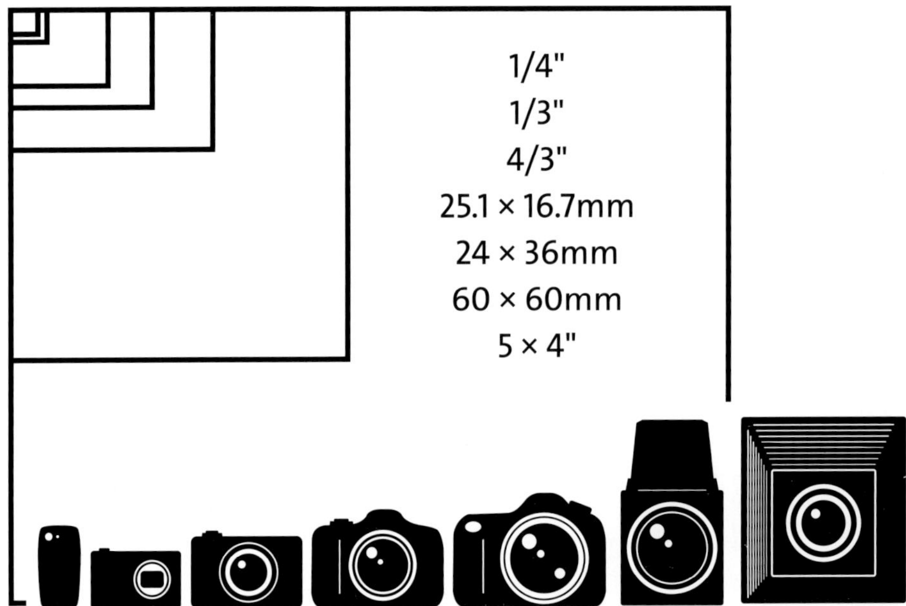

Sensor and negative sizes, from cell phone to large format camera

When deciding which camera type or format you want to work with, you should consider the subjects you prefer to shoot and/or how quickly (or inconspicuously) you want to work. Each type of photography has very individual requirements in terms of image quality and material. For example, photojournalists have a different set of needs from their equipment than photographers who shoot images of architecture.

Further Links

- Wikipedia: Film format *https://en.wikipedia.org/wiki/Film_format*
- Wikipedia: Cameras *https://en.wikipedia.org/wiki/Camera*
- Camerapedia *http://camerapedia.wikia.com/wiki/Camerapedia*

3.1   35mm

35mm cameras use film that's 35mm wide. These cameras usually expose frames that are 24×36mm. More rare models produce half-frame 24×18mm images, or panorama formats of up to 24×70mm.

In 1905, development engineer Oskar Barnack had the idea of using the cine-film available in the early 20th century for a new, handy-sized camera. Barnack, who later became the head of the microscope construction department at Leitz, loved hiking but suffered from asthma. He wanted a lightweight alternative to his 13×18cm bellows camera so he could more quickly and easily take photos on his tours through the mountains.

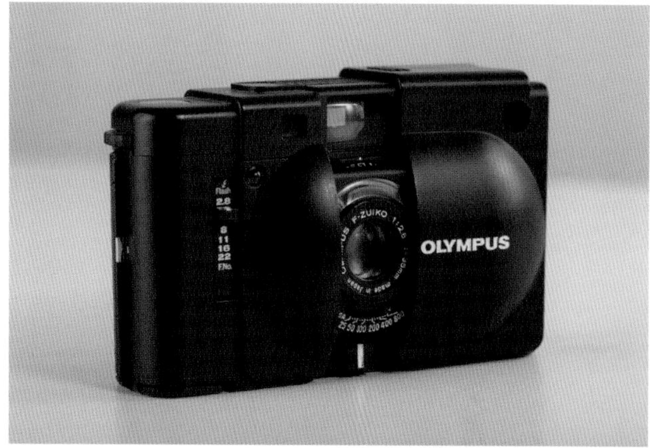

35mm Olympus XA

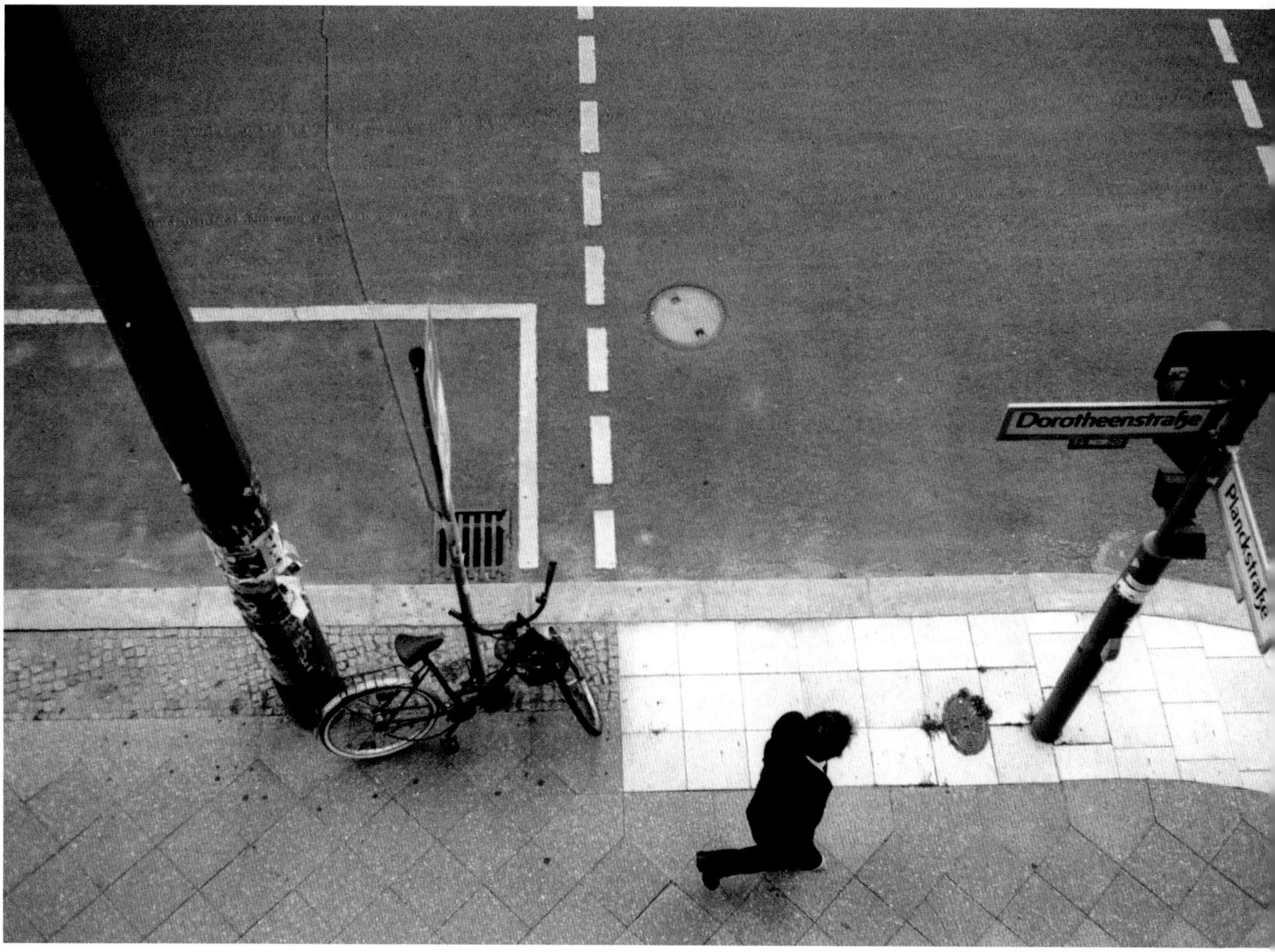

Dorotheenstraße, *35mm on Kodak Tri-X*

It took until 1924 for the first 35mm camera, designed by Barnack, to be mass-produced by Leitz. The Leica (Leitz Camera) was introduced to the public in 1925 at the Leipzig Spring Trade Fair. With it began a new era in documentary photography and photojournalism.

3.1.1   The Film

35mm film is wound onto a spool (plastic these days, metal in the past) and stored in a lightproof cartridge. Nowadays, you usually buy this film ready-made in cartridges. Common units have availability for 24 or 36 pictures. Disposable cameras sometimes offer 27 pictures. Buying film by the meter and winding it yourself used to be very popular among pros and dedicated (and price-conscious) amateurs. This method is still available today—especially with black-and-white film—but it's used much less.

The cartridge with the 35mm film is placed into the camera and threaded into the winding spool either automatically, in the case of most modern cameras, or manually via the leader. Changing film halfway through a roll so you can use a different make or sensitivity of film is very complicated and rarely safe with many 35mm cameras. Rewinding often makes the film leader disappear completely into the film cartridge; and reusable cassettes, commonly used in medium format cameras, are used quite rarely for 35mm cameras. Authorized dealers can reprogram some high-end cameras to leave the tip of the film outside the cartridge following automatic rewinding.

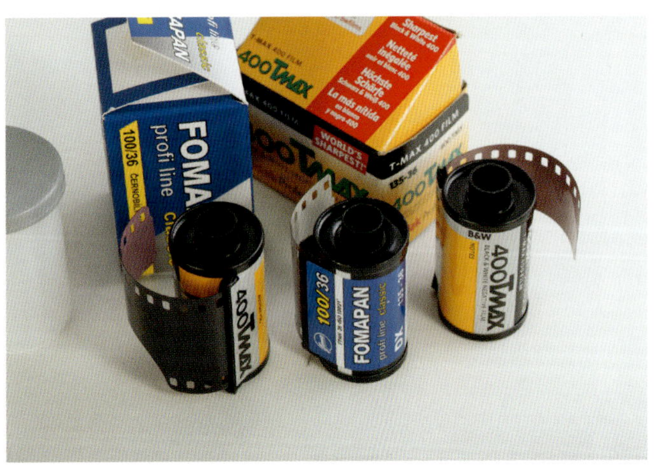

35mm film

Thanks to their small format and quick film transport, 35mm cameras generally enable you to take a higher number of sequence shots in continuous mode than their larger film format brethren. The film cartridges take up less space, so the cameras can be built to be more compact. 35mm cameras are available in different designs; the most common types are single-lens reflex cameras, viewfinder/rangefinder cameras, and compact cameras.

3.1.2 Rangefinder

The rangefinder is still one of the lightest and quietest cameras, which is why it's very popular, particularly in street photography and photojournalism. With this camera type, the viewfinder is on the left edge of the camera, outside of the lens axis. It is usually in the form of a little lens located behind a (generally rectangular) glass window. You can look at the subject with one eye through this viewfinder and keep the other eye on the surroundings. That takes a bit of practice, but can often be an advantage when it comes to picking the right moment to shoot.

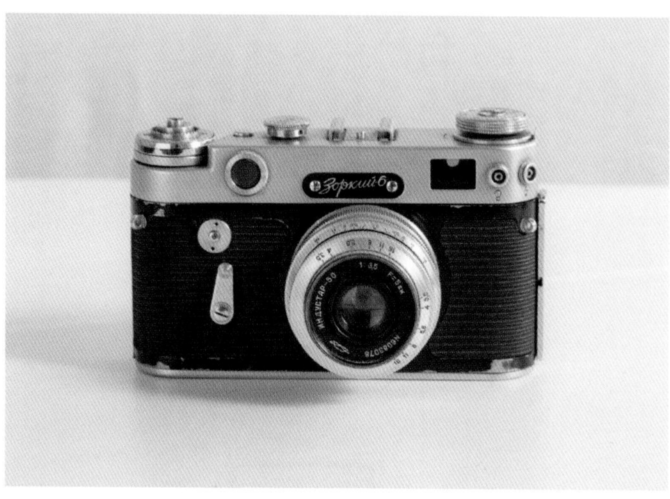

Rangefinder camera KMZ Zorki 6

A disadvantage of this camera design is that the picture you see in the viewfinder does not match the picture seen by the lens. This is referred to as *viewfinder parallax*. Some rangefinder cameras compensate for this disadvantage by displaying an illuminated box in the viewfinder that you can move around to display the part of the picture you want to capture.

Most cameras of this type can be focused via a superimposed image. While targeting the subject in the viewfinder, a second viewfinder simultaneously records a second image. This image is projected into the viewfinder image via a rotating mirror. Through a mechanical contact below this mirror that is linked to the distance setting of the lens, this "ghost image" can be moved around. Once both images line up, the picture is in focus.

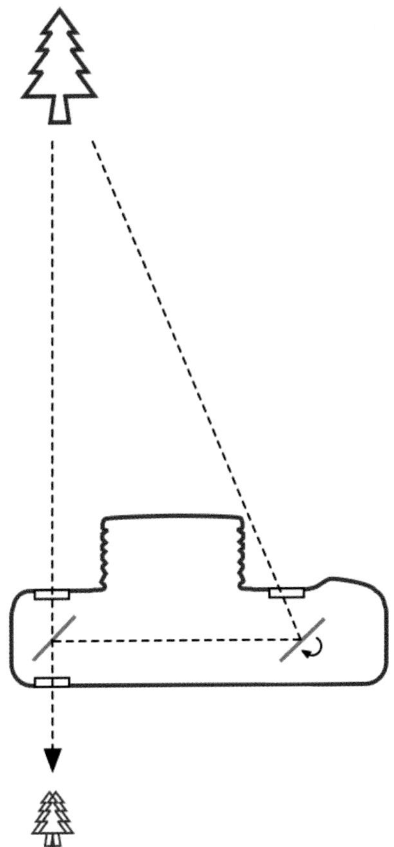

Rangefinder camera out of focus

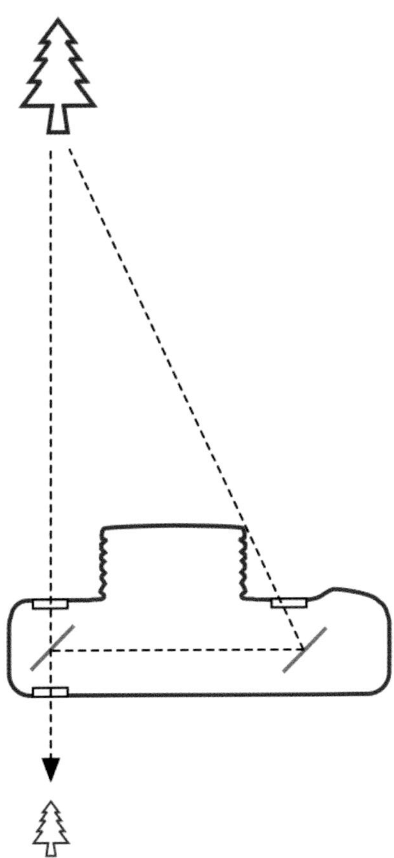

Rangefinder camera in focus

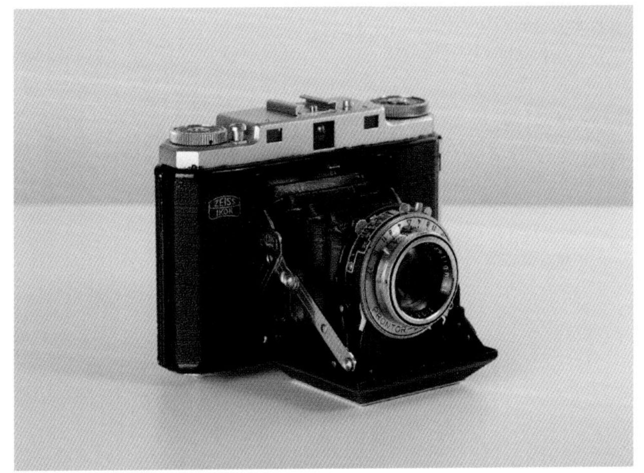

Zeiss Ikonta with non-coupled rangefinder

The viewfinder image in cameras of this type is usually very bright for exact focusing in low light, so compared to cameras with auto-focus systems, the manual focusing system of rangefinder cameras is advantageous in these situations.

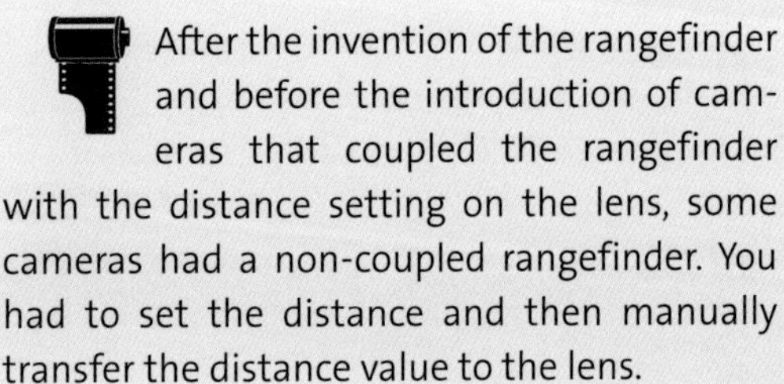
After the invention of the rangefinder and before the introduction of cameras that coupled the rangefinder with the distance setting on the lens, some cameras had a non-coupled rangefinder. You had to set the distance and then manually transfer the distance value to the lens.

Buying a Rangefinder Camera

Since the triumph of digital photography, we analog enthusiasts finally have the chance to buy film cameras at an affordable price. On camera stock exchanges, you can usually find at least one seller offering Leica-M models that are still pricey, yet affordable. Apart from Voigtländer, with the Bessa R cameras, Leica is one of the few manufacturers that still produces rangefinders for 35mm photography.

But there are plenty of other fish in the sea: On the secondhand market, the Yashica Electro 35 is a very interesting rangefinder camera with great optics for the cash-strapped photographer. Another exciting option—if somewhat idiosyncratic—is Leica replicas from Russia, e.g., by Zorki or FED.

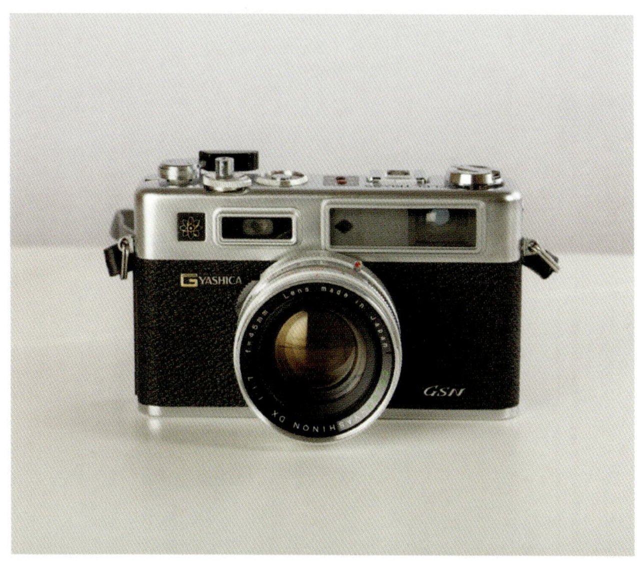

Yashica Electro 35

3.1.3   Single-Lens Reflex Camera

The first mass-produced version of the SLR came onto the market in 1936: the Kine-Exakta by a company called Ihagee, in Dresden, Germany. This was a model with a waist-level finder, in which the finder image appeared inverted. With the invention of the roof pentaprism, which produces an (again) inverted (and therefore upright) image, modern finder designs became possible. Now you can see the picture at eye level and upright.

This type of camera offers the photographer an exact look at the frame of view. The picture captured by the lens is redirected via a flip-up mirror to the viewfinder above it. As a result, you see exactly what the lens sees. What you see

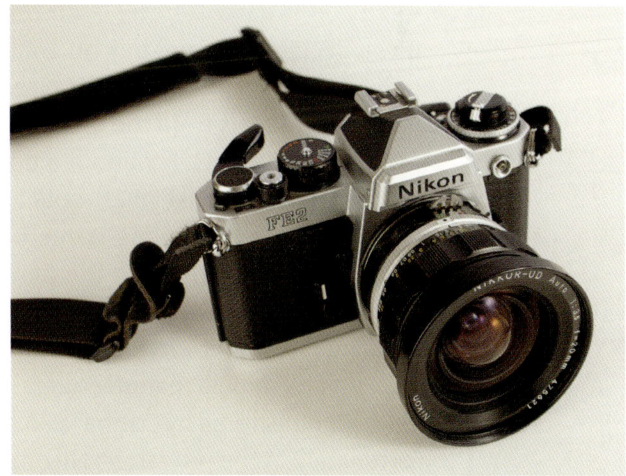

Single-lens reflex camera (SLR)

is what you get—if your camera has a finder with 100% congruence. With single-lens reflex cameras, you don't get the parallax error of the rangefinder cameras, because the viewfinder is on the same axis as the lens.

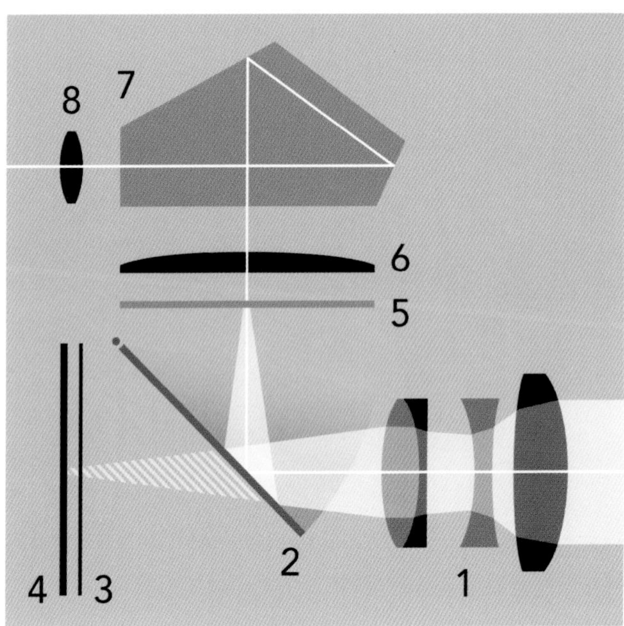

Schematic structure of a single-lens reflex camera, seen from the side

Buying Single-Lens Reflex Cameras

If you decide to (again) buy an analog single-lens reflex camera, you have the choice between second-hand models from the pre-digital era or their modern equivalents. For about a hundred dollars, you can get a robust, high-quality secondhand camera by one of the big-name brands—e.g., a Nikon FE2 or models from the Canon A series. If you get ahold of a suitable standard lens or other fixed focal length on a camera stock exchange or online auction platform, you're ready for analog photo excursions.

> If you are planning to buy a secondhand camera, have a look at the *Tips on Buying Cameras* section at the end of this chapter.

Only a few camera manufacturers still offer analog single-lens reflex cameras. The Nikon FM10 manufactured by Cosina (also sold as the Vivitar V3800N) is no longer in production. Fortunately, in the pro range, Nikon's portfolio still includes its analog flagship, the F6.

3.2   Medium Format: 6×6," 6×7," and 6×9"

Size Does Matter

In the past, medium format, in its various versions, was expensive and therefore used mostly by professional photographers and amateurs with deep pockets. Nowadays, secondhand medium format cameras have become more affordable. Often it's the tempting call of the larger format that draws hobby photographers from the digital realm (back) into the analog world. It's exactly what happened to us. In medium format, you make first contact with the greater quality, sharpness, and rich tonal range of larger formats.

Medium format has a greater area available for receiving light, with more crystals than there are on 35mm film. This format can save more light information, but also more image information. Also, the light-sensitive silver halide crystals are smaller in relation to the negative surface, which results in less visible grain.

The larger negative provides better image quality than the 35mm, but is still quicker and easier to process than the sheet film used in the even bigger formats. Due to the fact that the resolution capacity of the scanner does not have to be very high, hybrid post-processing is also quite affordable in this format. Suitable flatbed scanners are currently available for under 200 dollars.

The special charm lies in the option of being able to work with selective focus, even in wide-angle photography with a correspondingly open aperture. The following photo was shot with a Pentax 67, in which the normal focal length in relation to the 6×7 film format is approximately 100mm. The lens we used with 55mm focal length has about the same viewing angle as 28mm in a 35mm camera—but at the same time, it has the depth-of-field characteristics of the longer (55mm) focal length. Even at aperture 4, you get a depth of field that softly slides into blurriness.

Shot with 55mm on a Pentax 67

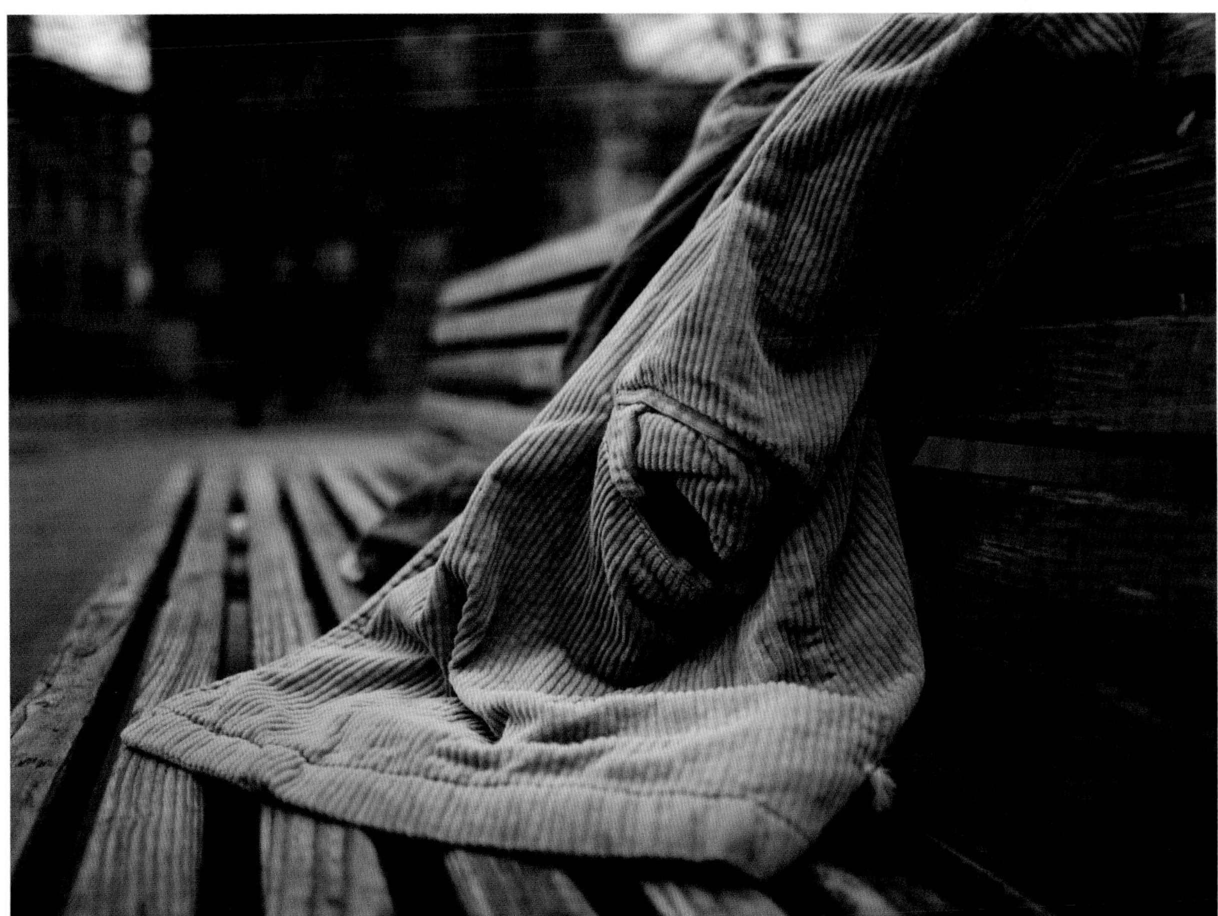

3.2.1   Film Types

Roll Film Type 120

Roll film is the most frequent variety of medium format film. Depending on the camera you're using, it can take about 15–16 exposures in 6×4.5 format (sizes in cm), 12 exposures in 6×6 format, 10 exposures in 6×7 format, and only 8 exposures in 6×9 format, the format used by many box cameras.

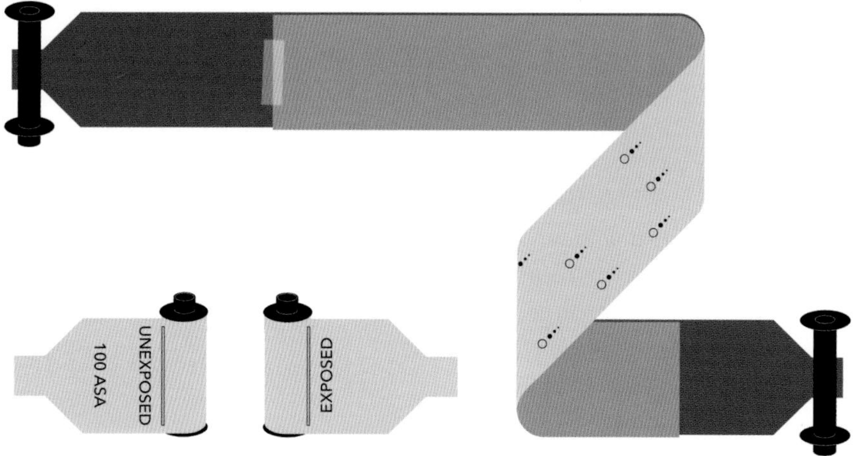

Medium format film with film spools, backing paper, and taped-on film

Roll film type 120 is 61.5mm wide and not perforated (unlike 35mm film). A strip of backing paper, matte-black to film side, runs along the filmstrip. They are taped together at the beginning of the roll. This paper strip is slightly wider than the film and acts as a screen so you can load film into the camera in daylight. There are printed rows of numbers for the different film formats on the back of the paper strip that, in combination with a viewing window in the camera back, replace the frame counter in simple cameras.

Roll Film Type 220

Occasionally, you also still find rolls of type 220, but not every camera can use it. Type 220 does not have the continuous paper backing—just paper strips taped to it at the beginning and the end. You can fit twice as much of type 220 as type 120 on the same spool. Cameras with a counter window in the back cannot cope with this film, but many system cameras offer replaceable backs or rotatable/exchangeable plates to compensate for the lower thickness caused by the lack of backing paper.

Roll Film Type 620

This type of film has the same length and width as roll film type 120, but the spools are a bit slimmer and not directly compatible with cameras built for 120-type film—and vice versa. If you pick up one of the popular Brownie 620 box cameras from the flea market and try to use 120-type film, you'll find that the film gets stuck in the camera sooner or later.

To fix this, you can modify film spools of type 120 film by removing the bulge on the edge. Alternatively, you can purchase old 620 spools on online auction sites or at flea markets, and then wind roll film type 120 onto the spools in the changing bag.

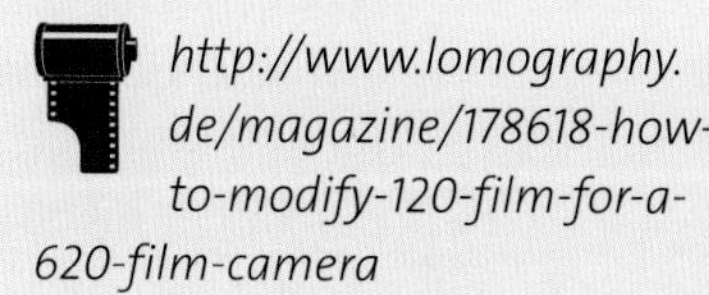

http://www.lomography. de/magazine/178618-how- to-modify-120-film-for-a- 620-film-camera

Film type 620 is no longer being mass-produced. You can find small quantities of type 120 wound onto 620-type spools offered by individual sellers on the Internet.

Roll Film Type 127

Type 127 is a 4.6cm-wide roll film introduced in 1912 by Kodak. Many box cameras, but also several twin-lens reflex cameras, such as the Baby Rolleiflex, use this narrow roll film. Like the wider type 120, it has a full-length paper backing with numbers printed on the back. As with type 120, these numbers are used for counting the frames in some cameras. The most common image format is 4×4cm with 12 exposures per film.

127 film is quite rare (e.g., as black-and-white film Rera Pan 100 127), but you can find some remaining stock from various brands online (e.g., the rare Rollei Retro 80S and Rollei Nightbird/Crossbird films). Film 127, the "baby roll film" format, can be used with corresponding frames in a 35mm projector. As the 4×4cm image is about 1.7 times as large as 35mm, slide film of this type (sadly, no longer in production) is referred to as "super slides."

3.2.2   Image Formats

6×4.5

The format 645 stands for negatives in the size of 6×4.5cm, with which you can fit up to 16 photos on a roll of film type 120. This is the smallest film format in the classic medium format, and the most economic in terms of exposures per film. The cameras are, for medium format, usually quite small, and therefore lighter than their corresponding cameras in the larger film formats. Some cameras of the 6×6-class also offer a mask for this smaller format.

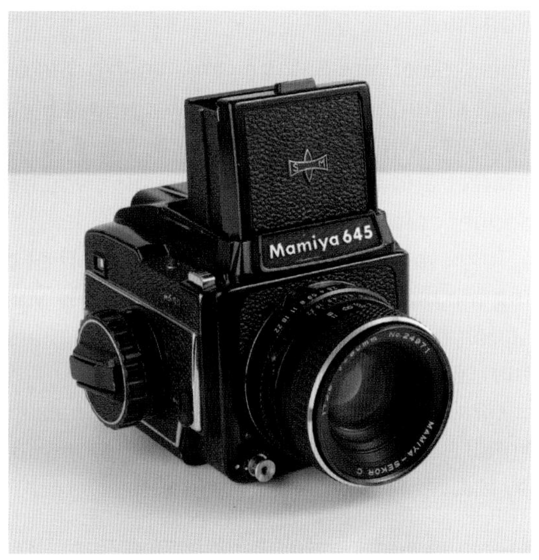
Mamiya 645

6×6

Square negatives are 6×6cm. This is surely the most popular medium format, and has a kind of cult status for many photographers. 12 exposures fit onto a roll of film type 120; 24 onto a roll of the more rare type 220. With this format, you'll always have a nice, symmetrical frame to compose your shot in whether you're in landscape or portrait orientation. However, if you are used to the aspect ratio of 35mm film, it can be quite challenging to find exciting compositions for the square format. Also, because all common paper formats for printing are rectangular, you end up with quite a lot of wasted space when printing square pictures.

For the square image format, there are cameras in all price classes, starting with plastic cameras from the universe of lomography (Holga and Diana) and cameras by the brands Pentacon and Kiev (sometimes lovingly referred to as "Eastern European divas" because of their particularities). Hasselblad is an example of a more expensive system camera.

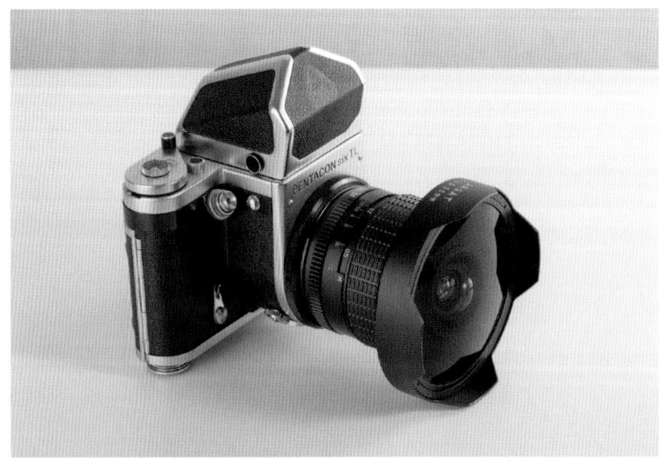
Pentacon Six TL with Arsat 30mm lens, image format 6×6cm

6×7

The format 67 stands for negatives sized 6×7cm. Ten exposures fit onto a roll of 120 film. This format is also referred to as "ideal format" because its aspect ratio is the perfect size for most paper formats when printing.

There are some exciting cameras for this negative size: the Pentax 67 (classic SLR form factor) and the Mamiya 7 (rangefinder), for example. For SLR heavyweights of this class, there is a persistent rumor that you can hardly shoot handheld because of the hefty mirror bounce. Personally, we have never found this to be a problem. The Pentax 67, which we refer to as "The Beast," is one of our favorite "always-in-the-bag" cameras. In moderate wide-angle (55mm focal length), you can easily get sharp images at up to 1/30 second.

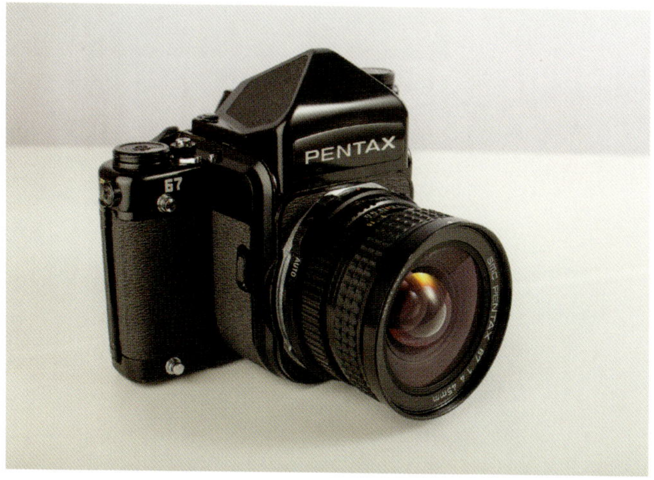

Pentax 67 ("The Beast")

6×9

The negatives of format 69 are sized 6×9cm. This is the largest of the medium formats (apart from the even wider panorama formats) and is sometimes referred to as "small large format." Many of the old box and viewfinder cameras use this format.

The format sizes mentioned above are always rounded values. The exact size of the exposures are as follows:

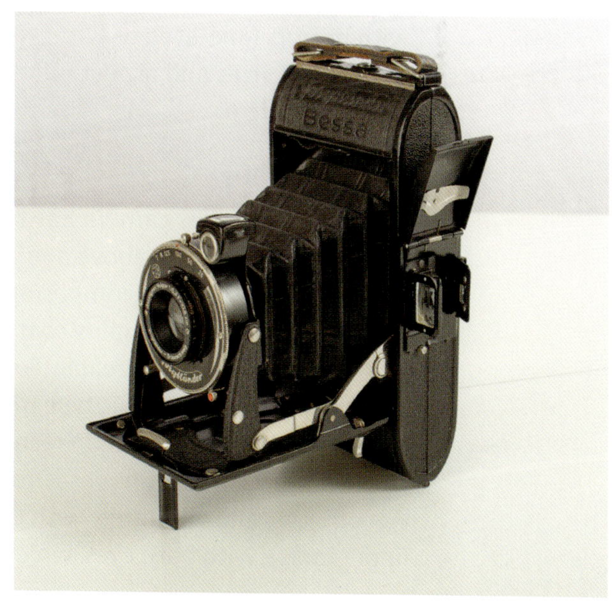

Voigtländer Bessa, film format 6×9cm

Roll Film Type 120, 220, and 620

Designation	Actual Size
6 × 4.5cm	56 × 41.5mm
6 × 6cm	56 × 56mm
6 × 7cm	56 × 69mm
6 × 8cm	56 × 77mm
6 × 9cm	56 × 89mm

Roll Film Type 127

Designation	Actual Size
4 × 4cm	38.1 × 38.1mm

3.2.3 Camera Types

Medium format cameras are usually larger and wider than 35mm cameras in order to be able to hold the larger-sized film material. For medium format, there are cameras with mirrors (one-eyed or two-eyed cameras), viewfinders, and rangefinders that cater to different sizes and aspect ratios of negatives. The most common formats are 6×4.5, 6×6, and 6×7cm.

Twin-Lens Reflex Camera

The twin-lens reflex camera has two lenses, one for composing and one for the exposure, usually arranged above one another. To get a really bright picture onto the focusing screen, the lens for composing is often faster, even though it may have a simpler construction or lower-quality coating. With a few exceptions (the Mamiya C series), the lenses are not interchangeable. For close-ups, you can often get add-on lenses.

For most cameras of this type, the finder is a folding, waist-level finder on top of the camera, with an integrated Fresnel lens to distribute the brightness evenly. The picture in the waist-level finder is reversed (left to right), so it takes a bit of practice to work quickly and accurately with the camera. On the other hand, you can see the entire finder image with both eyes, which makes composing easier.

The "two-eyed" construction makes it possible to use a fixed mirror in these cameras. No moving mirror means less noise and vibration when you shoot. You can shoot silently and "from the hip" with these cameras, which is handy for street photography since this style of shooting is generally less conspicuous. In a portrait situation, the photographer can have constant eye contact with the model because there is no camera between them, just like with large format. This makes many people feel less targeted and more relaxed.

Most twin-lens reflex cameras can be found in medium format for roll film type 120 or 220. They generally expose negatives in the 6×6 format. A few camera manufacturers also offer a small version for 35mm and 127 film formats.

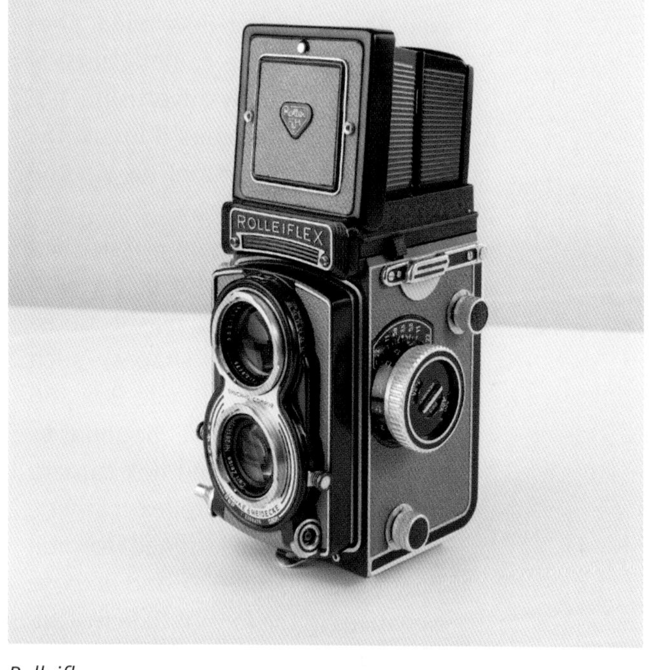

Rolleiflex

Single-Lens Reflex Camera

"One-eyed" cameras with mirrors are certainly among the most-sold cameras. In medium format, they often have the classic cube shape due to their high modularity (common brands include Hasselblad, Zenza Bronica, Rollei, and Mamiya). Their lenses, finder or prism modules, and film magazines are interchangeable. The flatter shape used in 35mm cameras is also available, both for cameras with a fixed pentaprism finder and cameras that offer the option of switching between pentaprism and waist-level finder (e.g., the Pentax 67 or Pentacon SIX).

Most of these cameras are more complicated to use effectively than a comparable 35mm camera. Few of these cameras have autofocus, and even the film transport is often manual. Integral exposure metering (partly with the function of automatic aperture control) is often only possible with a separate AE or measuring prism. The lower degree of automatization is usually not a problem, because these cameras are mainly used for landscape photography or photojournalism, not for sports photography.

Viewfinder or Rangefinder Cameras

The box cameras developed by Kodak are some of the oldest viewfinder cameras in medium format. These simple cameras, aimed almost exclusively at amateur and hobby photographers, were in production from 1900 to the late 1960s, and used the various roll film types. Later, it was more common for these cameras to use 35mm film. At the beginning of the box camera era, you would buy the camera ready-loaded, return it for processing complete with film, and then get the developed photos back with the camera already re-loaded. An early advertising slogan by Kodak summed it up neatly: "You press the button, we do the rest."

In addition to the classic box shape, there were also boxes with fashionably rounded plastic housing. Some special shapes, such as the two-eyed Bonita-Box 66 by Bilora, blurred the boundaries between the one-eyed box camera and the dual-lens reflex camera. Most boxes are designed for roll film type 120 or 620 and expose

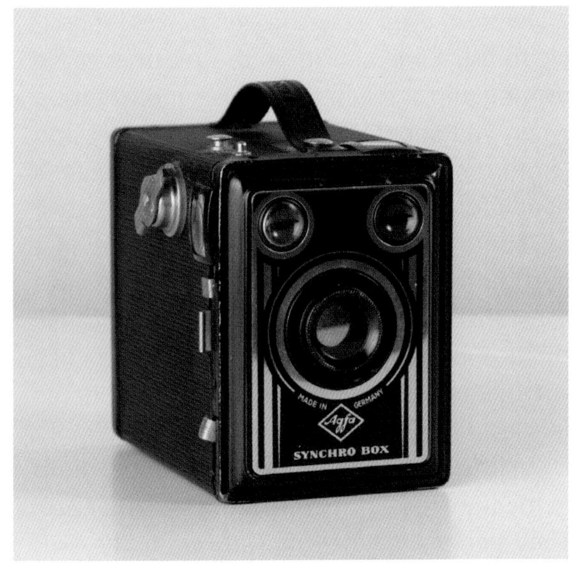

Box camera

negatives in the format 6×9cm. Later, foldable field cameras (bellows cameras), all with different qualities of finder mechanisms, lenses, and shutters, expanded the range of available cameras in every class from amateur to pro. At the top end of this range, there were press cameras for formats 6×7, 6×8, and 6×9cm with interchangeable film holders, lenses, and flashes.

If a camera has an optical finder with a focusing aid linked to the distance setting of the lens, it's referred to as rangefinder camera. In medium format, these models have a certain advantage regarding handling, size, and weight due to the absence of a mirror. A current representative of this camera type is the Fuji GF670 (outside of Japan, it's sold as the Voigtländer Bessa III), which exposes photos in the 6×6 and 6×7cm format.

3.3   Large Format: 4×5"

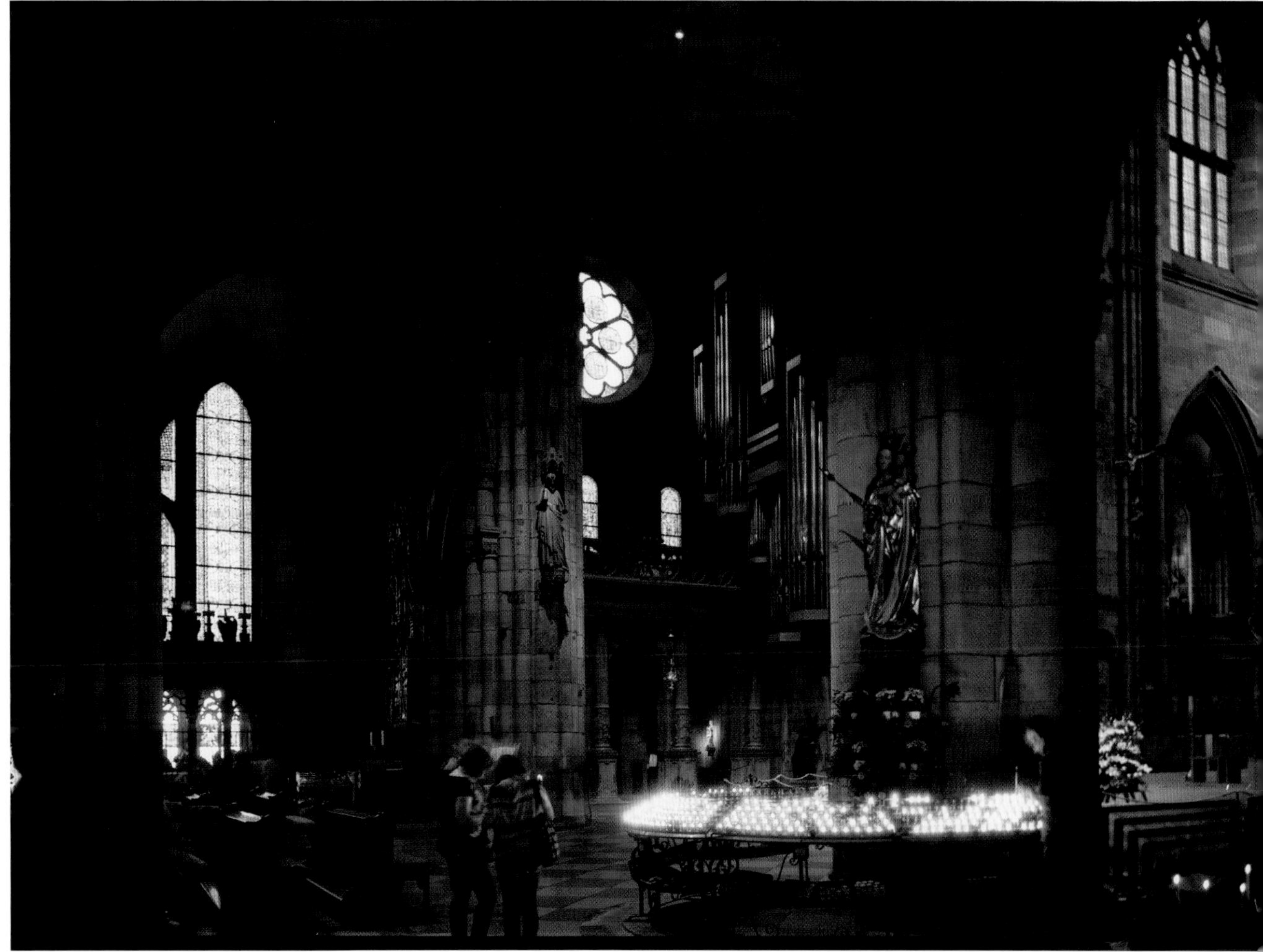

Freiburg Minster, Chamonix with 65mm

Now we move on to the premium class of film photography: the large format.

If medium format already offers a big leap in terms of quality compared to 35mm, the photographer can access an entire new dimension of detail clarity and rich tonal range if a negative can suddenly be a Letter/A4 size. As soon as you step into the world of large format, the negative size is theoretically unlimited. Some photographers even build their own cameras using film that's three feet wide, or work with specially cut X-ray film. Others convert car trailers into cameras and pour the required photographic emulsion themselves.

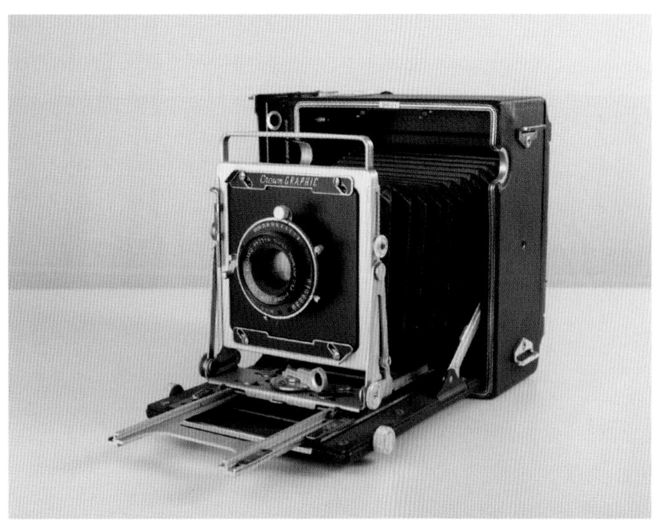
Graflex Crown Graphic, 4×5" press camera

Whether you use a 4×5-inch field camera, an antique studio camera, or a home-built large format giant, all cameras have one thing in common: They are beautiful and endlessly fascinating.

What is large format?

Large format starts with negatives sized 4×5 inches. Film for the German 9×12cm or 18×24cm formats is rarely available today, and the associated film holders sold on flea markets and camera markets are generally slow sellers. The international 4×5-inch format is currently the most widely used large format because the equipment needed for 5×7- or 8×10-inch formats is considerably large and heavy, and requires specific precision to use.

Cameras of this category are entirely mechanical and operated exclusively by hand. Each and every manual operating step has to be very precise, from loading and unloading the film cartridges to composing and focusing to measuring the exposure and finally, cocking the shutter and releasing it at the right moment. As a reader, you may ask yourself: "Why the heck should I go to all this trouble?" Having to do all these things yourself sounds tedious and awkward. With hardly any other camera do you ever have to think about the shutter or opening and closing a working aperture. Any halfway modern 35mm camera, whether analog or digital, will do the job for you. Even most medium format systems will guide you along. And now you're suddenly supposed to work through a long checklist just to take one single shot? Why should you bother?

One reason is certainly that the image quality and richness of detail that a negative of this size can accommodate far exceeds that of smaller formats. The smooth tonal value transitions and differentiated representation of light and shadow paths is another. Many photographers also feel compelled to tackle this task because of the great deal of control over composition and perspective that these cameras offer. For some people it can be intimidating, but for others it's a big playground.

The design of large format cameras gives you a large choice of possible settings that you don't get with 35mm or medium format camera. Thanks to their special construction (more on this later), they enable the photographer to precisely align focus planes and correct distortions. This makes the large format ideal for landscape, product, and architectural photography. Sports or street photographers, on the other hand, will probably find the slow process, the long exposure times, and the unwieldy equipment less suitable to their purposes.

Working with a large format camera takes you right back to the beginning of photography. In using this type of equipment, you'll become aware of aspects of photography that you were probably only implicitly aware of before. Getting to know the large negative format and the camera techniques that go with it is a great opportunity to dive deeper into your hobby.

3.3.1   Large Format Cameras

The supplies needed for large format photography can be purchased at an affordable price. You can buy a secondhand camera with one or two suitable lenses for a few hundred dollars. Even if you are buying a new camera, a complete set of equipment often costs less than a full-frame DSLR.

At first glance, large format cameras seem to be from a different era—that's part of their charm. Compared to a 35mm SLR, some of these cameras look relatively large and heavy. There are different kinds of large format cameras, the most common of which are the view camera with optical rail, referred to as a *monorail*, and the *field camera*. The camera housing for both types of camera consists of four important elements:

1. The film plane: formed by the *rear standard* with the ground glass for the settings mounted on it. During the exposure, it carries the sheet film holder, instant print film back, or roll film back.
2. The *front standard*: to which you can attach interchangeable lens boards with the camera lenses.
3. The light-proof, harmonica-like *bellows*: made of nylon or leather, these connect both standards.
4. The *baseboard* or optical rail: the front and rear standard are attached to it.

The distance between the two standards (referred to as the *extension*) determines the image scale:

- smaller extension = smaller image
- bigger extension = bigger image

You also use the extension to focus large format cameras. Usually, adjusting the front standard changes the focus, but in some cameras you can then fine-tune the sharpness by moving the rear standard.

Monorail

A view camera is mostly made of metal, and the two standards are attached to an optical bench in the form of a central rail (hence the name *monorail*). This optical rail gives you countless options for moving the front and rear standards relative to each other (tilt, swing, and so on). Common sizes for these cameras are 4×5, 5×7, and 8×10 inches. View cameras are usually used only in the studio due to their size and weight. Some models can be folded flat for transport, but for a day out with a view camera and tripod, you should either hire a strong assistant or consider acquiring a donkey.

Field Camera

A field camera is mostly made of wood or a mixture of wood and carbon fiber, so it's much lighter than a view camera. It can be folded to be very compact, and is easy to stash in a backpack or bag, which makes it great for landscape photography or city tours. Most types of field cameras allow fewer camera movements and, therefore, adjustment options than the highly flexible monorail camera.

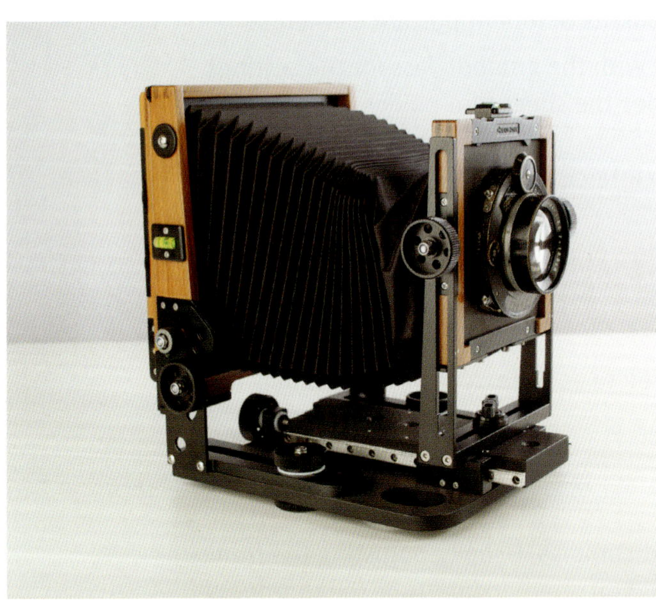

Chamonix 045N-2

Basically, a large format camera is just a dark, lightproof room with a lens on one end and a ground glass or film back on the other. The lens, in addition to its function during the exposure, also serves as a finder and projects the image upside-down onto the ground glass of the rear standard. To compose and focus precisely, you must avoid ambient light by hanging a black cloth over the camera back. As the photographer, when you disappear under that cloth you'll attract the attention of every passerby in the vicinity.

Taking a picture uses roughly the same process every time. You align the camera on the tripod, open the aperture and the shutter, compose the shot, and focus the important image areas via a loupe. Then you measure the exposure and set the required aperture and shutter time, close the shutter, and cock it (the sequence may differ depending on camera type). After inserting the film holder, you remove the dark slide, and trigger the shutter via a cable release.

Strangely enough, the difficulty of having to assess an upside-down image for com-position is an advantage. The unfamiliar view causes you to concentrate more on lines, areas, and the distribution of light and dark in the picture, and less on details. This may help you find clearer and more interesting compositions.

3.3.2   Film and Film Holders

Large format film is always supplied as sheet film. A pack usually contains 25 to 50 sheets of film packaged inside a box in lightproof plastic bags, often with paper in between each sheet. The individual sheets need to be loaded into suitable film holders in com-plete darkness. Each film holder can contain two sheets of film. Each sheet of film is protected from exposure by a dark slide that is only removed after the film holder is attached to the camera (in the dark) just before exposure.

The film holders for the 9×12cm and 4×5-inch formats are standardized in size as "International back," so they fit on practically all corresponding large format cameras.

Loading the sheet film holders can be done in a large changing bag or a completely dark room. It takes a bit of practice to get used to carrying out this procedure without being able to see.

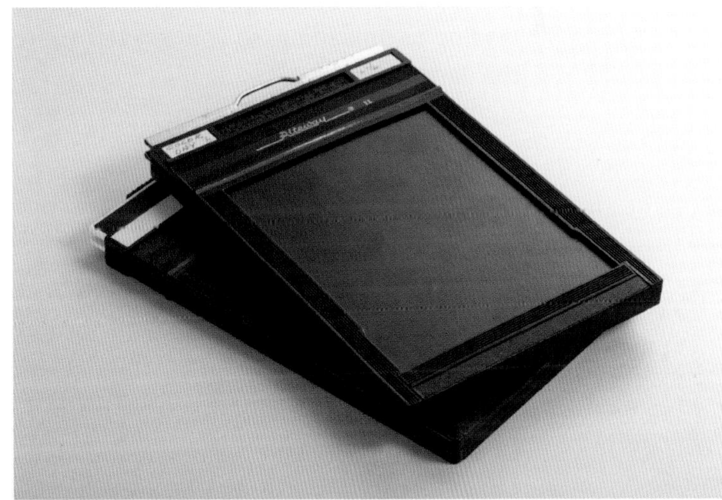

Large format film holders hold two sheets of film each

Notches

To make sure you load the film correctly into the holders, i.e., with the emulsion side towards the light, each sheet of film has a notch on one of the short sides. If you insert the film so the notch is at the top right or bottom left in portrait format, the emulsion is on the correct side.

The notches are specific to the various film types. The shape and pattern of notches forms a code that tells you which film you are loading or unloading, so you can tell, even in the dark.

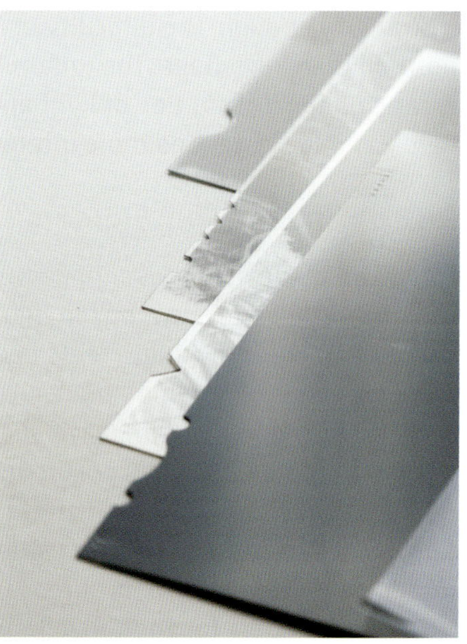

Top notch, right?

3.3.3 Camera Movement

For composing a shot with the large format camera, it helps to be aware of the various settings you can achieve by moving the two standards relative to each other.

Roughly speaking, you can divide these movements into two categories:

- Parallel movement up, down, or sideways (*rise*, *fall*, and *shift*): the front and rear standard can be moved independently from one another while staying parallel to each other. With these movements, you can control the composition and perspective.

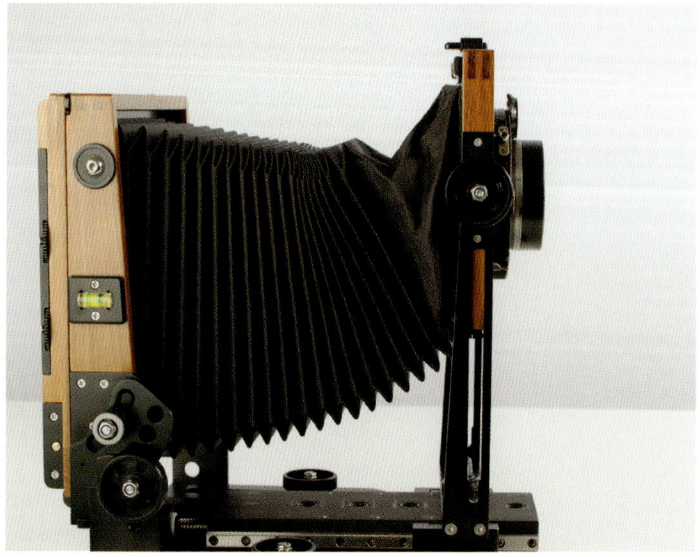

Front standard moved upwards in parallel to film plane (rise)

- Rotating the standards around their horizontal and/or vertical axes (*tilt* and *swing*): Swinging the front standard moves the focal plane, and tilting or turning the rear standard can compensate for or create perspective distortions. Remember: As long as the film plane is parallel to the subject you are shooting, parallel lines will be represented as parallel lines.

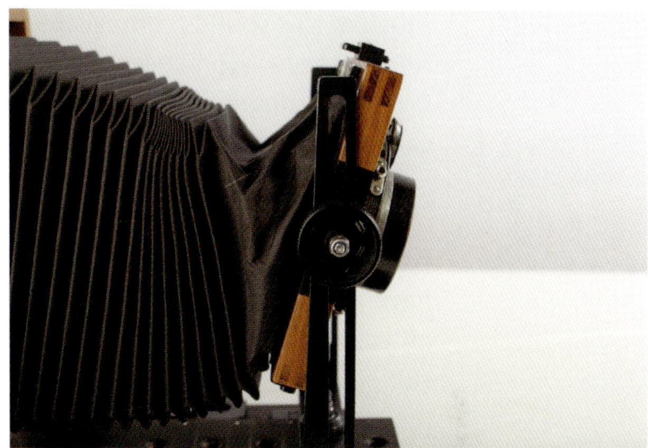

Front standard tilted to correct the sharp focus

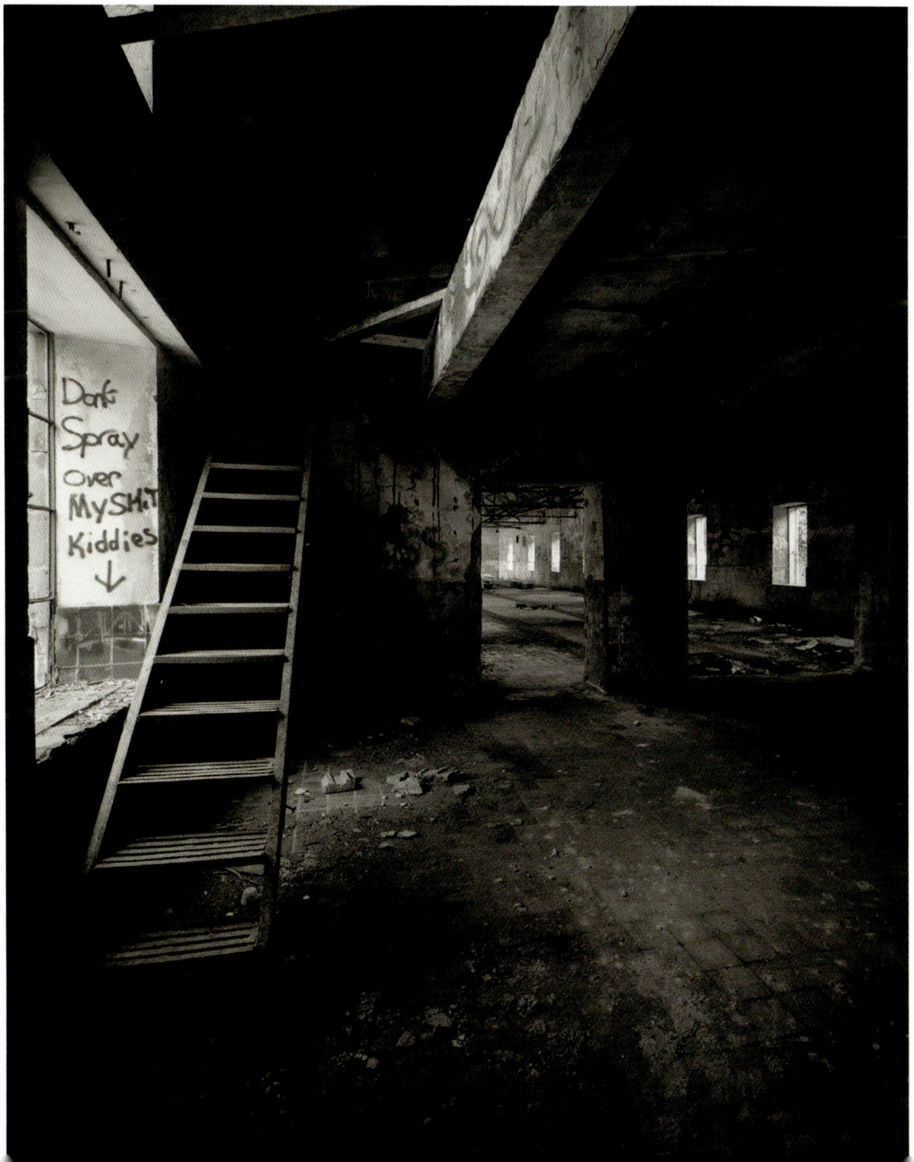

Large format picture— perspective corrected through front standard rise

Much of this sounds complicated in theory, but is quite easy to accomplish in practice. And as they say, practice makes perfect! The important thing is that the large camera gives you a degree of freedom and flexibility in capturing your own reality that no other camera system can achieve.

While you are playing around with these options and consciously slowing down when working through the many different steps, you have a lot of time to reflect and concentrate

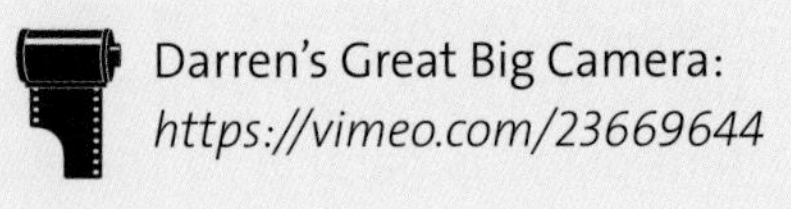

on your subject. You will quickly realize that you only want to go to all this trouble for subjects that really matter to you. At the same time, many photography basics will really sink in to your creative brain.

3.4   Tips on Buying a Camera

One of the easiest ways to get an analog camera at an affordable price is to buy one secondhand. More and more professional photographers are switching to digital or have already done so, and have abandoned their film-photography equipment. This gives many 35mm photographers the chance to get into medium format or even larger formats.

Apart from going to your local photo retailer, you can also try asking around among your friends and family. Many attics hold veritable treasures. You just have to find them. It can definitely be worth your while to ask the old-hand photographer around the corner about his former workhorses that may be gathering dust in the cupboard. You can also discover plenty of goodies online, both on the commonly used trading platforms and the various national and international online retailers. Once you have tracked down a secondhand gem or bought a new one, you are faced with a few important questions.

3.4.1   Light Seals

To produce a good photo, an analog camera has to fulfill certain requirements. To avoid blur, the film must rest as levelly as possible on the negative carrier. When transporting the film between pictures, leave enough space between exposures or individual photos could overlap. But don't leave too much space, or you'll waste film.

The most important job of the camera is protecting the film from light. That sounds simpler than it is, because light can easily sneak in and cause damage, especially in the camera back door where you insert the film. To stop this from happening, camera manufacturers have developed various ways of sealing the camera.

Labyrinth Seal

With the *labyrinth seal*, used mostly in older cameras, the light is trapped, so to speak, in several sheet-metal folds. It peters out and cannot reach the inside of the camera. Camera back doors with these light seals usually prevent unwanted light quite well. The only possible problems are a bent back door or the black paint that is supposed to absorb light flaking off the seal.

Foam Seal

Foam materials were invented in the 1960s. Since the 1970s, camera manufacturers have been frequently using them for light seals in

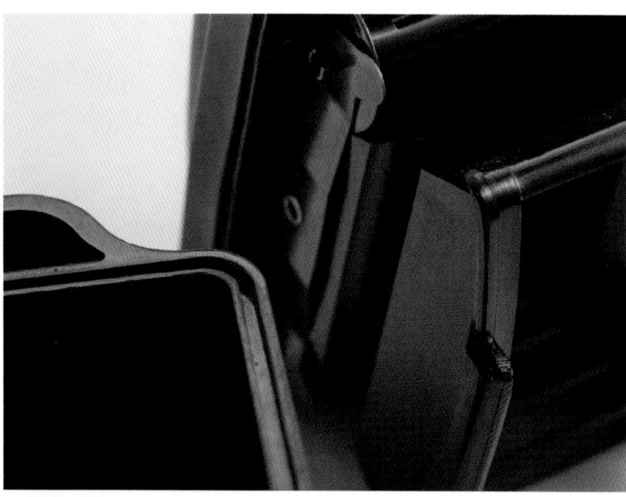

Labyrinth seal, Bilora Boy

addition to mirror dampeners. Sadly, they prove vulnerable as they age. When these materials were new, none of the manufacturers had long-term experience with them, so now, a few decades later, the seals on some of these cameras are disintegrating into sticky, crumbly bits. Sadly, and especially with online orders, you often find out if the light seals are okay only once you are holding it in your own two hands.

If you like DIY, you can create a seal yourself. New, custom-made seal kits are available on eBay for many popular camera models. Plus, you can look around online for instructions on how to change the seal yourself, but be aware that it does require a bit of patience and skill.

Velvet or String Seal

Some cameras have light seals made of velvet. These have a wider surface area to keep light out.

String seals use a mixture of labyrinth seal and a string, usually a thread of wool, into which the edge of the camera's back door presses when you close it. These wool threads are very durable and usually still lightproof after many years.

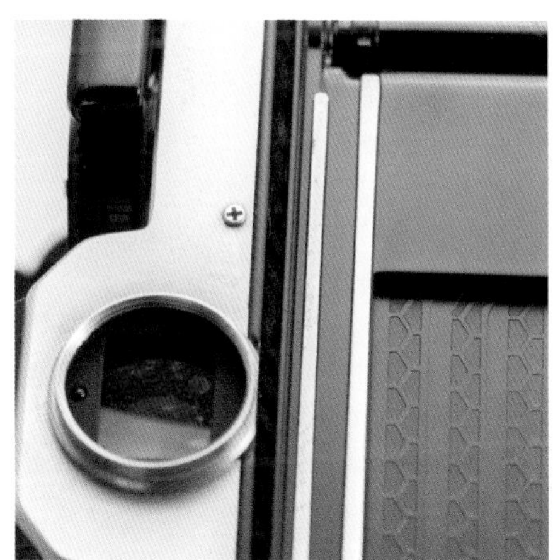

Light seal in form of black wool yarn

3.4.2 Shutters

Old, purely mechanical shutters often have their problems, too. In other words, older models don't consistently use the specified speeds. (Cameras from the 1970s onward are usually okay.)

Mostly you will find that the shutter speeds are slower than they should be, so it may happen that an exposure you set to 1/100 second is in fact 1/25 second long, and a second can actually last several seconds. Sometimes a shutter gets completely stuck.

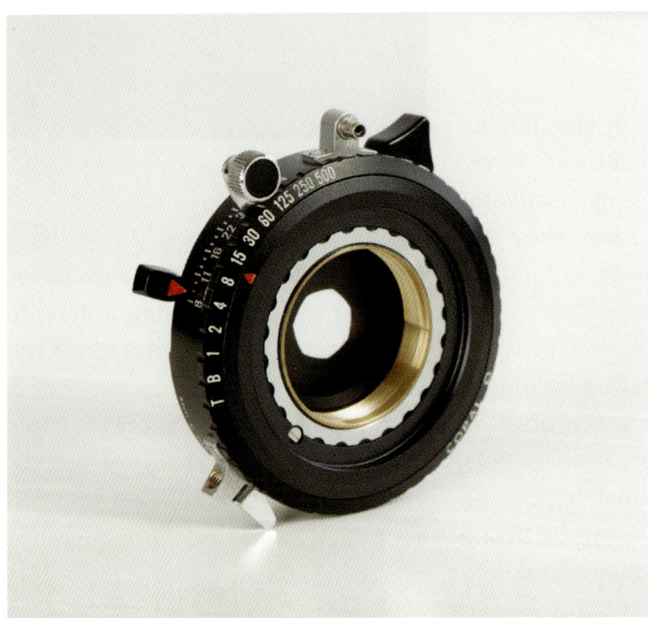

Copal-0 shutter from a large format lens

These flaws are probably due to the fact that while the camera was sitting in the attic for years, the lubricants used in the shutters slowly hardened. Plus, dust can accumulate in the shutters and slow down or even block them from moving. With a mechanical self-timer that works via a clockwork delay timer, you'll be able to hear the shutters running sluggishly.

There's another snag: These symptoms can be more or less noticeable depending on the season. In cooler weather, the shutters operate more slowly, while the summer warmth makes them work more smoothly again. To check if a shutter has problems with gummed up lubricants, you can try placing the camera on a warm radiator for half an hour to see if the self-timer runs more smoothly afterward. If you have the skill, you can find instructions online for anything from treating the seal with white spirit to taking it apart and cleaning it with alcohol and lubricating it with graphite powder.

But in serious cases of self-timer or shutter delay, the camera needs to go to an expert repairman.

You can try to prevent these problems by triggering the shutters regularly. We call it "shutter gymnastics." We make sure to take out all our film-photography cameras and use them regularly.

With the Shutter-Speed app from *photoplug.de* (iOS), you can measure your camera's actual shutter speed using your smartphone. It works via the phone's microphone and analyzes the shutter sound. With a little practice, and depending on the camera, this works amazingly well.

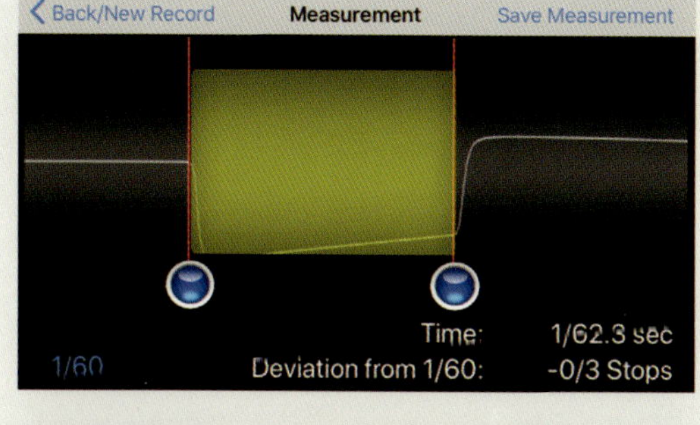

PhotoPlug's acoustic measurement of an old Agfa box camera resulting in 1/62 sec.

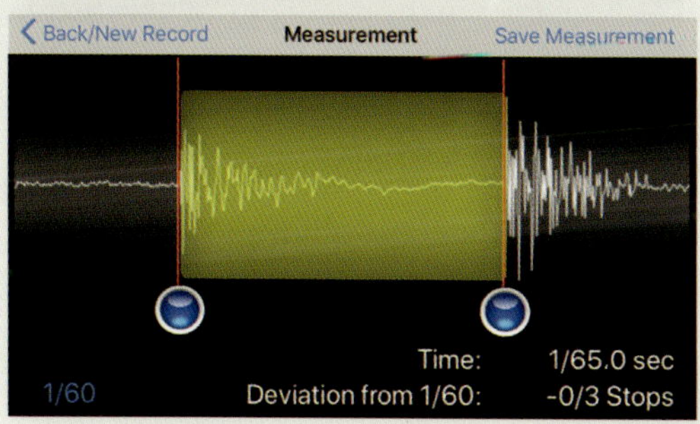

Using the Shutter-Speed app, the more precise acoustic measurement of the same camera was 1/65 sec.

Filmomat makes the PhotoPlug Shutter Speed Tester (*www.filmomat.eu/shop/photoplug-shutter-speed-testerphotoplug-verschlusszeitenteste*r). This is a small device that connects to the microphone/headphone jack on your smartphone. It contains a light sensor that detects the actual amount of light passing through your camera. With this, you can perform an optical, and even more precise, measurement.

3.4.3 Lenses

The third aspect you should watch out for when buying a used camera is the lenses—in particular, the glass and the mechanics.

The mechanical systems of old manual lenses are plagued by the same problems as the shutters in old lenses: The oil can gum up over the years, making them harder to focus, especially in cold weather. Despite claims to the contrary, dust that has collected on the optical lens is not usually a problem because it's far away from the plane of focus and won't be visible in the picture. The real problem is what's referred to as *lens fungus*, a fungus that can affect glass surfaces in objective lenses, especially if they are stored in damp conditions. This fungus feeds on materials used in making cameras and camera lenses, such as leather, glue, fibers, and lubricants.

You can recognize lens fungus by the telltale thread-like patterns on the glass, which resemble cobwebs. Once lens fungus has formed, it can potentially be removed from glass surfaces if you can reach them, but you may have to sacrifice the antireflective coating, if there is one. Lens fungus in between lens elements that are bonded together is very hard or impossible to remove. To prevent lens fungus, you should always store cameras and lenses in dry conditions. For long-term storage, it's a good idea to pack the lenses with little bags of silica gel as a desiccant.

Silica gel is easy to order online. You can collect the little bags of silica gel that sometimes comes in the packaging of new textile products and electronics.

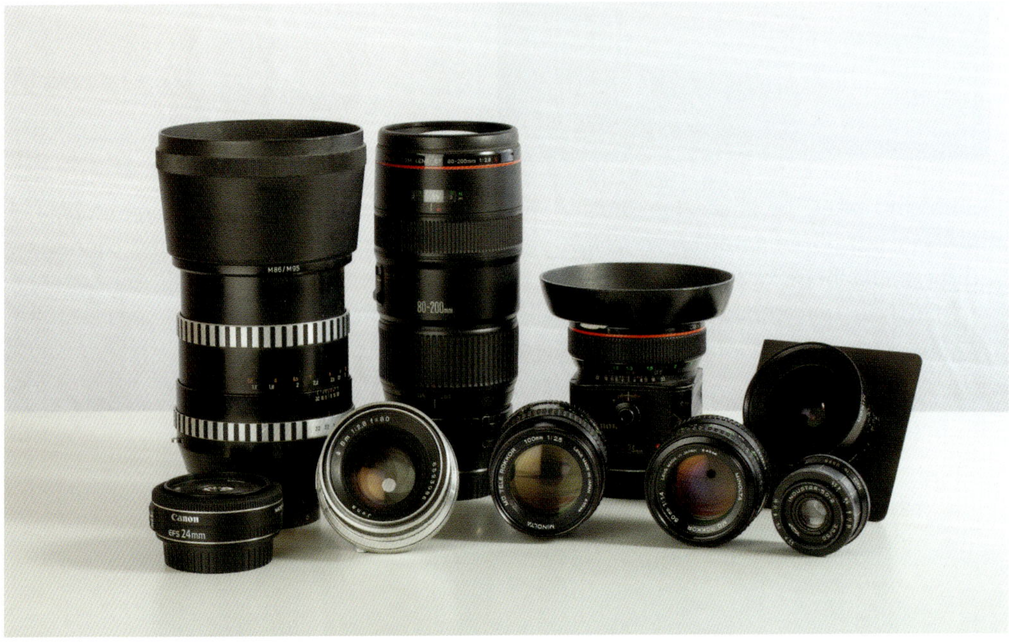

Photographic lenses: 35mm, medium format, and large format

Crowdfunding: We are often asked our opinion on photo-related crowdfunding projects. Platforms like Kickstarter, Indiegogo or GoFundMe allow companies to present product ideas in various stages of development, from pretty brass-colored Petzval lenses or classic-looking cardboard cameras taking pictures on Instax film, to autonomous flying drones that will one day be able to stream our every sporting activity live on the internet.

Crowdfunding is a fantastic vehicle for market research and financing. It allows companies to gauge interest in a future product. At the same time, manufacturers can use the money raised to advance at least some of the development costs, or even allow future customers some influence on the direction of product development.

Companies such as Peak Design, Intrepid, or Lomography are good examples of the success and customer loyalty that are possible with crowdfunding. On the other hand, we have also had to witness failed photography and videography-related campaigns. For example, several campaigns for cool lifestyle camera drones either resulted in products that fell far short of expectations, or some of them never came to fruition.

Crowdfunding as a form of financing does not necessarily guarantee the fans that they can look forward to a functioning product (or any product at all) in the end.

Of course, we like to support products that we find interesting. Often something beautiful and practical actually comes out of it. However, we always have to remind ourselves that we are not buying a product when crowdfunding, but that we are betting that the manufacturers will manage both development and production as well or better than they promised us at the beginning of the campaign.

In the end, however, we must be prepared to exchange our financial investment not for goods, but for a story. This story can then possibly tell how unexpectedly difficult it is to produce things that not only work, but are also meant to deliver on their promises.

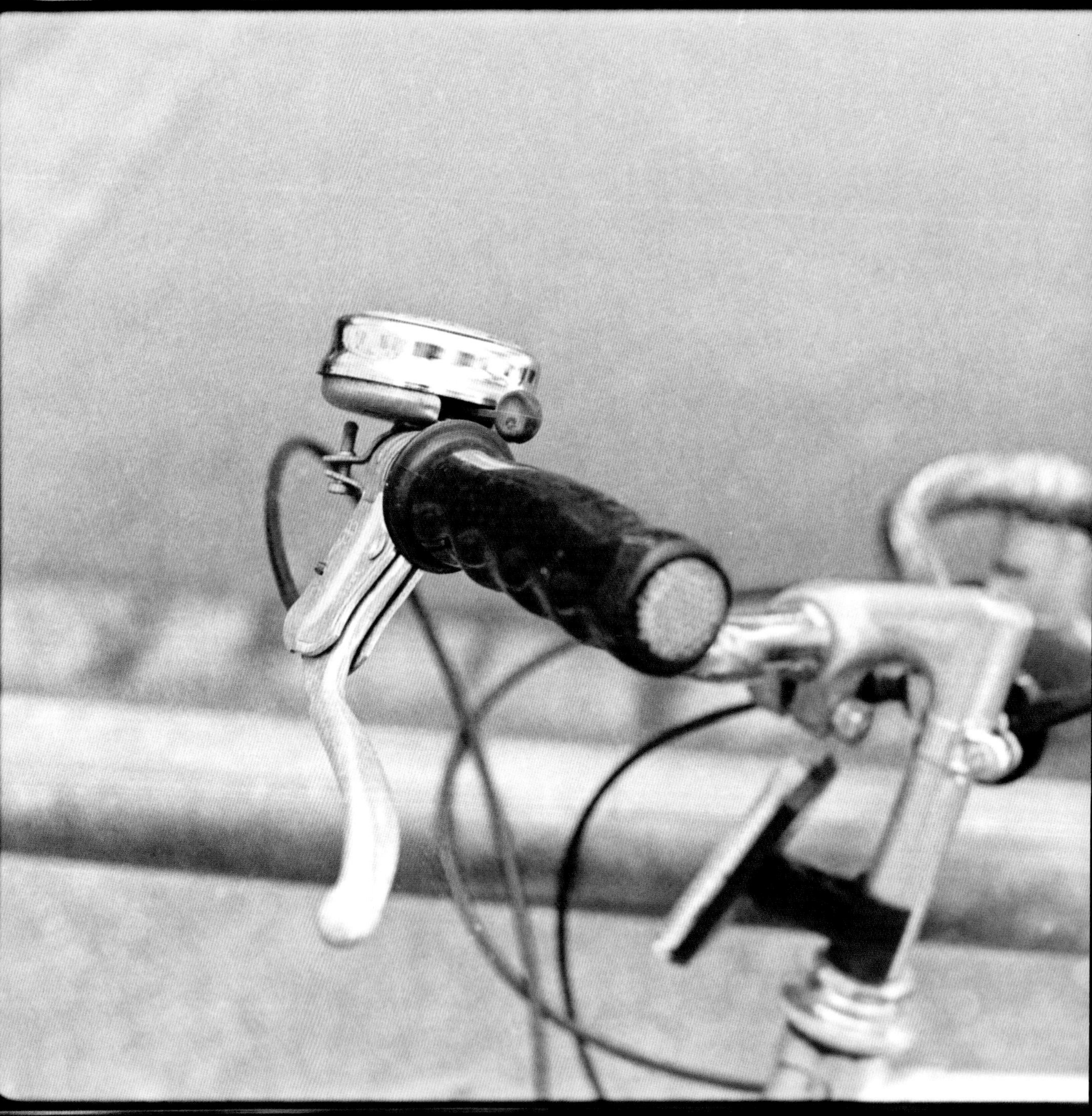
11A
12

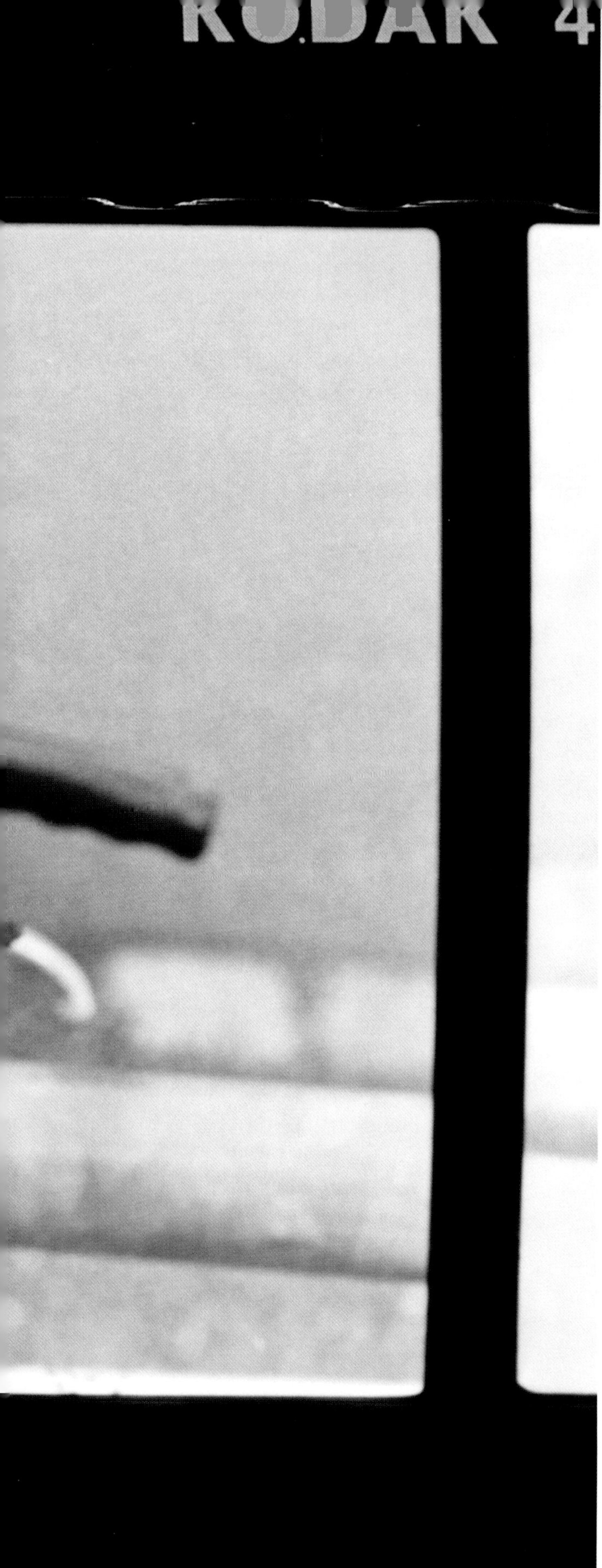

4
Exposure

Photography without light is like fishing without water—relatively pointless.

Light sources emit visible and invisible rays, and objects reflect a percentage of these rays back. A specially shaped piece of glass bundles parts of this light and projects an image onto grains of silver salts, triggering a chemical process that causes them to change and turn black in the exposed areas.

Without light, we would not be able to take photos. Light is technically necessary, but can also be used creatively. Light has direction, intensity, and color temperature. It can be emitted by a point or area source of light.

In school, you probably learned that you can mix the colors of light. The white sunlight consists of light of different wavelengths, and every monitor is composed of many small red, green, and blue pixels that can work together to represent almost any visible color. For the exposure, the intensity (and color) plays a very important role—particularly the intensity of image areas important to the photographer. Generally, it's the subject in the picture that we want to expose correctly. With the digital camera, you can check the result directly on the display. That makes it much easier to correct exposure errors quickly and take a second shot.

It's a whole different story if you are out shooting with a 1950's Voigtländer Bessa. The camera offers neither a preview nor a light meter, and you'll need to feed it the right settings before it can give you a picture with the right exposure.

4.1   Stops

In the world of photography, you often hear people talk about aperture stops, exposure values, f-numbers, f-stops, or just stops. All these terms mean basically the same thing, and refer to a relative unit for measuring the exposure. In brief: If someone says, "Expose one stop brighter!" or "Open up one stop!" it means, "Let in twice as much light!"

The term *aperture stops* refers to the aperture, but you can also change the exposure via the shutter speed, ISO, or a combination of all three values.

Here are a few examples:

Original	Change	Result
f/8, 1/100 second	one stop brighter	f/8, 1/50 second
f/16, 1/100 second	two stops lower	f/16, 1/400 second
f/4, 1/25 second	three stops darker	f/11, 1/25 second
f/4, 1/25 second	three stops darker	f/4, 1/200 second

Aperture, shutter speed, and ISO value have a triangular relationship. It's referred to as the *exposure triangle*.

For example, if you increase the shutter speed by one stop and simultaneously reduce the aperture by one stop, the exposure stays the same. But the smaller aperture changes the depth of field, and the longer exposure changes how movement is represented in the picture.

> The controls of modern digital cameras work in 1/3
> stops. So, one full stop is three clicks, and this applies
> to the aperture in the same way as the shutter speed
> and the ISO value. This makes adjusting the exposure very
> easy because you just have to count the clicks.

4.2   F-Numbers

The f-numbers with their strange fractions and odd notation are quite easy to understand and even easier to work out. Important for understanding the numbers, especially their inverse nature (bigger numbers mean smaller apertures), is knowing that their sequence describes a relationship between the focal length (f) and the size of the aperture opening.

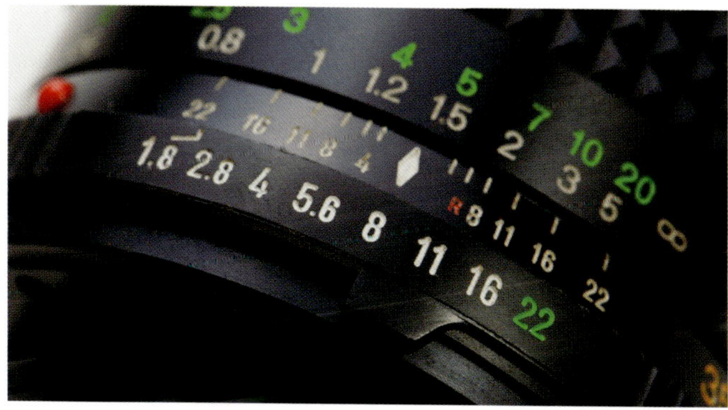

Aperture ring, Minolta 35mm F1.8

You can easily work out the f-numbers yourself by looking at every second number. Each of these numbers is double the previous, apart from a small rounding-down between 5.6 and 11.

F-numbers (full aperture stops)								
1.4	2	2.8	4	5.6	8	11	16	22

F-numbers (every other aperture value)				
.4	2.8	5.6	11	22
2	4	8	16	

So if you want the exposure to be two aperture stops brighter or darker, you simply need to double or half the aperture number. That's a quick way of working out the f-numbers for an aperture stop.

4.3   Light Metering

Before we get into the topic more deeply, it's important to familiarize yourself with the two fundamentally different approaches to light metering: reflective metering and incident metering.

4.3.1   Reflective Metering

With reflective metering, you are measuring the light reflected back towards the camera by the subject. This method is used by all cameras with integrated light meters. The aim of the light meter (exposure meter) is to get whatever is in front of the camera onto the film in such a way that the exposure is as much within the film's contrast range as possible. That works best if you choose an exposure that gets the average light of the scene into the middle brightness range.

Reflective metering is not entirely without problems: In the same light, differently reflective subjects in front of the camera result in different light meter readings, so the light meter is initially a gray meter. The result is that a white wall will be depicted as gray, and so will a black curtain. This rather technical approach contradicts our creative view because we know that white walls are white and not gray. Instead of the white wall, imagine a black cat in a coal cellar. Again, the light meter will try to get the exposure right in technical terms, and again the exposure will end up in the medium gray range.

The light meter always tries to do its job: getting the exposure as perfect as possible and making the best use of the film's contrast range. Modern light meters in both analog and digital cameras try to use integrated computer databases to recognize what's in front of the camera and compensate accordingly. This is referred to as matrix metering or evaluative metering, but in the case of the black cat in the coal cellar, even these systems can't cope.

So, your job is not to just blindly apply the results of the light metering, but to interpret them and adapt them accordingly before you transfer them to the analog camera. Then, you can decide to expose the picture of the cat in the cellar darker than the light meter is indicating. For a white cat in the snow, you would need to pick a lighter exposure than the light meter indicates.

4.3.2   Incident Metering

While reflective metering gives different results from picture to picture depending on what you point the camera at, the results of incident metering are much more consistent. Incident metering measures only the intensity of the (incidental light) light that falls onto the subject. In this case, it's completely irrelevant if the subject is black, white, or striped.

With incident metering, black subjects are depicted black in the photo, and white subjects are white. Everything is in its proper place in terms of exposure. But even incident metering is not entirely free of problems. To measure precisely, you need to be where the subject is. You can only get a good result if you are measuring in the same light that's illuminating the subject. That may be fairly easy if you are shooting a portrait in the studio, but spontaneous snapshots are trickier. In landscape photography, for instance, you can't just take your light meter and drive over to a far-off mountain to measure the light several miles away.

With a bit of experience, incident metering can still work for landscape shots. However, in certain situations you can also use proxy metering to work out the incident light: If the mountain several miles away is in full sunlight and the lighting condition is the same where you are shooting, you can assume that the light intensity is the same in both locations and take the reading from where you are.

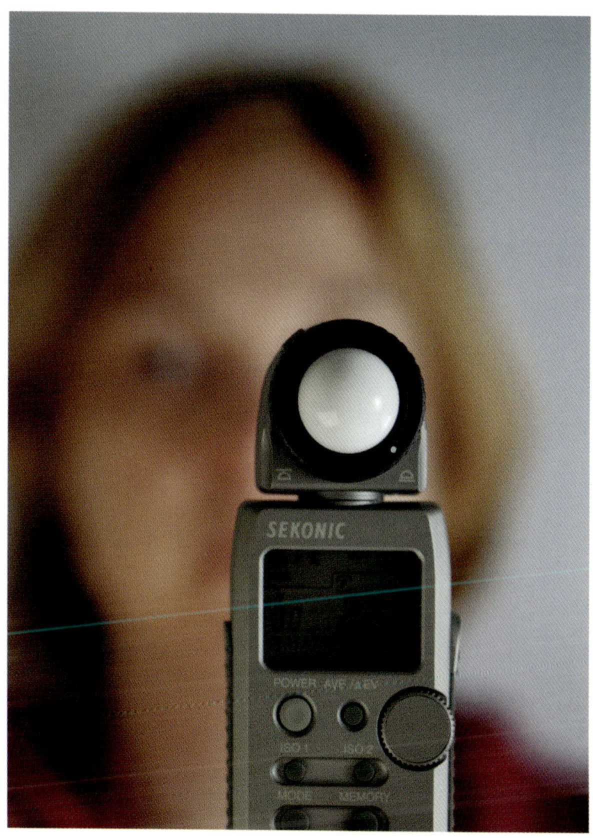

Incident metering with a modern light meter

The following sections will show you how to achieve good exposures in such situations.

4.4   Without Light Meter

First, let's make things easy. Before the light meter was invented, people still managed to take photos with good exposure. Photographers simply used figures based on their experience or compensated for minor exposure errors later in the darkroom during processing or enlargement. These empirical values were then turned into a few rules of thumb that are still applicable today.

4.4.1   Sunny 16

The Sunny 16 goes back to the time when cameras did not have light meters, but is still as valid today as it was 50 years ago.

The approach is simple. First, the camera needs to be in manual exposure mode (M).

1. Load a film with an ISO value suitable for the lighting situation (ISO 100, for example, for sunny situations).
2. Set the exposure time to the reciprocal value of the inserted film: For ISO 100, set it to 1/100 second; for ISO 400, set it to 1/400 second.

That's all you need in terms of preparation. Now you just have to set the following aperture depending on the lighting conditions:

Aperture	Light	Shadows
f/16	full sun	sharp edges
f/11	slightly overcast	soft edges
f/8	cloudy	hardly visible
f/5.6	very cloudy	not visible

This rule works for both analog cameras and modern digital cameras.

4.4.2   Looney 11

The Looney 11 is based on the Sunny 16 and designed for shooting pictures of the moon. Such a special case throws any light meter, so this rule of thumb comes in handy.

Again, follow the same steps as before. Start by setting your camera to manual exposure mode (M).

1. Load a film with an ISO value suitable for the lighting situation (ISO 400, for example, for night time).
2. Set the exposure time to the reciprocal value of the inserted film: For ISO 400, set it to 1/400 second; for ISO 800, set it to 1/800 second.

That's all you need in terms of preparation. Now you just have to set the aperture depending on the lighting situation to see the moon in all its beauty:

Aperture	Light
f/11	full moon
f/8	half moon

This rule works for both analog cameras and modern digital cameras.

4.5   With Light Meter

Nowadays, we usually work with a light meter. You can either use the light meter inside your digital camera, or if you want to be a bit more hands-on, you have options, as you'll see in the following sections.

4.5.1   Handheld Light Meter

At flea markets, in camera exchanges, or online, you will often find secondhand light meters. With a few exceptions, they work fine.

Without Battery

For a while, selenium was used as light-sensitive material in light meters. This material creates electricity from light, which made it ideal for light meters that worked without batteries. Sadly, many secondhand selenium light meters are only good for the museum these days, because selenium ages over time and loses its properties, especially if it's constantly exposed to light and has not been stored in a dark drawer.

So beware—especially if the light-meter reading differs significantly from your digital camera's reading.

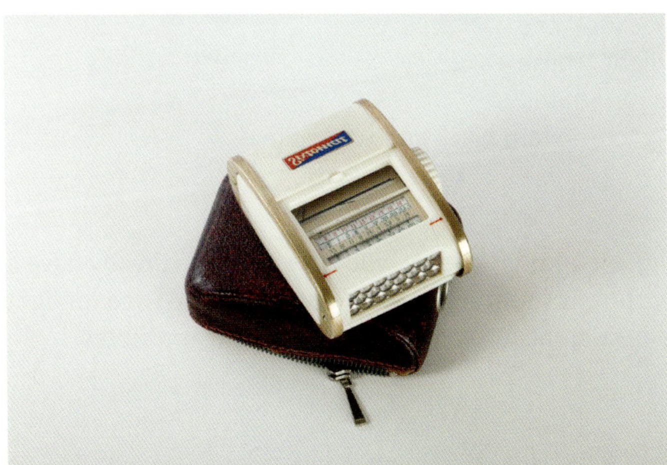

Sixtomat light meter with selenium cell

> To test a used handheld light meter, proceed as follows: Set the metering method of your digital camera to center-weighted and the camera itself to mode (P). Aim the camera at an evenly and diffusely illuminated white wall, so the wall fills the entire viewfinder. Then, touch the trigger lightly to start your camera's light meter. Remember the measured ISO, time, and aperture values. Take the same measurement with the handheld light meter (at a similar distance from the wall, with the same illumination) and read the determined values. These values should be, at most, half a stop different than the values measured by the digital camera. This test is not highly scientific but should help you detect faulty light meters.

Battery-Powered

The prime example of a used, battery-powered handheld light meter that still works very well today is the Lunasix 3 (known as Luna Pro S in the USA) by Gossen in Germany. Millions of these meters have been sold since 1966.

The electronics of the Lunasix 3/Luna Pro S are designed to be used with mercury batteries, which may be hard to find today. Gossen offers a battery adapter, so you can use two silver oxide batteries instead (type Varta V 76 PX or Duracell D 357 H). The adapter takes care of battery size and also contains a diode for the correct battery voltage.

Caution: Light meters from the time of orthochromatic film (generally pre-1950) do not measure red light because the film was not sensitive to red light. These meters are only suitable to a limited extent, including light metering for modern black-and-white film.

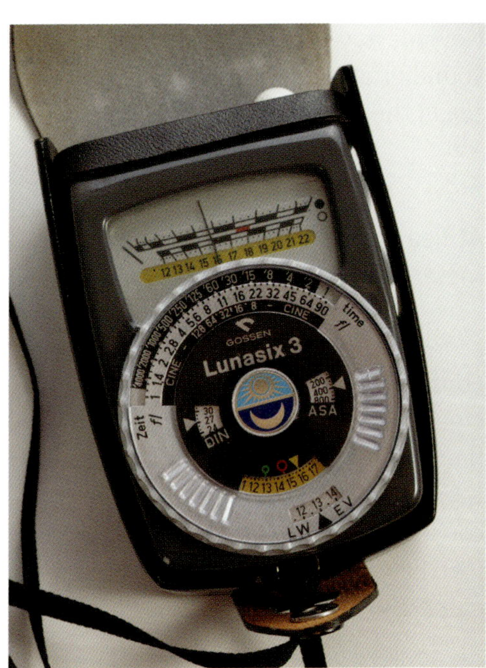

Light meter Gossen Lunasix 3

4.5.2   Smartphone

If you don't want to cart around yet another gadget, you may find you already have a light meter in your pocket. Any current smartphone with camera can be used for light metering. You can get suitable apps in the relevant marketplaces and app stores.

As an example, let's take a look at the Pocket Light Meter app for the iPhone. It works pretty much like many other light metering apps:

1. Select two of the three exposure parameters—in this example, aperture 8 and ISO 100.
2. Aim the camera at the scene you want to expose.
3. Read the third parameter (here, 1/250 second shutter speed) and transfer the value to your camera.

For Android, we have had recommendations for the Light Meter Tools and Lightmeter apps.

4.5.3   Gray Card

If you have an 18% gray card, you can use it for white balance as well as for light metering. The reflectivity of the card is calibrated to 18%, which is also the value the light meter is set to.

Again, the procedure is easy:

1. Place the gray card directly in front of or next to the subject.
2. Measure with the light meter directly off the gray card. Make sure you are as close as possible without letting your own shadow fall onto the gray card. The card should fill the picture frame.
3. Set the camera to the measured values.

Pocket light meter for an iPhone

4.5.4   Professional Light Meter

In the professional league—particularly for studio work—photographers use light meters that can deal with normal (continuous) incident metering, reflective metering, and also metering for flash units. The measured values can be stored in the memory to determine average exposures from multiple readings. With interchangeable domes, some light meters can be converted to highly accurate spot meters. The price for such a device is usually several hundred dollars.

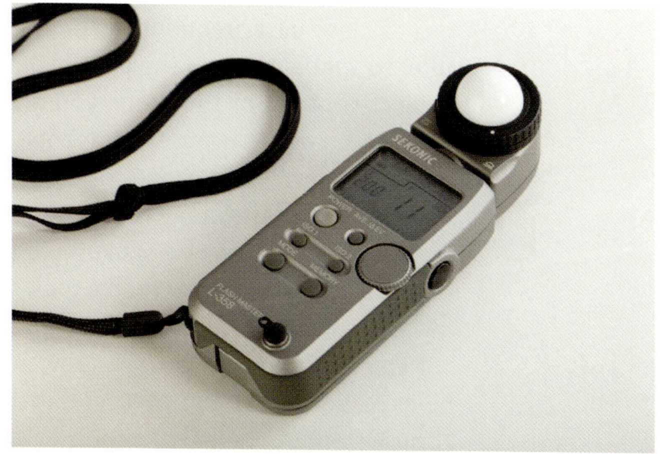

Sekonic L-358

4.6   Light Metering with the Zone System

The Zone System is not just about the creative aspect of film photography, but also the chemical, technical, and economic aspects. If you deal with film photography, you will come across the Zone System sooner or later. Be warned: There is a lot of voodoo floating around the Internet regarding the Zone System, and it causes confusion among newbies. In this chapter, we will use some examples to show you how easy working with the Zone System can actually be.

The Zone System was developed by the U.S. photographers Ansel Adams and Fred Archer. It is designed to get the contrast of the subject in the picture (taken in analog large format) as comprehensive as possible in the finished positive image, from exposing the negative to processing the film and enlarging the photo. Particularly in large format, experiments and failed shots have always been expensive and time consuming. By creating a system for this process, photography results became more predictable, and the amount of work and cost involved in the process was reduced. Parts of the Zone System can also be applied to smaller formats.

Simplified Zone System

Describing the details of the Zone System would go way beyond the scope of this book, but we want to take a closer look at the first part, so it's usable for other formats, as well. It's all about the right exposure of the picture. With film photography in particular, getting the exposure right is important because you can't just take a quick look at the histogram, adjust, and take a second shot to correct. The Zone System is an important tool that makes it extremely easy to get the exposure right where you want it to be.

Let's clear up a frequent misunderstanding: The zones in the Zone System do not refer to spatial areas in the picture, but brightness levels. The Zone System divides the subject contrast of the scene you are shooting into 11 zones numbered with Roman numerals. Zone 0 is pure black, zone X is pure white. In between, you have different brightness levels. Each zone corresponds to one aperture stop difference in exposure.

The middle of the range is defined as zone V and represents medium brightness. Light meters are set to zone V. For example: in diffuse light, if you point your light meter at an evenly lit white wall and then expose the picture with the settings shown by the light meter, your negative will render the area with medium brightness in zone V.

If you now measure an 18% gray card instead of the white wall and shoot it, it will be exposed correctly in zone V; but the white wall will be too dark. That's where the Zone System can help us. As soon as you're comfortable with which zone makes certain subjects looks best, you can get the exposure correct straight away without having to experiment.

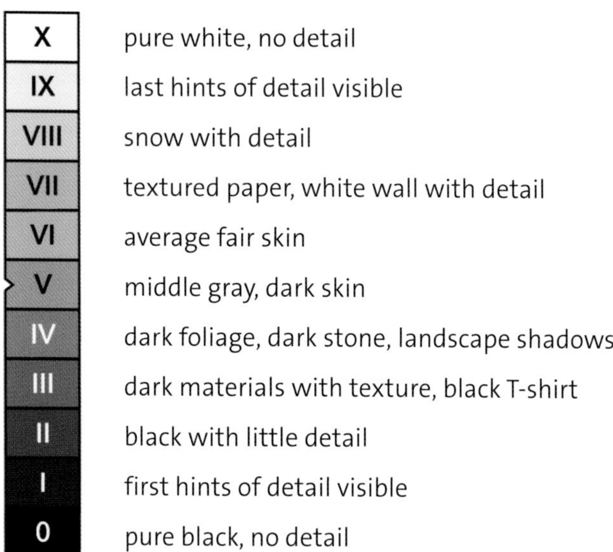

X	pure white, no detail
IX	last hints of detail visible
VIII	snow with detail
VII	textured paper, white wall with detail
VI	average fair skin
V	middle gray, dark skin
IV	dark foliage, dark stone, landscape shadows
III	dark materials with texture, black T-shirt
II	black with little detail
I	first hints of detail visible
0	pure black, no detail

The 11 zones of the Zone System

Examples

Using the Zone System table, let's take another look at that white wall. We now know that our light meter feels drawn to zone V. But the white wall wants to be in zone VII, so it needs to be exposed two stops higher. Let's assume our light-meter reading of the white wall resulted in the following exposure: ISO 100, f/8, 1/400 second.

Now all we need to do is correct this exposure two stops upward compared to the measurement. For the correction, we could theoretically use any of the three parameters (ISO, aperture, or shutter speed). But because we put a film with ISO 100 into the camera and aperture 8 offers the desired depth of field, we'll adjust the shutter speed two whole stops upward. So, we double the time twice: ISO 100, f/8, 1/100 second. The photo we expose now puts the white wall into zone VII.

Let's work through another example: We are sitting in the audience and want to shoot a photo of a concert on stage. The musicians are lit brightly, and the big black curtain behind the stage shows a bit of detail but is mostly black. The light meter looks at the whole scene, the black curtain is large compared to the lit musicians. The light meter determines the following exposure: ISO 800, f/4, 1/50 second. Again, the light meter has tricked us and will expose the black curtain as zone V, i.e., as middle gray. So the musicians will be hopelessly overexposed.

The table shows that the black curtain will have detail somewhere between Zone II and III. So we correct the exposure downwards, this time via the aperture. Instead of f/4, we use f/8: ISO 800, f/8, 1/50 second. The curtain will now be correctly exposed.

For the Zone System, spot metering is ideal. Spot metering uses only a small part of the scene for the measurement, so you can measure precisely even from a distance. If you don't have a spot meter, you need to get closer to your subject for the measurement. You can also use the spot meter from your digital camera.

The Gray Card as Reference

What to do if there are neither white walls nor black curtains for you to use as reference for light metering? You can bring along your own reference in the form of an 18% gray card (available in photo retail stores). This gray card is already in zone V, which makes life easier for you. Hold the gray card into the same light as the subject for which you want to find the right exposure. The values determined via spot metering (or close-up metering with the normal light meter) can be transfered directly to the camera.

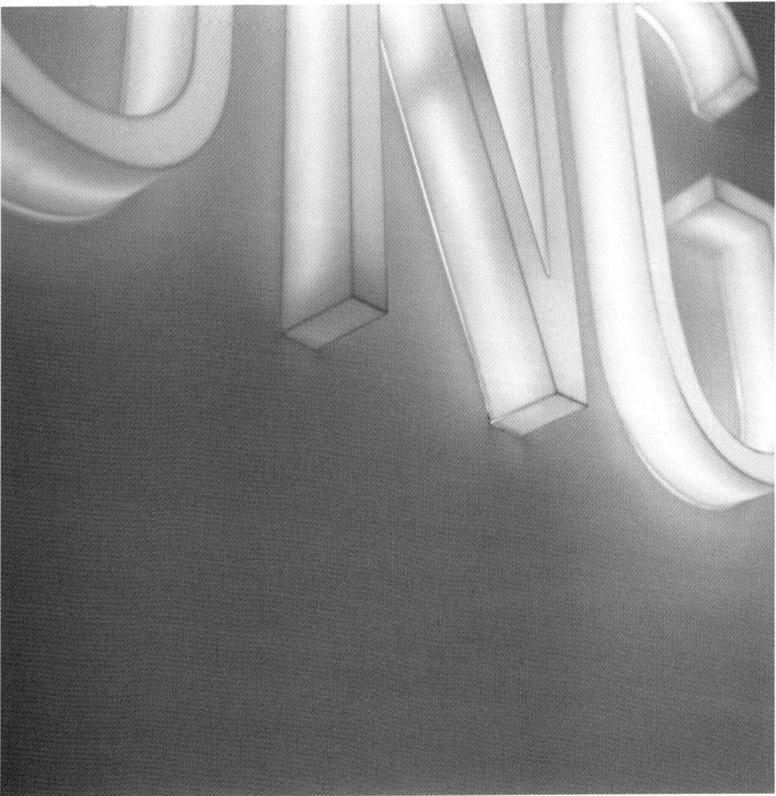

A white wall with an additional light source in the picture is a challenge for finding the right exposure. This issue is solved here via spot metering on the light source, and shifting the brightest areas to zone VIII. The wall then automatically falls in between zones VI and V.

Your Palm as Reference

We also carry another exposure reference point around with us all the time: the palm of our hand. Even in summer, it will never change in reflectivity. As long as we know which zone our palm is in, we can use it for light metering.

You simply have to work out just once what zone your palm is in. The easiest way is with a digital camera in exposure mode (M). First, set the camera's light meter to a diffusely lit gray card in such a way that the measurement is in the middle. Now, hold the palm of your hand into the light you're exposing for, and look at the scale of the light meter. Many fair-skinned peoples' palms are in zone VI, i.e., one aperture stop over the middle.

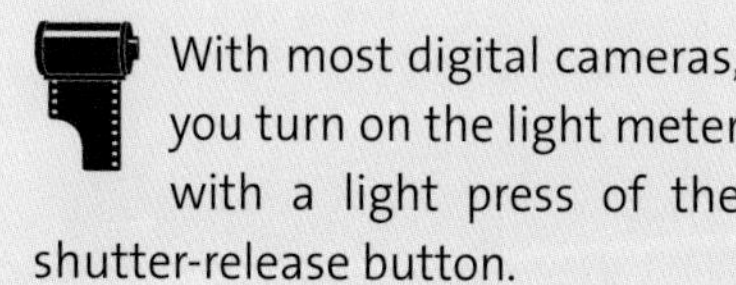

With most digital cameras, you turn on the light meter with a light press of the shutter-release button.

This is how you now measure the exposure:

1. Hold your palm into the same light that the subject is in.
2. Set the exposure so the light meter is one stop above the middle when measuring your palm.
3. Transfer the values to the camera.

Done!

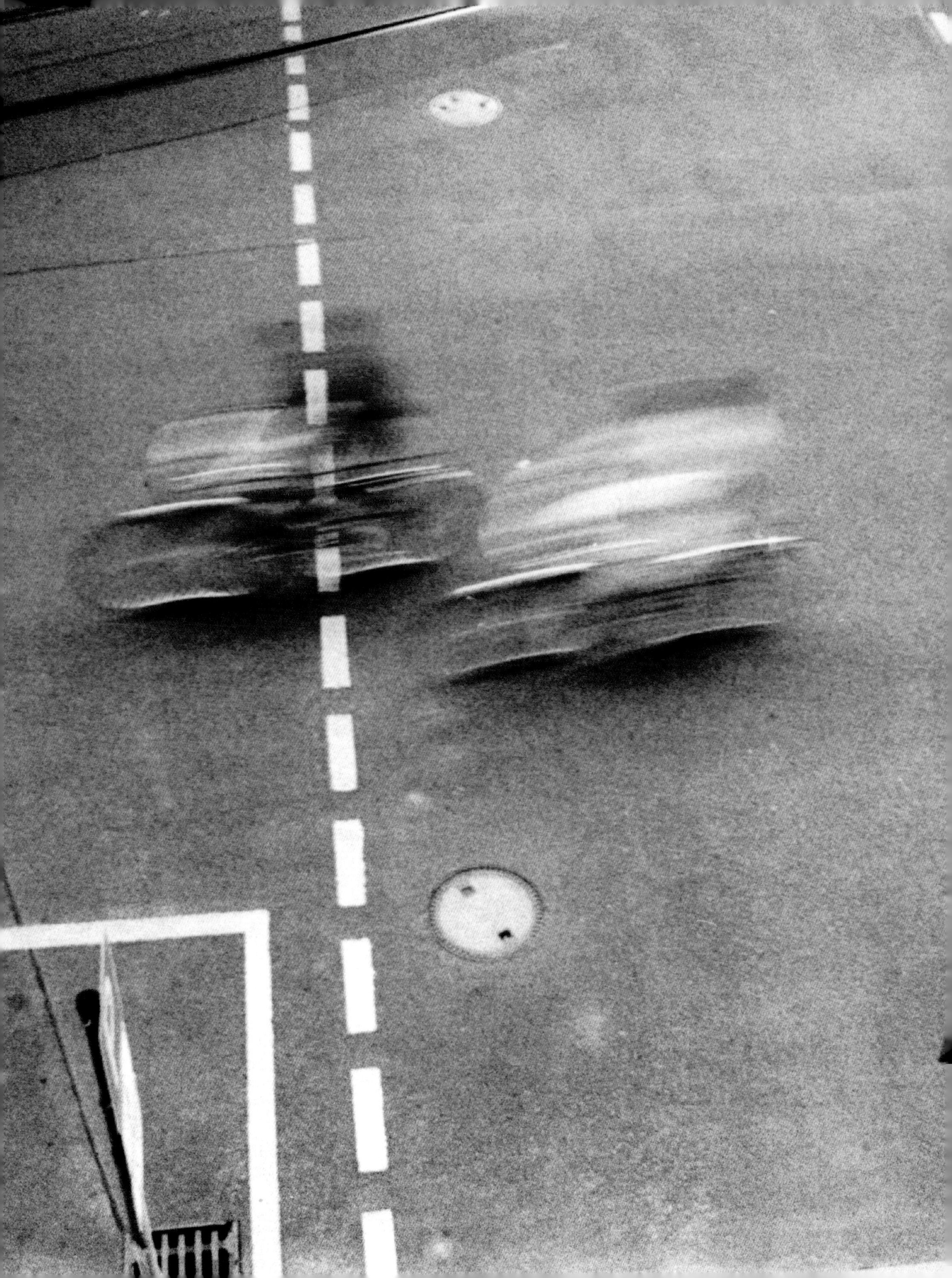

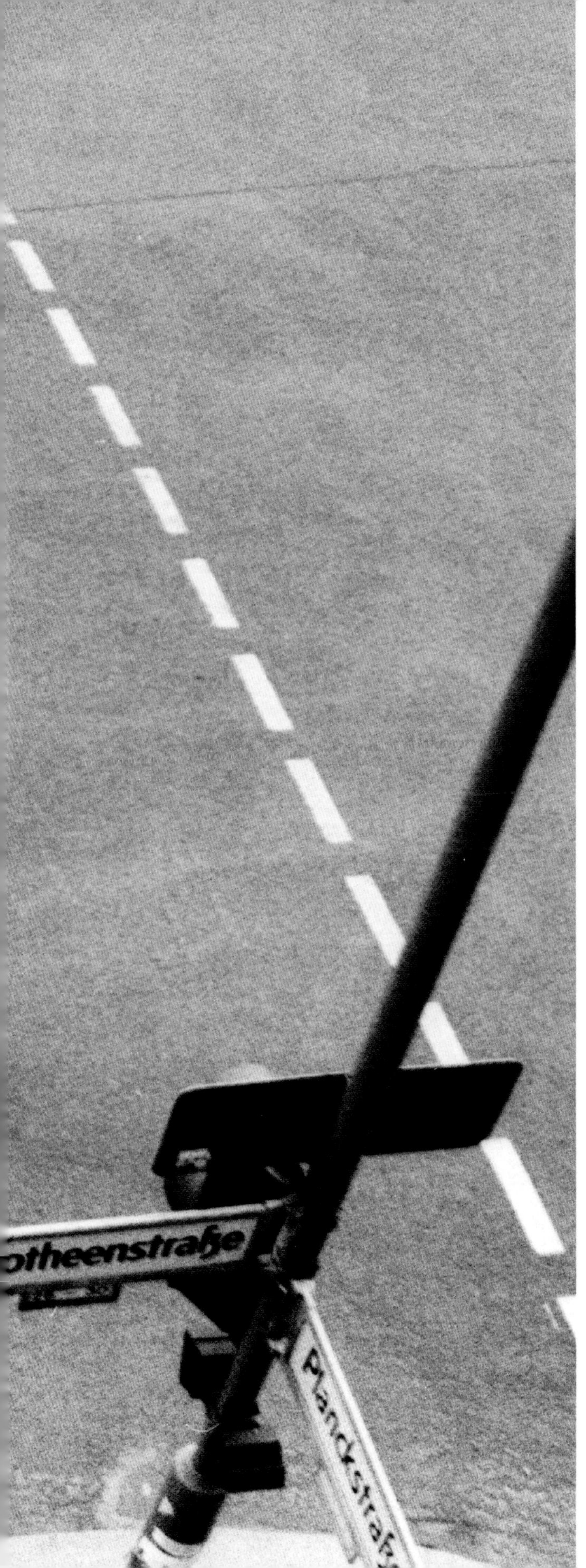

5
Film

If you look at a cross section of film under the microscope, you can see that it consists of multiple layers. First, there is the film base. Early types of film often had a base of highly flammable celluloid that made photography and storing film somewhat dangerous. Today, film does not explode any more because tri-acetate and polyester are used as film bases, instead.

During production, the film base is coated with several very thin layers of emulsion containing light-sensitive silver halides suspended in gelatin. Even black-and-white film usually has several layers of differently sized or individually shaped silver halides that serve to make the best use of the light. In addition to the light-sensitive emulsion layers, there are also protective layers and usually an anti-halation layer.

At one time, there was no gelatin of good enough quality for film production available in the United States, so for a while, Kodak became one of the largest operators of cattle ranches in the U.S.

The anti-halation layer absorbs light that would otherwise be reflected back onto the film by the film base or camera back wall, causing light edges (halation or halos) around the lights in the film. Depending on the film, the layer is applied to the back of the film or between the film base and the emulsion. The anti-halation layer increases the contrast options of the film considerably. There are also special types of film that either deliberately omit this layer for artistic reasons (they are referred to as AURA) or that have an anti-halation layer that is not particularly effective (for example Lucky, from China), so they tend still produce highlight halos.

Medium and large format film has an additional backing layer for stability. Plus, some manufacturers coat their film with an anti-curling layer to prevent excessive curling during the drying stage. All the emulsion layers of a black-and-white film taken together are about ten times thinner than a human hair.

Color film is even more complex in structure than black-and-white film, color film has separate layers for the colors cyan, magenta, and yellow, and these in turn each consist of two or three differently light-sensitive layers. Plus there are several filter and correction layers: the anti-halation layer, the protective layer and, depending on the film type, a backing layer, and perhaps a layer to prevent curling. A color film can have 10 to 20 layers and still be only several micrometers thick.

Making Kodak Film by Robert L. Shanebrook is a fascinating book on film manufacturing. *http://www.makingkodakfilm.com*

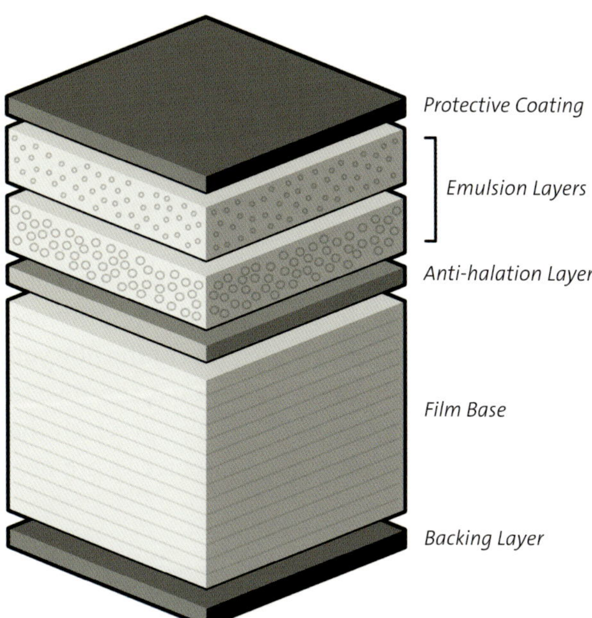

Schematic structure of a black-and-white film (not to scale)

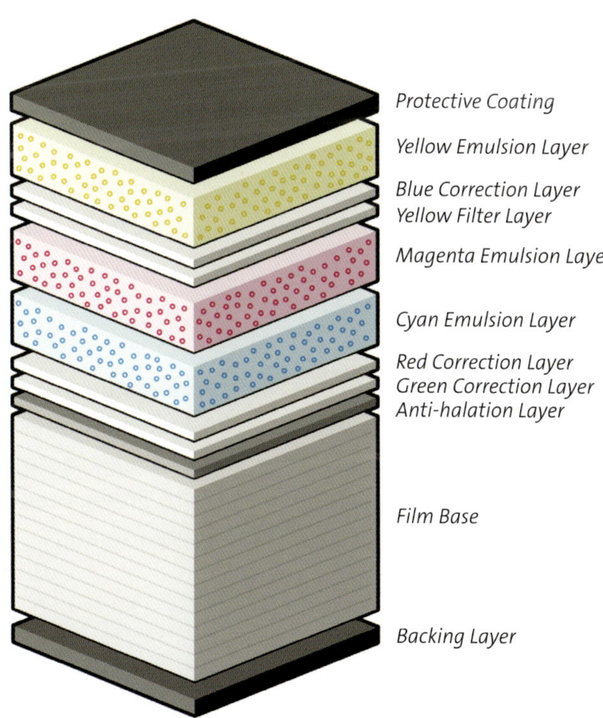

Schematic structure of color film

5.1   Black-and-White Film

If you decide to work with black-and-white film, the choice of film plays just as significant a role as the exposure settings on your camera. Depending on the aesthetic criteria that matter to you, or which style best suits your way of shooting and your favorite subject, it's worth playing around with the different types of film and finding out which one is best for you.

Each different film will have a different look in terms of the grain and tonal value characteristics, sharpness, contrast, ISO value, and nominal film speed. The interplay with different types of developer are another aspect to consider in terms of the film you choose. The question of which range of the light spectrum the emulsion is sensitive to is more important than the brand or manufacturer of the film. The way in which the film is sensitized has a great deal of influence on how the colors we perceive are rendered as shades of gray.

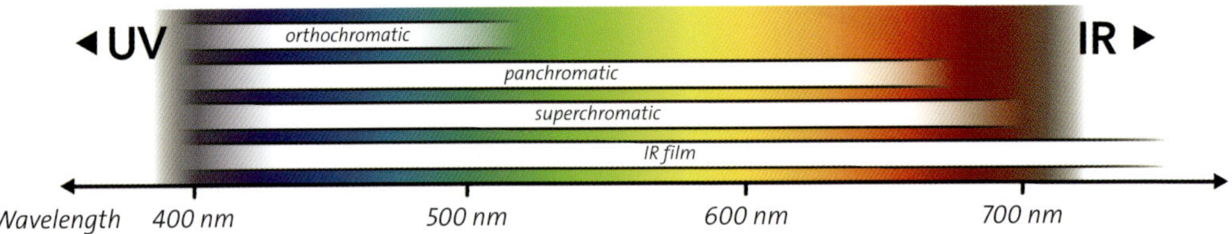

Film types and their spectral range

The human eye has its strongest spectral sensitivity in the yellow-green range. A photographic emulsion in which the silver grains have not been sensitized with embedded color particles is mostly color blind—it's only sensitive to the short-wavelength spectral range, around 380–420 nanometers (i.e., to blue light). Only subjects that reflect light of this wavelength are rendered in gray tones.

5.1.1   From Color to Black-and-White

Whether we are shooting digital or analog, or using color film or black-and-white film, the world around us is in color. The visible spectrum we perceive with our eyes is in between short-wave ultraviolet (UV) light and long-wave infrared (IR) thermal radiation. In between lies the complete rainbow, from violet and blue to green, yellow, orange, and red. This corresponds to wavelengths of about 380 to 780 nanometers.

The spectral areas of light

If we load a black-and-white film today, it will render the visible colors in as many shades of gray as there are shades of color perceptible to our eyes. That was different in the early days of photography. The early types of film were sensitive to only a fraction of the visible spectrum.

The white sunlight (color temperature around 5800 K) reaches us through a huge color filter—the atmosphere. Not all parts of the visible light spectrum can make it through the atmosphere evenly, so the color of the sunlight we see changes constantly. This is particularly noticeable in the morning and in the evening, when the sun is low in the sky and the light has to travel farther through the atmosphere.

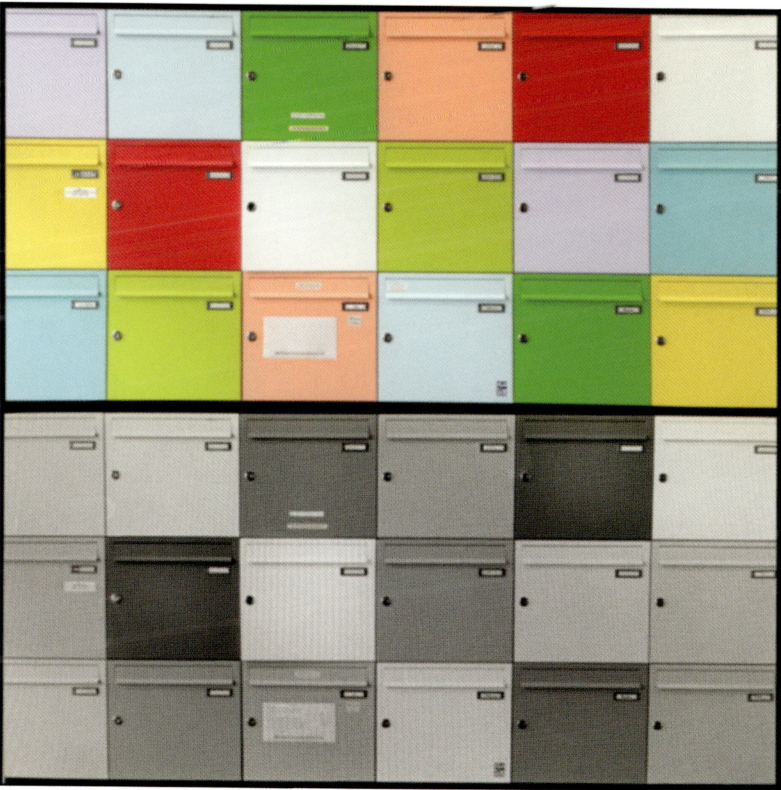

Even many modern black-and-white films render red quite dark and blue lighter than yellow

5.1.2   Orthochromatic Film

The name for this black-and-white film is derived from the Greek (*orthos* = right and *chroma* = color). An orthochromatic emulsion is highly sensitive to blue light, but by adding organic coloring, it has been sensitized to green and yellow light, as well. Light with a wavelength between 400 and 600 nanometers is rendered in shades of gray. As orthochromatic film is blind to red light, red objects are rendered black. An advantage of this insensitivity to red is that this type of film can be developed by inspection in red darkroom light, so you can see what you are doing. Orthochromatic film usually has a fine resolution with high contrast (Ilford Ortho+, Rollei Ortho 25, wephota Ortho 25, and Adox Ortho 25).

Telekia speciosa. *Example of a plant shot on orthochromatic film, Graflex Crown Graphic on wephota Ortho 25*

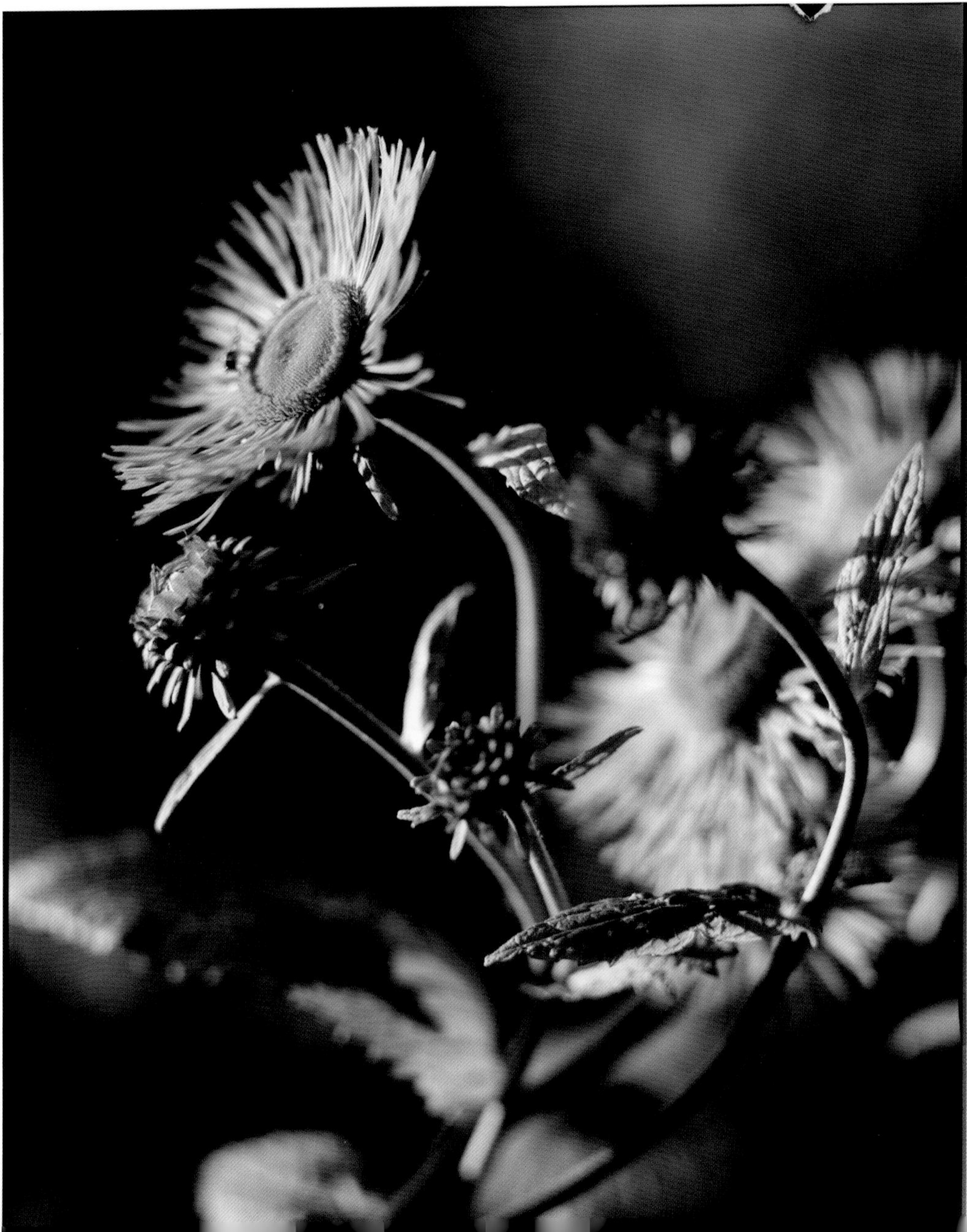

Incidentally, in the early days of film, this red blindness was the reason why actors and models had to wear different makeup than today. Red lips would have been rendered as black without special makeup, and red cheeks also looked dark. To achieve a more natural looking grayscale representation on film, actors wore blue and green makeup. Camera-people and directors had to use blue filters to be able to render the color red on film.

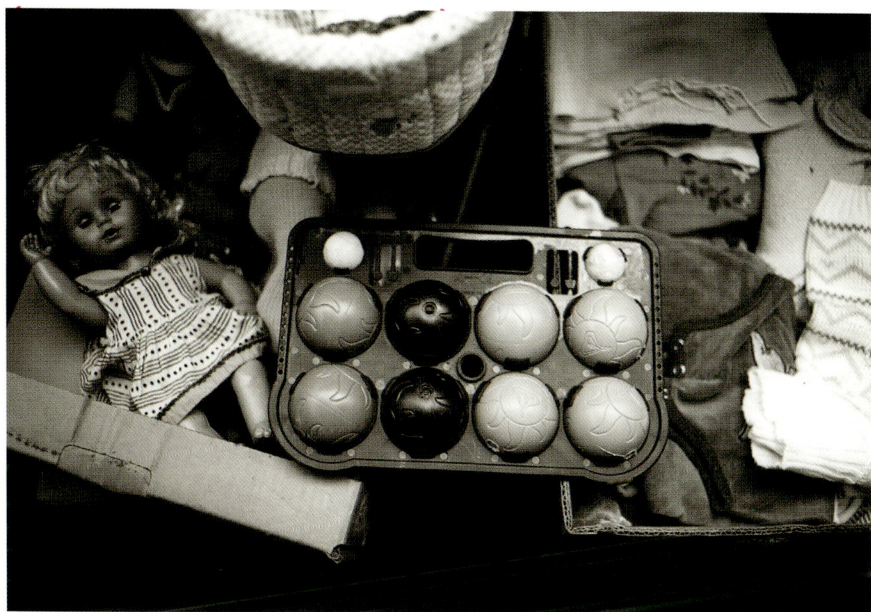

Green, red, yellow, blue: bocce balls on orthochromatic film

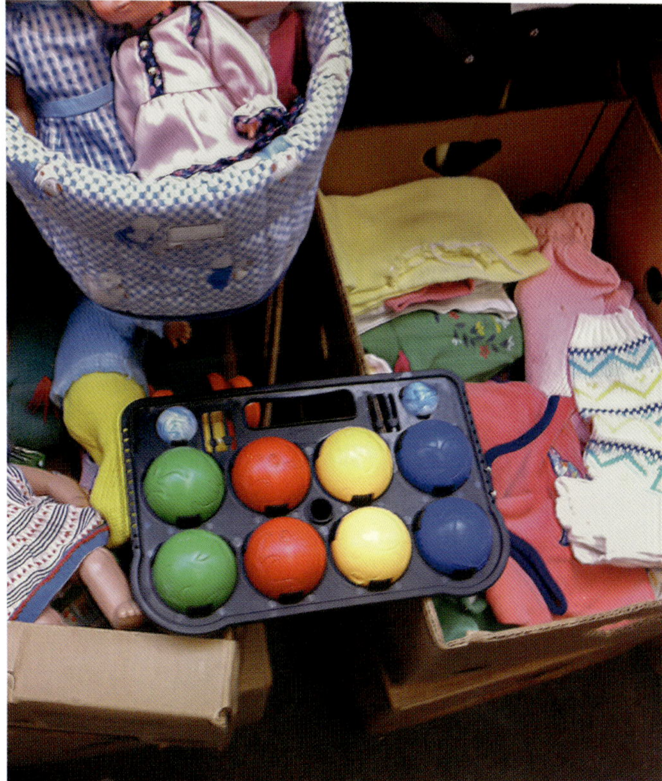

The same scene as a smartphone snapshot

5.1.3   Panchromatic Film

Panchromatic means sensitized to all visible light colors. While orthochromatic film is insensitive to red light, panchromatic film can render red objects in shades of gray because it is also sensitized to light wavelengths of up to 660 nanometers (in special cases, up to 750 nanometers; then it's sometimes referred to as super-panchromatic film), i.e., orange and red. Unlike orthochromatic film, classic panchromatic film has a slightly reduced sensitivity in the blue and green areas of the spectrum (490 to 540 nanometers). But the latter is still so strong that sky is often rendered very bright and clouds are hardly visible. If you are planning to use this type of film in landscape photography, you should consider using a yellow or orange filter. This will darken the blue sky and increase the contrast to the white clouds. Examples of panchromatic film are Tri-X 400, Kodak T-MAX, Agfa APX, Ilford HP5, and Ilford FP4.

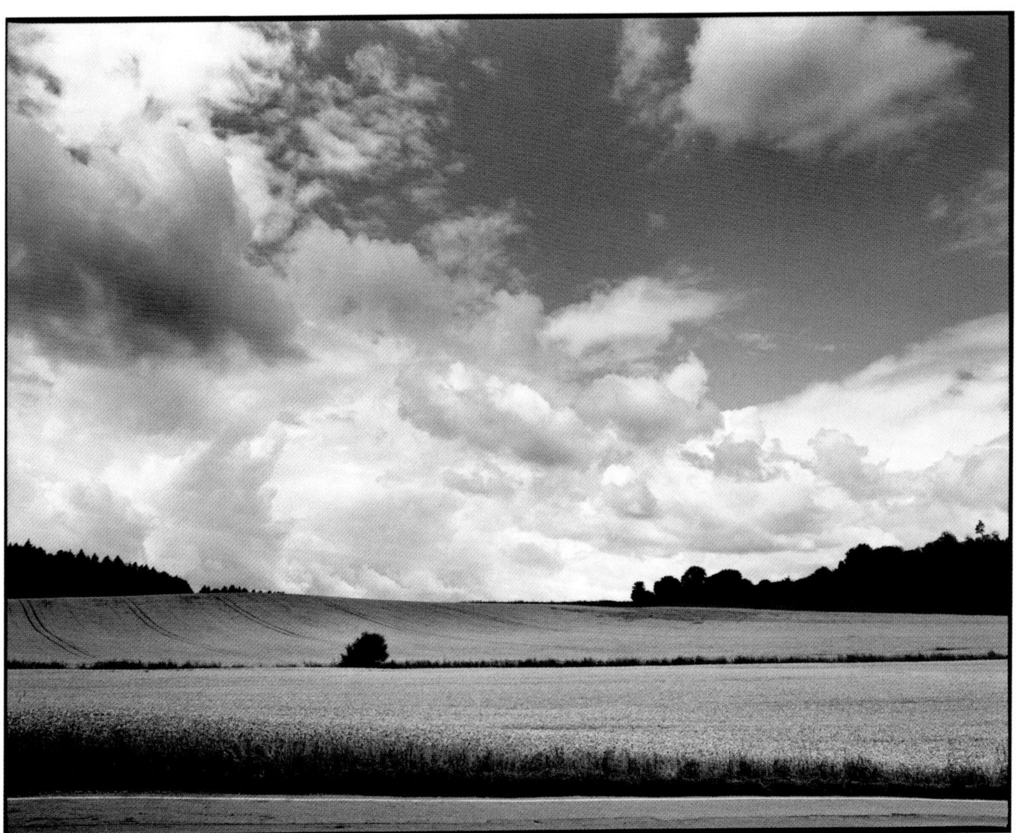

Field near Salem. Example of landscape shot on panchromatically sensitized film, Pentax 67 on Kodak Tri-X 400

Compared to the human eye and its predominant sensitivity in the yellow-green range, panchromatic film is more strongly sensitized in the red range. Film that shows reduced sensitivity in the red range of the spectrum—similar to the human eye—is referred to as orthopanchromatic or rectepanchromatic. Unlike orthochromatic film, red and black are not rendered as the same dark shade (Fuji Neopan 100 Acros, Adox CHS 100 II).

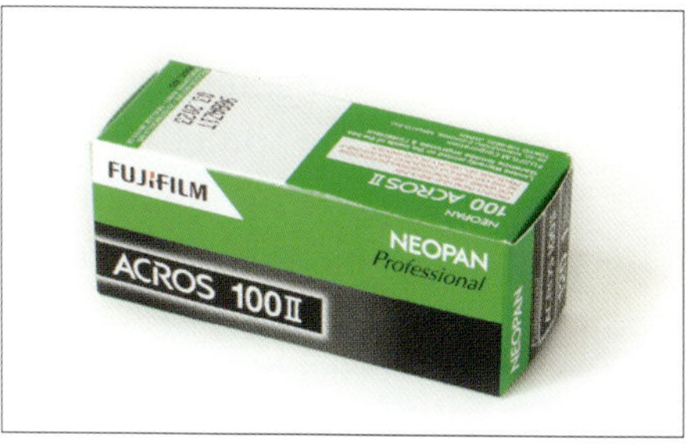

Orthopanchromatic in the 2nd generation: the Fuji Neopan Acros II

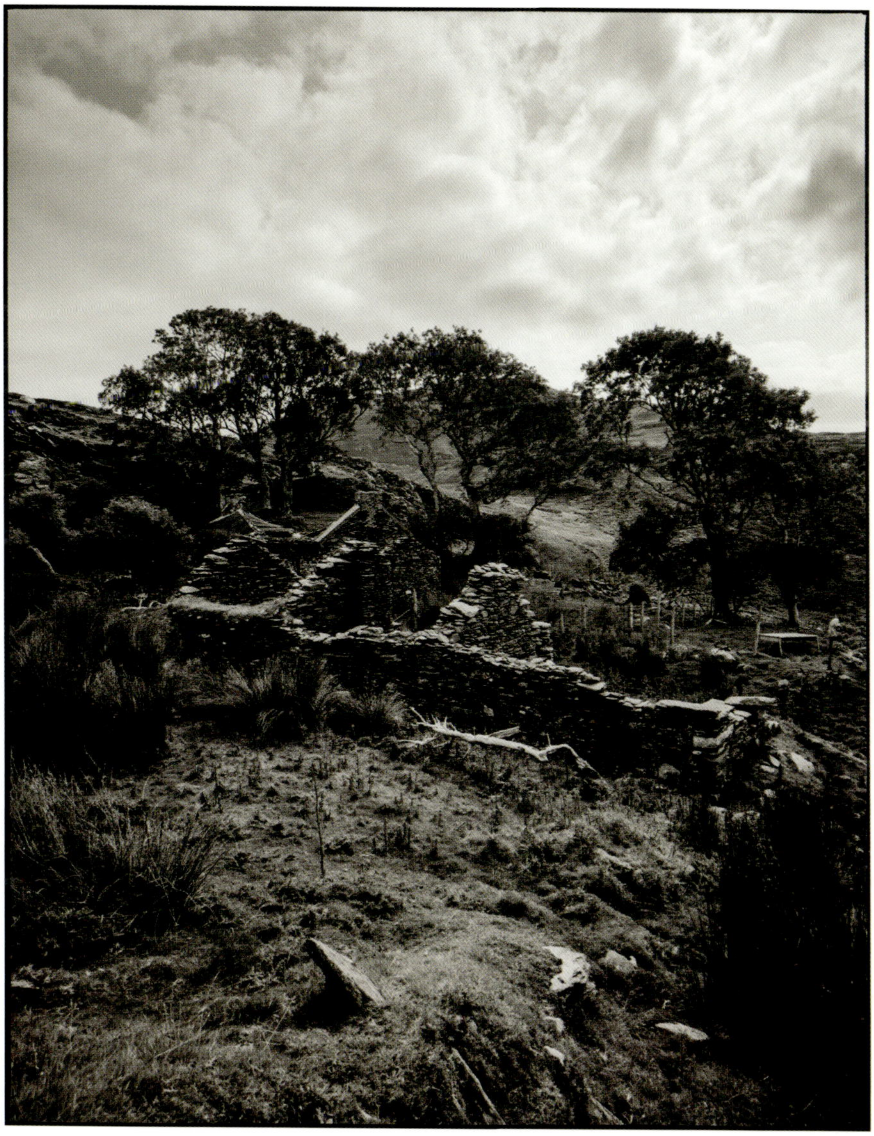

Abandoned. *Example of landscape shot on orthopanchromatic film, Pentax 67 on Fuji Neopan Acros 100*

Another variety of panchromatic film has greater sensitivity in the red range. These films, referred to as super-panchromatic, are sensitized in spectrum ranges of 680, and sometimes even up to 750, nanometers. They were originally designed for use in (warm) lightbulb light. When using dark red filters, you can sometimes even observe infrared-like effects, such as white foliage against almost black water surfaces.

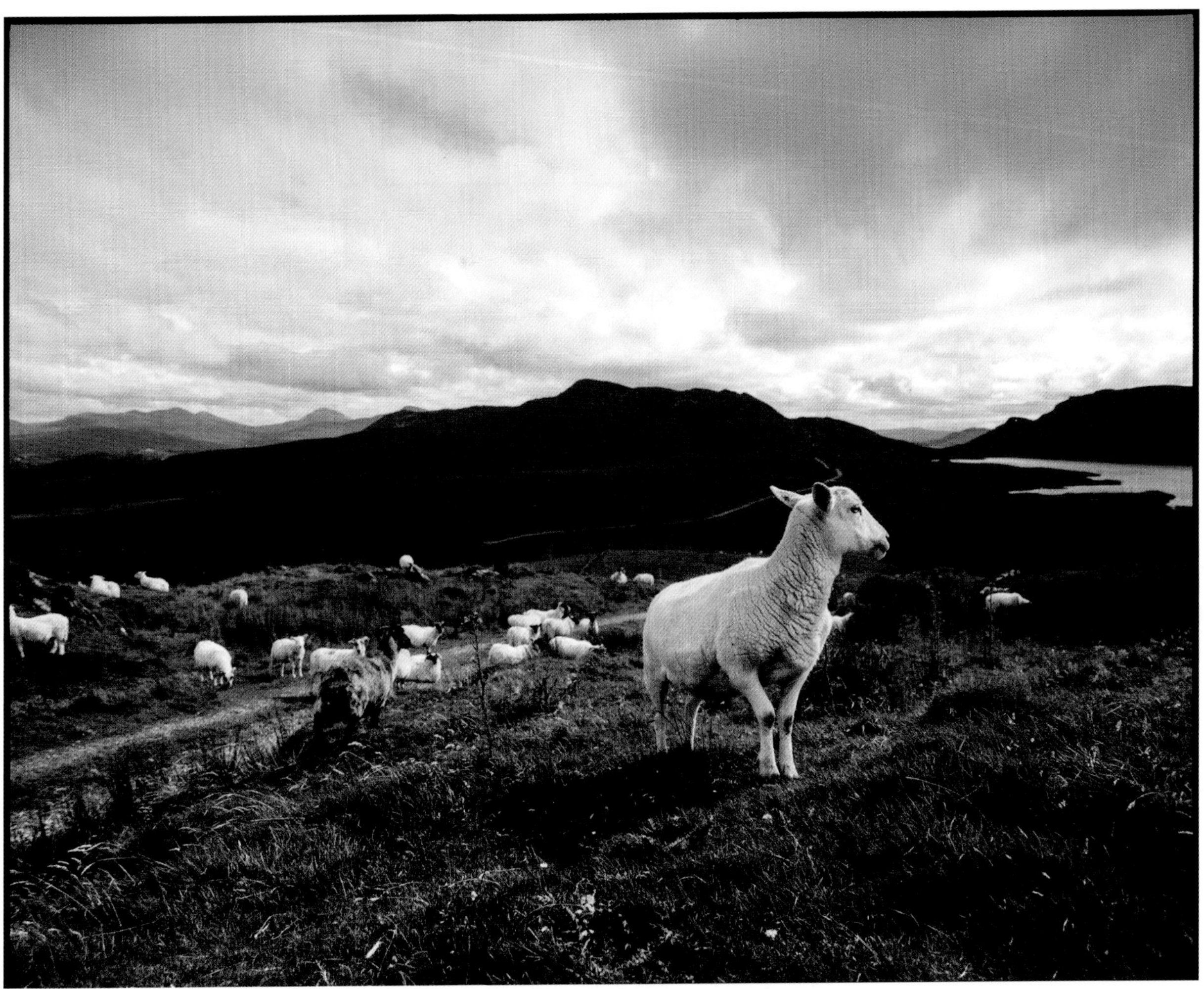

Flock of sheep in Donegal, Ireland. Example of a landscape shot on super-panchromatic black-and-white film, Pentax 67 on Ilford SFX 200

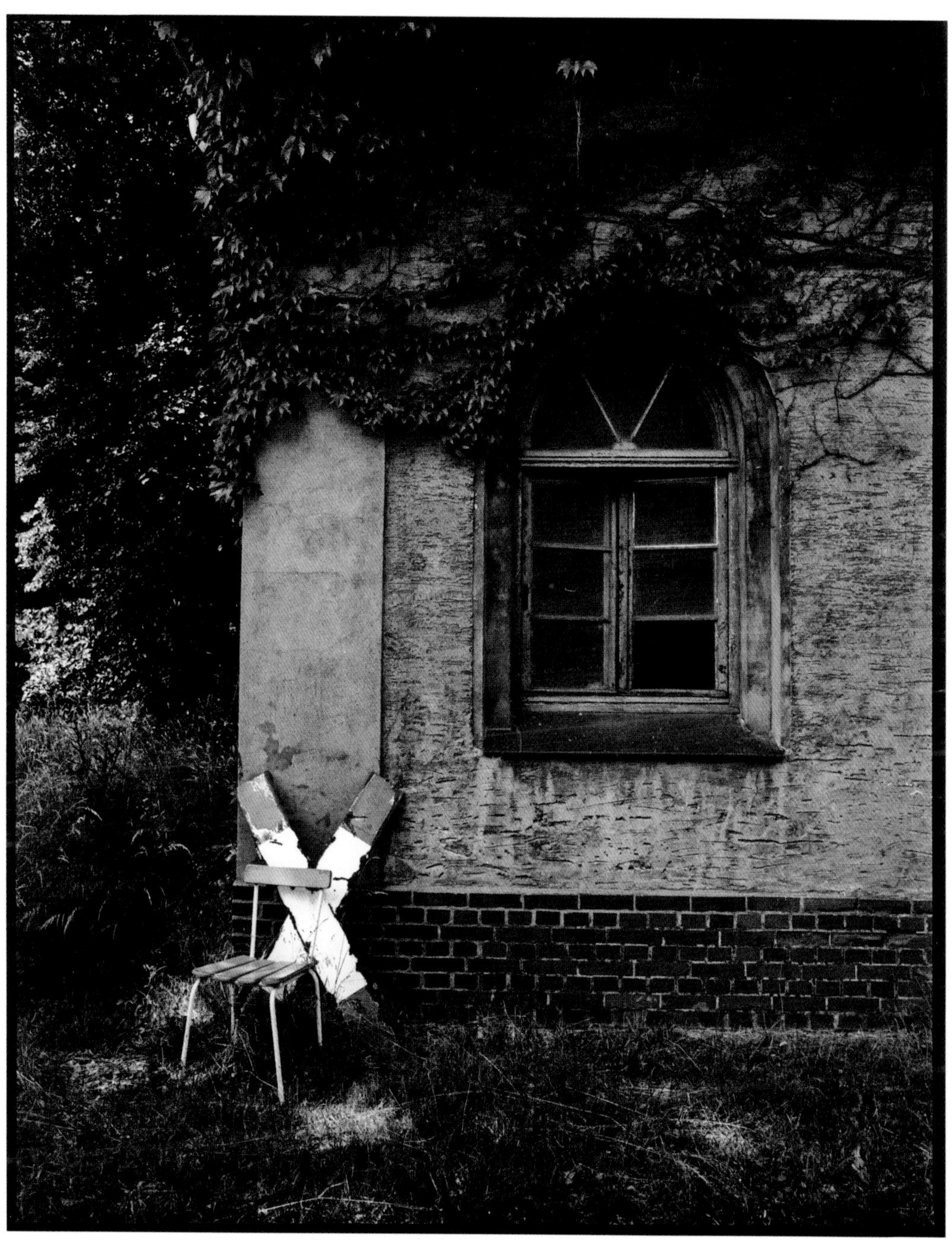

Example of a shot on super-panchromatic film. You can see the increased contrast caused by push processing, without losing detail in the shadows. Pentax 67 on Rollei R3 at ISO 1600

Most super-panchromatic film (with the exception of Rollei Retro 80 S) is frequently available as medium- or higher-sensitivity film (ISO 200 to 400). (Rollei R3, Rollei Superpan 200, Ilford SFX 200, and Foma Retropan 320 soft new are sadly no longer available.)

With the introduction of panchromatic film, it also became necessary to add a cover so you could close the red window for counting the exposures. Otherwise, the numbers printed on the backing paper of the film could be exposed onto the red-sensitive film by the light shining through the little window.

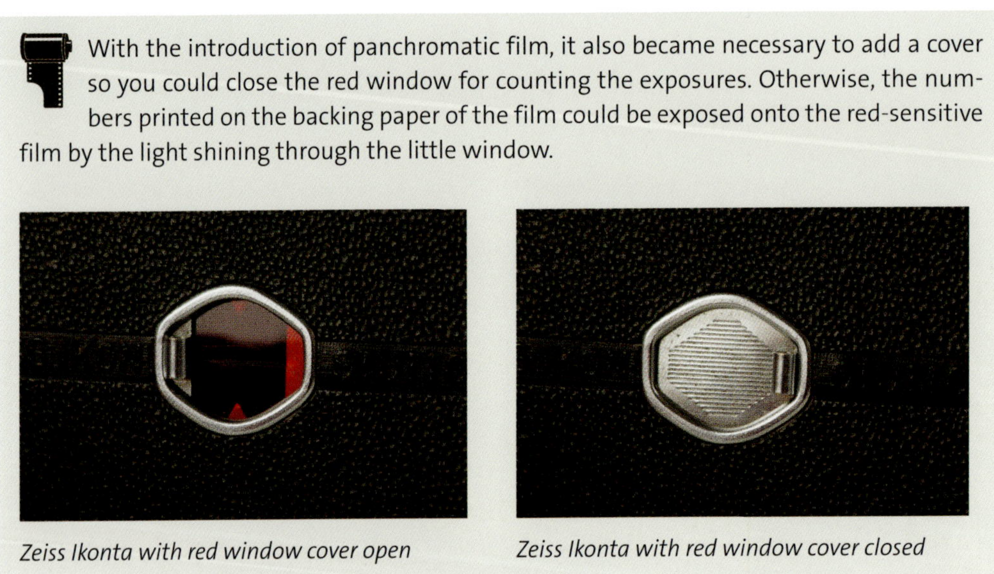

Zeiss Ikonta with red window cover open   Zeiss Ikonta with red window cover closed

5.1.4   Infrared (IR) Film

Classic panchromatic black-and-white film that is sensitive from the ultraviolet to red range of the spectrum is designed to render pictures as we visually perceive them. By using filters, you can manipulate how the tonal values are rendered, but you will not be able to achieve the dramatic effects that are possible when using infrared film. Infrared film is generally sensitized to the full light spectrum, but its sensitivity also goes into the infrared range, as the name indicates.

What sets this film apart from normal black-and-white film is how it records heat radiation. This is most noticeable in spring and early summer, when plants grow the most and a lot of photosynthesis takes place. A waste product of photosynthesis is heat or infrared radiation, and on films that have been sensitized to infrared rays, this increased heat generation results in better-defined shadows under trees and around dense vegetation. You can use IR film like normal black-and-white film and make use of this property, for example, when shooting gardens. Manufacturers usually specify on the packaging the nominal film speed for using this film without an IR filter.

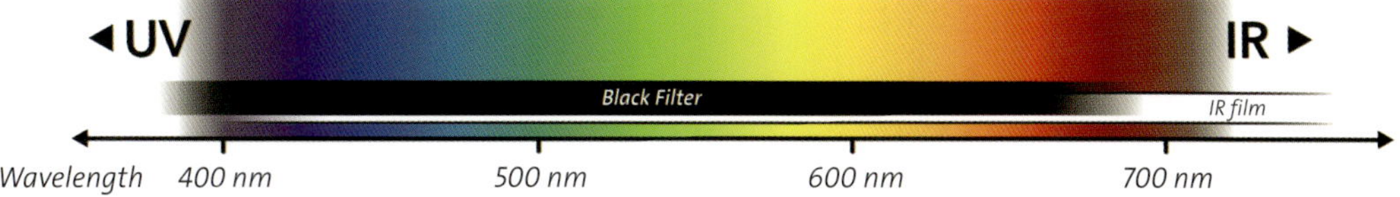

The black filter blocks out the light

If you use a black filter (actually, it's a very dark red filter), which blocks out visible light and lets through only infrared light of bigger wavelengths (depending on the type, >700nm), you can observe what's referred to as the *Wood effect* (named after a person, not the material): Green plants in sunlight are rendered almost white, and water areas or blue sky are rendered black. This effect produces dramatic pictures with strong contrast.

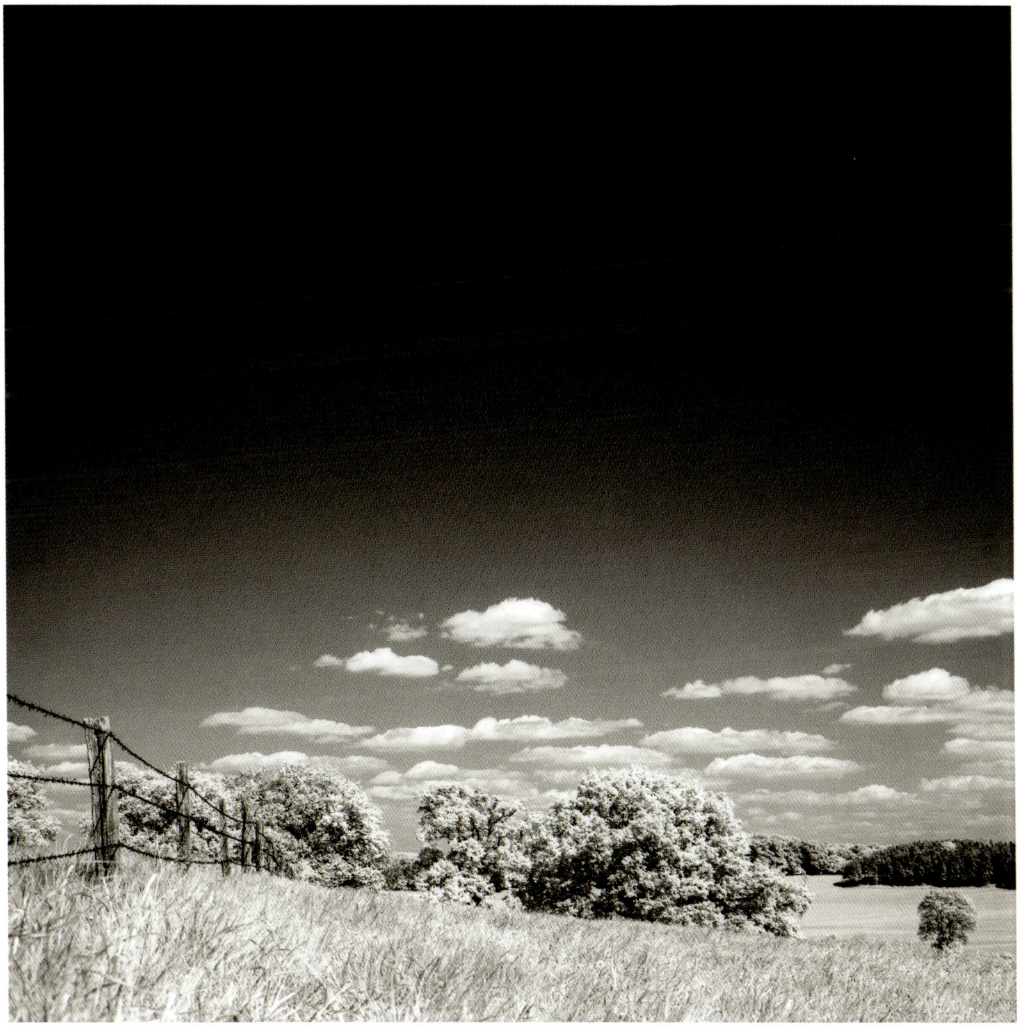

Photo:
Heinz Wille

5.1.5   Film with Aura Effect

Certain film brands, such as the Washi F and Washi I X-ray films or the Efke IR 820 aura (unfortunately only available in very small quantities via auction platforms), do not have an anti-halation layer. This can result in light reflection on the film base, which causes a halo or aura around the highlights. You can use this effect creatively.

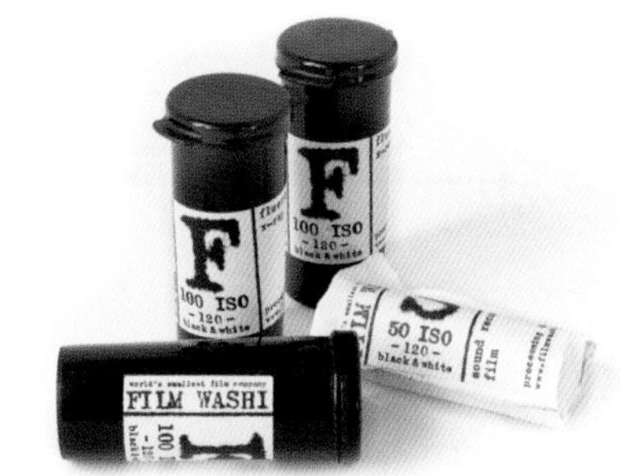

Washi offers two X-ray films without an anti-halation layer: Washi I and Washi F

Georgengarten Hannover on Washi F 100. The overexposure around the highlights fits atmospherically into the composition.

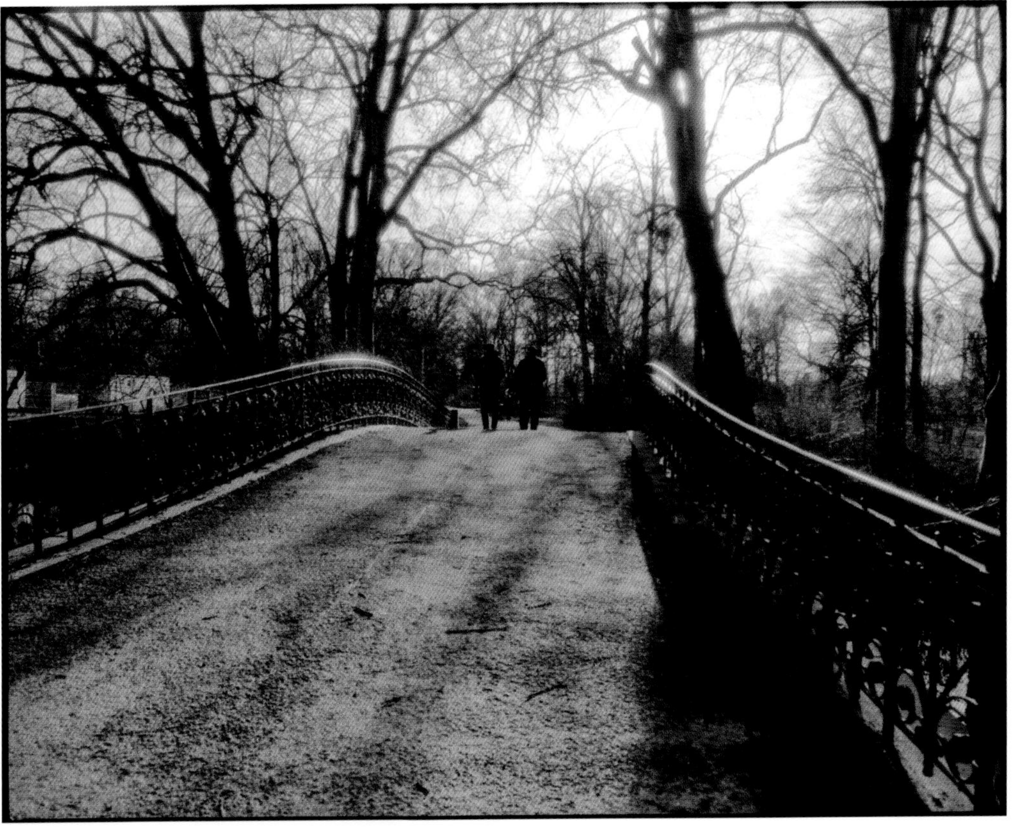

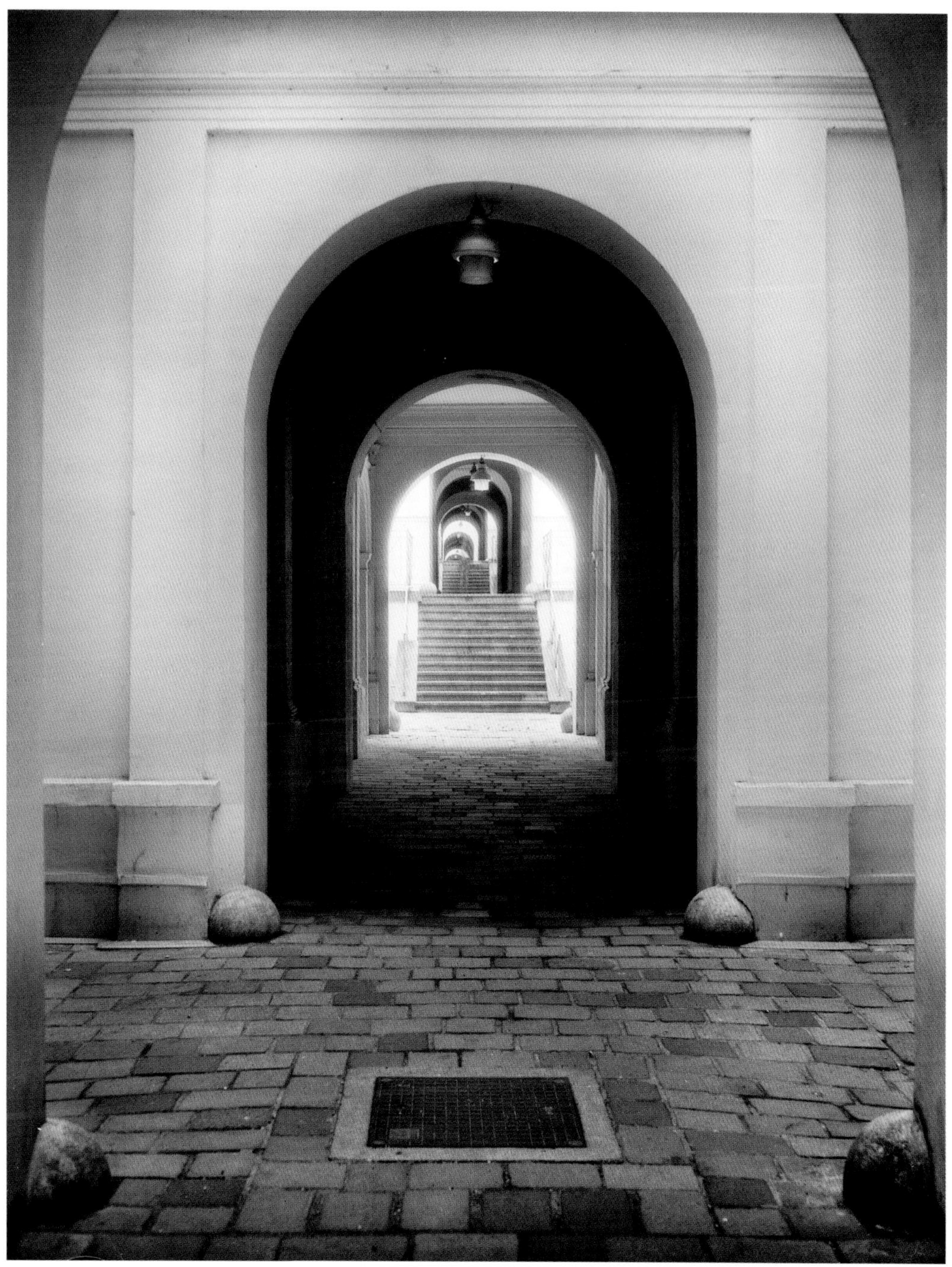

*Backyard
in Vienna,
Graflex Crown
Graphic on Efke
IR 820 aura*

Light Piping: Light piping is caused by unwanted exposure along the edges of the film. In medium format, this is more likely to be visible at the sides; in 35mm it can also be seen at the beginning of the roll. The principle is the same as with glass fiber. Reflections within the transparent film carrier allow the film to transport light from the edges into the image area. In 35mm, the film tab protruding from the cartridge can also carry light inside the cartridge this way.

Film manufacturers do a lot to prevent this light conduction from becoming a problem. For one thing, an anti-halation coating is applied to most films to reduce internal light reflections. Also, the film base often has dyes added to it that reduce internal light transmission.

In 35mm, light conduction can even expose through the transport holes to deeper film windings.

Of course, you can prevent light piping from becoming a problem: Change the film in shade if possible. With medium format make sure that the film remains taut when you change it and that the windings don't pop open. Also, wind 35mm film all the way back into the film canister before you take it out of the camera.

In the following table, we introduce a few common types of black-and-white film with their properties and areas of application.

Film	Properties	Areas of application
Adox Silvermax 100	Traditional black-and-white film with high silver content and medium sensitivity; good exposure latitude; orthopanchromatic characteristics; good detail contrast and high sharpness, clear film base. It can also be used as black-and-white slide film with appropriate reversal processing kit. Silvermax is only available as 35mm film.	Universal use; particularly for rendering a high contrast range.
Agfa APX 100 New	Available as 35mm film only. Panchromatic sensitized, reliable universal film with ISO 100.	Pushable up to ISO 200 and thus an all-arounder for many purposes.
Agfa APX 400	Available as 35mm film only. A panchromatic sensitized film that offers reserves at ISO 400 even in poorer lighting conditions.	Well suited for reportage, but also otherwise an all-arounder.

$\rightarrow$

Film	Properties	Areas of application
Adox CHS 100 II	Orthopanchromatically-sensitized black-and-white film with a traditional (single-layer) emulsion structure. This gives it broad exposure latitude and highly balanced tonal separation.	Like Silvermax, this film can be used as a slide film if developed using a reversal process.
CineStill BwXX	Variable-speed, classic black-and-white film with an ISO sensitivity of 250 in daylight and ISO 200 in tungsten light; comparable with the Eastman Double-X emulsion developed for cinema use; currently available in DX-coded 35mm cartridges.	Has a similar look and feel to Kodak's Plus-X emulsion, which ceased production in 2010.
Fuji Neopan Acros 100 II	Medium-speed, fine-grained black-and-white film with ortho-panchromatic sensitization; good reproduction of details, great edge sharpness, and balanced contrasts.	Monika's favorite film for landscape photography.
Ilford Delta 100/400	Panchromatic black-and-white film with flat crystal technology and a characteristically fine grain; comparable to Kodak T-MAX.	Particularly suitable for architecture and landscape in 35mm.
Ilford Delta 3200	Panchromatic black-and-white film with flat crystal technology; clear but still esthetic grain.	Suitable for indoor photography or in locations where light is limited.
Ilford FP4+ 125	Medium-speed black-and-white film with panchromatic sensitization.	A classic for any situation.
Ilford HP5+ 400	Higher-speed black-and-white film with panchromatic sensitization, the work horse among the black-and-white films; pushable up to ISO 3200, but also great for pull processing.	A classic in photojournalism; always works well.
Ilford OrthoPLUS	Black-and-white film with ortho-chromatic sensitization and speed ISO 40 in artificial light, ISO 80 in daylight; crisp contrast and plenty of detail.	Well suited for architectural photography.

→

Film	Properties	Areas of application
Ilford SFX 200	Medium-speed black-and-white film with super-panchromatic sensitization when used with a dark red filter, such as a Kodak Wratten 89B or similar.	Universal use; great for landscape photography.
Ilford XP2 Super	Chromogenic black-and-white film, processed with C-41 process; grainless film with very smooth look.	Universal use; great if you need quick industrial processing.
Kodak Tri-X 400	Higher-speed film with panchromatic sensitization; moderate, well-accented grain and plenty of character; high exposure latitude and easily pushable up to ISO 1600.	Safe choice for any photographic situation.
Kodak T-MAX 100/400	Medium- and higher-speed film with panchromatic sensitization; can be pushed one stop without adjusting processing time and recipe. The flat crystal structure ensures very fine grain. Good for pull processing.	Great film for landscape and architectural photography.
Rollei Infrared 400	Sensitized to 795nm, Infrared is a film for infrared-like effects, but without the distinct shadowing common to its genre. When exposed and developed to nominal speed, the film shows a high-contrast reproduction and fine grain.	Landscape photography, for Wood effect with a dark red filter, or even architectural photography.
Rollei Ortho 25 (comparable to Wephota Ortho 25 and Adox Ortho 25)	Low-speed and exceptionally fine-grained black-and-white film with orthochromatic sensitization, steep contrasts, and extraordinary sharpness.	Popular for scientific photography; we've also used it in macro photography.

Black-and-White Film

Film	Properties	Areas of application
Kono! Recorder 100-200	A black-and-white film with randomly distributed pre-exposed numbers and letters. Provides high-contrast images with surprising effect. Only available as 35mm film with ISO 100-200.	Experimental black-and-white photography.
Lomography Kino Potsdam	A negative film from the cinema film range with ISO 100, classic emulsion, good sharpness, and fine grain.	A film for artistic as well as documentary black-and-white photography.
Lomography Kino Berlin	Higher sensitivity negative film, with ISO 400 and classic emulsion. Like Lomography Kino Potsdam, it was developed as a cinema recording film. The material shows accentuated grain with good tonal reproduction and sharpness.	Monochrome all-purpose weapon for a wide variety of motifs.
Revolog SNOVLOX	Black-and-white effect film with ISO 200 and hand-incorporated glitches reminiscent of snowflakes.	Experimental black-and-white photography.
Washi F 100	X-ray film with ISO 100, which, according to the manufacturer, was originally used in pulmonary diagnostics. Orthochromatic sensitized film with medium to strong contrast and visible grain. Due to the lack of an anti-halation layer, the film exhibits a pronounced diffusion effect. Aura-like overexposures form around the highlights.	Exciting in landscape and street photography. The over-lighting effects bring a very unique, sometimes-unreal atmosphere to the image.

→

Film	Properties	Areas of application
Washi W	The first and thus quasi "original" Washi film with orthochromatic characteristics. A hand-coated carrier of Kozo paper shows a distinct fiber structure and steep contrast. The sensitivity of the material varies between ISO 3 and ISO 25, depending on the lighting conditions and the developer used.	Suitable for landscape, urban, or still life photography. The texture of the paper creates a painting-like appearance.
Washi V	Panchromatic film on Gampi paper base. The exposure latitude is increased compared to Washi W and the film has a nominal speed of ISO 100. The structure of the paper is finer than Washi W.	Suitable for landscape photography or all those subjects that benefit from soft contrast and visible texture.
Washi I	A double-sided, coated X-ray film originally developed for non-destructive industrial material testing. Nominal speed is ISO 80. Washi I is high contrast with fine grain. An anti-halation layer is missing.	A very unique aesthetic for landscape, urban, portrait, or still life photography.
Washi S	According to the manufacturer, feature film soundtracks are normally recorded on material comparable to this film. It has ISO 50 and a reduced sensitivity in the wavelength range of red light (up to 620nm).	A film for those who prefer hard contrast with the finest grain.
Washi Z	With a spectral sensitivity of up to 750nm (extended red range), Washi Z belongs to the super-panchromats. Originally developed for mapping green areas in aerial photography, this film features good green value differentiation and balanced contrast.	A film suitable for landscape photography. A Wood effect is observable with a dark red filter.

Special Film

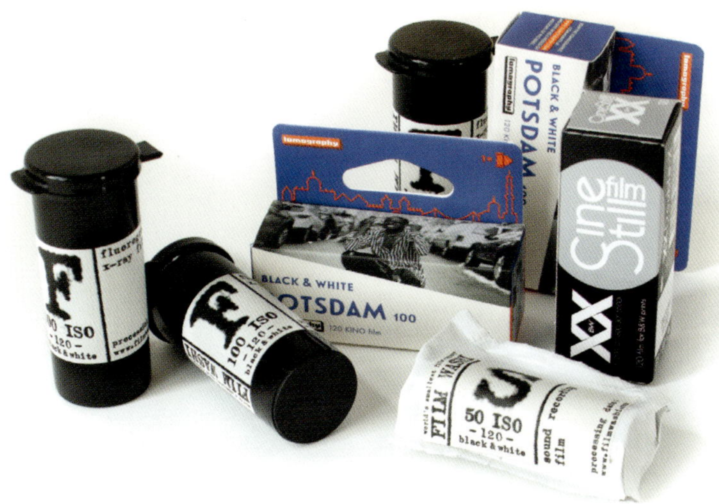

A small selection of black-and-white films beyond the classics

5.1.6   Color Filters

Depending on which film you choose and its particular spectral sensitivity, color will be rendered as shades of gray in different ways. In early photographs, when film was almost exclusively sensitive to blue light, you could, for example, rarely see clouds in the sky. The orthochromatic film was unable to distinguish between blue sky and white clouds. Even today, blue light is almost always rendered brighter than green or red tones. That's why we like to use filters in front of the lens in black-and-white photography, to prevent parts of the blue spectrum from reaching the film.

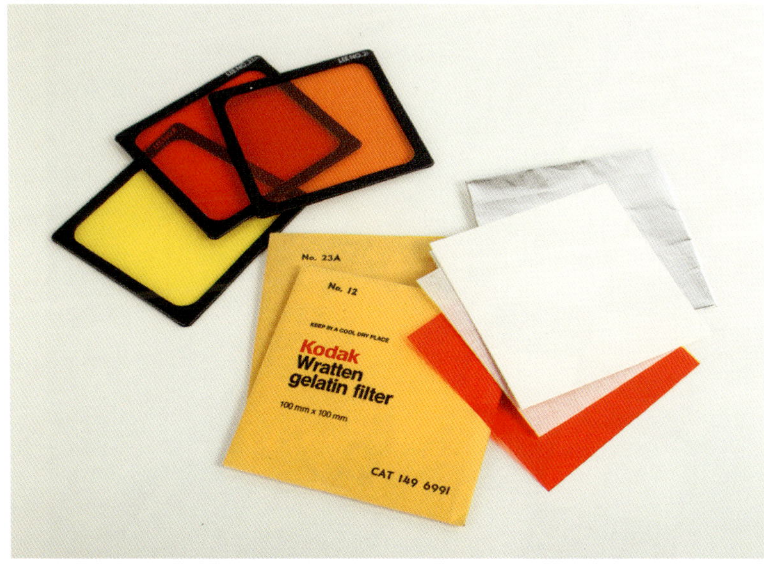

Color filters and gelatin filters

Today, color filters ("gels") are made of glass, polycarbonate, or plastic foil. Older color filters (e.g., Kodak Wratten) were made of gelatin and had to be kept absolutely dry. The term *gel* for filter foil goes back to the time of gelatin filters, and is still used today.

With a red filter, you get a dark or almost black sky with a great contrast to the white clouds. Plus the red filter increases the distance vision. To get a weaker version of this effect, you can use an orange or yellow filter.

Photo with red filter

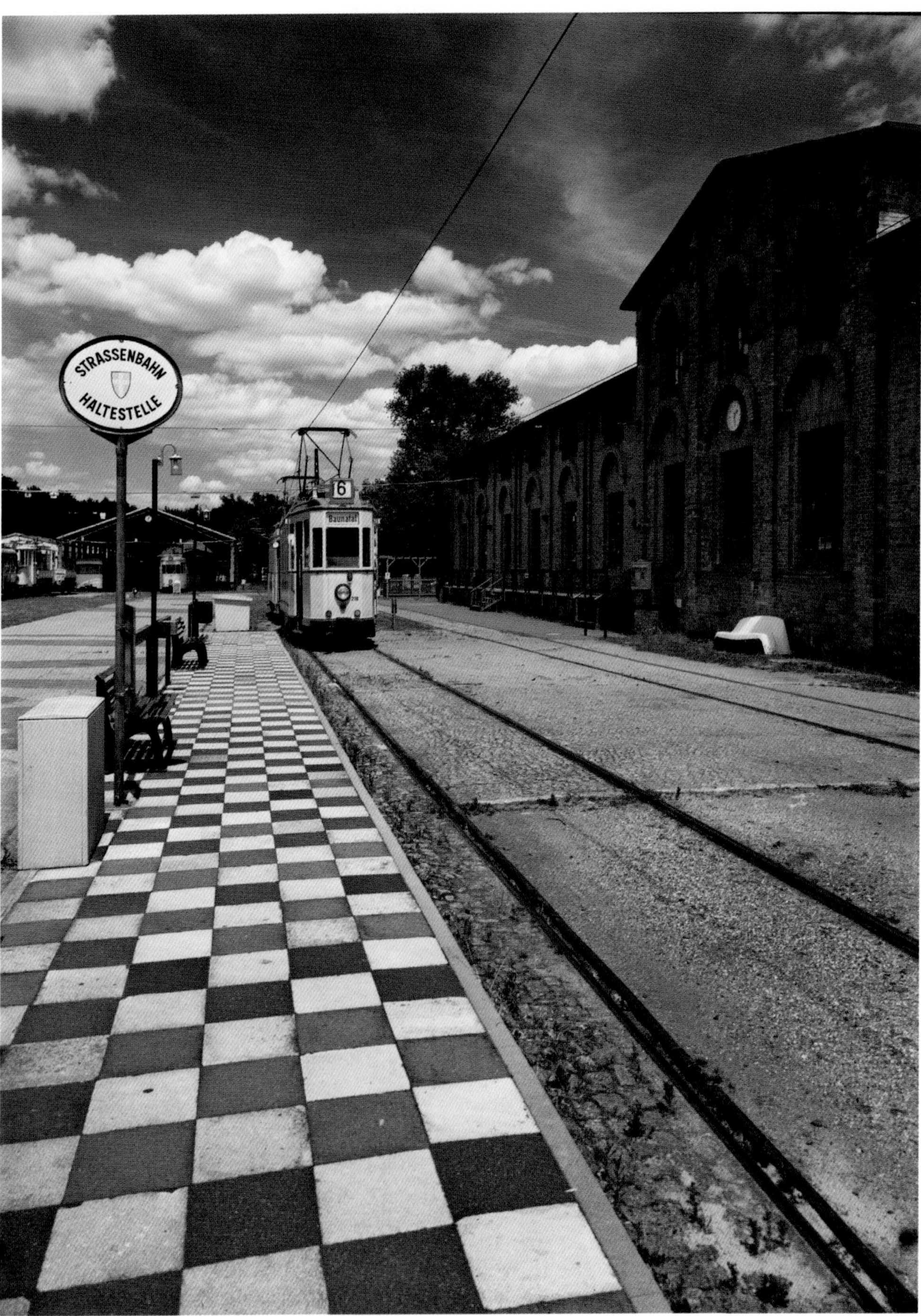

Light Metering with Color Filters

Color filters extend the exposure because they always result in a reduction of incident light. A red filter, for example, blocks out blue and green light. We need to factor in this light loss in our exposure metering. Many manufacturers specify a filter factor—the correction factor by which you need to extend the exposure—for their filters. A factor of three means adjusting by three aperture stops, so a measured exposure time of 1/200 second is reduced by 3 stops to 1/25 second.

If you cannot find a specified factor, here is a table with a (very approximate) rule of thumb for correction factors:

Yellow	+1 stop
Orange	+2 stops
Red	+3 stops

Proceed as follows: Measure the exposure as usual, and then correct the value by the number of stops shown in the table. If your specific filter produces results that are too dark or otherwise unsuitable, do a small exposure bracketing and then remember the correction value that provides the best photo taken with this filter.

Some photographers measure the exposure through the filter to factor in the light loss during metering. That can work, but depends to a certain extent on the spectral sensitivity of the processing meter and how much it matches the speed of the film used. We have had some unexpected results, particularly when using red filters.

5.2   Color Film

While black-and-white film offers a wealth of film speeds, processing options, and creative variations, the processing methods for color film are much more standardized. The commonly used method of developing color film was designed for industrial mass processing. In 1996, the German industrial photo lab CEWE processed more than 2 billion color pictures alone (according to their own statistics). The only way to cope with such quantities is to fully standardize the processes involved.

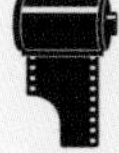 In industrial labs, the day with the highest throughput was always the Tuesday after the holidays. The holiday film rolls were handed in to the drugstore on Monday morning, and arrived at the lab for processing on Tuesday.

5.2.1 Color Negative Film

Over the years, different standardized color processes have become established. Today, only the C-41 process is left. All C-41-rated color negative films, regardless of the brand, can be machine-processed fully automatically in suitable chemicals. Processing times and even temperatures are normed. The associated processing machines are integrated and compact enough (a footprint of less than ten square feet) for local use. Processing and enlarging a color film ("dry to dry") can be carried out within one hour.

For manual processing, you can get *press kits*. These are differently sized packets with all the chemicals you need for processing color film at home. Color negative film consists of several layers of color emulsion and filters that interact during the exposure, and divide the picture into its yellow, magenta, and cyan parts. Each of the three base colors is represented by up to three layers of silver halides of differing sensitivity, just as in black-and-white film. In addition, the color film has dye couplers that form color in the relevant places when the exposed silver is processed.

The color film undergoes a special bleach bath after processing (usually a combination of bleach bath and fixer, also known as "blix" (bleach + fix), which removes the black (exposed) silver and only leaves the colors in the film. Color film is also referred to as grain-free because the bleaching removes the silver image completely.

If need be, you can also process color film with black-and-white chemicals. The result is a (very dense) black-and-white image that usually scans reasonably well.

The orange mask often causes color issues in the analog-digital hybrid process. Rollei offers a daylight color negative film, the Digibase CN 200, which managed to eliminate this mask. After scanning, you no longer have to make complex color corrections.

Orange Mask

If you look at a processed color negative film, you will notice its orange tint. This is caused by a combination of different mask dyes that the film contains to compensate for color errors. The analog color enlargement process is matched to this mask so the prints look color corrected. In digital post-processing, this mask can get in the way, and will need to be color corrected after scanning. In contrast to color positive film (slide film), color negative film has a great exposure tolerance and usually forgives exposure errors of several aperture stops without sacrificing too much image quality.

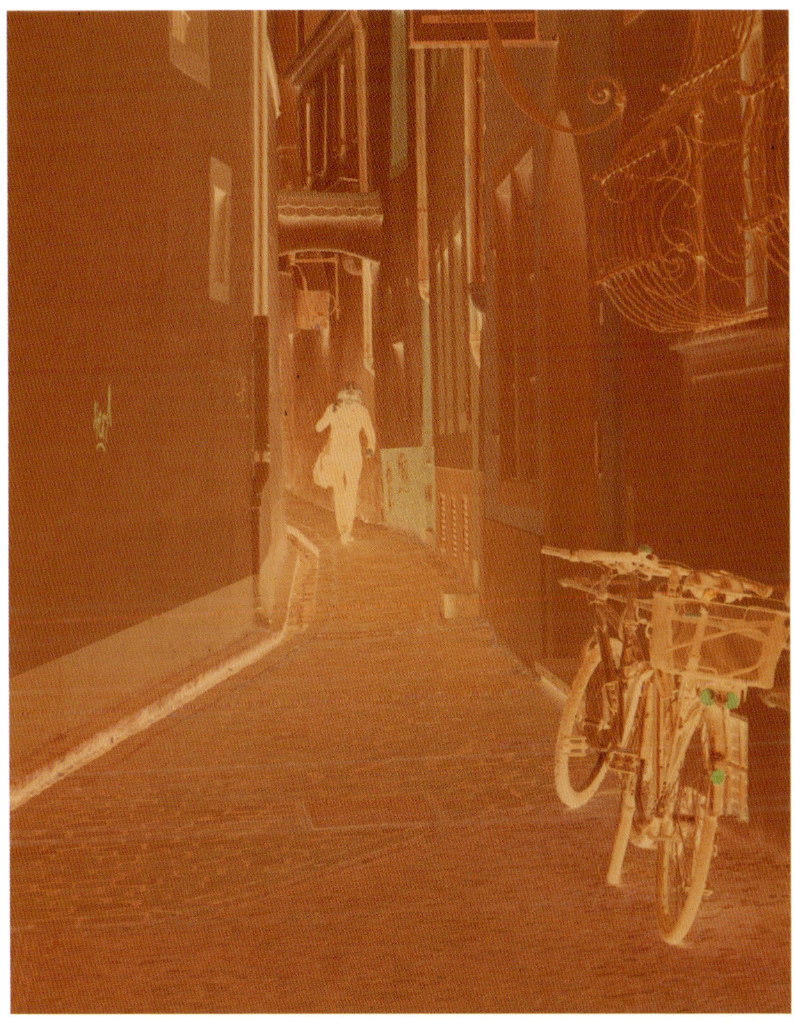

Orange mask,
Kodak Portra 160

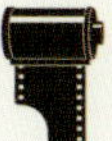 **Cinefilm:** Even today, numerous films are still shot on analog material. Many filmmakers, such as Quentin Tarantino, Christopher Nolan, and JJ Abrams swear by the characteristic look of classic film stock. The professionals prefer to shoot on 35mm, 65mm, or 70mm film. Kodak Vision3 is often used.

Cinema film is now also available for 35mm and 120 roll film. It has also become increasingly popular among photographers. Cine film offers a good dynamic range and a relatively large amount of latitude in digital post-processing. This makes it easy to give your results a specific look.

Ex works motion picture film comes with an additional protective layer on the back of the film. This so-called remjet layer protects the material from light flashes caused by static charge as well as from being damaged by the film camera during its brisk run. It also acts as a halation protection layer and, in addition to what is known as Light Piping (page 80), also prevents over-illumination from appearing around the highlights. Film material with a remjet layer is developed in the ECN-2 process.

The CineStill company offers colored cine film material with the remjet layer removed. This means that these films can also be developed in the C-41 process.

5.2.2   Slide Film

The reversal of the image is a typical process in film photography. Anything that's black on the film is going to be white on the finished picture through exposure or digital reversal. That's not the case with a reversal film, with which the negative is reversed directly onto the film to get a positive image again.

The layer structure of reversal film (also referred to as color positive, slide, or transparency film) is almost identical to that of negative film. Today, slide film is developed using the E-6 process. An additional reversal step in processing turns the negative into a positive image.

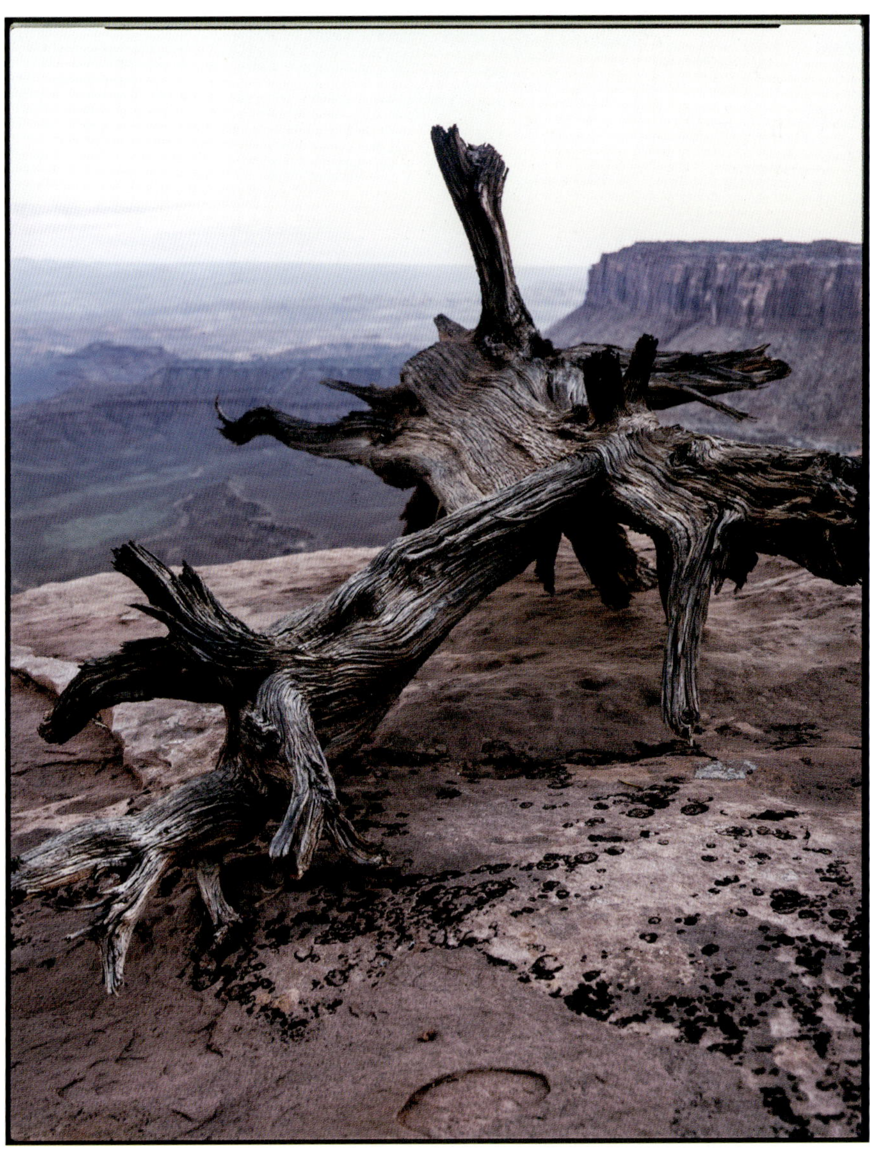

Canyonlands National Park, Graflex Crown Graphic on Fuji Provia 100F

Precise Exposure

While color negative film shows an enormous exposure latitude and can easily handle incorrect exposures of up to several aperture stops, slide film is much more sensitive. To avoid demanding too much or too little from its low contrast range during the shot, the exposure should be absolutely spot-on. You will be rewarded with brilliant colors and a vibrant picture. Slide film offers some advantages over color negative film. Slide emulsions have finer grain and provide better sharpness with greater overall resolution, making them ideal for really big enlargements.

A slide is "finished" as soon as it has been developed, so no further processing steps are necessary. To view a slide, all you have to do is hold it up to the light, although using a projector enables you to enlarge it as much as you like at levels of image quality that even the very best digital projectors cannot equal. You can also make direct monochrome prints from slides using specialized papers such as HARMAN Direct Positive and Imago Direct. Slides produce extremely high-quality scans that can be presented as large-format display slides or printed on RA-4 silver halide paper, Ilford Galerie Digital Silver paper, or using an inkjet printer. Prints from slides offer the same fine grain, excellent sharpness, and high resolution of the original.

Kodachrome

We also want to mention what is possibly the most legendary slide film of all time: Kodachrome, which Kodak made from 1939 to 2009. Kodachrome was the first commercially available slide film with natural color representation. Its fine grain, ability to reproduce vivid colors, and archival longevity made it the film of choice for many professional photographers.

Unlike other reversal film processed via the E-6 process, Kodak used its proprietary K-14 method for Kodachrome. In contrast to the C-41 process, K-14 was more demanding in terms of chemicals and machinery (the original K-14 processor required floor space of over 1,000 square feet), this film could not be developed in the local lab around the corner. It had to be sent to Kodak or a special lab for processing.

Black-and-White Slides

Black-and-white slides make a fascinating addition to the other film types on offer. Similar to color slides, they provide unparalleled brilliance and images appear almost three-dimensional. The range of options in this particular field has grown enormously in recent years.

ADOX Scala 160 BW is an optimized successor to the now obsolete Agfa Scala 200X film; and Fomapan R 100 is a great monochrome slide film that you can develop at home using the dedicated Foma reversal kit. Many specialists offer online development services or home development kits for these kinds of films.

Maco (macodirect.de, also in English) offers a reversal kit based on chemicals manufactured at the Agenzia Luce specialist lab in Italy.

5.2.3   Other Types of Film

In addition to the normal versions of negative and positive film, there are also a few oddballs and special treatments with which you can turn normal film into something special.

Redscale

Depending on the exposure, redscale film creates results in surprisingly deep reds and oranges. You don't even need special film for it, because redscale film is just normal color negative film that has been wound in reverse so it's exposed from the back. Color film consists of several color, filter, and correction layers. When exposing it from the back, the color and filter layers are exposed in reverse order, producing the corresponding effect. You can buy redscale film ready-made or simply wind color film in reverse yourself in the changing bag.

Cross Processing

Color negative film (process C-41) and slide film (process E-6) are almost identical, apart from the red mask of the color film. The reversal—turning the negative into a positive—happens as an additional chemical step during processing. Because both types of film are structured almost identically, you can also cross process them, i.e., process the slide film in the C-41 chemistry intended for color negative film and the color negative film in the E-6 process.

Slide film works particularly well and can be enlarged just like a normal negative after the C-41 process. The results are very interesting, depending on film and exposure, and can produce high color saturation, strong contrasts, rough grain, and strong color shifts. If you hand in slide film to be cross processed in the drugstore, please write clearly "C-41 Process Please!" onto the film pouch—perhaps even directly onto the film cartridge with a waterproof pen.

Some labs charge extra for cross processing. You do not usually have to pay extra if you are using slide film sold as C-41 and designed specifically for cross processing, such as Rollei Crossbird.

Go ahead and play around with overexposing and underexposing when cross processing. Some types of film shift from predominantly red tones to green tones with different exposures.

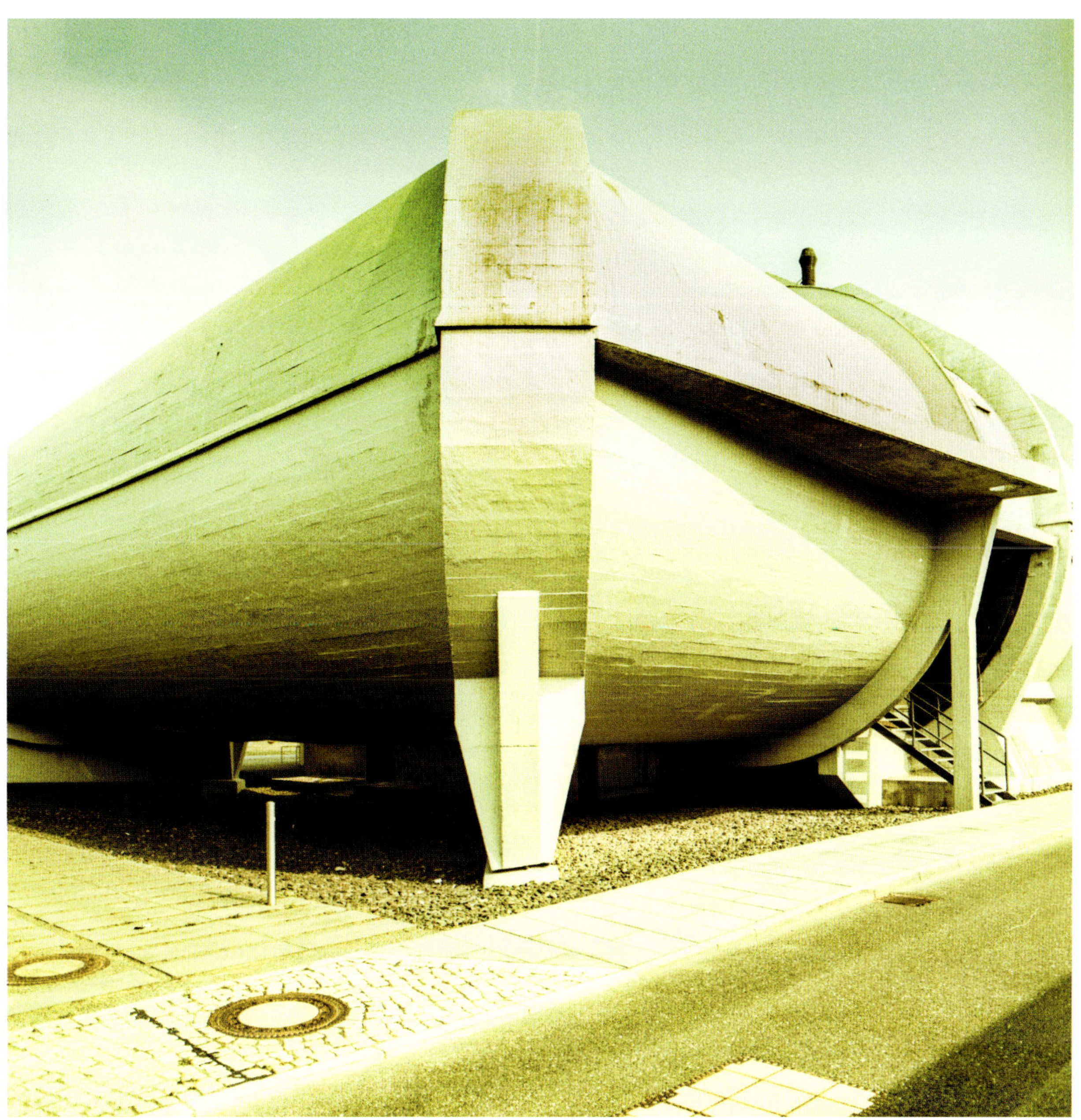

Wind tunnel in Berlin Adlershof, Rollei Crossbird

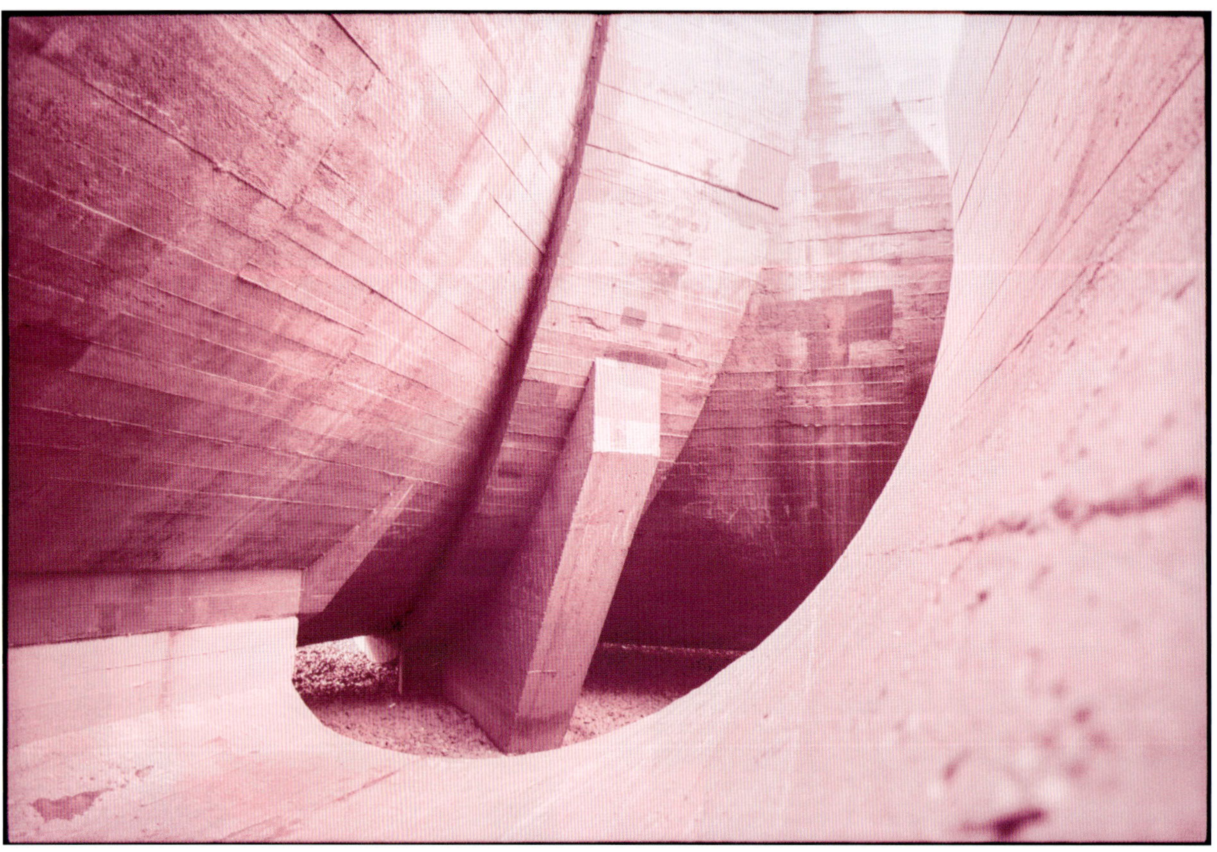

Wind tunnel in Berlin-Adlershof, Germany. Fuji Sensia 100 @ ISO 50, cross developed in the C-41 process. Here you can clearly see the difference from the Rollei Crossbird. The Sensia shows strongly saturated magenta on cross development.

Chromogenic Film

Chromogenic film is black-and-white film that is developed in the C-41 process designed for color negatives. This film can be processed in any color photo lab anywhere in the world that uses the normal color process. That makes processing much shorter and simpler. Plus, chromogenic black-and-white film has a very high exposure latitude, just like color film. Incorrect exposures are rare.

These advantages are offset by the disadvantage of standardization: The entire creative potential of black-and-white processing with its many different developers, temperatures, and times, and the resulting possibilities regarding contrasts and grain, is now eliminated.

Film	Properties	Areas of application
Adox Scala 50	Ultra-fine grained superpan-chromatic Black-and-White slide film with very high resolution and excellent sharpness. Scala 50 can be developed in the ADOX Scala or Foma reversal kit.	Suitable for most applications, thanks to its fine grain and high sharpness; for example in fashion, architecture, or landscape photography.
Foma Fomapan 100 R	Medium-sensitive, pure black-and-white slide film with ISO 100, developed using the Fomapan BW reversal kit.	Due to good tonality and high sharpness, it can be used almost everywhere where more sensitivity is not needed.
Fujichrome Provia 100F	Vivid but natural colors and fine color gradation; very sharp; high detail rendition.	Universal use, especially if you want to print the photo.
Fujichrome Velvia 50	Extremely fine-grained, contrast-rich brother of Provia with highly saturated colors.	Universal use, especially for architecture and landscape.
Fujichrome Velvia 100	Fine-grained, medium-speed film; saturation similar to Velvia 50.	Universal use, especially for landscape photography.
Kodak Ektachrome E100 VS	Medium-sensitivity daylight slide film with extreme sharpness, very fine grain, and highly saturated colors.	Ideal for outdoor use, especially landscapes.

Slide Film

In this and all other tables, we only reference films that we use ourselves, films that we find particularly interesting, or films whose performance we can adequately judge. The tables are not intended to be exhaustive or in any way definitive.

Film	Properties	Areas of Application
AgfaPhoto Vista plus 200/400	Medium- and high-speed film with good skin color rendition.	Good all around; available in many supermarkets and drugstores.
CineStill 50Daylight Xpro C-41	Sharp, fine-grained color negative film based on Kodak movie stock; available in rolls or 35mm cartridges; not DX-coded; provides fine highlight details that tend to overexpose due to the lack of coating on the reverse.	Great for portraits and landscapes.
CineStill 800Tungsten Xpro C-41	High-ISO tungsten film based on Kodak movie stock; available in rolls or 35mm cartridges; lack of coating on the reverse can lead to halo effects in highlights; pushable up to ISO 3200.	Great for tungsten available-light situations (clubs, bars, gigs, nighttime street scenes, etc.).
Fujicolor Superia 200	Medium-speed film with natural color rendition; moderate color saturation.	The classic always-in-the-bag film; available in most supermarkets.
Fujicolor Superia X-Tra400/X-Tra400	Higher-speed film; characteristics comparable to Superia 200.	For snapshots in lower light conditions and/or moving scenes.
Fujicolor Superia 1600	Highest-speed film.	Indoor photography, especially suitable for events such as concerts, festivals, etc.
Kodak Ektar 100	Medium-speed film with very fine grain, neutral color rendition, and natural skin tones.	Universal use in good light conditions (fair weather film).
Kodak Portra 160	Medium-speed film with unsurpassed skin tone rendition.	The portrait film (but our absolute favorite film in other respects as well).
Kodak Portra 400	Higher-speed film with the good skin tones typical for Portra.	Portrait, fashion, and travel photography.
Kodak Portra 800	High-speed film; fine to push to ISO 1600 according to the manufacturer.	Portrait, fashion, and travel photography.

→

Film	Properties	Areas of Application
Silbersalz35 50D	Factory-new and unaltered Kodak VISION3 motion picture film stock for use in photography. Development takes place in the ECN-2 process. https://silbersalz35.com Daylight film with ISO 50. With purchase, one acquires a voucher for development and scanning services.	A daylight film for lots of light and good scope for digital post-processing. The manufacturer recommends overexposure by one f-stop.
Silbersalz35 250D	Factory-new and unaltered Kodak VISION3 motion picture film stock for use in photography. Development takes place in the ECN-2 process. https://silbersalz35.com Daylight film with ISO 250. With purchase, one acquires a voucher for development and scanning services.	Medium-sensitivity daylight film. Good scope for digital post-processing. The manufacturer recommends overexposure by one f-stop.
Silbersalz35 200T	Factory-new and unaltered Kodak VISION3 motion picture film stock for use in photography. Development takes place in the ECN-2 process. https://silbersalz35.com Tungsten film with ISO 200. Shots with incandescent light are possible without a filter. With purchase, one acquires a voucher for development and scanning services.	Medium-sensitivity film for artificial light. The manufacturer recommends overexposure by one f-stop.
Silbersalz35 500T	Factory-new and unaltered Kodak VISION3 motion picture film stock for use in photography. Development takes place in the ECN-2 process. https://silbersalz35.com Tungsten film with ISO 500. Shots with incandescent light are possible without a filter.	Higher-sensitivity film for artificial light. The manufacturer recommends overexposure by one f-stop.

$\rightarrow$

Film	Properties	Areas of Application
Silbersalz35 125T Edition Vivid 500	Limited edition. Tungsten film with ISO 125. The development is carried out in the ECN-2 process. https://silbersalz35.com	Medium-sensitivity film for artificial light. The manufacturer recommends overexposure by one f-stop.

Color Negative Film

Film	Properties	Areas of Application
CineStill REDRUM 120	Limited edition redscale film with ISO 200 for medium format.	Overwrapped color negative film exposed through the orange mask. For dramatic images in red, yellow, and orange tones.
Fujichrome Astia 100f	Only available expired and as remnants, usually online; slide film with finer tone.	With expired BBD, particularly popular for cross processing; tends to have a strong pink and magenta cast.
Kono! Delight ART 100/400	Medium/high-sensitivity color negative film with color cast. Available as 35mm and 120 roll film.	A film for those who like color shifts.
Kono! Original Sunstroke, Moonstruck, Candy, Monsoon, Galaxy, or Mirage	Pre-exposed 35mm films with a wide variety of color effects. The films with an ISO between 100 and 400 are all DX-encoded and developed in the C-41 process.	For experimental photography.
Rollei Crossbird	Medium-speed slide film with ISO 200 based on the Agfachrome RSX II 200 emulsion. It is labeled C-41 specifically for cross processing (which avoids extra charges in the lab). This film has been discontinued, and only remainder stock is available.	Cross processing; for pictures with green tones in the shadows and warm yellow-orange highlights.
Rollei Redbird 35mm film	Medium-speed redscale color negative film with ISO 200.	Experimental film for color appearances between warm red and complete color distortion.

Special Film

5.2.4 Who Makes These "Special" Films?

Today, there is still an active market for analog film stock. Some films cease production, others make a comeback, and new products and "creative" films (with appropriately high-flown marketing blurbs) regularly hit the shelves.

The three major manufacturers—Kodak, Harmann/Ilford, and Fujifilm—concentrate on a relatively narrow range of products. Smaller manufacturers, such as Film Ferrania in Italy and Adox in Germany, produce films with a limited selection of emulsions, which they offer in a range of formats.

It is tricky to find out who is really responsible for the often fanciful labeling on today's analog films. Some dealers refer to Agfa Gevaert in Belgium for certain Rollei films. On the other hand, current Agfa films are said to originate from British production. It can be assumed that pairings of this kind change from time to time, which is why you can find different information in the film photography forums.

If you want to play a bit of detective with 35mm films, you can check the website http:// industrieplus.net/dxdatabase. There you can search for the so-called "DX code"—the 6-digit number that is printed below the barcode on 35mm cartridges—or by the film name. (With some relabeled materials you have to peel off a label underneath the film tab to find the barcode as well as the DX code)

The underlying databases for DX code or film name searches use different sources, so the results do not match in every case.

For black-and-white films, you can also compare the development parameters (developer, dilution and times) to get at least an idea, which emulsions are similar. For those who would like to get first hints, please refer to the the page "Notes" with the table "Equivalent Films" at darkroom-solutions.com.

As you can see, there is plenty of room for speculation. What truth can be deduced from it is questionable. The only thing that can be said with certainty: Do not believe everything that is in marketing texts and be prepared to spend one or two extra euros for relabeled possibly expired standard material.

5.3   Instant Film

With instant film, we distinguish between two types: peel-apart and integral film.

Peel-Apart Film

Peel-apart film is mostly used in large format photography. The film consists of two parts: the negative and the positive. The exposed image is pulled out of the film back after the exposure. While you pull it out, two steel rollers squish a paste with developer chemicals between the two parts of the film, and the processing begins. After a processing time of a few seconds to several minutes, you peel apart the two halves to get your photo. Due to lack of demand, Fujifilm has ceased production of its peel-apart instant picture film. New55, too, has ended its famous large-format peel-apart film project.

Integral Film

Polaroid is the integral film most of us probably remember best. This film contains everything needed for instant pictures. In addition to the picture, the film cartridge comes with a battery that provides power for the camera. The Polaroid film integrates everything that's needed for the picture. You do not have to peel anything apart or dispose of any negatives. After the exposure, a motor in the camera ejects the picture forwards and processing starts automatically. After a few minutes, you have a fully developed photo.

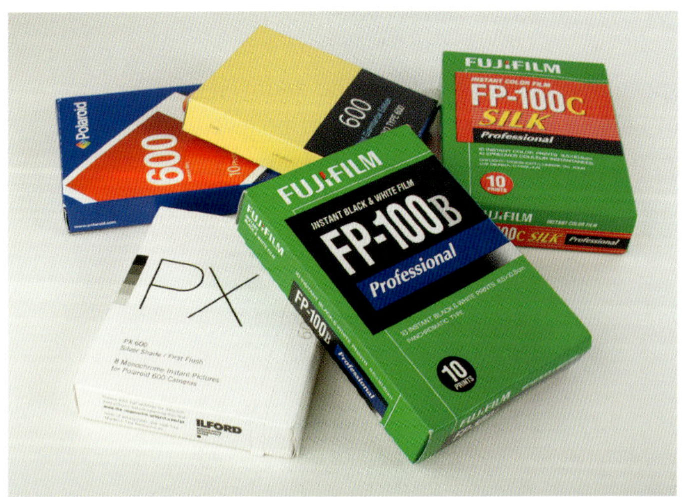

A selection of instant film packs (some are no longer available)

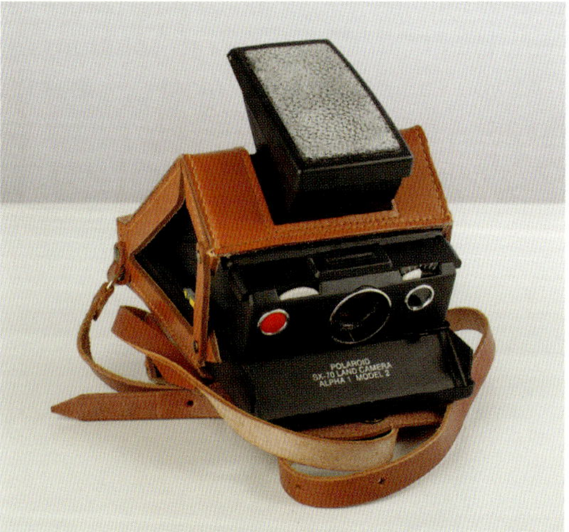

Polaroid SX-70 uses integral film

Polaroid Spirit 600 CL with Impossible PX600 Silver Shade, First Flush

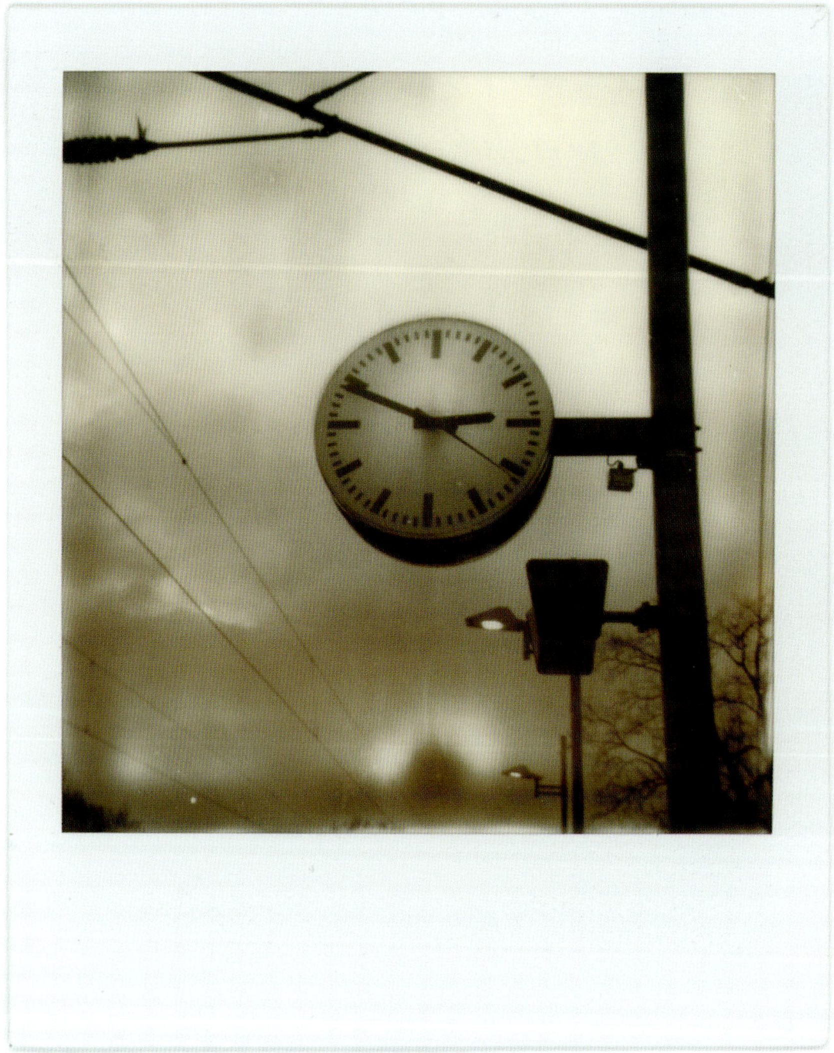

Polaroid Spirit 600 CL with Impossible PX600 Silver Shade, First Flush

You often see people shake a Polaroid picture after shooting. That's not necessary at all. On the contrary: the movement can even have a negative impact on the processing. Instead, you should keep the picture still (a dark coat pocket is best) until the processing is complete.

Instant Photography Over the Years: It all started in 1948 with the Polaroid Land Camera, named after Edwin Herbert Land, the founder of Polaroid. After first becoming known for polarizing filters for use in eyeglasses, science, and photography, the company produced the first instant film from 1948 to about 1960. Initially in the form of "Roll Film," a rolled instant film that shares only the name with the 120 medium format now often referred to as "roll film." Roll Film was the forerunner of the later pack film, where the negative and positive had to be separated by hand after a short development time. Several versions and sensitivities followed, and eventually Polaroid even made pack film in color.

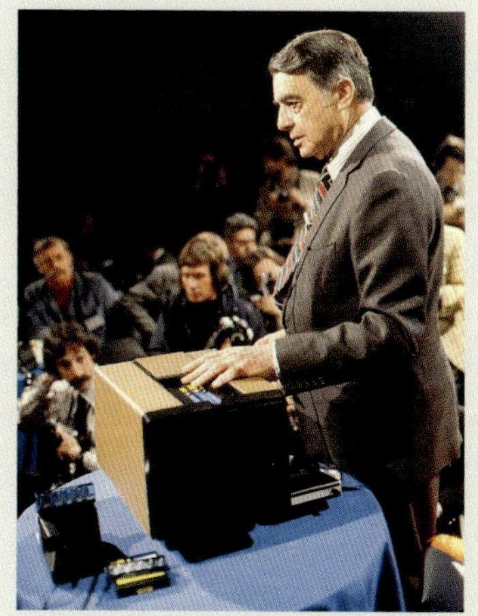

Edwin Herbert Land, inventor of instant photography.

Photo: Bernard Gotfryd, Source: Wikimedia

The next big innovation, from about 1972, was integral film. With pack film, photographers were required to separate the film by hand after a specified development time had passed. They then had to dispose of the somewhat caustic waste. With integral film, everything was neatly tied up in a single package per image. As if by magic, the film developed all by itself within a few minutes and at the end of the development time there was nothing to dispose of. Integration went so far that even the batteries to power the cameras were integrated in the film packages.

By the way, like with all other instant films, you don't really have to shake integral film to develop it.

Edwin Land had thoroughly patented his instant film system. So when Kodak tried to get a piece of the pie, they failed and had to discontinue and scrap their products. In the early 1980s, Fujifilm brought out their own pack film. Initially only on the Japanese market, later worldwide.

At the end of the 1990s, Fujifilm launched the enormously successful integral film Instax, which is now available in different formats: Mini, Wide, and Instax Square, which has dimensions that are very similar to the classic Polaroid picture.

In 2008, Polaroid went insolvent. Shortly after, The Impossible Project bought the last Polaroid factory in the Netherlands to continue to make integral film with new chemistry using the old Polaroid machines.

In 2017, the former Impossible CEO took over ownership of the Polaroid brand, bringing both brand and films back under one roof.

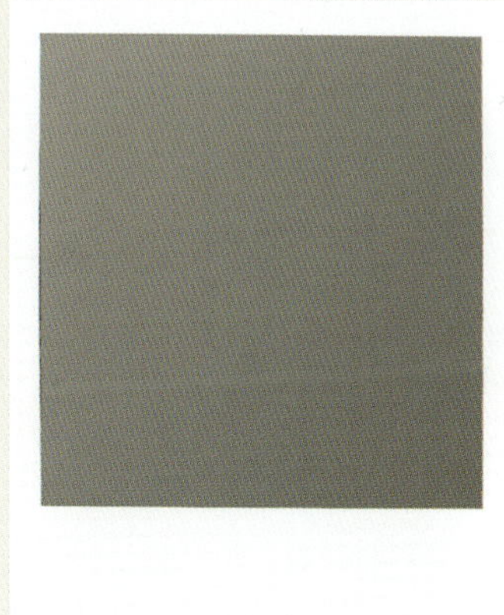

The Polaroid integral film became the epitome of the instant picture for several generations

The Impossible Project

After Polaroid declared bankruptcy in 2008 and announced that integral film would no longer be produced, The Impossible Project was founded to continue producing instant film. They purchased 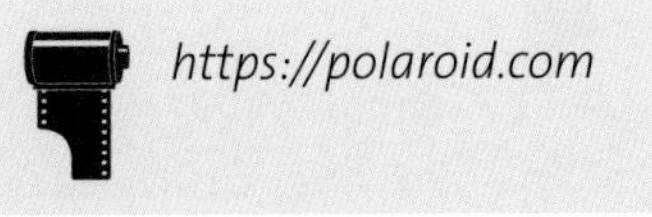

the last Polaroid production site in the Netherlands and have been producing various types of film for the different Polaroid cameras since then. The main shareholder at The Impossible Project has acquired the rights to the Polaroid brand, and the two brands now appear under the single Polaroid Originals label. Since then, it has rebranded to Polaroid.

Fujifilm Instax

Fujifilm's Instax products are the best-known and most successful instant picture products on the market today. The color films are available in three formats—Mini (46×62mm), Square (62×62mm), and Wide (62×99mm)—and Mini format is available in black-and-white too. In addition to a range of cameras, Fujifilm also sells two printers that can output digital image files on Instax Mini and Square film. MINT, Lomography, and Leica also sell cameras that are compatible with the Instax system. Since its introduction in 1998, Instax has become a global bestseller. As of March 2018, Fujifilm sold seven million Instax cameras and more than 45 million packs of Instax film.

Film	Format / Type	Features
Fuji Instax Mini	Instax Mini Dimensions: 8.6 x 5.4cm Image size 6.2 x 4.6cm	Color integral film with 10 exposures and a nominal sensitivity of ISO 800. Available in a variety of frame colors or decors (including White, Black, Airmail, Rainbow, Pink Lemonade, and Sky Blue).
Fuji Instax Mini Monochrome	Instax Mini Dimensions: 8.6 x 5.4cm Image size 6.2 x 4.6cm	Black-and-white integral film with 10 exposures and a nominal sensitivity of ISO 800. The fine grain structure supports high image sharpness.

→

Film	Format / Type	Features
Fuji Instax Square	Instax Square Dimensions: 8.6 x 7.2cm Image size 6.2 x 6.2cm	Color integral film with 10 exposures and a nominal sensitivity of ISO 800. Available in white and black frame colors.
Fuji Instax Wide	Instax Wide Dimensions: 8.6 × 10.8cm Image size: 6.2 x 9.9cm	Color integral film with 10 exposures and a nominal sensitivity of ISO 800. The fine grain structure supports high image sharpness, vibrant colors, and natural skin tones.
Polaroid Originals Color i-Type Film	i-Type (film without battery) Dimensions: 10.7 x 8.8cm Image size: 7.9 x 7.9cm	Integral film for 8 color images and a nominal sensitivity of ISO 640. Fine details and balanced colors; available in different frame colors and decors.
Polaroid Originals B&W i-Type Film	i-Type (film without battery) Dimensions: 10.7 x 8.8cm Image size: 7.9 x 7.9cm	Integral film for 8 black-and-white images and a nominal sensitivity of ISO 640. Strong shadows and soft highlights.
Polaroid Originals Color 600 Film	600 (film with battery) Dimensions: 10.7 x 8.8cm Image size: 7.9 x 7.9cm	Integral film for 8 color images and a nominal sensitivity of ISO 640. Available in different frame colors and decors.
Polaroid Originals B&W 600 Film	600 (film with battery) Dimensions: 10.7 x 8.8cm Image size: 7.9 x 7.9cm	Integral film for 8 black-and-white images and a nominal sensitivity of ISO 640.
Polaroid Originals Duochrome Edition Blue 600 Film	600 (film with battery) Dimensions: 10.7 x 8.8cm Image size: 7.9 x 7.9cm	Integral film with ISO 640 for 8 Duochrome images in black and cyan tones with a black frame.

→

Film	Format / Type	Features
Polaroid Originals Duo-chrome Edition Yellow 600 Film	600 (film with battery) Dimensions: 10.7 x 8.8cm Image size: 7.9 x 7.9cm	Integral film with ISO 640 for 8 Duochrome images in black and yellow with a black frame.
Polaroid Originals Color 600 Film Round Frame Edition	600 (film with battery) Dimensions: 10.7 x 8.8cm	Integral film for 8 round, color images and a nominal sensitivity of ISO 640.
Polaroid Originals Color SX-70 Film	SX-70 (film with battery) Dimensions: 10.7 x 8.8cm Image size: 7.9 x 7.9cm	Integral film for 8 color images and a nominal sensitivity of ISO 160. A film with fine structure for rich colors and contrast.
Polaroid Originals B&W SX-70 Film	SX-70 (film with battery) Dimensions: 10.7 x 8.8cm Image size: 7.9 x 7.9cm	Integral film for 8 black-and-white images and a nominal sensitivity of ISO 160. A fine-grained film for situations with enough light.
Polaroid Color 8x10 Film	Large format Dimensions: 12.8" x 8.5" (32.5 x 21.5cm) Image size: 9.5" x 7.5" (24.1 x 19cm)	Integral film for color images in 8x10-inch format and a nominal sensitivity of ISO 640. Ten exposures per pack. Processing this film requires special equipment.
Polaroid B&W 8x10 film	Large format Dimensions: 12.8" x 8.5" (32.5 x 21.5cm) Image size: 9.5" x 7.5" (24.1 x 19.0cm)	Integral film for black-and-white images in 8x10 inch format and a nominal sensitivity of ISO 640. Ten exposures per pack. Processing this film requires special equipment.

Instant Film

5.4   ISO—The Film Speed

The ISO number on the film packaging (the nominal film speed) is a guideline on how to set the exposure meter so the film gets the optimal amount of light. If the film box says ISO 400, set the exposure meter to ISO 400, and all will be well.

But you can do much more. Exposing the film should not be seen as completely independent from the subsequent processing. Take a quick look at the Massive Dev Chart online database, which is a source for processing recipes (see page 160). As an example, let's look at a common combination of film and developer: Kodak Tri-X 400 and Kodak HC-110. Instead of just one recipe for processing, the Massive Dev Chart will offer a long list of dilutions, processing times, and temperatures. This list includes ISO 200, 250, 320, 400, 800, 1600, 2400, 3200, and 6400.

If you have only ever dealt with digital photography, this may astonish you. Why should you change the exposure of the film? After all, there is no little wheel to adjust the film speed. The secret lies in processing. If we expose Tri-X at ISO 1600 instead of its nominal speed of ISO 400 (in other words, we give it 2 stops less light by setting the exposure meter accordingly), then we can process it later with the corresponding recipe to get a useful result. This is referred to as push processing. We could just as well expose the film for ISO 200 instead of ISO 400, giving it twice as much light. This type of compensation is referred to as pull processing.

So why do the film manufacturers bother specifying film speeds at all? In an ideal case, these film speed numbers mean that the film shows the biggest possible contrast range at the corresponding exposure. More important is the creative potential hidden within this information.

Push/Pull

Changing the exposure and using various ways of processing causes different results. Push processing increases the contrast; pull processing increases the film's contrast range. Night shots that have been pushed over several aperture stops tend to show deep blacks and a strongly increased contrast. But you need to expose very precisely. The contrast range of a pull processing, on the other hand, can sometimes be so big that exposure errors are hardly possible.

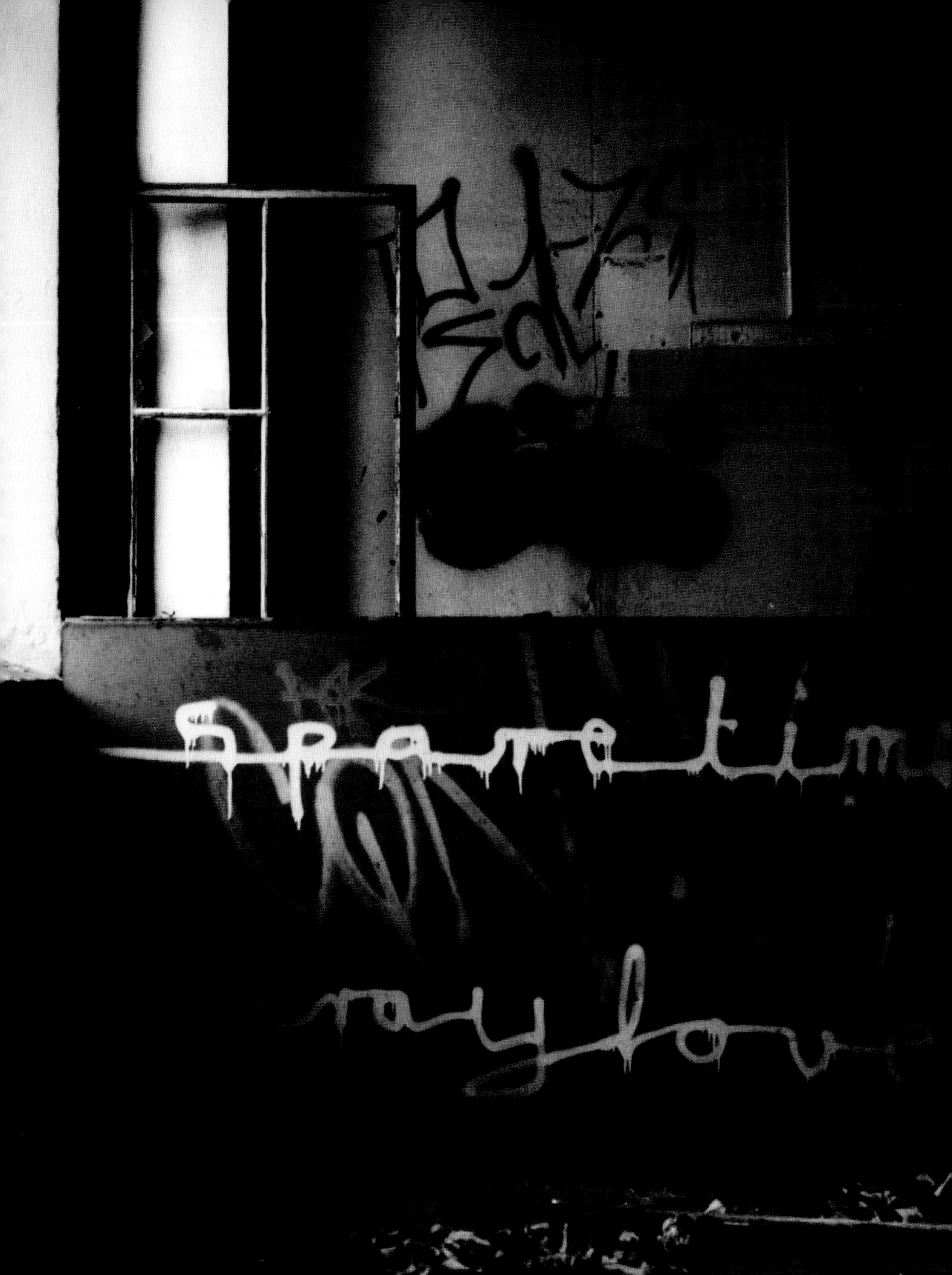
spare tim
ray lo

6
In the Laboratory

After shooting, the next step is developing the film. Basically, you have three options: an industrial laboratory, a professional lab, or processing the film yourself.

6.1   Industrial Laboratory

The most convenient option for developing is having someone else do it. One option is to use industrial labs. In the 1990s, there were quite a few of these around, but not many are left now. Industrial labs specialize primarily in processing color film, particularly color negative film, using the C-41 process. This process is standardized and can be done almost fully automatically by machines.

To send your color film to an industrial lab, you can just hand it in at the drugstore around the corner. The film is collected and sent on to the lab. A few days later, you get your film back, developed and with prints, if you ordered them. With an industrial lab, you do not have much control over treatment, contrasts, and colors of your pictures. And even if the service offers black-and-white options, we think that black-and-white film does not really belong in the industrial lab.

6.2   Professional Laboratory

There are still many professional labs that offer all kinds of analog and digital services and products, and even cater to special requests. Options include printing on baryta paper, large format processing of all kinds, and negative scanning. Plus you can have pictures framed, mounted, laminated, or printed digitally in large format on many materials, from canvas to aluminum panels to acrylic glass. Just type the term *professional photo lab* into your search engine, and you may be surprised by how many hits you get.

6.3   Processing Yourself: Black-and-White

Black-and-white processing is easy, quick, and relatively straightforward to do at home. By choosing a developer and having full control over all other developing parameters, you can directly influence the results. That's not possible in any photo lab.

The process itself is very easy and quicker than you think. With a bit of practice, the right tools and knowledge, you can easily develop five films in 20 minutes. Here we will give you step-by-step instructions of what you need for getting the results you want.

6.3.1   Overview: Negative Processing

First of all, here's an overview of the developing process:
1. Get all your equipment ready: the changing bag, scissors, tongs, a measuring jar for the liquid, the developer concentrate, and the fixer.
2. Wind the film into the developing tank. This has to be done in absolute darkness. Watch out for glow-in-the-dark sports watches, clocks, smartphones, and smartwatches.

3. Close the developing tank. Don't forget the center column—otherwise the tank won't be lightproof.

4. Optional: Pre-wash the film with tap water at approximately 20°C/68°F. After a few minutes, you can pour the water down the drain.

5. Dilute the developer with the right amount of water, according to your chosen recipe.

6. Now the developing starts. Pour the diluted developer solution into the developer tank. Agitate the tank constantly for the first 30 seconds, then agitate it again every minute for about 5 to 10 seconds. At the end of the developing time, pour the spent developer into the waste canister.

7. Intermediate rinse: Fill the developer tank with tap water at about 20°C/68°F, and agitate it for about a minute. Then, pour the water down the drain.

8. Fill the tank with fixer, and agitate it the same way you did for developing: at first constantly, then every minute. Depending on the strength of the fixer, this process takes 3 to 10 minutes. When you're done, pour the fixer back into its container. You can reuse it several times.

9. Wash the film in clear tap water for 10 minutes, and treat it against lime spots if required.

10. Hang the film on a line to dry. The best place for this is a dust-free room.

6.3.2   Chemicals

Types of Developer

People often ask us if there is an ideal combination of film and developer. Frequently, the answer is "it depends." It depends on your personal preferences—and these can be completely different depending on the subject, light situation, and your mood.

Many of the wisdoms you find online are to be taken with a healthy pinch of skepticism. Before you take statements, such as: "Developer XY is unsuitable for push processing" or "Developer XY makes clumpy grain" at face value, you should definitely try different combinations yourself. For example, platforms such as filmdev.org in combination with Flickr offer you the option of looking at the pictures that result from specific film-developer combinations, so you can see for yourself.

You should think about the right type of developer for your negatives early on, not just when you take the exposed film out of the camera. Depending on what kind of negative characteristics are on your wish list, you should ideally make your choice even before you go out shooting with your camera. There are three factors that influence your picture in terms of contrasts, tonal values, and fine or rough grain: the emulsion of the film you choose, the exposure, and the choice of developer. Negative developers have different properties that influence the result of the development. They can be grouped by certain characteristics.

Compensating Developers

A compensating developer is a slow-acting negative developer with a lower level of alkali and a weaker concentration of developer substance compared to other developer types. A slower development results in better detail in the shadow areas in combination with slightly moderated highlights. This has a compensating effect on the contrasts.

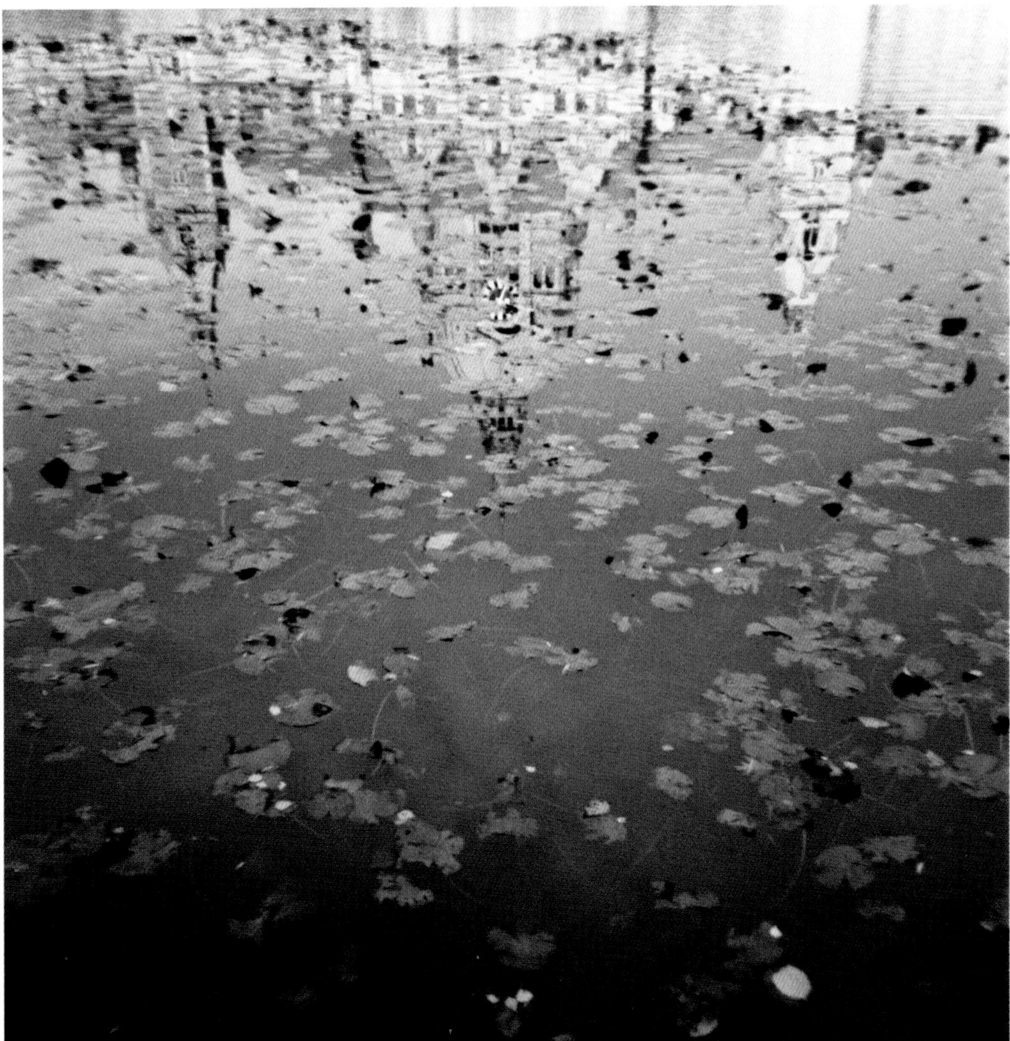

Shot with the Box, in Tetenal Ultrafin Blue

Compensating developers are suitable for scenes with a high contrast range: a shadowy alleyway at noon on a hot summer's day, backlit shots, and the like. A strong dilution of developer substance and a correspondingly longer developing time also have a compensating effect on the negative contrast. The developer substance becomes exhausted more quickly in the highlights, but the shadows are developed for a longer period of time.

Fine-Grain Developers

Fine-grain developers contain additional substances that can dissolve silver halides. These halides are reduced to silver and accumulate on the latent picture, making the film grain appear finer and less pronounced. These developers do not usually make full use of the film sensitivity, but result in negatives with a fine, even grain and show good sharpness performance.

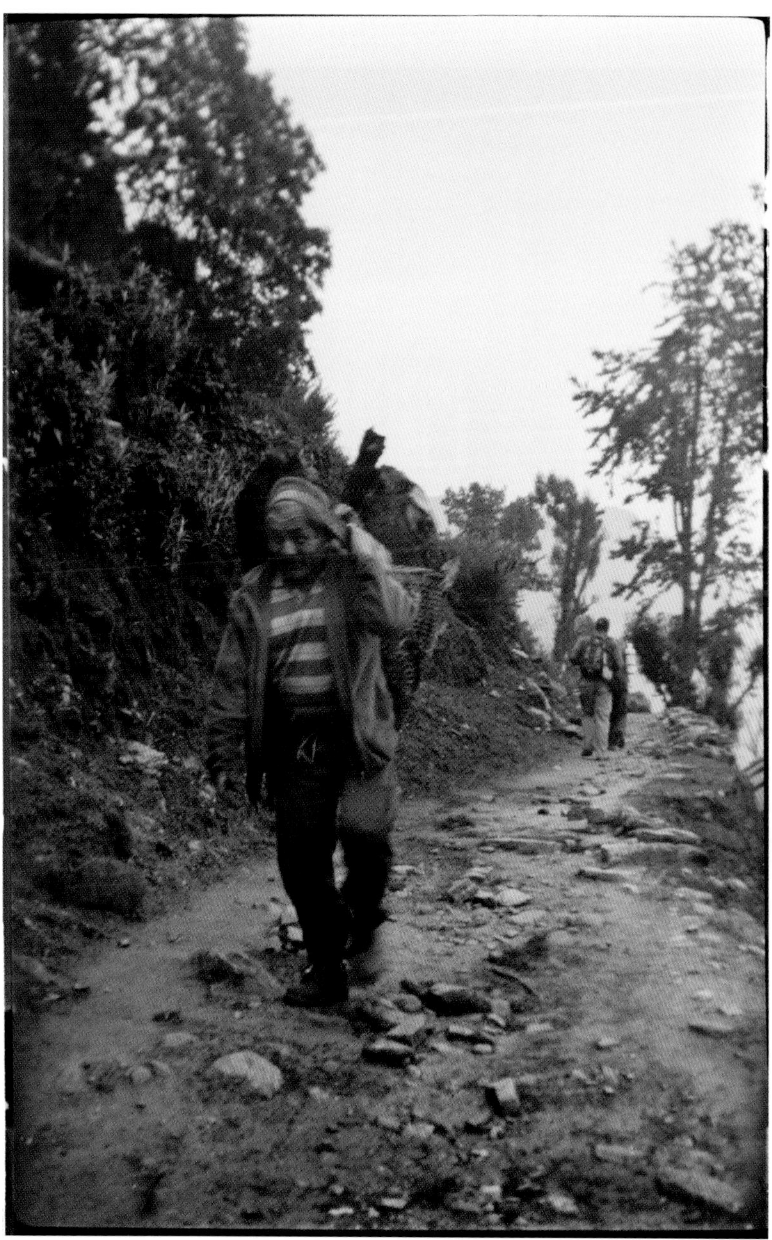

Agfa Synchro Box in Calbe A49 fine grain developer

Important: A fine-grain developer can only influence grain to a limited extent. If the emulsion of the film you chose already has rough grain, even the best fine-grain developer is not going to change that.

Universal Developers
Universal developers hardly affect the nominal film speed and show good tonal gradation. They are a happy medium between making best use of the film speed and providing sharpness and fine grain.

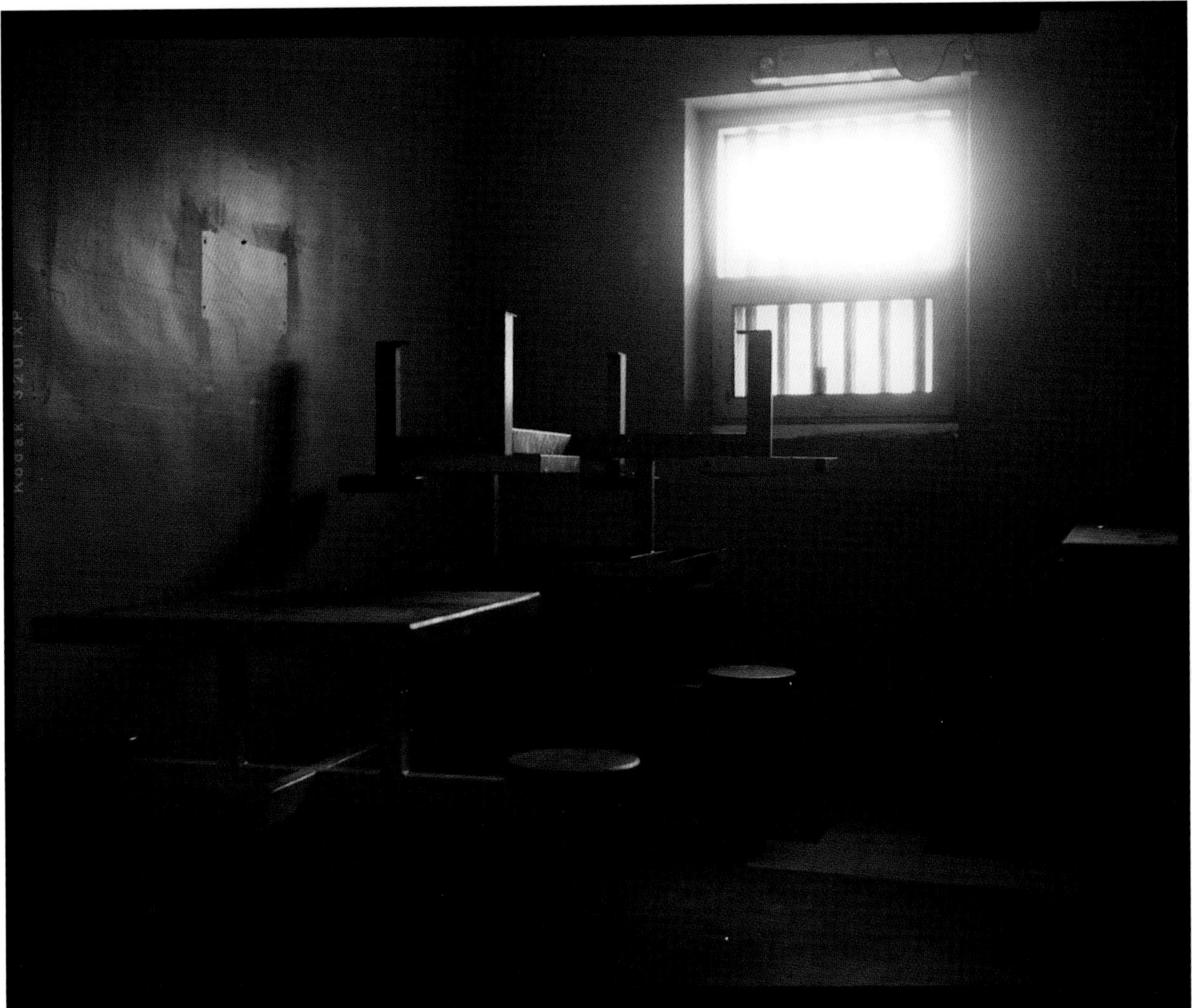

Graflex Crown Graphic, large format in Kodak HC-110

Industrial Developers

We use the term *industrial developers* to describe developers that have been on the market for a long time. They are available internationally and are generally produced by larger companies. The manufacturers of these developers are often also film manufacturers. The companies include Kodak, Agfa, and Ilford. Industrial developers are usually very well documented, so you can go online and easily find data sheets, user reports, and developing recipes (often with pictures).

Agfa Rodinal

Agfa Rodinal was introduced in 1881 and is the oldest known industrial developer. Agfa ceased production of the original Rodinal products; however, ADOX acquired the formula and has continued production of products that match the original Agfa quality. Similar products are also available (some of which use the original formula) and are sold under brands such as Calbe, Compard R09, and ADOX APH 09.

Rodinal and its derivatives are sold as a liquid concentrate. The working solution can be prepared quickly and in the desired quantity and concentration for immediate use. The concentrate is very inexpensive and will keep pretty much indefinitely—although all manufacturers include a best-before date. The liquid gets darker over time, and sometimes crystals accumulate at the bottom of the bottle, but this has practically no impact on the use and results.

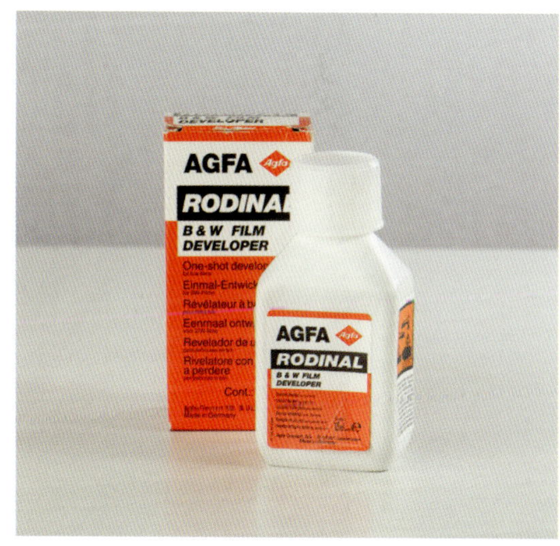

Agfa Rodinal is only available as a clone today

The developer has a slight sharpness-increasing effect and makes good use of the film speed. Typical dilutions for standard developments are 1:50 and 1:25. Many photographers use a dilution of 1:100 or lower when it comes to contrast-compensating stand developments of 60 minutes and longer. For us, it has become an all-purpose weapon when we want fine grain and balance when pushing film by two stops. When faced with unlabeled ("What did I expose this film at again?") or unknown material (film from the flea market), we resort to a 60- to 90-minute stand development in Rodinal 1:100. The results have always been convincing.

You can find recipes for developing in Rodinal for practically all commercially available black-and-white film. It is a developer you should always keep around.

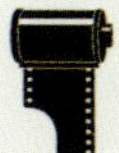 There is a DIY Rodinal clone that you prepare with Paracetamol. See the Parodinal recipe on page 123.

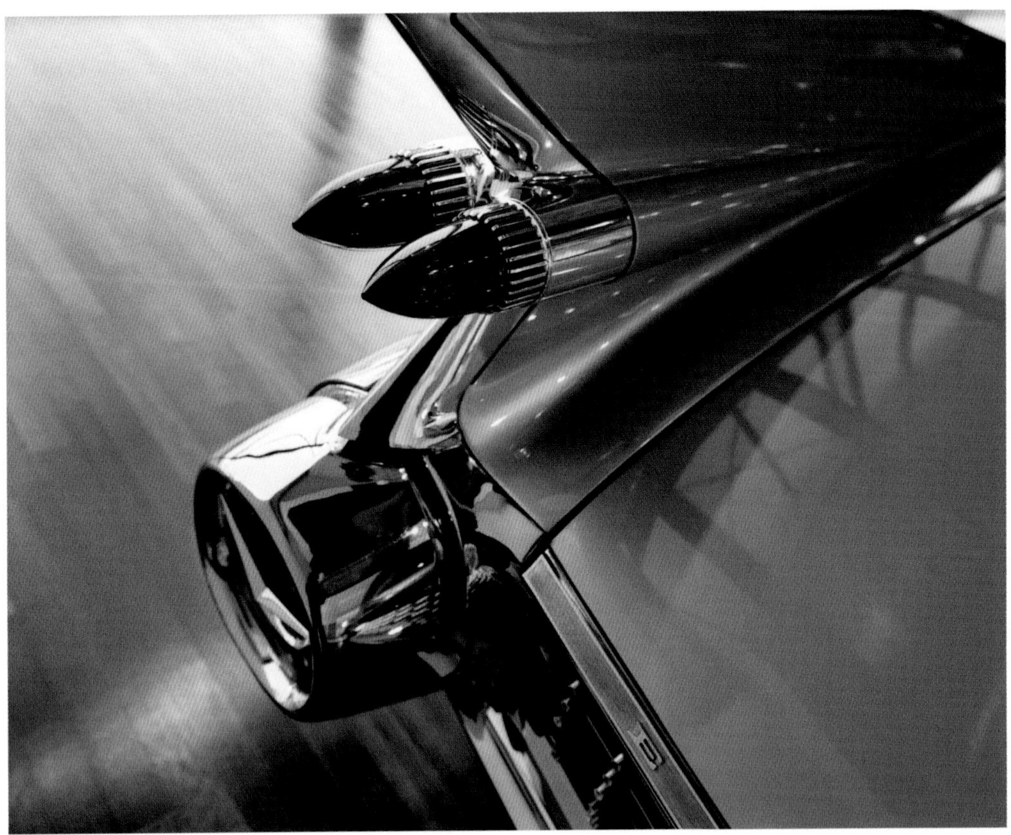

Vintage tail fin. Pentax 67 on Kodak Tri-X 400 at ISO 1600, stand developed in Rodinal

Kodak D-76

This developer is based on metol-hydroquinone and one of the classic film developers. It has been on the market since 1927 and was one of the most popular developers in the 20th century. It belongs into the category of fine-grain developers, and it is particularly popular these days among photojournalists who prefer working on 35mm film. Ilford ID11 and the GDR-manufactured Orwo F19 are also based on this recipe.

Kodak D-76 is supplied as powder developer and has to be prepared as stock solution before you can develop. You mix the powder with warm water (approx. 50°C/122°F). Then the solution has to cool down before you can use it. Properly stored, the stock solution will easily keep up to six months. You can use it as one-shot developer or regenerate the stock solution.

The Kodak D-76 is a developer with a wide range of applications. There are recipes for any commonly used black-and-white film and push processing. We use it a lot for pull processing if we want to revel in particularly subtle shades of gray.

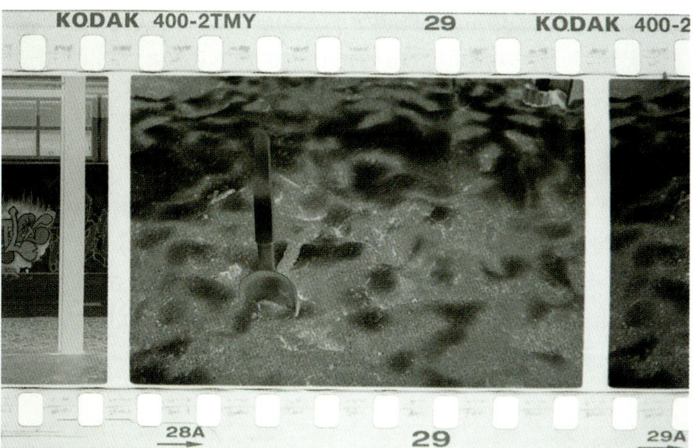

Kodak T-MAX 400 developed in D-76, pulled three stops to ISO 50. There is ample detail in both shadows and highlights. This is the negative...

Kodak D-76 is a classic fine-grain developer. We use it often for pull processing.

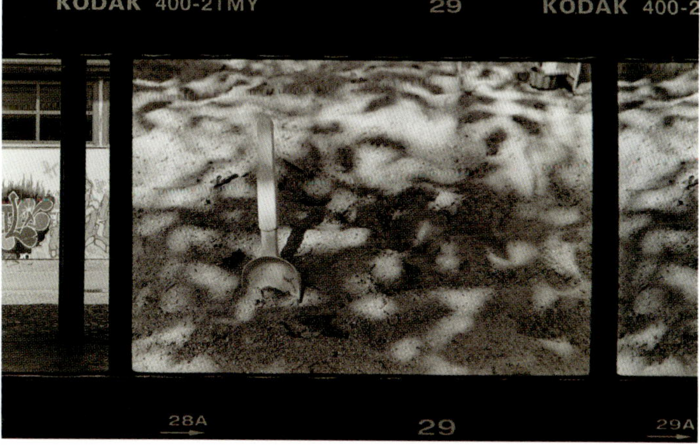

...and after conversion to positive

Kodak XTOL

Kodak XTOL is a two-part powder-based developer for black-and-white film. It was introduced in 1996 as the successor to D-76 and is based on a derivative of ascorbic acid (vitamin C) rather than the potentially carcinogenic hydroquinone used in its predecessor. XTOL can be mixed, stored, and used at room temperature. Under proper conditions, the solution can be stored for up to six months.

The stock solution consists of a mixture of two components (A and B) and can be used undiluted for developing. You can use it diluted 1:1 for one-off developing or for adding to a stock solution. Kodak sells packages for making 5 or 50 liters.

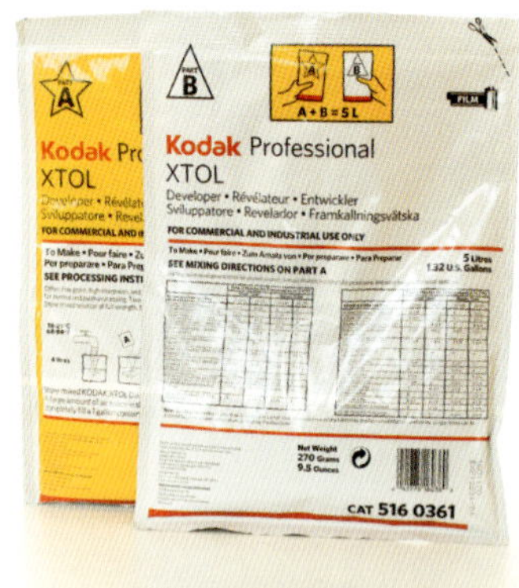

Kodak XTOL is a universal developer based on ascorbic acid

Like D-76, XTOL is a fine-grain developer. The authors of *The Film Developing Cookbook,* Stephen G. Anchell and Bill Troop, claim that XTOL provides 10% more enlargeability than D-76 while retaining sharpness and visible grain. Using diluted XTOL produces negatives with increased sharpness and better shadow detail.

XTOL utilizes a film's sensitivity to the full. According to Anchell and Troop, Kodak particularly recommends XTOL for developing T-MAX film, although it is pretty universal and works well with just about any black-and-white film at nominal speeds, or for push and pull processing (see section 6.39 for more details on these techniques).

Other Developers

Developer recipes and makes are still available today in abundance. You are probably going to find your favorites very quickly. In addition to Rodinal and D-76, we frequently use various other developers. In our bar of photo chemicals, there is always a bottle of Kodak HC-110, which we like to use especially for developing Kodak Tri-X 400. At nominal film speed and at a push of one or two stops, we get negatives with clean details and good contrasts. HC-110 is similarly indestructible, and we happily use it far beyond its best-before date.

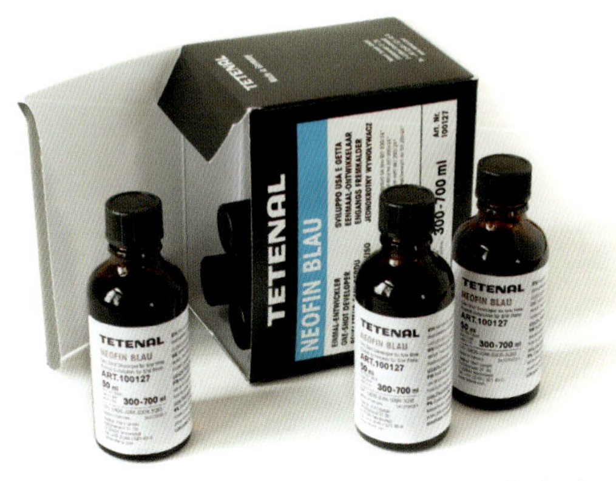

Tetenal Neofin Blue: A single-use developer for high resolution and pronounced sharpness

Due to their good storage stability, we also always have one or more powdered developers available. This includes Kodak XTOL, a developer that does it all. And for fine grain, we use ADOX ATOMAL 49 (previously known as Calbe or Orwo A49). For optimal results when developing modern delta or flat crystal film, we use T-MAX developer, which works particularly well with T-MAX film by the same brand. If we need to tease out a tad more sharpness from medium to low-sensitive films, Tetenal Neofin Blue is used.

Caffenol

As described in previous sections, there are countless developers that have been around for decades. In addition, innovative, smaller developer makers keep introducing developers with interesting properties. So why think about more alternatives?

It's not the price. With many of the established recipes, developing a black-and-white film costs less than a dollar. It's more likely to be the fascination of experimenting with substances that are available in most households and, in doing so, satisfying the inner child in analog photographers. The first time we heard about using coffee to develop film, our curiosity was roused and we went straight to the search engine.

The idea of using coffee as an alternative developer substance was born in 1995 at the Rochester Institute of Technology (RIT). Dr. Scott Williams's technical photographic

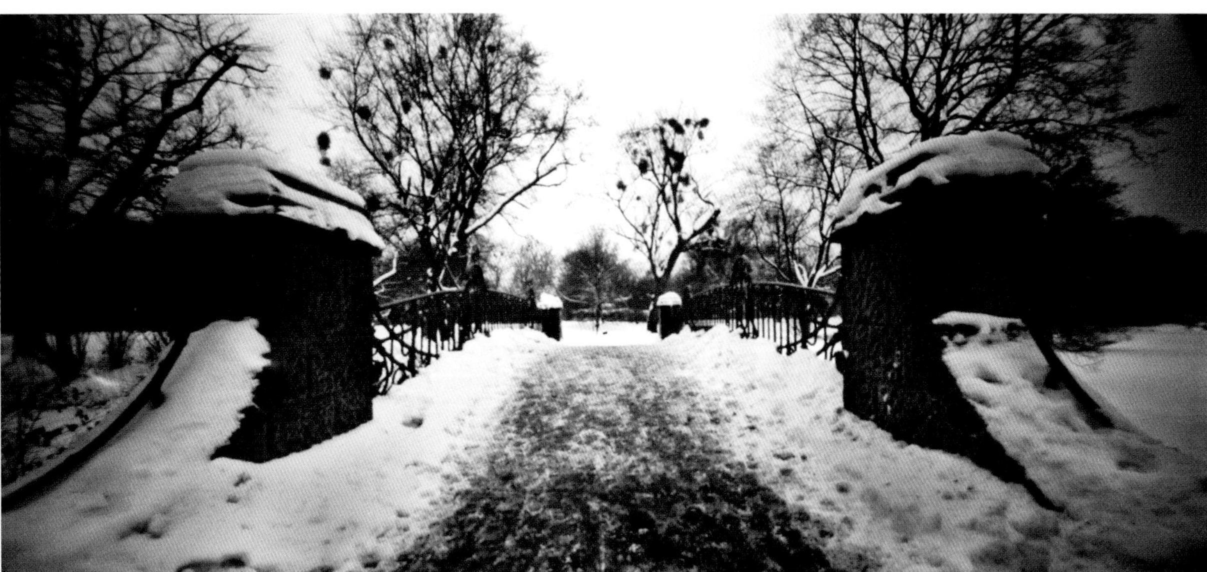

Bridge. *Holga 120-PWC on Kodak T-MAX, developed for 15 minutes in Caffenol-C-H*

chemistry class had the task of identifying non-traditional developers. They tested various household substances for suitability. Success came when they began experimenting with liquids containing caffeine. Both tea and coffee developments showed results—coffee yielded the best quality.

The reason that coffee gets us going in the morning and is also able to reduce silver bromide to metallic silver lies in the presence of various phenols: amongst others, caffeic acid, which resembles well-known developer substances such as catechol. The chemistry course came up with a developer recipe based on coffee and a mixture of sodium bicarbonate (baking soda) and potassium hydroxide. The latter two ingredients serve mostly as buffers to stabilize the developer during the process at a pH-value of 9. The developing time was approximately 25 minutes. The mixture wasn't named back then, but was basically the original version of Caffenol.

Although the recipe created by RIT does work as developer, the recipe has been revised a few times. Cheap, instant coffee based on Robusta beans has a greater acid content, and evidently works better than the nobler version with Arabica beans. By adding vitamin C, an active developer substance also contained in industrial developers such as XTOL, you can increase the image contrast and shorten the processing time. Using washing soda (calcined anhydrous soda, i.e., sodium carbonate, soda ash) instead of baking soda yields more reliable results. Instant coffee is available from the discount store; washing soda and vitamin C in the drug store. Only potassium bromide is sometimes a bit harder to get. You can try ordering it in your local pharmacy or online via eBay.

We have been working from day one with the recipes provided by Reinhold G. on his English-language website *http://caffenol.blogspot.com*. They have never let us down yet.

Preparing Caffenol developers is very easy, provided you follow the specified quantities in the recipes and mix the ingredients in the right order. An inexpensive food scale is great for weighing the ingredients. For preparing and mixing, we usually use something like a half-gallon plastic bottle. You can easily mix all the ingredients by shaking the bottle thoroughly.

Please make sure you are working with gloves and protective goggles! Although the substances used are household items and freely available, you definitely do not want to get the stuff into your eyes.

1. Add the washing soda to the water, and stir or shake until the soda has dissolved. This procedure releases heat (exothermic reaction). As you are aiming for a target temperature of 20°C/68°F in the finished solution, the water should have a starting temperature of about 17°C/63°F. After mixing, open the bottle lid carefully.
2. Stir in the vitamin C powder. You may see small bubbles forming. Wait until they have dissolved.
3. In developer recipes for higher-speed film, you also add potassium bromide.
4. Add the instant coffee. Mix everything well; the coffee dissolves slowly.

Now start developing. The Caffenol preparation will not keep very long. You should use it within a few hours.

Caffenol: Recipes
The standard recipe for low- to medium-speed film up to ISO 100 is:

Caffenol-C-M
- Water: 1 L
- Washing soda: 54 g
- Vitamin C: 16 g
- Instant coffee: 40 g

A good starting value for the developing time is about 15 minutes (at a developer temperature of 20°C/68°F). We always get scannable results at this value for different brands of film. Regarding the agitation of the developing tank during developing, we stick to the normal procedure: continuous movement during the first 30 seconds, then swirl the tank three to four times after every minute. The all-purpose weapon for film over ISO 100 with a slight increase in film speed is Caffenol-C-H. Adding potassium bromide prevents fogging.

Caffenol-C-H

- Water: 1 L
- Washing soda: 54 g
- Vitamin C: 16 g
- Potassium bromide: 1 g
- Instant coffee: 40 g

Developing time and agitation is the same as for Caffenol-C-M.

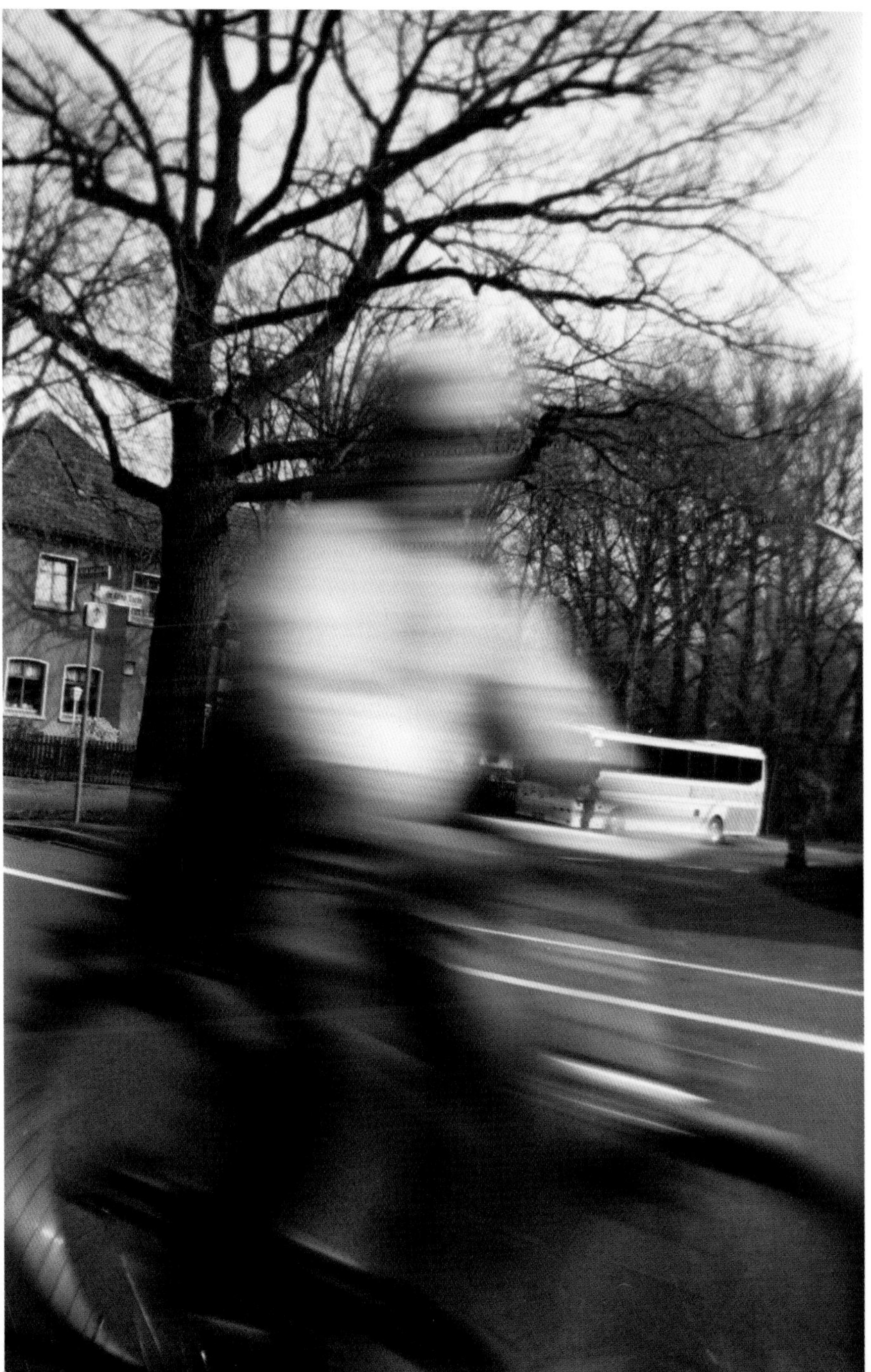

Cyclist. *Agfa Synchro Box on Shanghai GP3 100, developed for 15 minutes in Caffenol-C-H*

For push processing or finer grain through reduced agitation, a stand development is ideal. Caffenol aficionado Reinhold of *caffenol.blogspot.com* offers a recipe for this:

Caffenol-C-L
- Water: 1 L
- Washing soda: 16 g
- Vitamin C: 10 g
- Potassium bromide: 1 g
- Instant coffee: 40 g

If we use industrial developer for stand developments (and we often do), the time is typically 60 to 90 minutes—depending on how much we want to push the film. The starting value for this recipe is around 70 minutes, which has resulted in balanced negatives, both for processing at nominal film speed and with push processing of 1 to 2 stops.

For the agitation, we again use our own method: continuous movement for the first 30 seconds, then park the tank and swirl it two or three times after half the developing time has passed. With all recipes, the stop bath, fixer, and rinse are done just as they are for classic developing. We particularly like using the coffee developer for processing our lo-fi negatives (pictures we shot with low-tech cameras like the Bo or a pinhole Holga).

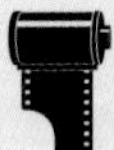 Modified recipes and other refinements of Caffenol development can be found at *https://www.caffenol.org*

Important: The use of Caffenol is not limited to pictures shot with simple or non-existent lenses. This developer is a fully fledged alternative to industrial developers. Impressive examples of pictures developed in this manner can be found online at:

- *https://caffenol.blogspot.com*
- *https://figitalrevolution.com*

Vitamin C, Parodinal, and Others
Ascorbic acid, a.k.a. vitamin C, can also be used as a developing agent. Industrial developers such as Kodak XTOL use it. Roger K. Bunting, a chemistry professor at Illinois State University and author of the book *The Chemistry of Photography,* describes how you can prepare a developer using vitamin C tablets and washing soda. Admittedly, this developer will not result in award-winningly fine-grained negatives, but supposedly yields a good range of detail, as Bunting explains in his article, "Coffee, Tea, Or Vitamin C: Kitchen Chemistry In The Darkroom." This article can be found on shutterbug.com.

Vitamin C
- Water: 250 ml/ 1 cup
- Vitamin C: 8 tablets of 1000 mg vitamin C each
- Washing soda: 15 g/5 TSP

The developing time is 30 minutes and the tank should be agitated every 30 seconds.

In addition to the various Rodinal clones that are available nowadays, there is also a simple method of making this developer yourself from cheap and easily available ingredients. The developer, known as *Parodinal*, is supposed to be similar to Rodinal in its characteristics. We have not tried it ourselves, but here is the recipe:

Parodinal
- Water: 250 ml/ 1 cup
- Acetaminophen (Paracetamol): 30 tablets of 500 mg each
- Sodium sulphite (calcined/anhydrous): 50 g
- Sodium hydroxide (calcined/anhydrous): 20 g

Tablets often have a wax coating that does not dissolve very well in water and can form a deposit on the negatives, so it's a good idea to use powdered Paracetamol for preparing the solution. Mix the ingredients in the order specified by the recipe and let them sit for 72 hours in a closed container before use. Developing times and dilution probably correspond to those of Rodinal. (Source: *digitaltruth.com*.) If you type *parodinal* into your search engine, you are quickly going to find other recipes, for example, those that add potassium bromide to prevent fogging.

Please make sure you are working with gloves and protective goggles! Although the substances used are household items and freely available, you definitely do not want to get the stuff into your eyes.

Adventurous film photographers like to experiment, and evidently won't stop at anything. On the Internet, you can find reports of experiments with developing film in Winenol (red wine, usually with added washing soda and vitamin C) or urine. We leave it up to you to decide if and how much of this you want to try out yourself. Perhaps you will even come up with other new ideas.

German Specialists

The recipes of the big industrial developers by Ilford or Kodak have been adapted over the years to the current makes of film and emulsion types, but we probably can't expect innovative developments here. If you are looking for something special, it's worth having a look at the comparatively small, innovative developer companies in Germany—for example, the companies Moersch-Photochemie, or SPUR. In addition to compensating two-bath developers, the range offered by Moersch-Photochemie also includes three different layer-staining developers. These types of developer include additives whose reaction products stain the film's gelatin layer (usually yellow or brown).

SPUR Schain + Partner currently offer nine different negative developers for black-and-white film. The universal developer SPUR UFP is a product you can use both for developing negatives and for printing slides.

As you can see, you have many options for harmonizing subject, lighting situation, film, and developer. You should certainly try out the many specialities available on the market.

Fixer

As you can see, film can indeed be developed with household items. But you are probably going to search in vain if you try to find fixer components in your kitchen cupboards.

The fixer bath has the task of washing the unexposed silver salts (that have not been reduced to black silver during processing) out of the film. To do so, the fixer transforms the silver bromide, which is not very water-soluble, into a form that can be washed out easily with water.

In addition to some other possible ingredients, modern fixers usually contain sodium thiosulfate and/or ammonium thiosulfate. Plus, many fixers also contain an acid component to neutralize the alkaline developer.

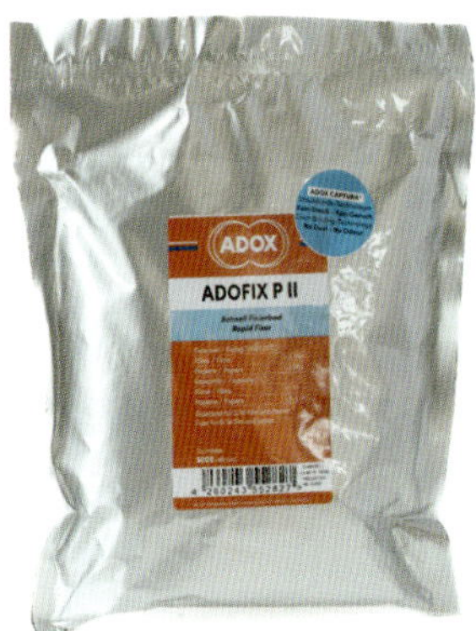

ADOFIX P II Express powder-based fixer can be used with black-and-white film and paper

Stop Bath

The stop bath is used to interrupt the developing process. It is particularly useful for developing photographic paper in the darkroom. As you are developing by inspection, you can use the stop bath effectively to prevent overdeveloping.

A stop bath is usually an acid solution based on acetic acid or citric acid, which quickly neutralizes the alkaline developer. As a side effect, less developer chemistry gets into the fixer bath, so you can use it for longer. In our daily practice of film developing, stop bath does not get used. A short rise after the first developing step does the same job for us and has proved to be just as effective.

Wetting Agent

To avoid water stains on the film, particularly in areas with hard water, people
often recommend using wetting agents.
The main ingredient in common wetting
agents are surfactants, which help the
water run off the film more quickly. The
film dries faster and has noticeably fewer
lime spots after drying. Wetting agents are simple to use: One drop is enough for a
large bowl of water. You briefly dip the film into it as a last step before drying.

Although household washing-up liquid is also made mostly of surfactants, you should not use it as wetting agent for film because of its skin-friendly, emollient components.

There are different wetting agents that have other components, as well. Some contain an anti-fungal ingredient that is supposed to prevent fungi growing on the film
in humid storage conditions. Some manufacturers also add a hardener to make sensitive emulsions more resistant to mechanical stress. From our point of view, the biggest
advantage of wetting agents is that they make the film dry more quickly. While the film
is hanging up on the line, the slightly sticky emulsion is particularly vulnerable to dust
particles and lint. The shorter the drying time, the less dust can accumulate on the film,
and the less time you need later for retouching.

But our personal experience also shows that not all films are compatible with all wetting agents. Some combinations even produce marks instead of preventing them. That's
why we like to play it safe and use distilled water for the last "washing cycle" instead.

You can experiment a little bit for yourself here to see if your favorite combo of wetting agent and film works well together. If worst comes to worst, you can still rescue a
spotty film by washing it again in distilled water.

Water

Strictly speaking, even water is part of the chemistry, because depending on your local
conditions, tap water can have different levels of hardness. To ensure your film devel-
ops consistently despite different water hardness levels, most developers contain a
water-softening agent. The makes that do not will have this listed in the data sheet.
These are usually prepared with distilled water.

6.3.3   Hardware

To develop film, you need a few pieces of equipment. You can use some household items, but for working with chemicals, it's a good idea to mark the used utensils clearly and then use them exclusively for developing film.

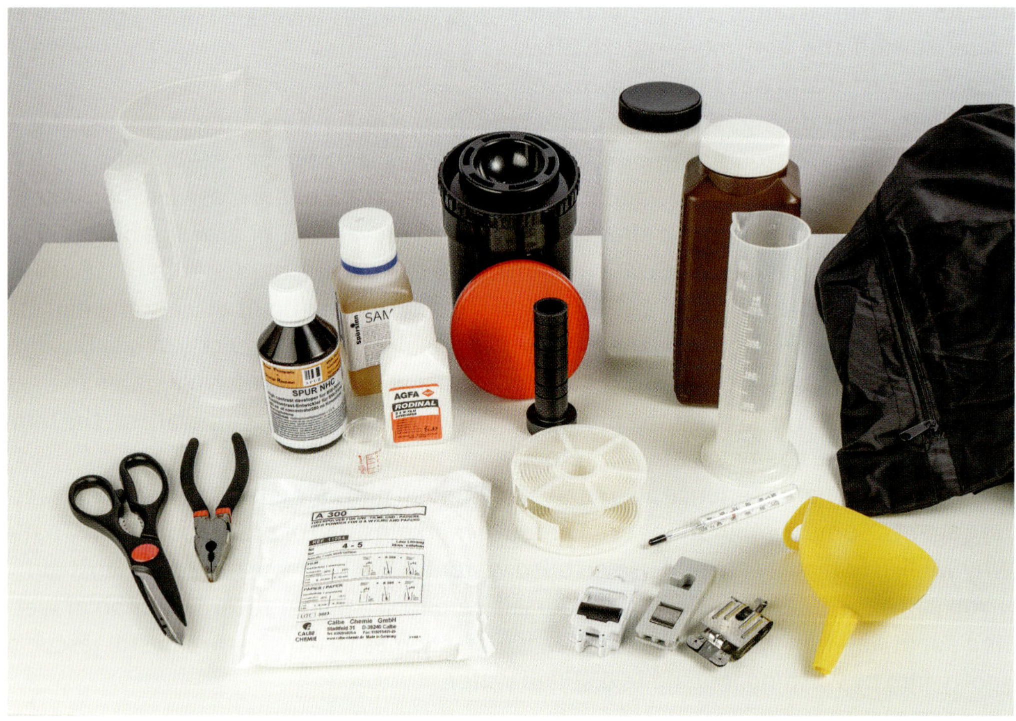

Utensils for use in the laboratory

We use a few large plastic boxes with lids for keeping developer chemicals and utensils clearly separate from the rest of the household items.

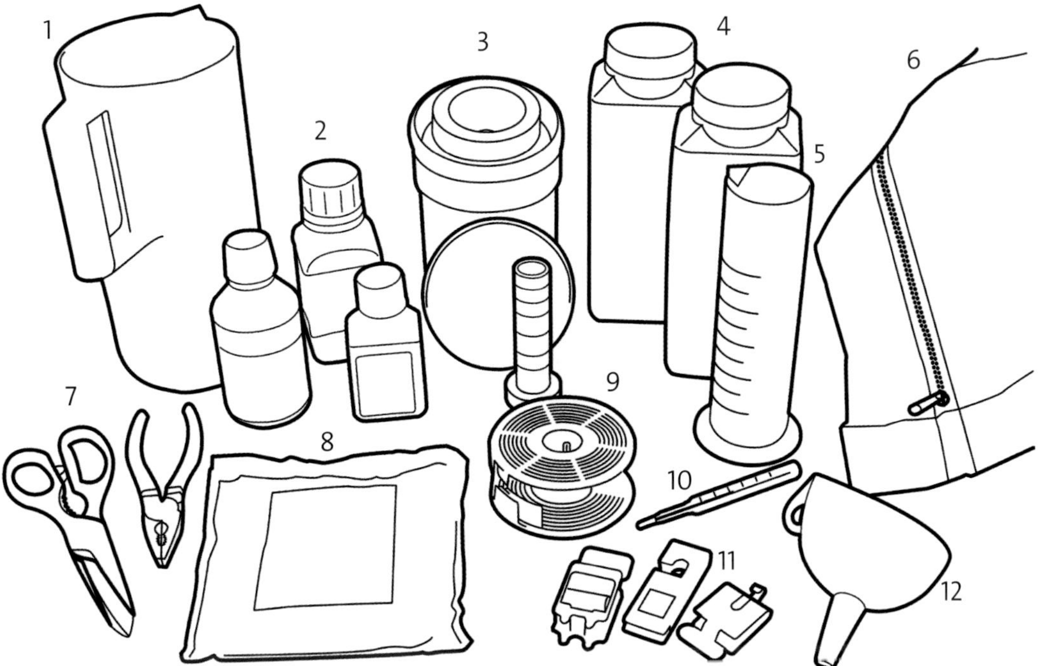

From back left to front right:

1. Measuring jug
2. Developer concentrate
3. Developing tank (with center column)
4. Developer and fixer bottle
5. Measuring cylinder
6. Changing bag
7. Pliers and scissors
8. Fixer powder
9. Film reel
10. Thermometer
11. Film clips
12. Funnel

Measuring Jug

A large measuring jug is useful for measuring amounts of liquid that would not fit into the smaller measuring cylinder.

Thermometer

Depending on the recipe, you develop film at different temperatures (usually at 20°C/68°F). Many developer starter sets already come with a thermometer.

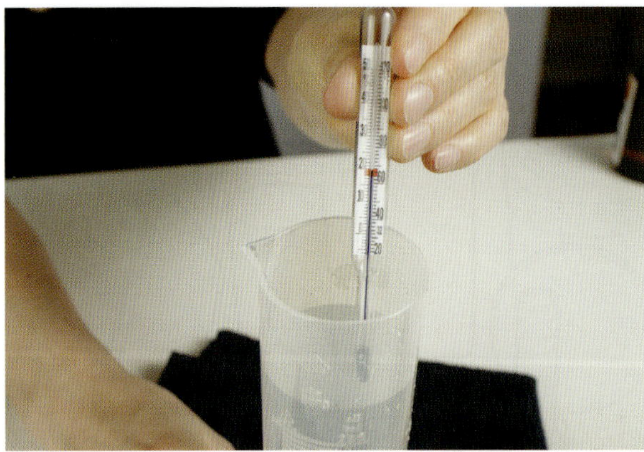

Analog thermometer

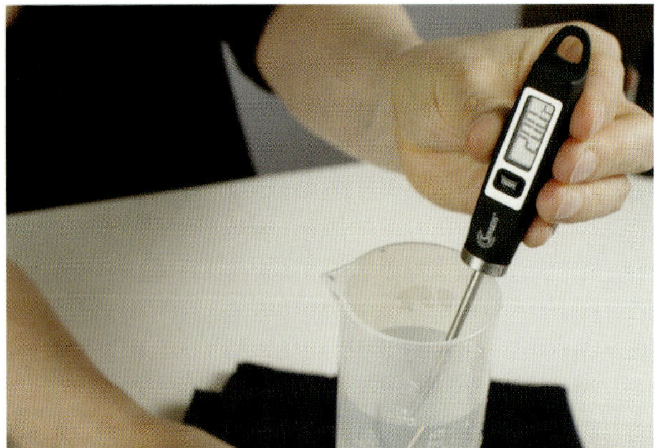

Digital thermometer

If you use, for example, a digital meat thermometer, make sure you mark it accordingly so you don't accidentally use it for food.

Developing Tank

The developing tank makes it possible to pour liquids in and out while the film inside the tank is enclosed in its light-tight interior. All the wet processes happen here: developing the film, fixing, and the final rinse. Thanks to the light-tight design, you can do all this in normal light. Only winding the film into the tank has to be done in absolute darkness.

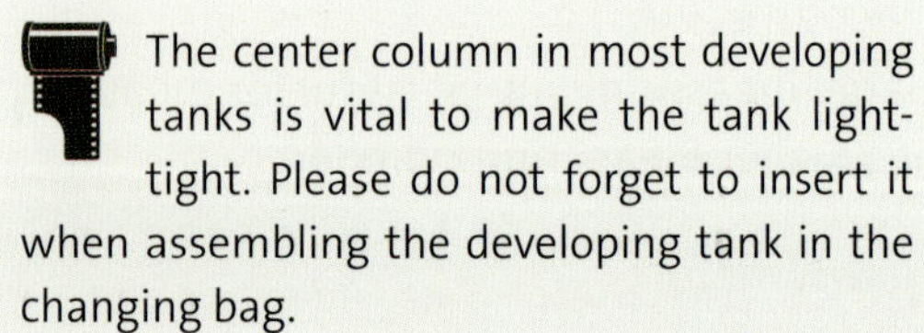 The center column in most developing tanks is vital to make the tank light-tight. Please do not forget to insert it when assembling the developing tank in the changing bag.

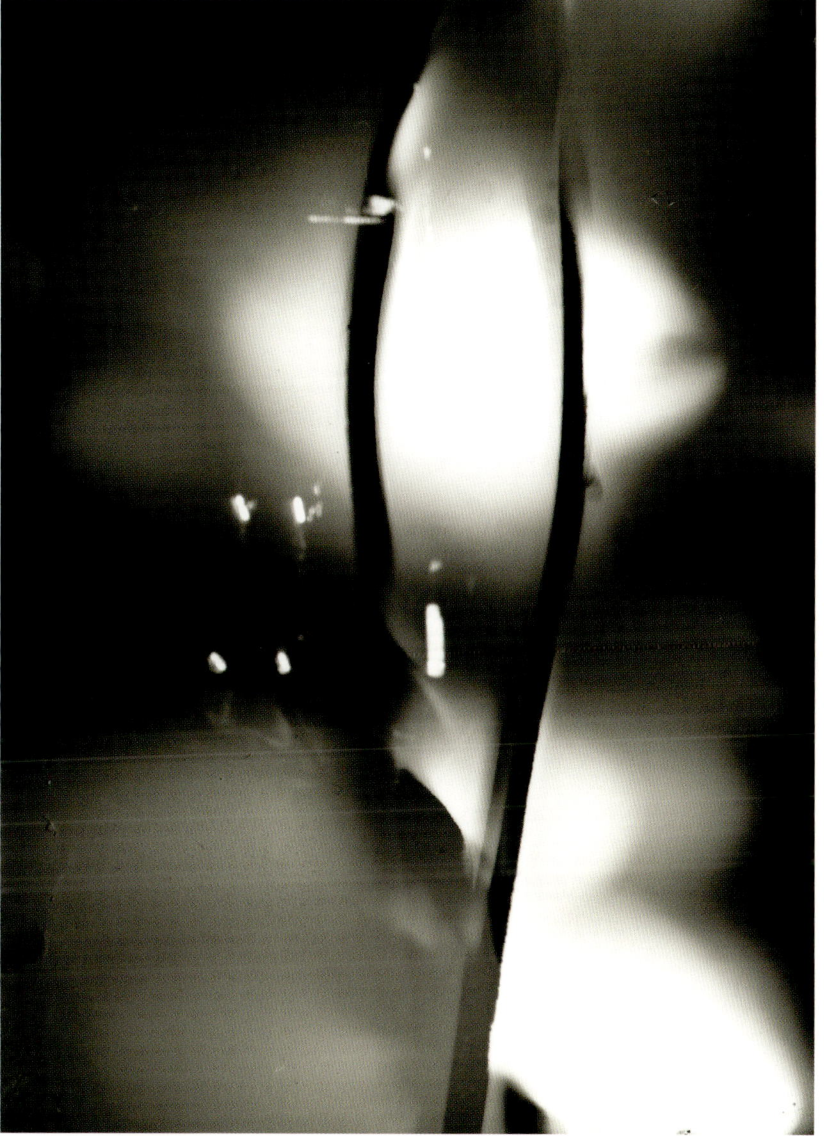

"Accident" caused by forgetting the center column. The light got in through the opening and exposed the film in an uncontrolled way during development.

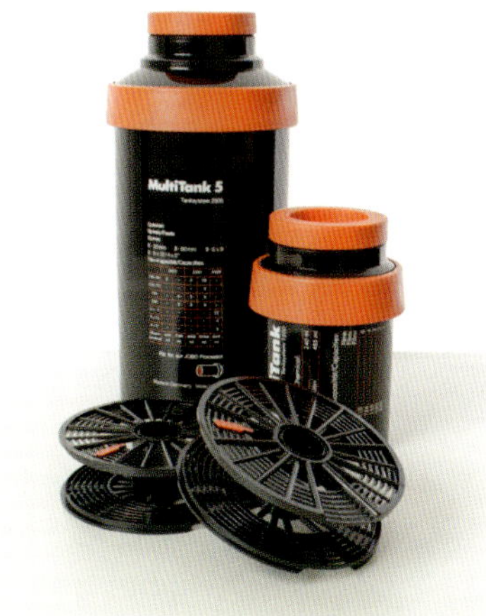

The JOBO system offers various sizes of developing tanks

Tank Systems

We commonly use developing tanks from several manufacturers: JOBO, Paterson, and Kaiser. The tanks differ in size and diameter of the film reel inserted into them, and the lids also have different locking mechanisms. Plus, most manufacturers offer developing tanks in several sizes. The largest tank by Paterson can hold up to eight 35mm films at once for simultaneous development. The smaller tanks from the common starter sets usually hold up to two reels, each with a 35mm film on it.

Film Reels

The plastic reels ensure that the developer chemicals can wash over the film evenly from all sides inside the tank. The reels are spirals to prevent the filmstrip overlapping itself.

The film is usually pushed onto the reel from the outside, and there are corresponding guides and mechanisms to help with this. For example, Kaiser reels have little steel balls on the guide tabs to prevent the film from slipping back out when you wind it. The width of the spiral

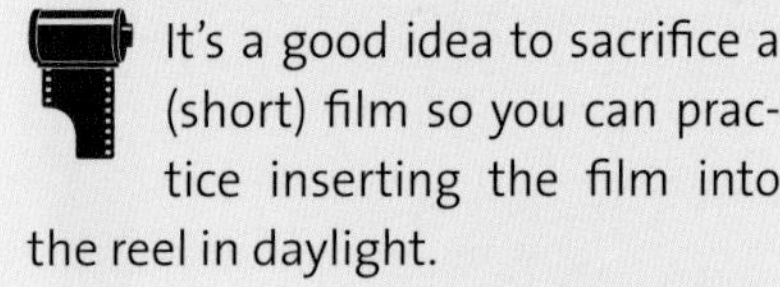
It's a good idea to sacrifice a (short) film so you can practice inserting the film into the reel in daylight.

is adjustable so you can insert different widths of film. The reels we use take film in 135, 120 (and 220), and 127 format. If you want to develop the narrower 110 format, you usually have to resort to DIY. Inventive developers have adapted existing reels by shortening the shaft along the reel axis.

Large Format Inserts

For large format sheet film, JOBO offers the sheet film reel 2509n, which can hold six sheet films in the 4×5 inch format. For this reel, you need a JOBO 2500 developing tank. There is also the MOD54 (*http://www.mod54.com*), a large format insert with which you can also load six sheet films. This is designed for the Paterson system.

Trays

Orthochromatic film can be developed on inspection under red safety light. This is a good option for unusually sized or particularly big sheet film (large format). Instead of a light-tight developing tank, the film is developed in the

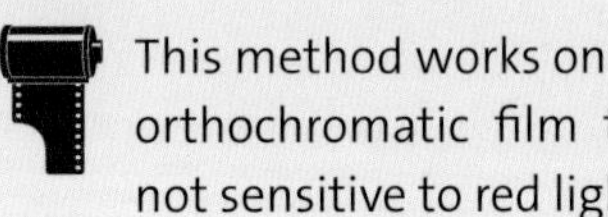
This method works only with orthochromatic film that is not sensitive to red light.

darkroom in a developing tray. This makes it possible for you to stop the development, if necessary, with a stop bath.

You need to handle the film very carefully using this method. The gelatin layer of wet film is very vulnerable to mechanical damage.

Changing Bag

The changing bag is not mandatory for inserting film into the developing tank, but it makes the task much easier. It looks a bit like an extra-large black T-shirt that has been sewn up at the head hole and is closed via a zipper along the bottom. You insert your arms through the "sleeves" and work in the dark while sitting at the table in daylight. The armholes have tight-fitting elastic closures to make them light-tight. Higher-quality changing bags feature double walls and two zippers to form a kind of airlock. The light-tight fabrics used in these models also keep out infrared light.

For working in the changing bag, it helps to prepare a plan, and, above all, have all the tools you need ready to go. For example, to insert 35mm film, you need to have a pair of pliers in the bag for opening the film cartridge and scissors for cutting off the film leader.

To make sure you can find all the things in the changing bag, it's best to always set them up in the same way. For example, we always put the developing tank at the back on the left, and the scissors and pliers go to the back on the right. The film cartridge goes on the right. To wind the film, we reach out for each tool we need, place it in front of us and then return the tools to their place inside the changing bag after use. This approach is especially helpful if you are going to wind several rolls of film or if you're working with large format film holders inside the changing bag.

You can get changing bags in different sizes. There are also other versions available, for example, pop-up darkroom tents, which are similar to light tents for product photography. We personally find the normal double-skinned changing bag the best.

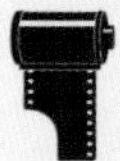 Make sure you take off your watch, fitness bracelet, or smartwatch before working in the changing bag. Imagine your screen lighting up with a new notification while you are trying to load a film.

Bottles

Bottles for mixing and/or storing the chemicals are either made of polyethylene (PE) or glass. Caution: PVC bottles are not suitable for photo chemicals. It's essential to label them and keep developer and fixer bottles separate. That's the only reliable way to prevent contaminating the developer with fixer, which would make it unusable. Bottles with darkroom chemicals are usually brown or black to keep out the light.

Measuring Cylinder

The measuring cylinder is a graduated cylinder for measuring liquid. The easiest way of using it is to pour the required amount of developer concentrate into the measuring cylinder, and then top it off with the desired amount of water.

Example: For a dilution of 4+1 (4 parts water and 1 part developer) and a total required

To prepare larger quantities of fixer, the commercially available 5 liter/1 gallon bottles of distilled water are handy. We do not pour away the distilled water they come with. Instead, we use it for the final rinse to prevent lime spots on the film.

amount of 200 ml, you first pour 40 ml developer (200 divided by 5) into the measuring cylinder and then top it off with 200 ml water. The working solution you have created can be stored in a developer bottle until you want to use it.

Funnel

We also label the funnels we use with "developer" or "fixer" to prevent cross contamination, as mentioned above.

Squeegee

Starting to develop films usually begins with buying a complete developing set that includes the most important equipment, from developing tank to measuring cylinder and film clips. Sadly, these starter sets often also include tools that can do more harm than good.

The film squeegee falls into this category. It is meant to wipe water off the freshly developed film with its two rubber lips to help the film dry more quickly. In theory, that's a great idea, but in practice, it really isn't. You will throw out this tool as soon as you have used it with a trapped dirt particle in it that leaves a long scratch mark in the still vulnerable wet emulsion of the film.

Film Clips

The freshly developed film should go on the line to dry. A normal washing line will do fine. Choose a line that does not shed fibers that could get stuck to the wet film emulsion. To attach the film to the line, you can use ordinary laundry pegs. If you like a bit more luxury, you can also use special film clips. These are usually sold in pairs, with an extra weight on one of them. This heavier clip goes at the bottom of the film to make it hang nice and straight during drying and prevent it from curling up. Developer starter kits usually come with two film clips.

Protection

Gloves

When dealing with darkroom chemicals, you need to keep everything very clean. Depending on the substances used, you should avoid skin contact. Disposable gloves are available in drug stores for a reasonable price, and can offer protection. Nitrile gloves are particularly suitable.

Safety Goggles and Eye Bath

Darkroom chemicals are by no means harmless. Particularly in their undiluted state, the concentration of developer or fixer can be quite high. If these chemicals come into contact with sensitive mucous membranes, for example in the eye, you need to act quickly. We always keep a bottle of saline solution in the darkroom, together with an eye bath attachment. Luckily, we have never needed to use it. To make sure it does not get this far, it's a good idea to wear safety goggles when working. These protective goggles are inexpensive and available from various online retailers.

Waste Canister

In many countries, you are not allowed to dump chemical waste down the drain. Depending on the amount and type of the components, darkroom chemicals have to be disposed of as hazardous waste.

For collecting and disposing of small quantities of these chemicals, 1-gallon (5-liter) canisters made of polyethylene (PE) work well. The cheapest way of getting these canisters is using the ones you can buy with distilled water in them. Empty PE canisters that you can buy in the DIY store are more expensive.

Of course you can also use other containers. But please ensure you label them clearly and keep them out of the reach of children. Please note, the waste containers should not be made of PVC because this material is corroded by darkroom chemicals.

6.3.4 General Procedure for Film Processing

Clean and Safe

Working cleanly has top priority when developing film, particularly if you do your developing in a room with other purposes, like your kitchen. Remember to be meticulously careful to keep food well away from chemicals. You also need to wash all working surfaces thoroughly after developing, and put all the cloths and towels you have used into the wash.

Please also take note of the hazard symbols printed on the relevant packaging. They warn you of skin irritation or chemical burns (wear gloves!) and point out that some ingredients are environmentally hazardous.

Hazard symbols, old and new

Do Not Mix

You have to make absolutely sure that the different chemicals do not mix. This would not result in an explosive mixture, but even just a few drops of fixer are enough to make freshly diluted one-shot developer unusable. If that happens to you, you cannot develop even a single film in the developer.

In practice, it proves a good idea to label all bottles clearly and assign each one to a separate step in the procedure. Only use the bottle labeled "developer" for developer, and keep the fixer in a separate bottle, too. If bottles, measuring cylinders, or thermometers come into contact with both developer and fixer, you need to ensure that you wash them particularly well to prevent fixer from getting into the developer. For rinsing them, it's enough to use clean tap water that can then also go down the drain.

Tools

Medium format film is easiest to wind onto the spool: You don't need any special tools, because you neither have to free the film from a metal cartridge nor cut it to size. The film is usually attached with a piece of tape on the backing paper and you can just tear it off with your fingers.

For 35mm film, you need a bit more effort. Here you usually need pliers to open the film cartridge and scissors for cutting the film straight at the front and separating it from the plastic reel at the back. A normal pair of flat pliers from the spare parts section of the DIY store will do fine. Some people also use a hook-type bottle opener for opening the cartridge.

If you have not rewound the film fully into the cartridge, you can also just pull it back out through the slot. But we would recommend opening the cartridge, because you can then take out the film all in one go, and there is less risk of scratching up your film. You can also get special darkroom tools that let you pull out a rewound film through the cartridge slot. We tested them and did not find them really necessary.

Curious fact: Sometimes you get 35mm film (such as the Chinese brand Lucky) with such a loose cartridge that the side lid falls off almost by itself when you squeeze it.

Mise en Place—Setting Up

In restaurants and TV cookery shows, the *mise en place* is the indispensable set-up to make sure everything goes smoothly. All ingredients are prepared in the right portions, and in the ideal case, the cook just has to throw them all together in the right order.

It's a good idea to make this approach a habit for developing film, too. There is nothing more annoying than having your hands in the changing bag to pull the film out of the cartridge, only to find that the scissors are still out on the table. (Incidentally, if that happens to you, you can just stick the film into the developing tank for a while. As long as you have remembered to insert the center column, the film is protected from light.)

Take care to ready everything you are going to need: the tools, the developing tank, a bottle each for developer and fixer, the undiluted developer, the cylinder for measuring, the thermometer, the timer, and a jug of water at the right temperature. A bit of care when setting up will save you a hectic rush later on, so you can work safely and stay relaxed.

Mixing the Fixer

Because fixer keeps for a long time and can be reused several times, it's a good idea to mix it in advance. You can buy fixer either as liquid concentrate or in powder form to be dissolved in water. For our usual throughput, we always use a 1 gallon canister like the ones you get with distilled water. We fill it with tap water and add the fixer powder, then put the lid back on and shake the bottle until the powder has thoroughly dissolved. If you are using liquid fixer concentrate, just read the package insert for the right dilution. Most fixers can be used for both film and photo paper, but in a different dilution.

Diluting the Developer

Unlike the fixer, which can be prepared days or weeks in advance, the developer, once diluted, should be used within a few hours. Most one-shot developers lose their potency quite quickly once diluted. We usually dilute the developer just before we are going to use it.

Some types of developer can be used several times and need to be replenished with new developer before the next use. Important: If not otherwise specified, please use normal tap water for diluting the developer. Very few developers require distilled water. The reason? Most developer concentrates contain a softening agent, the same as in laundry detergents. It makes sure that the developing results stay consistent even with different grades of water hardness. If you are working with already softened water, the softening agent does not have anything to do and may have a negative effect on the processing result.

Before you start diluting the developer, you first need a recipe that tells you the ratio of developer concentrate or stock solution to water. Such recipes can be found on the film data sheet that comes with the film (usually as overview on the inside of the box), or can be downloaded online from the manufacturer's or retailer's website.

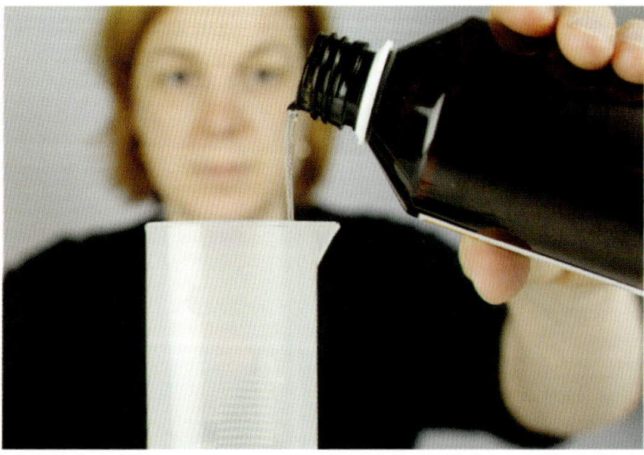

Measuring developer concentrate

The recipes always refer to a specific combination of film and developer, and look something like this:

1:25, 12 min @ 400

That means that the mixing ratio of developer concentrate and water is 1 to 25 and the developing will take 12 minutes if the film was exposed at ISO 400. If nothing else is specified, you can assume a water temperature of 20°C/68°F.

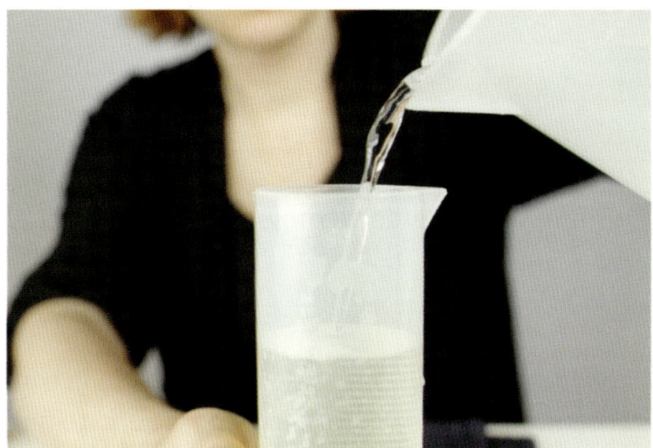

Diluting with water

To find out the total quantity you need, have a look at the bottom of the developing tank. It will usually say how much liquid you need for which type of film, and the number of film reels needed to keep the film covered with liquid during developing. Let's assume you need 700 ml of solution in total. Then the amount of developer you need would be 700 divided by 25. That makes 28 ml.

That's all the math you need. The rest results automatically from how you proceed:

1. Measure the required amount of developer in the measuring cylinder.
2. Top off the measuring cylinder with water until you have the required total amount of liquid.

That's it. If the measuring cylinder is too small, just top it off several times. So for a measuring cylinder that can hold 200 ml, you would proceed as follows to get a total amount of 700 ml developer:

1. Pour 28 ml of developer into the measuring cylinder.
2. Fill up the cylinder to the 200 ml mark and pour the mixture into the developer bottle.
3. Fill up the measuring cylinder twice more with 200 ml and then once more with 100 ml, and pour the water into the developer bottle each time.

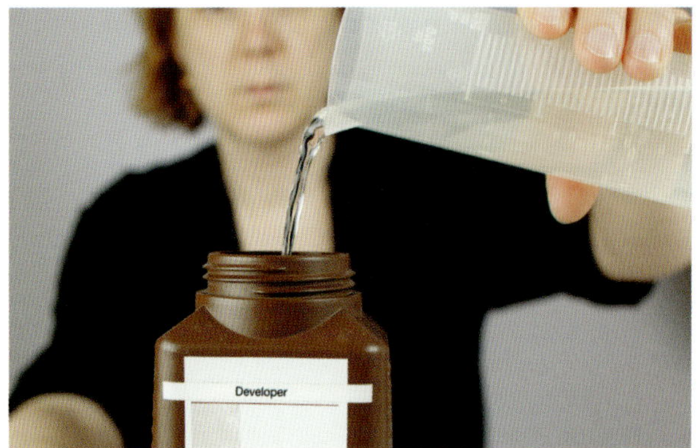

Small deviations in the mixing ratio or in the temperature (of up to 10%) do not usually have any visible effects on the result. Especially in the beginning, don't worry too much if everything isn't accurate to the last millimeter. You will still get acceptable results even with small deviations.

Pouring the mixture into the developer bottle

Swirl the developer bottle to mix everything well. The bottle now contains 700 ml of developer.

Orderly Changing Bag

As we have already mentioned, it's a good idea to always put your tools and film in consistent places inside the changing bag. Then you don't have to rummage around to find what you need and you won't forget anything. You will realize how important that is if you accidentally expose the film because you have put together the developing tank without inserting the center column because it wasn't in its proper place. It also allows you to check very quickly if you have all the required tools in the changing bag.

If you are not using a changing bag, and are loading the film in a darkened room, keeping order is even more important. In the changing bag, things cannot get very far away from you, but if you have ever been crawling around on your knees in the dark, groping around the floor for a center column that rolled off the table, you are going to remember these words.

Shaken or Swirled?

If you look online at the corresponding message boards, forums, or social networks, it becomes clear very quickly that you can easily get into hot water with certain topics. In particular, there seem to be many diverging opinions as to how you should shake, tilt, or swirl the developing tank during the various developing steps (or if you should do so at all).

Generally, agitating the developing tank during developing, rinsing, and fixing has the important task of replacing exhausted chemicals on the film with fresh ones, or getting enough clean water through to speed up the diffusion processes. We have opted for a pragmatic approach: We do what always works for us and what has yielded very good results. If something has caused problems, we avoid it. For that reason, we swirl the developing tank during development, moving from the wrist, a few times to the left, a few times to the right, to ensure the liquid can spread all around the spirally wound film.

Once when we tilted the tank completely (referred to as *inverting*), the film spool slid upward on the center column, so only half the film was fully developed at the end. We don't shake, ever. Shaking causes foam, which gets in the way during developing.

Sequence

The sequence of steps for the *inversion* or *swivel* method of developing black-and-white film is always the same.

Loading the Film—Medium Format

First, you load the film onto the reel.

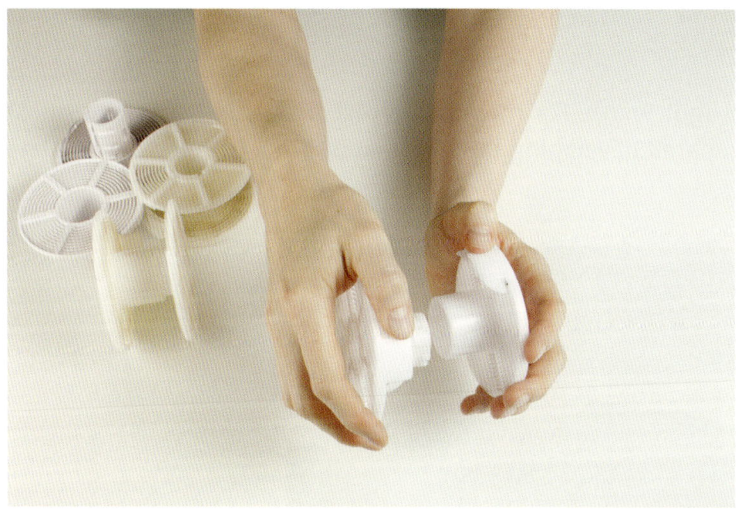

Assembling the reel

An important tip in advance: Practice these steps in daylight first. For our workshops, we always keep a few rolls of cheap "sacrificial film" handy (Shanghai for medium format. The film does not survive this experience, but it's all for the good cause of preparing the darkroom rookies for working in the changing bag.

Take the reel out of the developing tank and close it again. Leave the center column in the tank so you can easily find it again and won't accidentally forget to put it back in.

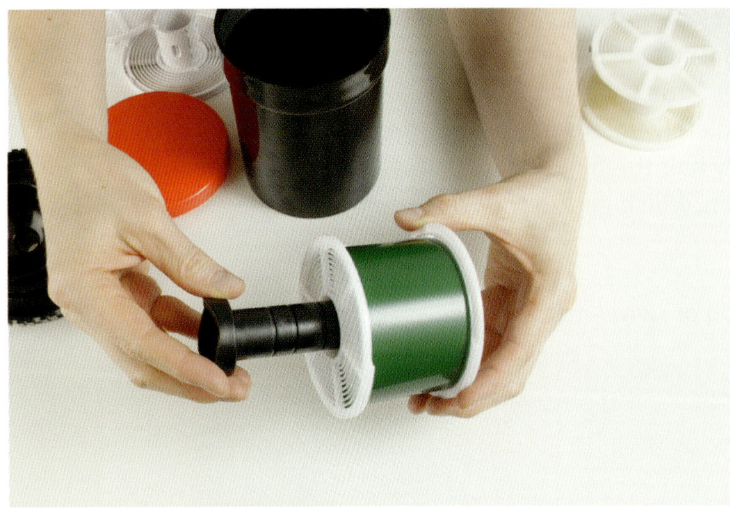

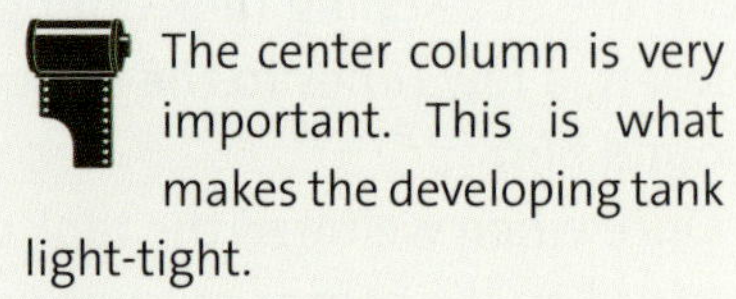

The center column is very important. This is what makes the developing tank light-tight.

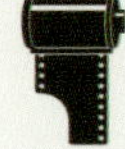

Keep a bit of old film ready to test if you have set the reel to the correct width.

Don't forget the center column!

Adjust the reel to the right width. For medium format, it's usually the outermost notch. Now place the prepared developing tank, reel, and film into the changing bag and close both zippers.

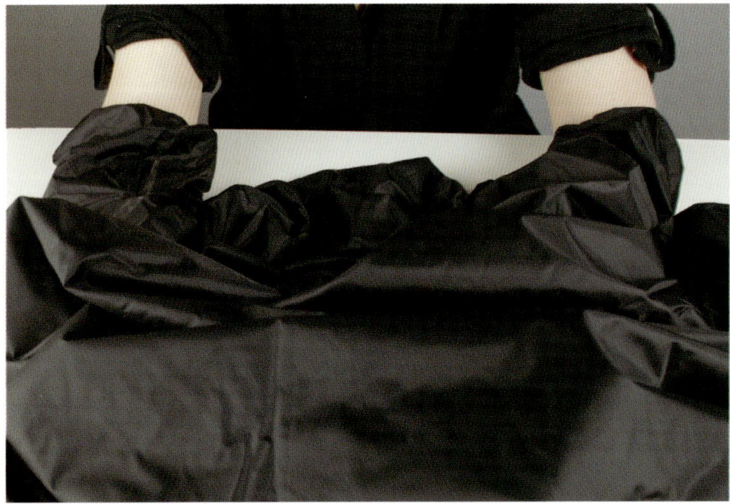

Both arms in the changing bag

Roll up your sleeves and push both your arms into the changing bag up to your elbows. From now on, you should not take out your hands until the film is all wound and the developing tank is closed and light tight.

It's a good idea to take off your watch, smartwatch, or fitness bracelet before working in the changing bag. Otherwise, you run the risk that your next notification might leave its traces on the film.

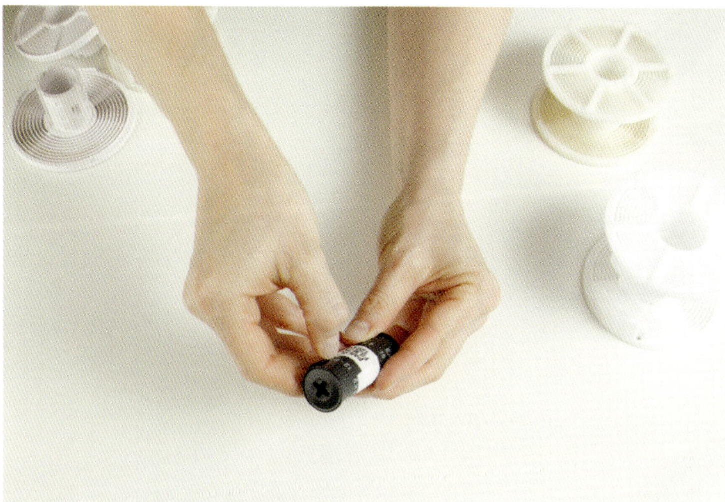

Slit open the tab

Inside the changing bag, slit open the sticky tab on the film roll with your fingernail or use a previously prepared tool. Unroll the backing paper until you can feel the beginning of the film.

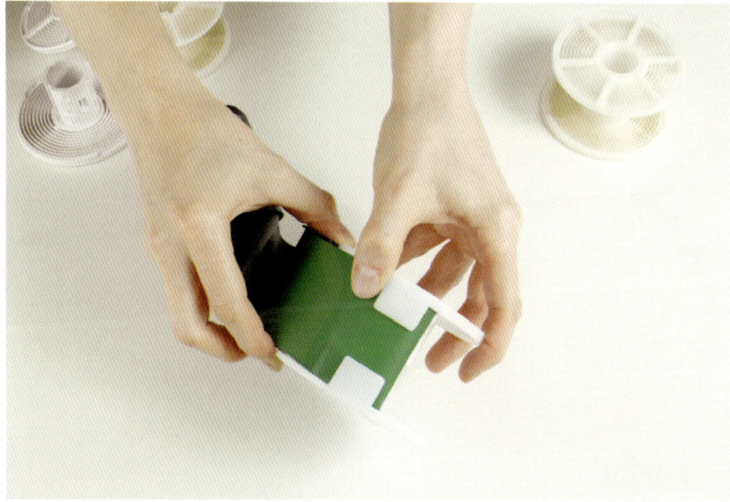

Insert the film into the reel

 Quick Tip: When you take a 120 roll film out of the camera, fold the tapered paper tip inward before you tape it down. This produces a small protrusion that you can easily find with your fingernail when loading the film into the spool inside your changing bag.

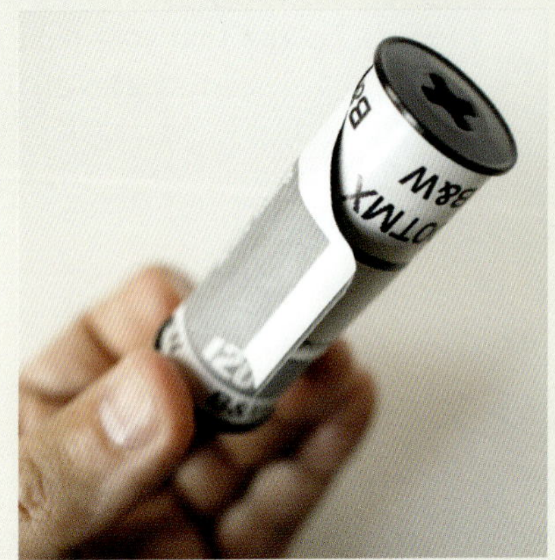

The tip of the film roll...

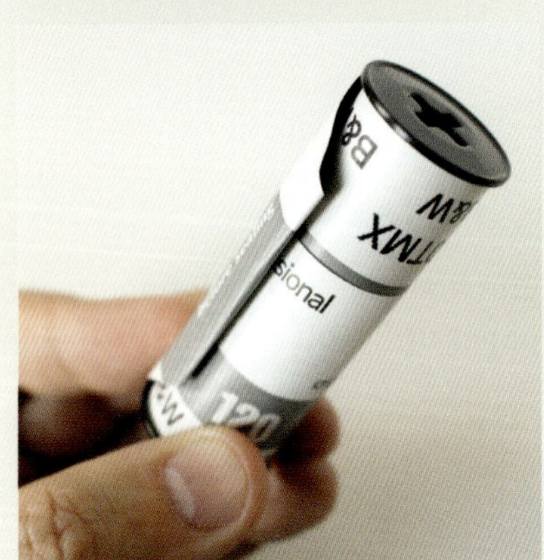

...folded inward...

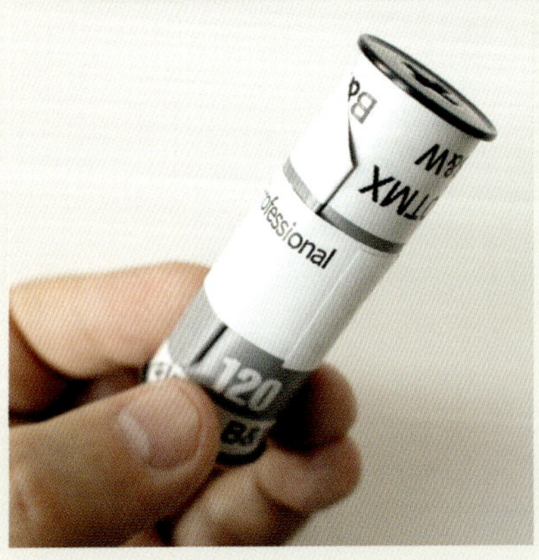

...and taped down

Now, hold the reel so the openings for inserting the film point towards you, and insert the film into the openings. Depending on the system, the reel will grip the film and prevent it from slipping back out (for example, Kaiser reels do this). You can also use your index finger to hold the film in place through side recesses on the reel.

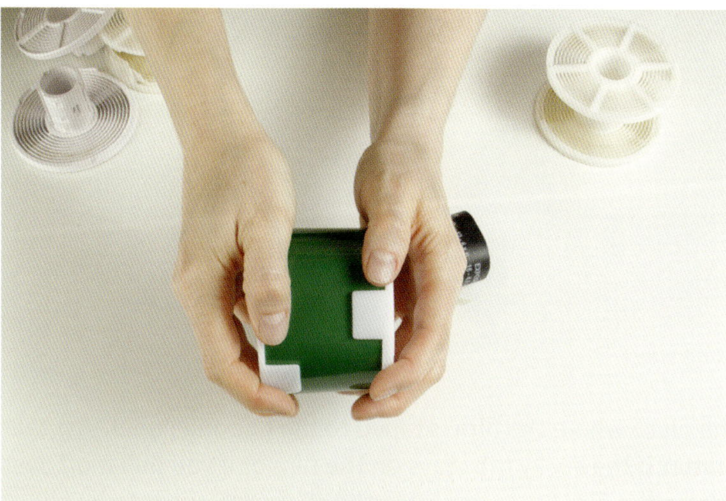

Wind up the film with rocking movements

Now start twisting the two sides of the reel in opposite directions by rocking them back and forth, and at the same time. Hold the film in place with your thumb or forefinger on opposite sides of the reel. The rocking movement winds the film into the spool bit by bit.

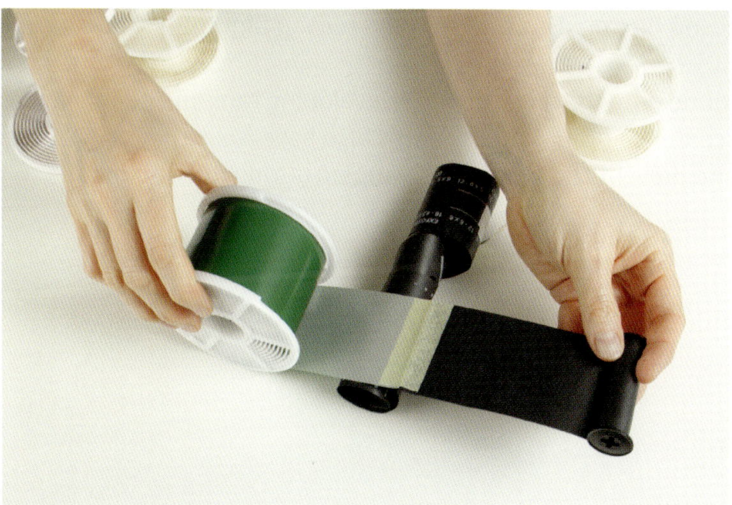

The end of the film is taped to the backing paper

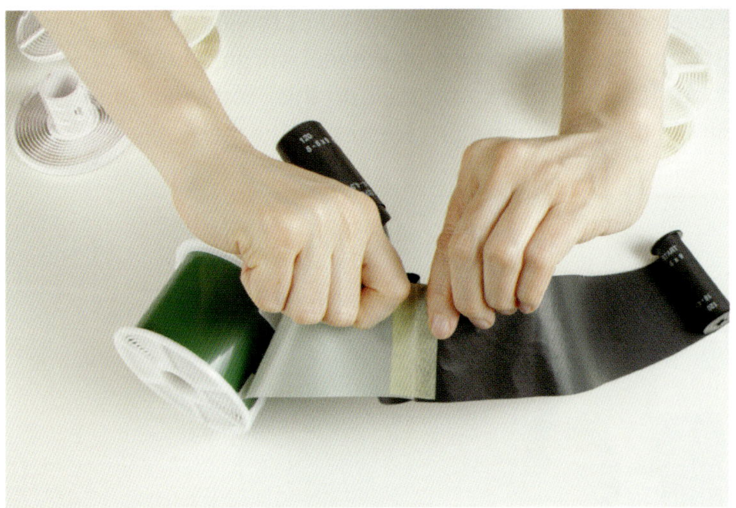

Tear off the film from the backing paper

Once you have reached the place where the film is taped to the backing paper, just tear the film off. It does not matter if the sticky tab stays on the film or if you pull it off. Just remember, when you hang up the film for drying later, the sticky tab needs to be hanging down, so the water dripping down from it does not run onto the film and cause streaks.

If you are not sure if you have inserted the film or the backing paper onto the reel, just try to rip the remaining bit. If you can rip it, it's paper; if you can't, it's film.

The JOBO developing tanks have a special feature: Their very wide reels hold two medium format films of type 120 behind one another. Proceed as follows: Open the little plastic stopper at the side of the reel. Thread the film onto the reel until the beginning touches the middle. Now close the stopper, and push the second film on. This prevents the second film from slipping over the first.

Once the film is fully wound onto the reel, open the developing tank and push the reel all the way down on the center column. Some systems also have a clip that goes at the top of the center column to prevent the reel from sliding up during developing.

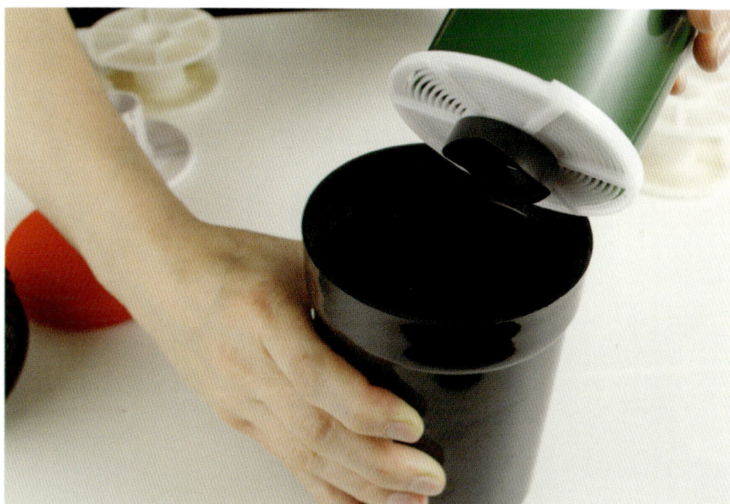

Put the reel and center column into the developing tank

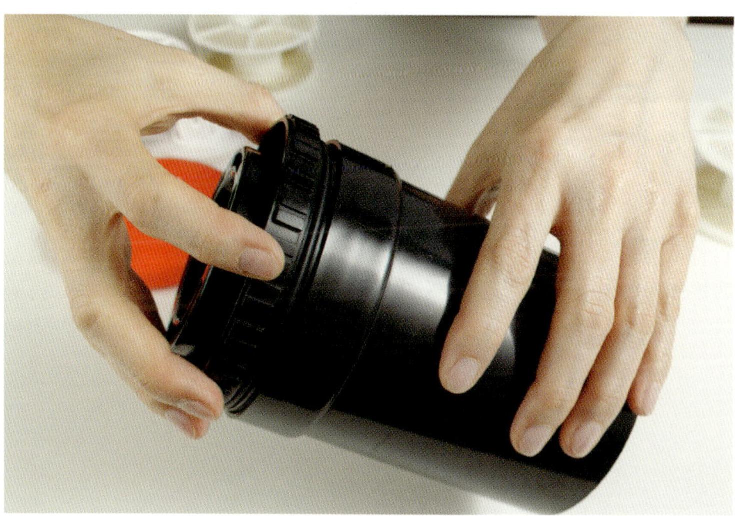

Close the developing tank

After you have closed the developing tank, check again that there is no film left in the changing bag. Then you can take your hands out and open the zippers.

Loading the Film—35mm

The setup for 35mm film is exactly the same as for medium format. The only difference is the width of the reel. Set it to the inner notch, and it will fit for 35mm. Do not forget to put a pair of pliers and scissors into the changing bag, as well.

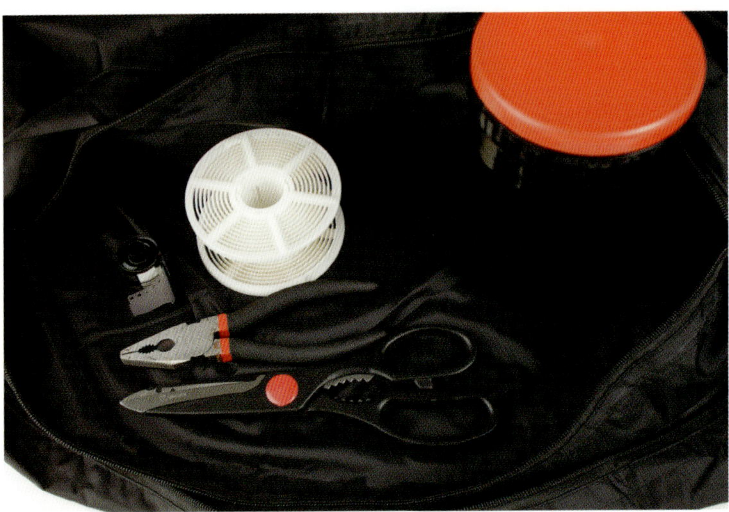

Put all important items into the changing bag

Inside the changing bag, your first task is to crack open the film cartridge. The best way is to grip it with the pliers on the end where the film's core does not stick out. Now you can pull off the cartridge lid with the pliers.

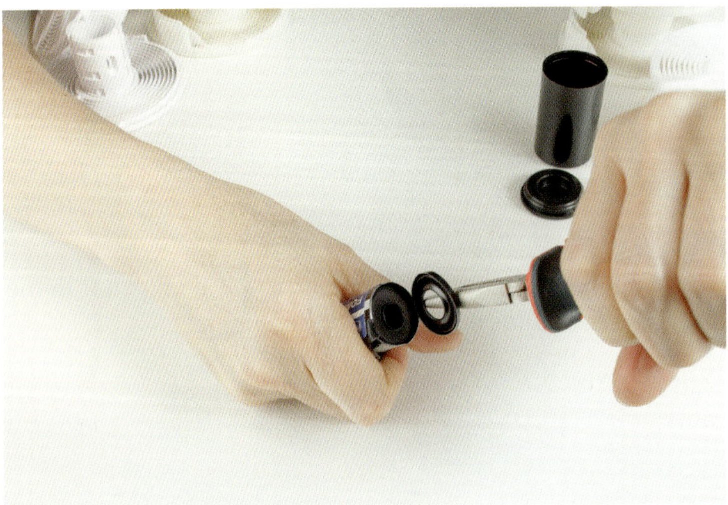

Crack open the cartridge with pliers

Now you can take the whole rolled-up film out of the cartridge in one go. Alternatively, if you did not rewind the film fully, you can pull it out of the cartridge through the slot. There is some risk of scratching, but it's not very likely, because film emulsion is quite robust when dry.

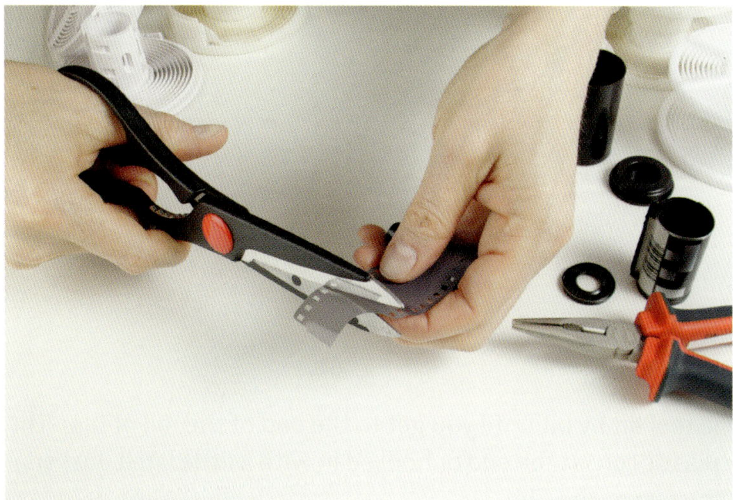

Cut off the front leader

Take the scissors and cut off the film leader at the front so the film is straight. It is not obligatory, but you get bonus points if you get the cut straight between the perforations and cut the edges of the film slightly diagonally. Then the film will slide onto the reel more smoothly and be less likely to snag.

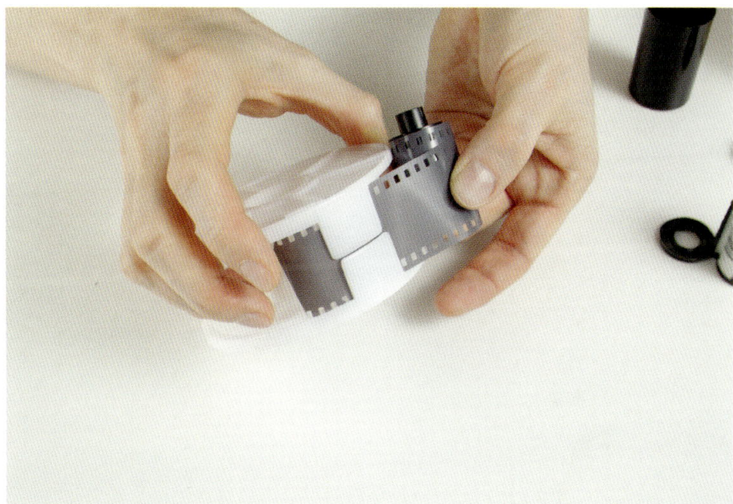

First insert the film...

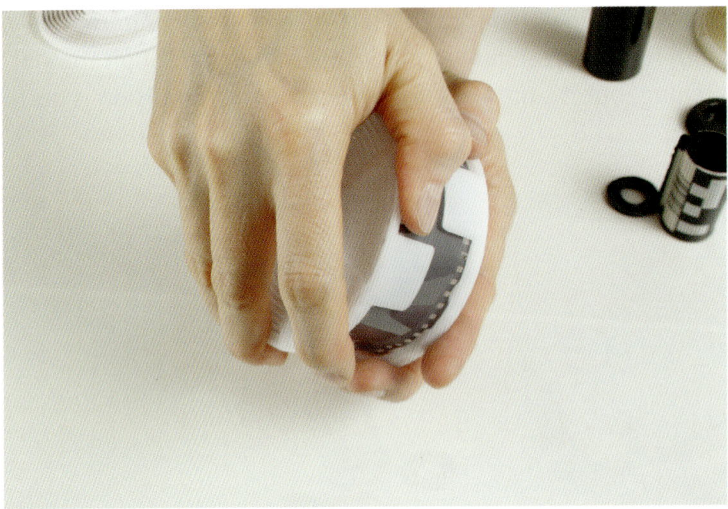

...then wind it

Now, rock the film onto the reel bit by bit until you get to the end of the roll of film. The film is either taped to the plastic core at the end or hooked in with a little latch. Just snip off the end, and wind up the rest of the film.

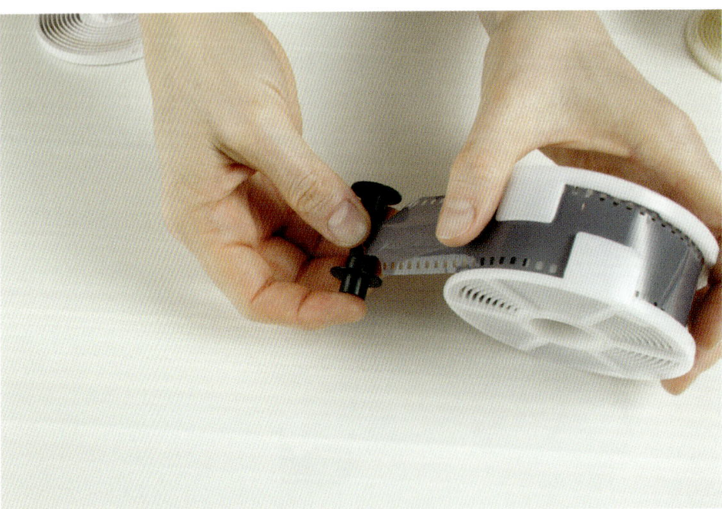

The end of the 35mm film...

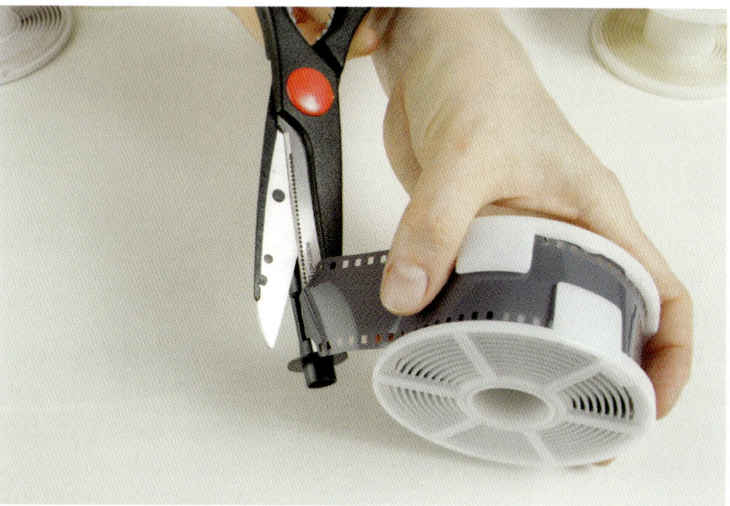

...just gets snipped off

The other steps are the same as for medium format: Put the reel onto the center column, and insert it into the developing tank.

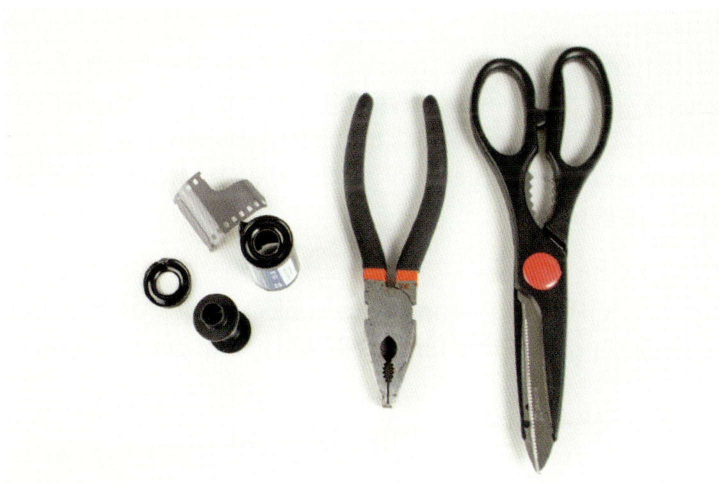

What's left at the end

At the final check, you should have only the following items left in the changing bag: scissors, pliers, an open cartridge, a cartridge lid, the small plastic core the film was wound on inside the cartridge, and the snipped-off film leader—and of course, the closed developing tank with the film wound onto the reel.

If It Snags

During the first few attempts at getting the film onto the reel, things don't always go smoothly and the film sometimes refuses to cooperate. Some films are wound so tightly that they lean into the reel too much during winding and get stuck. If that happens, it usually helps to roll the film in the opposite direction inside the changing bag to make it less curly.

Another reason for this can be moisture, either because your hands are sweaty or because it can get a bit hot inside the bag. Moisture makes the gelatin-based film emulsion a bit sticky, and the film can snag.

If that happens: DON'T PANIC. Stay calm, and try to bash the reel with the flat side down onto the table a few times inside the changing bag. This loosens the film, and you can keep winding. If this does not help and you can feel your hands get even sweatier while trying to wrestle the reel into submission, then you can, for example, just stick the film into the developing tank as it is (remember the center column!) and close the tank. Now that your film is safe, you can take your hands out and dry them.

If you use disposable rubber gloves to roll your film onto the developing spool, all the sweat you produce will end up inside the gloves rather than on the spool and the film. You can use the same gloves during developing too.

To prevent too much moisture, we like to put a few packets of silica gel into the changing bag, especially in summer.

If you are developing several films in a row, the freshly cleaned reel may be the cause of the moisture. Even if you do your very best to dry it off, tiny droplets of water will remain in the nooks and crannies of the reel and stick to the film you insert next. A hair dryer can help: Just blow warm air onto the reel until it's dry. Even better, invest a few dollars and buy one or several spare reels.

Pre-Rinsing

The next step is pre-rinsing. This step is optional and is the subject of much debate, but it is said to prepare the gelatin layer on the film for developing and to wash off part of the anti-halation layer.

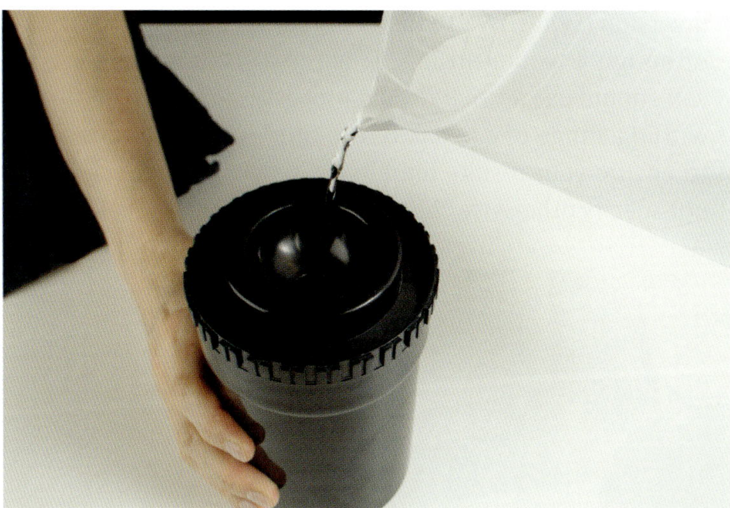

Performing the optional pre-rinse

The anti-halation layer is added to the back of the film during the manufacturing process. It prevents light from reflecting off the film surface, which could cause halos around the highlights. Some types of film omit this layer. They are usually marketed under the description *Aura*.

For pre-rinsing, just pour warm water (20°C/68°F) into the developing tank until it's full. Swirl the tank around a few times, then let it stand for one to two minutes. Then pour the water down the drain. Depending on your film, the anti-halation layer has different colors, so the water you drain away may be turquoise, green, or dark blue.

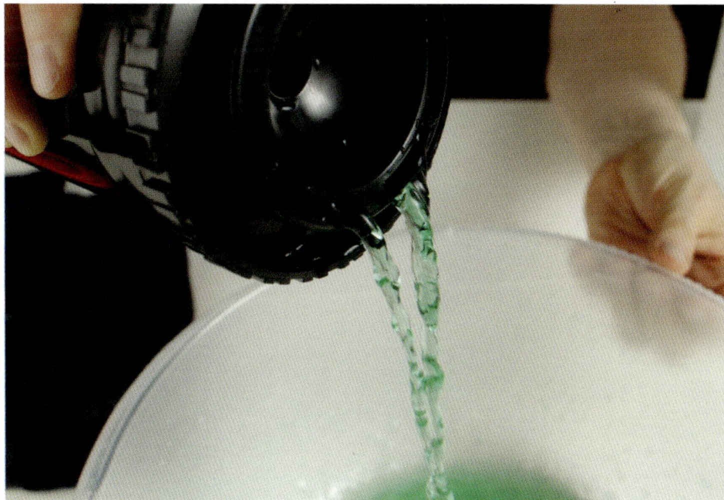

Drain the pre-rinse water

Depending on the make of film, the water you pour away after pre-rinsing can have different colors. If you have forgotten which film you have inside the tank, you may be able to tell from the color of the water.

Taps are hardly ever able to provide a constant temperature. We always prepare a large bowl of water at the right temperature and then refill the jug with it during development.

Inversion (Swivel) Method

Although the pre-rinsing is not particularly time-critical, you should use a timer during processing. Try to at least stay within a range of +/− 10% of the time specified in the recipe to ensure your results remain consistent. If the recipe does not specify otherwise, it's for inversion (swivel) development.

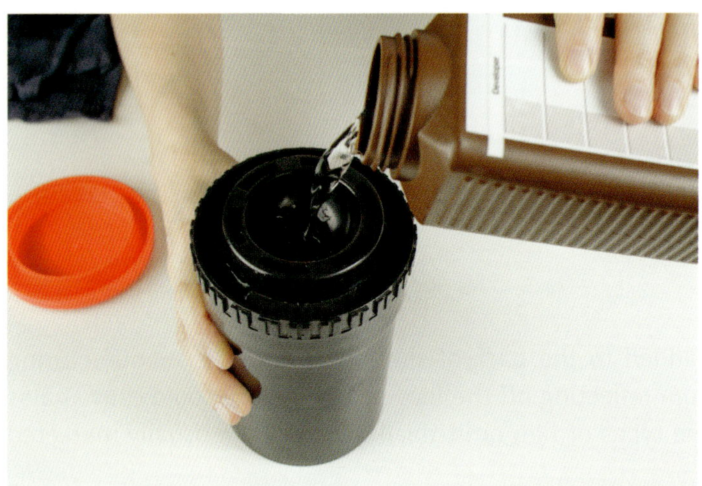

Add the developer

Add the developer to the developing tank swiftly, and start the timer. Now agitate the tank continuously for half a minute.

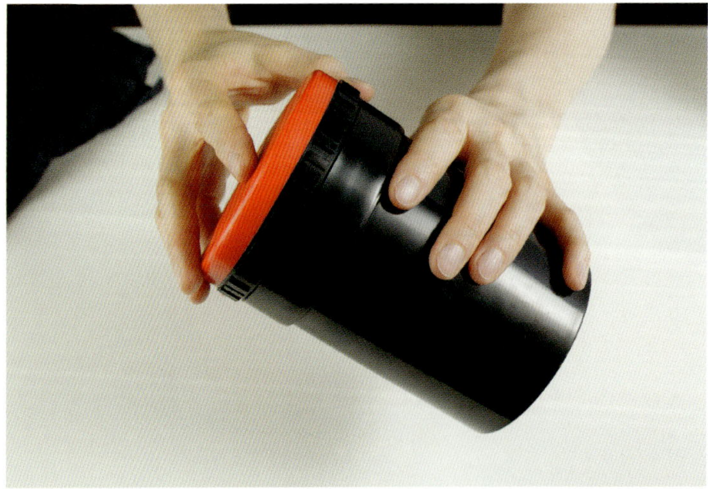

Swirl the tank

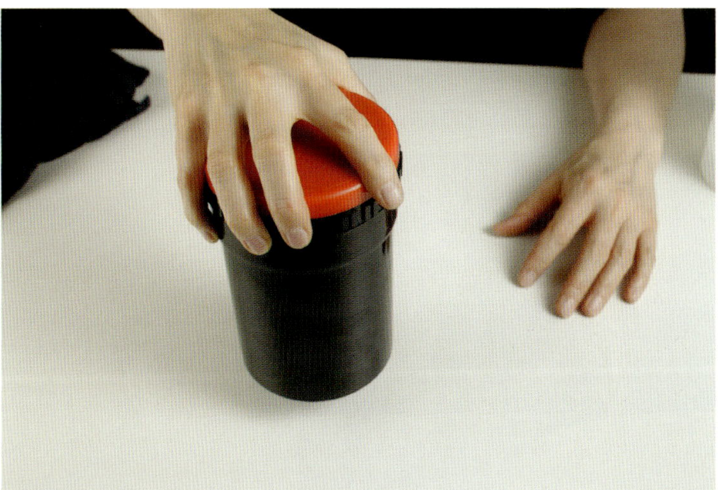

Rap the tank on the table

Rap the developing tank on the table to dislodge any air bubbles stuck to the film. Then swirl the tank every minute for about 5–10 seconds, tap it onto the table again, and repeat this procedure until the specified developing time is over. If you prefer to invert the developing tank fully instead of just swirling it as we do, then you need to make sure the lid (usually red) is on the tank, otherwise you'll have to mop the floor later.

If you work quickly, it does not really matter if you start the timer before or after adding the developer, because the time can vary a bit with most film-developer combinations without producing dramatically different results.

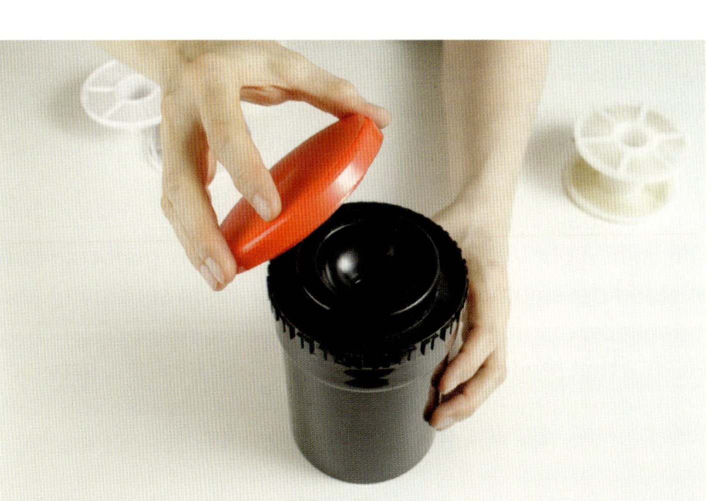

This lid prevents spills when inverting

The purpose of the agitation is to get fresh developer into contact with the film, because while it's standing, the chemicals are slowly getting used up as they interact with the film.

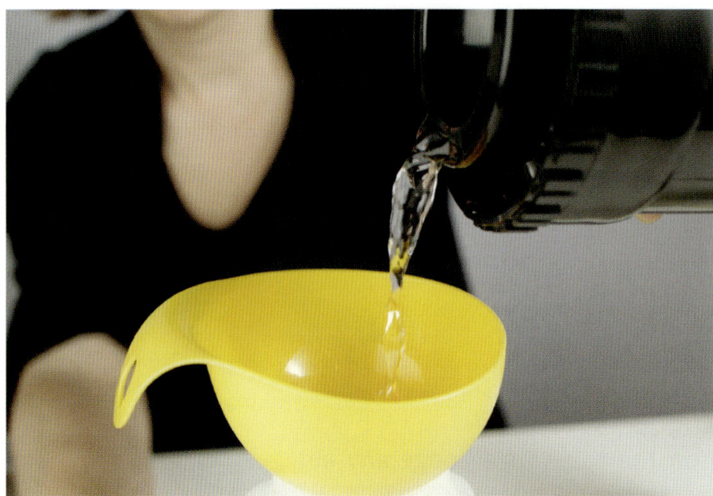

Pour the developer into waste canister

Once the developing time is over, pour the developer from the developing tank into the waste canister.

Stand Development

Stand development is an interesting alternative to regular inversion development. This technique uses heavily diluted developers and correspondingly lengthened development times of between 30 and 90 minutes. In rare cases development can take several hours.

Apart from the initial agitation that takes place within the first minute of development, this process involves virtually no further agitation, and the film is left to stand—hence the name.

When using Rodinal developer, this method results in noticeably less grain and slightly lower edge sharpness. Two major advantages of stand development are a slight increase in sensitivity and improved shadow detail. However, there are some developers (such as Kodak HC-110) that produce more grain when used for stand development. Stand development is very straightforward because you have plenty of time, and five minutes more or less really doesn't matter.

By developing for a longer time or at a higher temperature, you can influence the contrast of the film. As a general rule, longer developing times or higher temperatures increase the contrast. We will get back to this when we discuss push processing (see page 176).

Initially, the stand development is the same as the agitation method: Pour the developer into the developing tank, then agitate it for half a minute. Rap the tank onto the table, and put it aside for half an hour. After those 30 minutes, agitate the tank for 10 seconds and then put it aside for another half an hour. Repeat this procedure until the time specified in the recipe has passed.

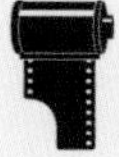 Stephen Schaub at figitalrevolution.com on stand development: *http:// figitalrevolution.com/category/ stand-development*

Typically, our stand developments take 60 to 90 minutes, depending on film, developer, and intended result. We have even left the developing tank outside in the snow over night to see what would happen and were pleased to see strong contrasts the next morning. Feel free to play around to your heart's content.

Again, you pour the developer into the waste canister when the time is up.

So how does it work? The developer depletes slowly during the long development time, which is great when you are developing shots of high-contrast subjects. Where the film has been exposed to a lot of light (i.e, where the film itself is very dark), the developer is used up fast. However, the lack of agitation means that no fresh developer reaches these details, so these areas don't burn out. Conversely, the developer depletes less rapidly in shadow details, which develop slowly and steadily.

Please note, a regular stand development process takes about 60 minutes, but this can easily be extended to 90 minutes or more, depending on the results you are aiming for.

In our experience, 60 minutes is a universally useful development time for:

- Films you find in old cameras
- Films with unknown exposure parameters
- Developing different film types in a single tank

You can even use this technique to produce differing ISO sensitivities on a single roll of film.

Rinsing

At this point, the development is finished. But when you drain off the developer, the developing does not stop all of a sudden, because there is still a bit of developer in the tank and in the film's gelatin layer.

To achieve highest precision, reproducible results and to neutralize the alkaline developer to ensure the acid fixer does not go off too quickly, people used to pour stop bath into the developing tank at this point.

Trace amounts of photo chemicals in the rinsing water are fine to go into the sewer system in most countries. But larger amounts of developer and particularly fixer should not be poured down the drain. Best to check the wastewater regulations in your location.

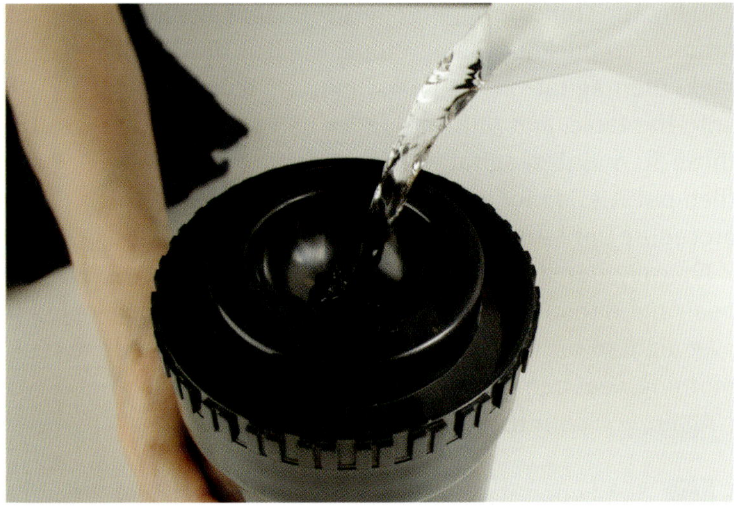

Rinse

We find it's enough to fill the developing tank with water and swirl it several times. That also slows the developing process, even if it does not stop it as quickly and suddenly as with the stop bath. This step takes only half a minute, and then you can tip the water down the drain.

Fixing
The fixer washes the non-exposed silver out of the film.

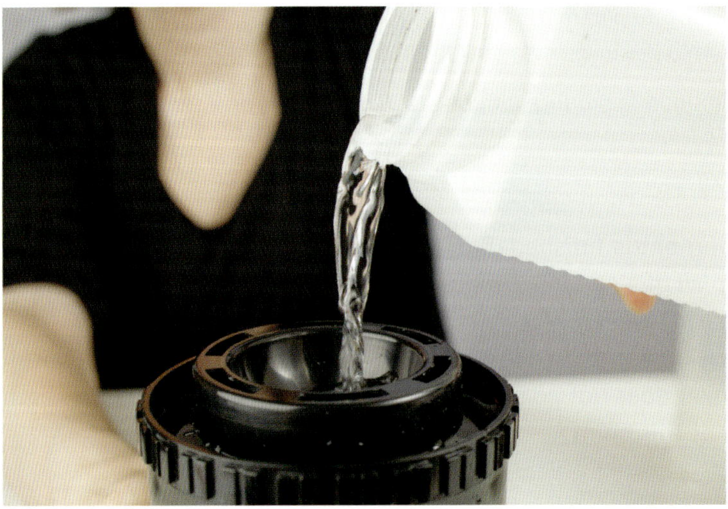

Add fixer

Pour the fixer into the developing tank and proceed as you did with developing. First, swirl the tank for half a minute, and then agitate the tank every minute. This turns the previously opaque film transparent in the places where the fixer has washed out the unexposed silver. This step is not particularly time-sensitive. Depending on which fixer you are using and how fresh it is, a film can be fully fixed after one or two minutes. Older fixer that has already been used several times takes a bit more time.

If a film just does not want to turn clear, this may be due to exhausted fixer, or to the film itself. With some film bases, it's normal that they look slightly foggy while wet.

Interestingly, after about only one minute in the fixer solution, the film is no longer light sensitive, so you can go ahead and open the tank and visually check if the film is done or needs a bit longer. If you see a milky, sometimes slightly yellow haze, the film has been insufficiently fixed.

If you notice a few days or months later that the film was not fully fixed all the way through, you can simply fix it again.

Our usual fixing times are three to five minutes. But even if you leave the fixer in for 15 minutes, you won't do any major damage. Once the film is fixed, you can pour the fixer back into its bottle or canister.

Final Rinse

After development, intermediate rinse, and fixing, the remainder of the photo chemicals has to be washed out of the film thoroughly. Only then will the material have good archiving properties. Opinions diverge regarding how and for how long this final wash should be done. The methods vary from special cascades that rinse the film for a long time with hoses and running water to special tilt rhythms, for example, the "Ilford method." If you swear by this method, by all means stick to it. It certainly won't be wrong.

We heard from Ilford sources that their recommendations regarding washing the negatives were designed to use as little water as possible to get the thiosulfate level of the emulsion below the threshold of 1.4 micrograms per square meter in order to make the negatives suitable for archival storage.

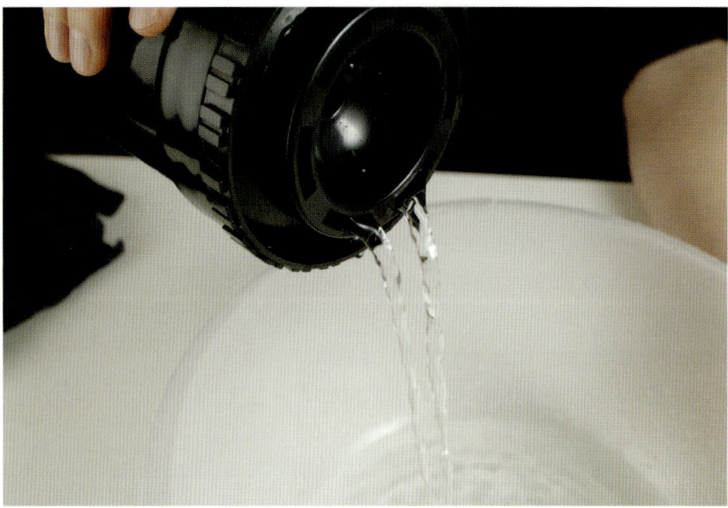

Final rinse

For us, the final rinse usually looks like this: We fill the developing tank with tap water twice, swirl it a few times each time, then tip it out again. This removes the largest part of the remaining fixer from the tank and the film. Then we take the film out of the tank, complete with reel (and center column), and place it into a large tub, bucket, plastic bowl, or large sink of water for 10 to 20 minutes, and agitate it occasionally. Now the film is ready for drying.

Post-Treatment

Before drying, you may also want to treat the film while it's still damp. A special hardening bath is supposed to make the emulsion less susceptible to scratching when dry.

A wetting agent reduces the surface tension, so water runs off more easily. This prevents lime spots. Some wetting agents also contain antifungal agents and make the film more suitable for storage. In our experience, not all wetting agents are compatible will all films. Some combinations even have the opposite effect and cause spots during drying. You just have to try it out and experiment. Our secret tip is to put the film briefly into distilled water. (That's the water that was originally in the 5-liter/1-gallon waste canister.)

Drying

Now the film can go onto the line to dry. The emulsion is sticky while damp, so it collects dust easily. Particularly with regard to scanning later, it's a good idea to dry the film in as dust-free an environment as possible.

Hang up the film on the line by attaching it with a film clip or laundry peg, and clip another peg to the end of the film so it doesn't flap around and get stuck on anything. If you are drying roll film, make sure that the end with the sticky tab hangs downwards. Otherwise water can drip from the sticky tab onto the film and cause streaks.

Some types of film curl up terribly during drying, even lengthwise; others hang nice and straight. You can only really tell once the film is completely dry.

Also, avoid hairdryers and other drying aids. You are only going to regret it later when scanning or optimizing during post-processing.

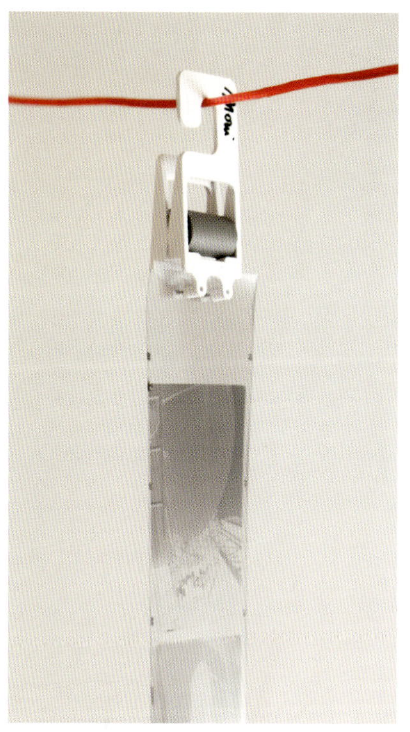

Film on the line

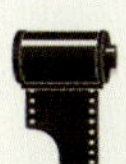 Let the (cold) shower run for one to two minutes in the bathroom. This takes a lot of dust out of the air without generating steam.

Another tool some people use to make the film dry more quickly is the squeegee included with many developing sets. As mentioned above: *Don't* use this tool! The emulsion is very vulnerable to scratching while wet. Even a tiny particle of dirt caught on one of the rubber lips of the squeegee can be enough to mar the entire length of your film with a nasty scratch.

Recipes

The two following tables list example recipes for different films and developers. The first table is for developing film according to the nominal film speed, and the second is for push and pull. If not specified otherwise, these recipes always refer to a temperature of 20°C/68°F and a *normal agitation (constantly for the first 30 seconds, then every minute).*

Film	Developer	Dilution	Exposure at ISO	Time in min.	Comments
Agfa APX 100 New	Adox Atomal 49	Stock solution	100	9:30	Fine grain, balanced grayscale gradation, good use of film speed, well-scannable negatives
Agfa APX 100 New	Rodinal or similar	1+50	100	10:00	Good shadow detail, balanced contrasts, well-scannable negatives
Fomapan 100	Adox Atomal 49	Stock solution	100	7:00	Good use of film speed, fine grain, good shadow detail
Fomapan 200	Adox Atomal 49	Stock solution	200	9:00	Good use of film speed, fine grain, good shadow detail
Fuji Neopan Acros II	Rodinal or similar	1+50	100	13:30	Sharp, high-contrast development with good tonal range and moderate grain
Fuji Neopan Acros 100 I	Kodak HC-110	1+31	100	5:30	Results comparable to those achieved using Rodinal
Ilford HP5 PLUS	Kodak XTOL	1+1	400	12:00	Good detail in negatives, fine grain, moderate contrasts
Kodak Tri-X 400	Kodak HC-110	1+31	400	7:30	Moderate, well-accented grain, full tonal range, balanced negatives
Lomography Kino Potsdam	Rodinal or corresponding derivative	1+100	100	60:00	Stand development
Washi F	Rodinal or corresponding derivative	1+50	100	13:00	High-contrast development, uniform grain

Example recipes for nominal film speed

Film	Developer	Dilution	Exposure at ISO	Time in min.	Comments
Kodak T-MAX 100	Kodak T-MAX developer	1+4	800	5:00	Push, at 24°C/75°F
Kodak Tri-X 400	Kodak HC-110	1+31	1600	16:00	Push, hard contrasts
Kodak Tri-X 400	Kodak HC-110	1+31	800	11:00	Push, moderate contrasts, Tri-X-typical grain
Kodak Tri-X 400	Rodinal or similar	1+100	1600	90:00	Push, stand development
Adox CHS 100 II	Kodak HC-110	1+31	200	7:30	Sight push, even, well-distributed grain, fine grayshades, moderate contrast
Ilford HP5 PLUS	Kodak T-MAX developer	1+4	50	1:30	Pull, good distribution of midtones
Kodak T-MAX 400	Kodak D-76	1+1	50	7:20	Pull, extremely fine contrasts, good distribution of midtones
Kodak T-MAX 400	Kodak T-MAX developer	1+4	100	5:00	Pull, develop at 24°C/75°F, stock solution: no further dilution after developer has been prepared

Recipes for push and pull processing

Washing Up and Drying

Last but not least, it's time to clean up.

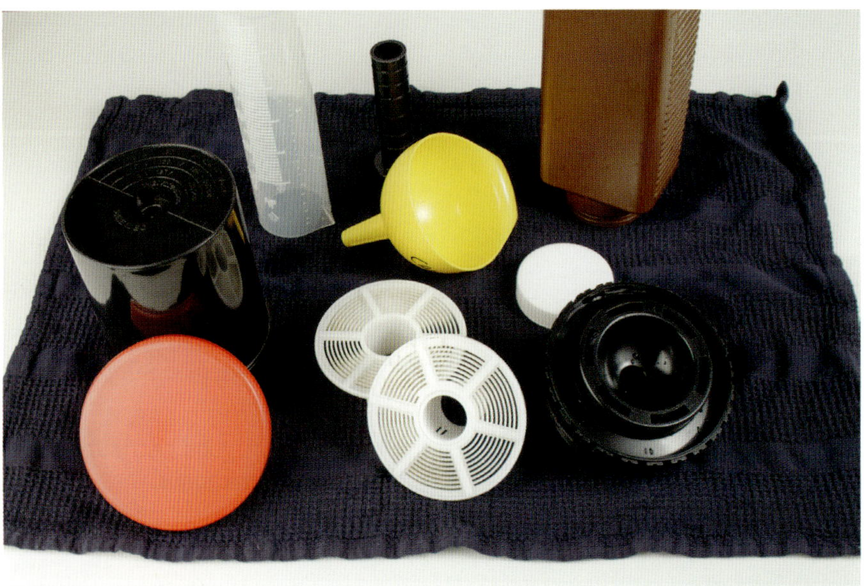

Clean up at the end

Rinse all items thoroughly with water. You don't need washing-up liquid, and it can get in the way for the next developing process if you have not rinsed it off well enough.

Disposing of Chemicals

In many countries, photo chemicals should not go into the sewage system, and you are required to dispose of them in a hazardous waste facility. You should play it safe and check your local regulations.

Developer

The quantities of developer used by a hobby photographer are relatively small compared to those produced by the industry in photographic processes. But even small quantities of developer need to be collected and disposed of separately in some places.

Fixer

The silver salts dissolved in the fixer are poison to the bacteria that do such an important job in sewage treatment plants. That's why the fixer should not go down the sink but needs to be collected instead. Larger labs use special systems to recover the silver. For hobbyists, this is not worth it.

Stop Bath

Stop bath should not pose a problem and can generally go down the sink.

Film Washing and Washing Up Water

The water you use for rinsing and washing the film contains highly diluted traces of chemicals and can safely be poured down the sink. The same applies to the washing-up water you use for cleaning the developing utensils.

Wetting Agents

Wetting agents mostly consist of surfactants, just like washing-up liquid. The most important difference is that the washing-up liquid also has moisturizing agents that are good for your skin. These additives are not good for film, though. The surfactant concentration in the wetting agent bath is much lower than when washing up, so you can safely pour it down the sink.

For disposing of photo chemicals, the previously mentioned 5-liter/ 1-gallon polyethylene (PE) canisters are ideal. You can buy these in a DIY store filled with windshield cleaner or distilled water.

If you have developed a taste for analog photography and have already shot some large format (4×5-inch) sheet film, you are sure to have noticed how expensive dedicated sheet film developing tanks are. You can, however, develop sheet film using regular developing tanks without special sheet-film spools—a tank made for two 35mm spools is large enough. The only additional gear you need is a handful of rubber bands.

The things you need in your changing bag are:

- Your 4×5-inch negatives
- One rubber band per negative
- The developing tank and its center column

You can set your spools aside, as you don't need them for this method.

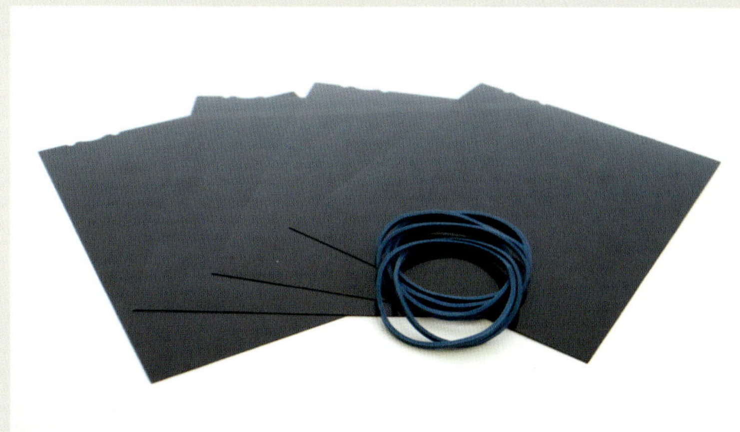

If need be, you can develop sheet film using just a regular developing tank and rubber bands.

→

In the changing bag, roll your negative so the ends (i.e., the short sides) meet, then use one of the rubber bands to keep it rolled up. Make sure the emulsion side faces inward so the rubber band doesn't produce unwanted stripes on the developed negative (if the notch in the film sheet is at top right, the emulsion is facing toward you). The rolled negative kind of looks like a taco.

Open the developing tank and arrange the rolled negatives around the center column. Now put the lid back on. The development process is just like the one for 35mm and medium format films, using the same pre-wash, develop, and interim wash steps. Following fixing, you need to open the tank, take out each negative, and shift the rubber band slightly down each "taco" before replacing them in the fixer solution. This ensures that no fixer gets left under the rubber bands and prevents unwanted stripes that show up when you make prints or scans later on. After a couple of minutes, the places previously covered by the rubber bands will be fixed too, so you can now pour out the fixer and do the final wash. Congratulations, you have just developed your own large format negs!

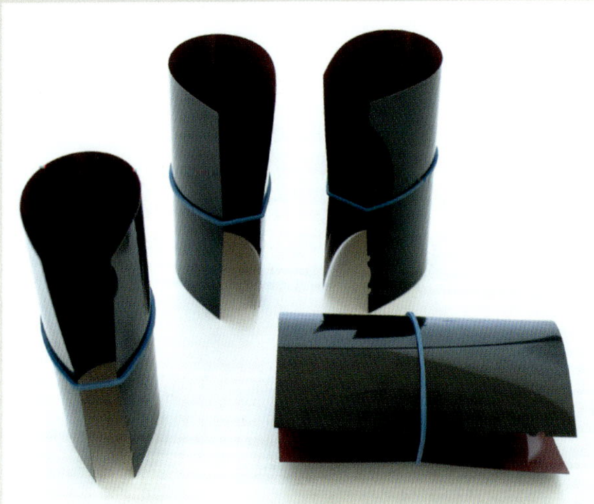

Roll your negatives so the ends meet. The rubber bands used to cinch bunches of spring onions are ideal for making sheet-film "tacos."

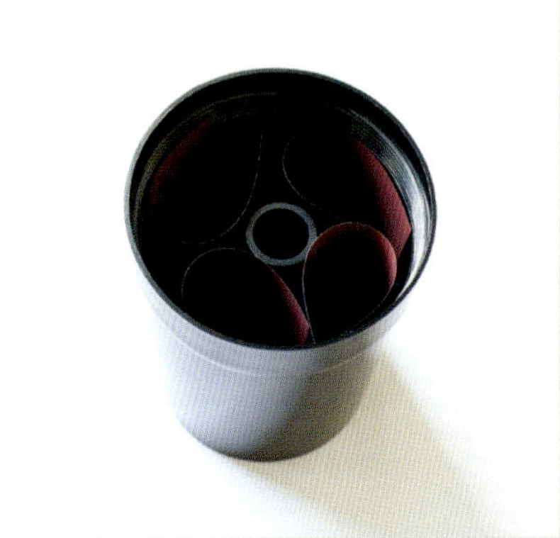

You can develop up to four sheet-film "tacos" in a single tank. The development process is the same as for 35mm and medium format films.

6.3.5 Dust

After the first time digitizing film, most people realize that even small specks of dust can lead to big problems. The smaller the negative, the more the tiny things will matter. We have already addressed the topic of dust here and there in this book. However, after several requests, we have decided to bundle all that information in one place for your reference.

What Is Dust?

Under the microscope, dust consists of a multitude of different particles. You can find anything from pollen and Sahara sand to soot particles, skin flakes, and microplastic fibers from fleece jackets. And the next time a sunbeam floods the room, it becomes apparent that freedom from dust is a mere illusion.

Dust in Photography

Contrary to popular belief, dust on the front of and inside of lenses rarely poses an issue for our negatives. The plane of focus is virtually always in front of the camera and never on or in the lens. Lens dust is therefore not sharp or visible in the images. Roger Cicala, head of Lensrentals, demonstrated this very nicely in an experiment that revealed even small snippets of sticky notes on the front lens of a lens were almost invisible under normal conditions. (For the full story, see his article *The Apocalypse of Lens Dust:* https://www.lensrentals.com/blog/2011/08/the-apocalypse-of-lens-dust.)

Dust and Film

When it comes to dust and film, we need to distinguish between two areas:

- Dust on the film: Even dry film can attract dust due to static charge. Fortunately, in this case, the dust does not remain permanently attached to the film. Static charge can be caused by plastic storage sleeves, for example, or by wiping the film with non-antistatic cloth.
- Dust inside the film: After development, film must dry. During this process, the very sticky emulsion, which consists mainly of gelatin, is exposed to the ambient air. Dust particles that land on the gelatin become part of the film as it dries. They can then no longer be removed. It is worth taking particular care here. This includes drying in an environment that is as dust-free as possible, e.g., in a bathroom after the cold shower has washed dust out of the air for a few minutes.

Dust During Scanning

Dust on the film and film holder can become a problem during scanning. Therefore, if possible, work with a lint-free antistatic cloth and antistatic gloves, a rubber bellows and a goat-hair brush. By the way, with a flatbed scanner, a few grains of dust on the glass are usually not a problem. The film holder holds the film a slight distance above the glass. This keeps the dust out of the plane of focus and therefore keeps it virtually invisible during the scan.

By the way, we advise against using compressed air from spray cans: First, it's quite possible that traces of the propellant will end up on the film. Second, the term compressed air is somewhat misleading. Depending on the gas used, the can contents are not only flammable when sprayed, but often also harmful to the atmosphere.

We have had good success removing dust from scanners and negatives using a soft goat-hair brush. Ours is a cosmetics brush. Dust clings to them nicely and occasionally shaking them out has been sufficient to keep them clean.

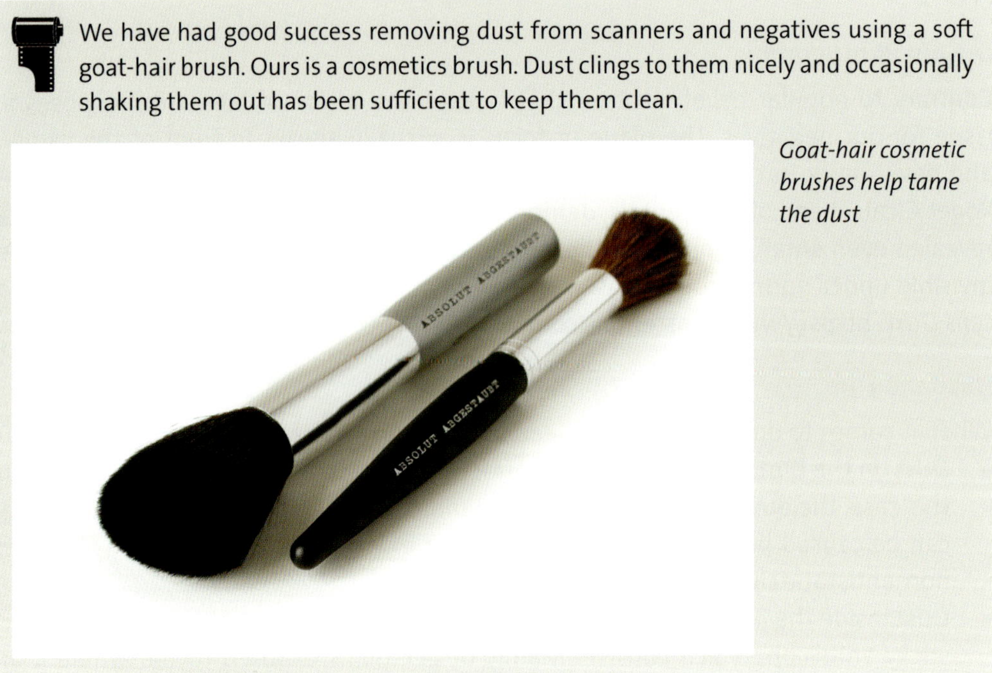

Goat-hair cosmetic brushes help tame the dust

Dust During Storage

After drying, the film is often placed in negative sleeves. These are available in various materials that have one thing in common: They protect the film from dust. We are fans of glassine-based sleeves. Not only are they more breathable than plastic sleeves, they also pick up less of a static charge, which comes into play especially when you pull the film out of the sleeve for scanning.

Our conclusion: A little effort in dust prevention is definitely worth it. Especially if it means that digital post-processing takes much less time afterward. But even with the greatest care, we still usually have to digitally stamp out a couple of specks of dust.

6.3.6   Troubleshooting

We like to compare developing film to baking a cake. You can't really tell if it was successful until the end. Because we have hardly any options of making corrections during development, it's possible for errors to occur. In the following sections, we describe a few typical problems and their causes.

The Film Comes Out Clear

Black-and-white film is supposed to show a negative image, i.e., it turns dark in the places where it was exposed. If the film comes out of the developing tank clear, without showing any picture, there are a few possible causes.

The easiest way to find the problem is to have a look at the image numbers at the edge of the film. These are exposed onto the film during the manufacturing process, so they are also images. If the numbers are clearly visible, it means that at least you have not made any serious mistakes during developing. In this case, something may have gone wrong during light metering and the film has been completely underexposed. With old cameras in particular, it can also happen that a shutter gets stuck or the film was incorrectly exposed for some other reason.

If you don't see the numbers, it may be because you have worked with too low temperatures during development. This makes the developing time considerably longer. If the developer got contaminated with fixer, this could also prevent the development from taking place properly.

The Film Is Black

If the film comes out of the developing tank completely black, then it has had too much light. That can be due to strong overexposure or a defective camera.

The Film Is Gray

The film base to which the emulsion is applied looks different depending on the type of film, and it's not always completely clear. Depending on the film, the clear areas can look gray after developing and fixing, but film can still change during drying, as well.

The Film Is Cloudy

If the film shows milky-cloudy areas, this is a sign that you have not fixed it for long enough or that the fixer has become exhausted. In this case, you can just put the film into the fixer bath once more and let it fix for a few more minutes. Then get rid of the old fixer and prepare new fixer for the next developments.

The Film Has Spots

If you see spots with clear outlines on the film after drying, these may be lime spots. To prevent lime spots, some people recommend using wetting agents. These consist of surfactants that reduce the surface tension and help the water run off the film more quickly.

Occasionally, certain combinations of film and wetting agents can make these lime spots worse. That's why we now prefer to omit the wetting agent, and instead put the film briefly into distilled water (from those 5-liter/1-gallon canisters) after the final wash. This has sorted out such problem cases for us.

Dust

Another form of marks are small, clearly delineated spots that are particularly visible after scanning. This is dust that got onto the film during drying. You can somewhat alleviate the problem by taking appropriate countermeasures, but you cannot completely avoid it.

During the time before digital photography, negatives had to be optimized, especially for big enlargements. This involved using (sometimes single-haired) brushes and special albumen glaze to retouch the negatives under a loupe. These days, we use the digital repair brush during photo editing.

The Film Curls Up

Some types of film have the tendency to curl up lengthways or sideways when they are damp or dry. That does not have to be a fault, but can get in the way. The reason for this behavior lies in the particular combination of film base and coating. The film base does not change when it gets damp during development, but the emulsion expands.

To make the film curl less, some brands of film have a special anti-curling layer on the side opposite the film base. The degree of curl can only be assessed once the film is completely dry. Some films curl and twist even when only slightly damp but hang completely straight on the line once they are fully dry.

The Film Has Streaks

Streaks and lines can have different causes. Fine, hard-edged lines that run lengthwise along the film can be scratches in the emulsion. These can happen if you have not been careful enough with the damp film. A tiny grain of sand trapped on the rubber lips of the squeegee can be the culprit.

Wider streaks can be caused by water (or traces of fixer) running over the film. This often happens if you do not fully remove the sticky tab from medium-format film when winding the film into the tank. When drying, the sticky tab should hang down because it's usually masking tape, which absorbs liquid during developing that can then drip off again later.

One Side of the Film Is Low in Contrast Lengthways

If the film is low in contrast along its length on one side and rich in contrast on the other, this is either because you have not used enough developer or the film was only half immersed in the liquid. It may be that the reel has slipped upward on the center column.

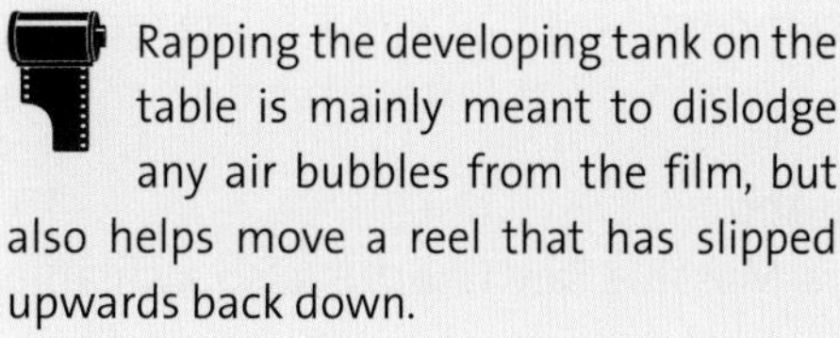

Rapping the developing tank on the table is mainly meant to dislodge any air bubbles from the film, but also helps move a reel that has slipped upwards back down.

The Emulsion Has Holes

To manufacture black-and-white film, extremely thin layers of gelatin containing silver halides, coloring, and other substances are applied to a film base in liquid form. After the manufacturing process, the film is usually dried thoroughly and left to solidify.

It has occasionally happened in the past that certain batches of film ended up on the market too quickly and then showed tears or other problems in the emulsion layer. The emulsion of such films has proved extremely sensitive during developing and sometimes comes away from the film base. In such cases, there is hardly anything you can do to compensate.

6.3.7   Digital Helpers

The Internet, our smartphones, and our smartwatches are important helpers in any situation. This also applies to film photography: There are several online sources and apps that can be very useful for developing. We will introduce a few examples here.

The Massive Dev Chart

The Massive Dev Chart (*www.digitaltruth.com/devchart.php*) is one of the first places to go if you are after any kind of developing recipes. This large database lets you enter the film and developer, and then displays suitable recipes.

The details of the database cover the type of film, developer, ISO value, dilution, developing times for different formats of the same film (35mm, medium format, large format), and the relevant temperature. Plus there is a field with notes for special instructions. If nothing else is specified, the recipes use a normal agitation rhythm and a temperature of 20°C/68°F. The recipes come from users of the database and have not all been checked. But we have always had good results with what we've found.

As App

The Massive Dev Chart is also available as an app for iOS and Android. In addition to the database, you also get a comprehensive developing timer and the option of adding your own recipes.

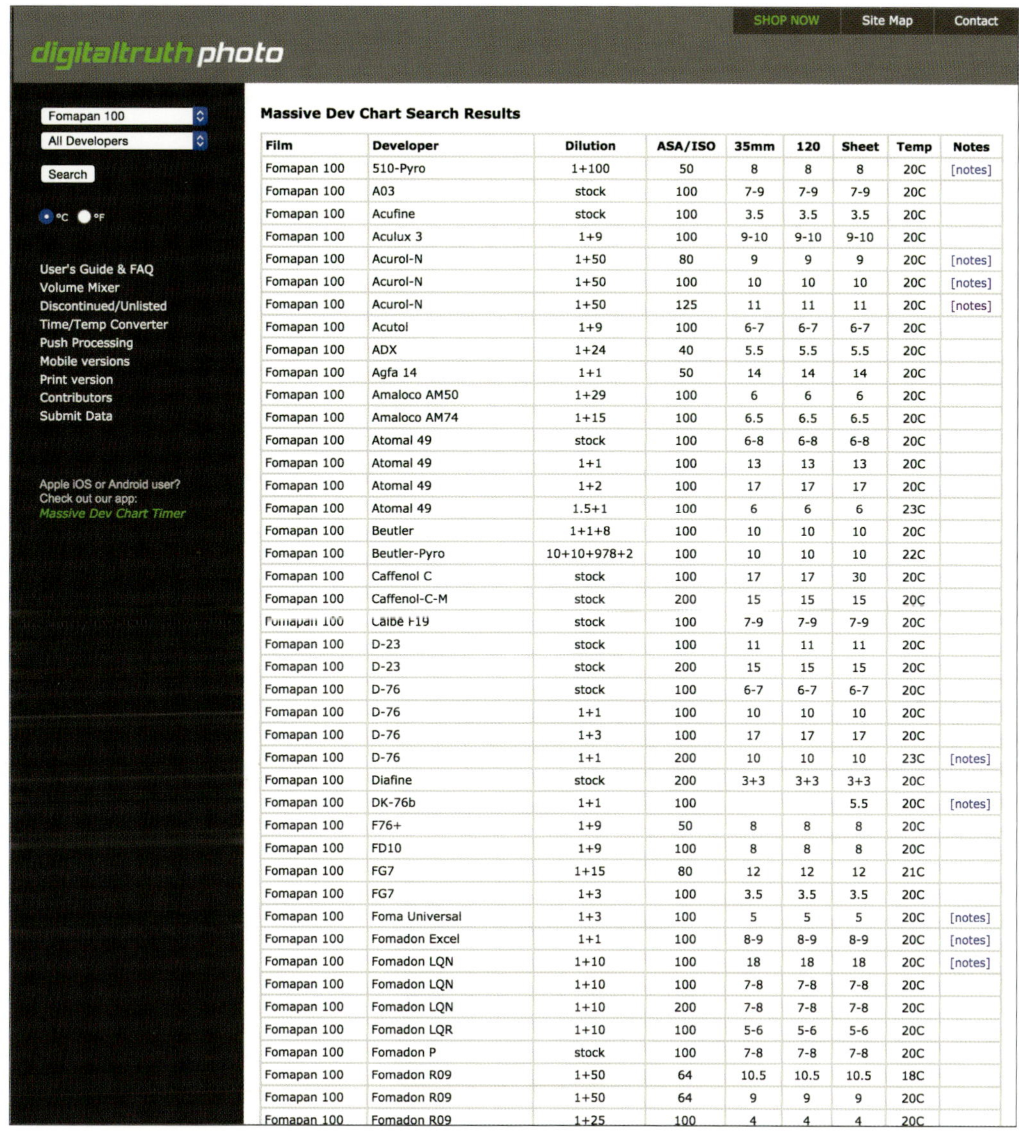

Massive Dev Chart Search Results

Film	Developer	Dilution	ASA/ISO	35mm	120	Sheet	Temp	Notes
Fomapan 100	510-Pyro	1+100	50	8	8	8	20C	[notes]
Fomapan 100	A03	stock	100	7-9	7-9	7-9	20C	
Fomapan 100	Acufine	stock	100	3.5	3.5	3.5	20C	
Fomapan 100	Aculux 3	1+9	100	9-10	9-10	9-10	20C	
Fomapan 100	Acurol-N	1+50	80	9	9	9	20C	[notes]
Fomapan 100	Acurol-N	1+50	100	10	10	10	20C	[notes]
Fomapan 100	Acurol-N	1+50	125	11	11	11	20C	[notes]
Fomapan 100	Acutol	1+9	100	6-7	6-7	6-7	20C	
Fomapan 100	ADX	1+24	40	5.5	5.5	5.5	20C	
Fomapan 100	Agfa 14	1+1	50	14	14	14	20C	
Fomapan 100	Amaloco AM50	1+29	100	6	6	6	20C	
Fomapan 100	Amaloco AM74	1+15	100	6.5	6.5	6.5	20C	
Fomapan 100	Atomal 49	stock	100	6-8	6-8	6-8	20C	
Fomapan 100	Atomal 49	1+1	100	13	13	13	20C	
Fomapan 100	Atomal 49	1+2	100	17	17	17	20C	
Fomapan 100	Atomal 49	1.5+1	100	6	6	6	23C	
Fomapan 100	Beutler	1+1+8	100	10	10	10	20C	
Fomapan 100	Beutler-Pyro	10+10+978+2	100	10	10	10	22C	
Fomapan 100	Caffenol C	stock	100	17	17	30	20C	
Fomapan 100	Caffenol-C-M	stock	200	15	15	15	20C	
Fomapan 100	Calbe F19	stock	100	7-9	7-9	7-9	20C	
Fomapan 100	D-23	stock	100	11	11	11	20C	
Fomapan 100	D-23	stock	200	15	15	15	20C	
Fomapan 100	D-76	stock	100	6-7	6-7	6-7	20C	
Fomapan 100	D-76	1+1	100	10	10	10	20C	
Fomapan 100	D-76	1+3	100	17	17	17	20C	
Fomapan 100	D-76	1+1	200	10	10	10	23C	[notes]
Fomapan 100	Diafine	stock	200	3+3	3+3	3+3	20C	
Fomapan 100	DK-76b	1+1	100			5.5	20C	[notes]
Fomapan 100	F76+	1+9	50	8	8	8	20C	
Fomapan 100	FD10	1+9	100	8	8	8	20C	
Fomapan 100	FG7	1+15	80	12	12	12	21C	
Fomapan 100	FG7	1+3	100	3.5	3.5	3.5	20C	
Fomapan 100	Foma Universal	1+3	100	5	5	5	20C	[notes]
Fomapan 100	Fomadon Excel	1+1	100	8-9	8-9	8-9	20C	[notes]
Fomapan 100	Fomadon LQN	1+10	100	18	18	18	20C	[notes]
Fomapan 100	Fomadon LQN	1+10	100	7-8	7-8	7-8	20C	
Fomapan 100	Fomadon LQN	1+10	200	7-8	7-8	7-8	20C	
Fomapan 100	Fomadon LQR	1+10	100	5-6	5-6	5-6	20C	
Fomapan 100	Fomadon P	stock	100	7-8	7-8	7-8	20C	
Fomapan 100	Fomadon R09	1+50	64	10.5	10.5	10.5	18C	
Fomapan 100	Fomadon R09	1+50	64	9	9	9	20C	
Fomapan 100	Fomadon R09	1+25	100	4	4	4	20C	

The Massive Dev Chart website: www.digitaltruth.com/devchart.php

darkroom-solutions.com

The "world's largest b/w film development time database" is available in German and English. Here, too, there is a seemingly endless combination of development recipes and times with associated tilt rhythms.

The database is also available as an app for iPhone and Android.

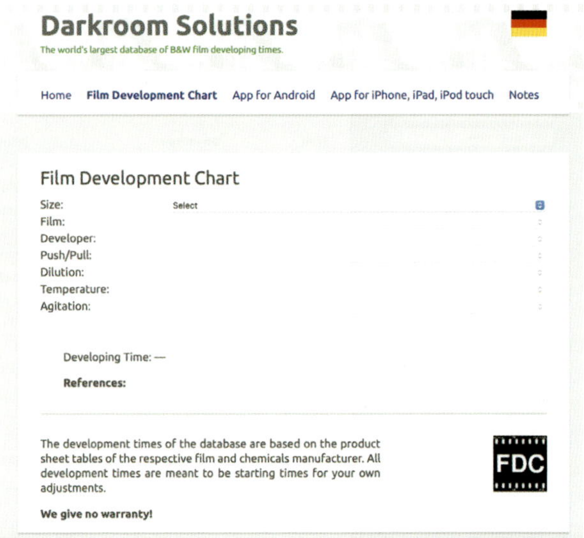

Film Dryer: Photo labs used to hang film to dry in a dedicated drying booth. Clean filtered (and sometimes heated) air was moved over the film. Not only did film dry quickly this way, but this method also kept it free from dust.

Commercial film dryers were not available for years. JOBO has now relaunched their MISTRAL film dryer. Depending on which drying chute you use, it will dry films from 35mm to large format in a dust-free environment.

If you lean more toward the DIY side, you can build one yourself. You will find fans and dust filters in PC accessory stores. Here's a picture of an older specimen from someone's dark room.

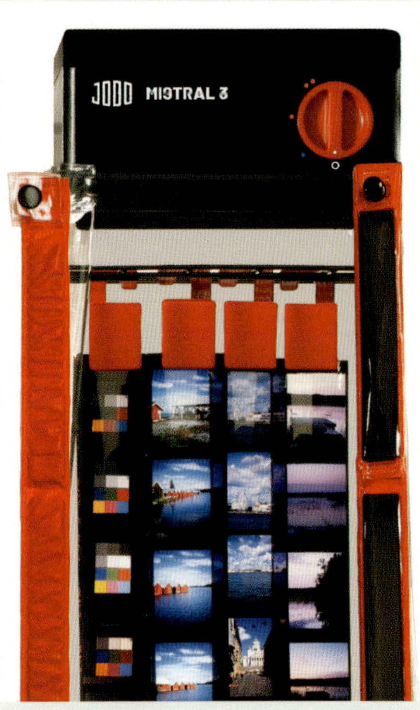

JOBO MISTRAL film dryer

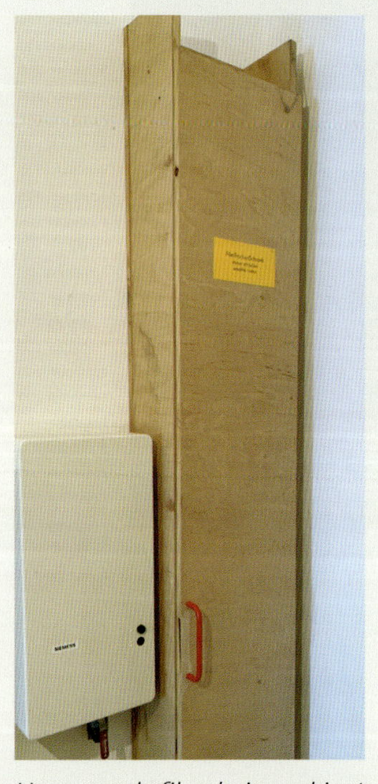

Home-made film drying cabinet

filmdev.org

Another popular online source for developing recipes is *filmdev.org*. The big advantage of this website is the example photos. Users can submit their recipes to *filmdev.org* and upload the photos that go with it to *Flickr.com*. Users can now search for films and recipes on *filmdev.org* and then immediately get a preview of what the pictures might look like if you use the corresponding recipe.

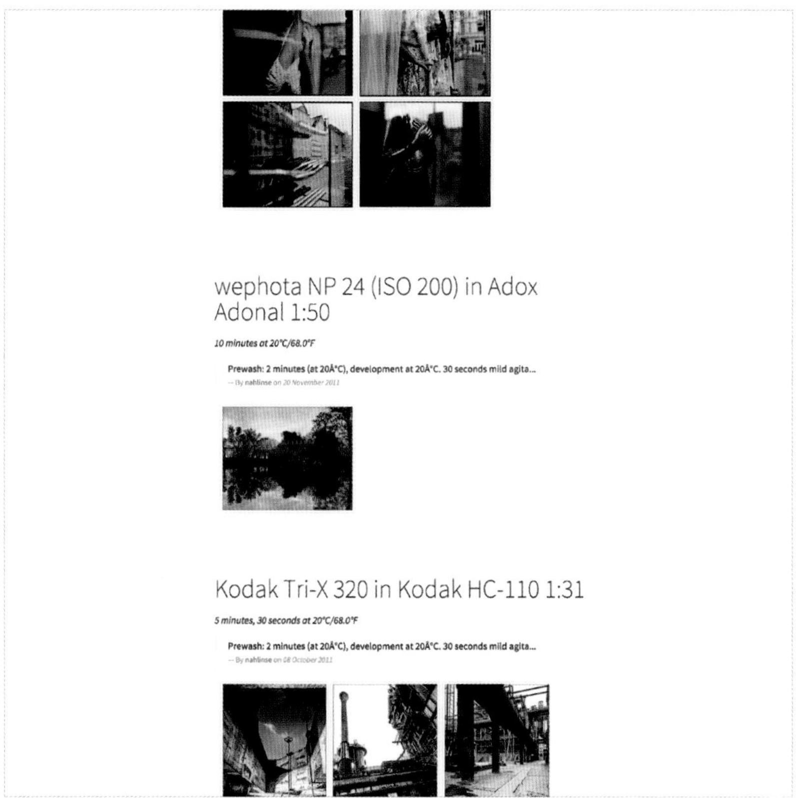

Example recipes at filmdev.org

The website also offers specialized lists, including:

- the most popular combination of film and developer *(http://filmdev.org/popular)*
- the most frequently used films *(http://filmdev.org/films)*
- the users' favorite developers *(http://filmdev.org/developers)*

You can use filters to quickly find your way around the website.

Timer Apps for Your Smartphone

- **Develop! (iOS):** The free app Develop! Film Development Timer supports multi-step timers and can also import recipes from *filmdev.org* in addition to offering its own recipes. Plus, you can create steps in any order in the app, including reminders for when to agitate the developing tank. Other special features offered by this app are the darkroom mode and the voice control that allows you to move on to the next developing step without having to touch your smartphone with wet fingers.
- **The Massive Dev Chart (iOS and Android):** This app contains the recipe database plus a multi-step developing timer for the standard developing steps. It also offers a darkroom mode that switches the app to red light.

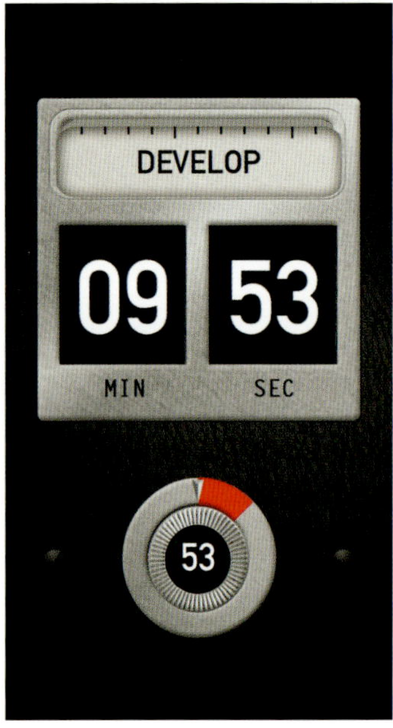

Develop!

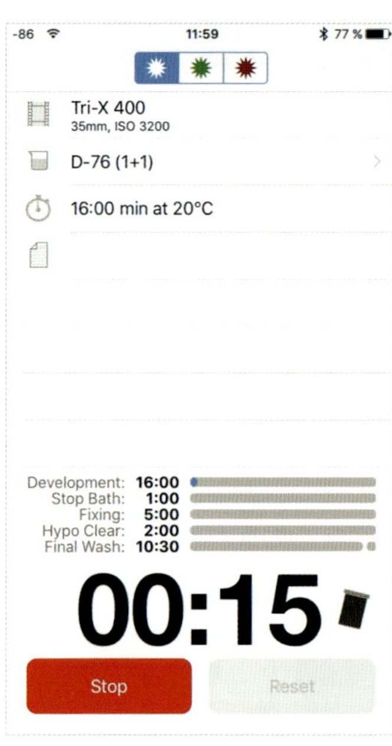

Massive Dev Chart

- **Film Developer Pro (Android):** This database for developing recipes is based on the manufacturers' recommendations. There is a calculator for determining times that are not covered by the database. Plus the app offers a development timer and a dilution calculator.

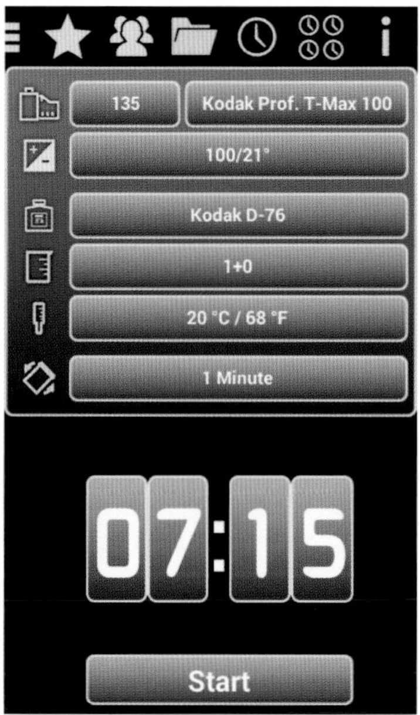

Film Developer Pro

6.3.8   Community

There are some online communities and projects about film photography that we want to briefly mention here.

Film Swap

You can find various groups online that are dedicated to random multiple exposures if you keyword search *Film Swap*. Usually, the first person exposes a roll of film, then rewinds the film and passes it on to the next person who then exposes the film a second time. Sometimes, even a third exposure takes place. The results are often surprisingly beautiful.

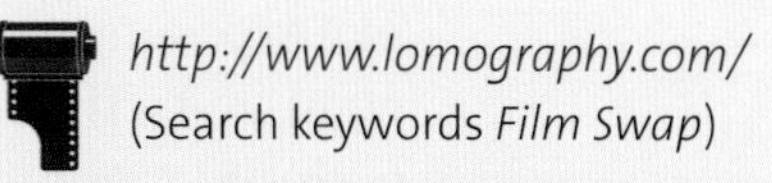

Filmdev.org

This free website offers a good platform where you can share your development recipes with others.

Pinhole Day

Every year, the last Sunday in April is Pinhole Day, to celebrate photography with the pinhole camera. You can upload your photos to the Pinhole Day website (*https://pinholeday.org*) where they find themselves in the best company with thousands of pictures from umpteen different countries.

Crowdfunding Projects

Various crowdfunding projects focus on film photography. Here is just one example:

Ferrania is a Kickstarter project for the salvage and continued operation of the Italian film-producing company Ferrania.

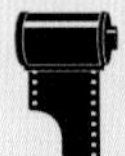

https://www.kickstarter.com/projects/filmferrania/100-more-years-of-analog-film?ref=nav_search

6.3.9   Push and Pull

The ISO sensitivity designated on the film (the nominal film speed) is not set in stone—it's more of a suggestion. Film is quite flexible, and both the push and pull processing expands not just the exposure limitations of the film but also the creative possibilities. Let's jettison the widely held opinion that push processing is only for increasing the film speed and has no other side-effects.

Push Processing

Many photographers resort to push if the light is no longer sufficient for normal exposure, such as with evening and night shots. This approach is justified for such situations, but you are not doing push enough justice with it. With push processing, the film gets less light than it should have—i.e., you set a higher ISO

The more aperture stops you push by, the more important good exposure becomes. The limited contrast range caused by the push causes even small inaccuracies in exposure to have disproportional effects on the result.

value on the light meter. To compensate, you adjust the parameters later during development. This could be by using a higher temperature, a weaker dilution, or a longer exposure time.

This treatment has at least one consequence: The contrast range of the film is reduced, so the picture's contrast becomes harder and the curve becomes steeper. You will find only very few gray shades in the midrange. If this was a digital photo, the histogram would look like a bathtub: lots of dark and bright areas, but not much in the middle.

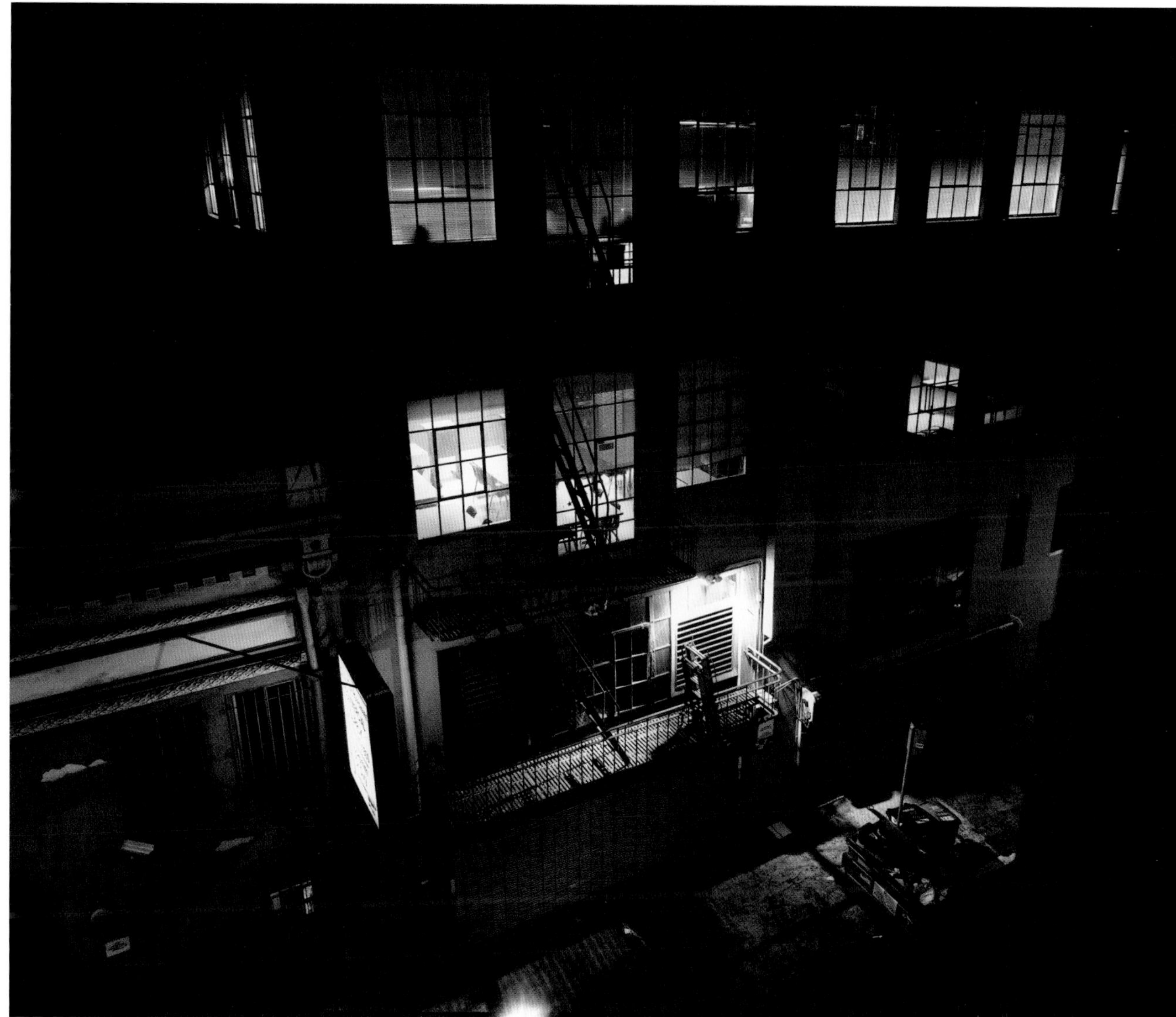

San Francisco backyard, 4×5-inch large format

Perhaps you know the Curves tool from digital image editing. You use it to control which brightness level in the original image is translated to which level of the resulting image. The x-axis of the curve describes the brightness curve of the original picture, and the y-axis shows the curve of the edited result. The neutral curve is a diagonal that represents all brightness levels neutrally. A steeper curve means that dark values are represented even darker and bright values even brighter. The contrast is increased.

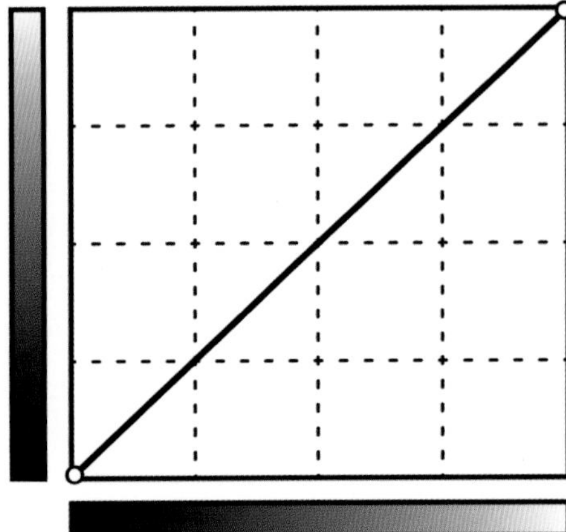

Neutral gradation curve

The push makes the curve steeper. As a result, the film may lose detail in the shadows and highlights, while the overall contrast becomes noticeably harder.

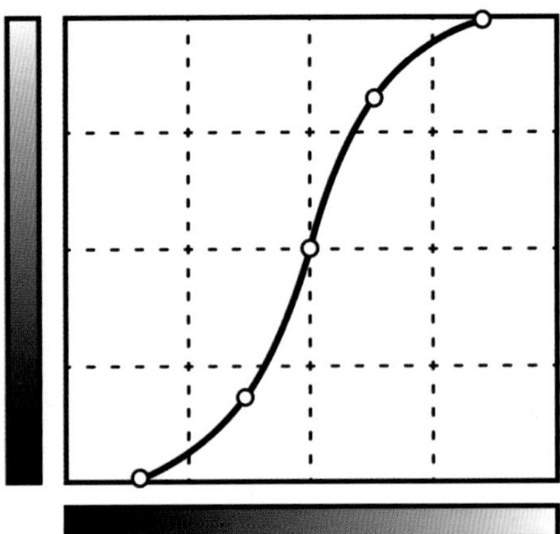

Push makes the curve become steeper and the contrast range narrower

With push, you are going to lose a bit of detail in the highlights and shadows due to the stronger contrasts. You will see the same effect in your image editing if you push the contrast slider to the right in an already contrast-rich photo.

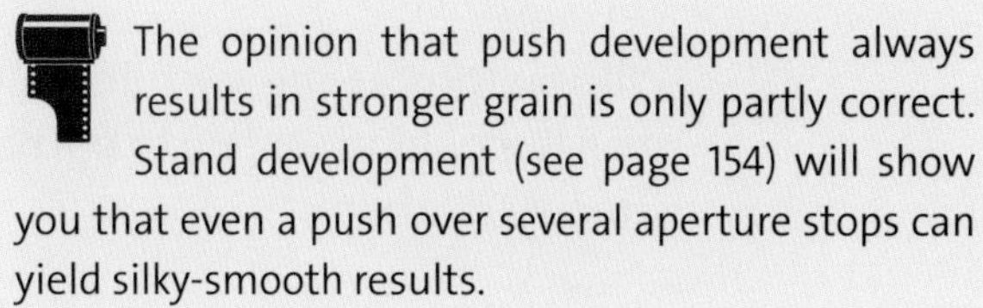

The opinion that push development always results in stronger grain is only partly correct. Stand development (see page 154) will show you that even a push over several aperture stops can yield silky-smooth results.

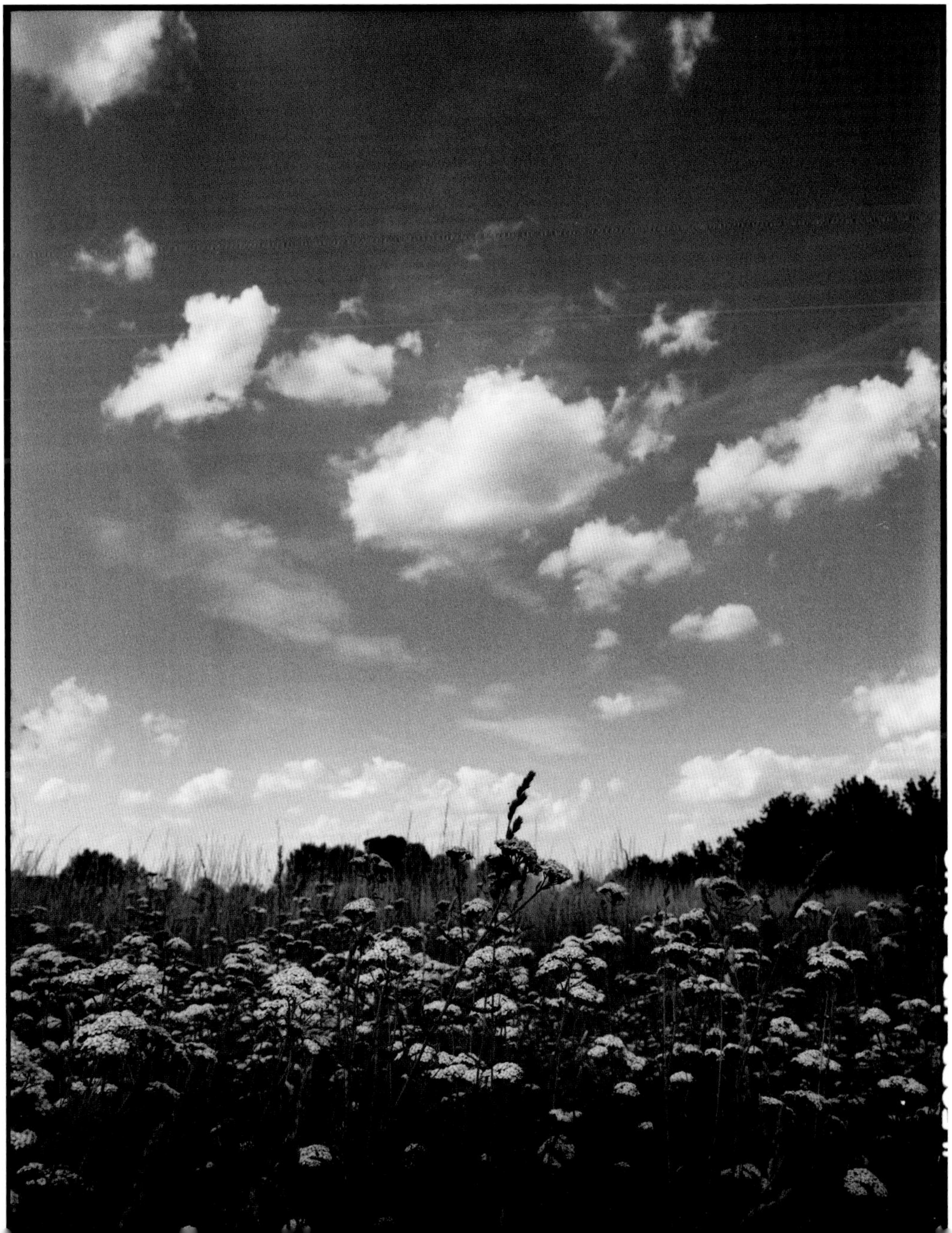

Incidentally, push processing gets particularly interesting if you use it where it does not (purely intuitively) really belong: for photos taken in bright sunlight. Go ahead and try it, and you can enjoy a very interesting contrast behavior.

Push in bright sunshine

Pull Processing

With pull processing, we turn it all on its head. During shooting, the film gets more light than it should, according to the packaging. Then we develop it for a shorter time or with stronger dilution.

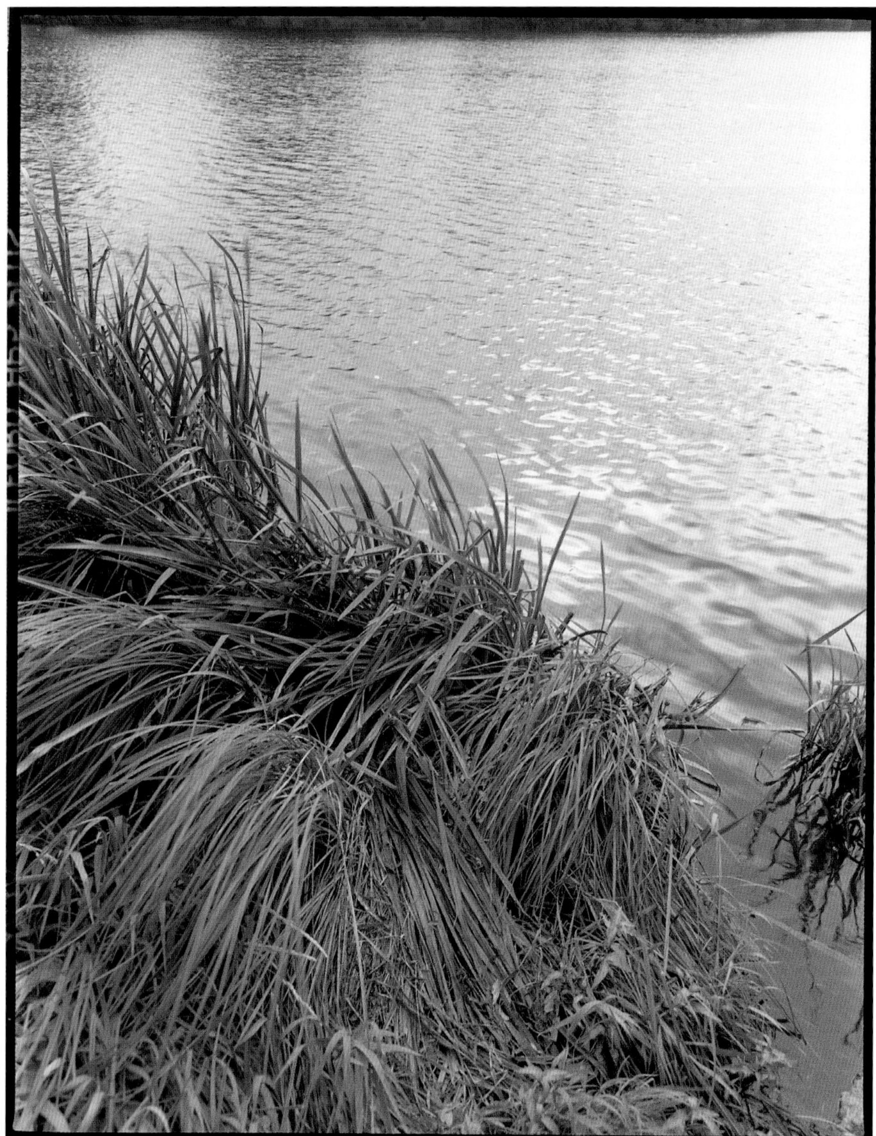

Pull in the late afternoon, Ilford HP5+

The result then shows very fine gray shades in the midtones. The film's contrast range increases with pull, and wrong exposures become practically impossible. When experimenting during a workshop, we tried shooting a high-contrast scene seven times, each time with a one-stop exposure difference, from 1/15 second to 1/1000 second. At the end, all pictures still clearly showed all the detail in the scene. Each of these pictures would have been suitable for post-processing both by scanning and by printing.

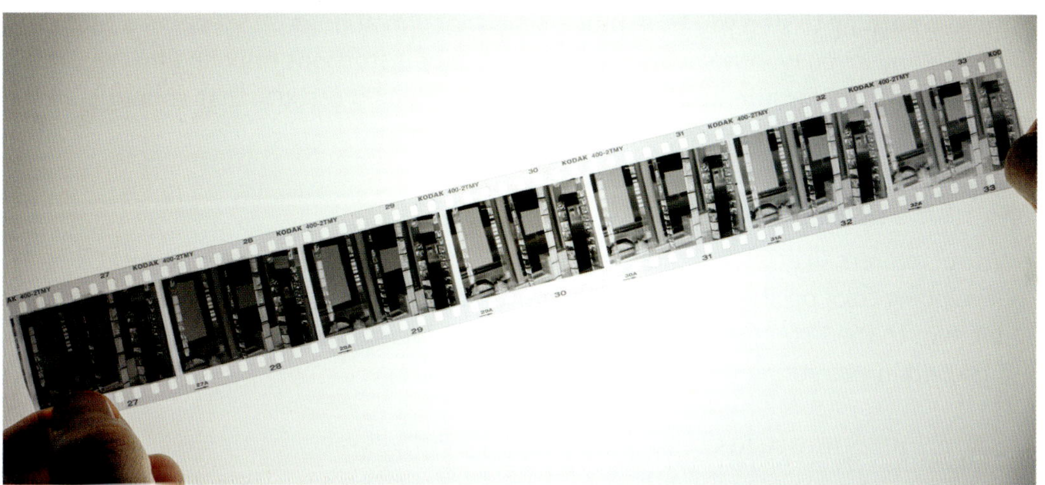

Kodak T-MAX 400, 3 stops pull to ISO 50, D-76 1+1 7:20 minutes. Exposure times from left to right: 1/15, 1/30, 1/60, 1/125, 1/250, 1/500, 1/1000 second.

Generally, it can be said that pull increases the contrast range the film can capture, usually far beyond the contrast range of the subject. The resulting negative shows a lower contrast range, which is usually an advantage when it comes to further processing.

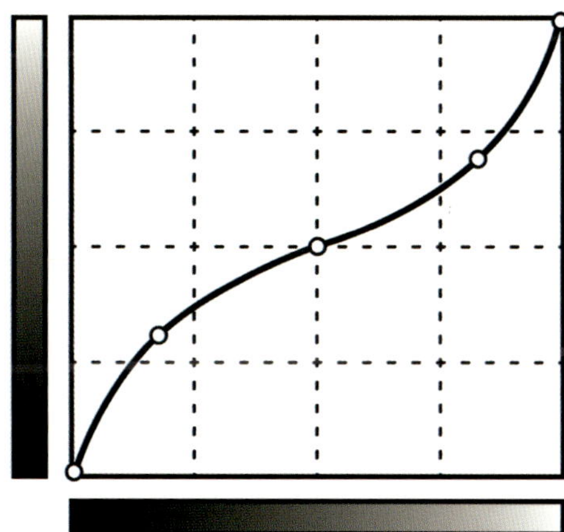

Low-contrast gradation curve

6.4   Processing Yourself: Color

Just about any photo lab can reliably provide color development in the C-41 or E-6 process. The process is so standardized that machines can carry it out automatically. Still, there is nothing to stop you from processing color film at home. It's a popular approach particularly if you want to deliberately create color distortions or push film (yes, it can be done with color film, too). First of all, you need a "press kit" that contains all the chemicals for successful home processing of color film.

6.4.1   The Typical C-41 Negative Kit

Manufacturers like Tetenal, Rollei, Fuji, or Compard offer different chemical kits for developing color positive and negative films. Packs range from the starter set for exactly one film to the 1 liter (which is sufficient for developing up to 12 films) to 15 liters. The kits contain everything you need in one simple package.

6.4.2   Temperatures

Depending on the chemicals and recipe you use, the development of color negative film usually takes place at about 38 °C/100° F and can tolerate only tiny temperature variations (less than 1° F, +/− 0.3° C) before you get color distortions. The times are also correspondingly short—usually 3 minutes and 15 seconds.

6.4.3   Step-by-Step C-41 Developing

This section details the individual steps involved in developing color film using the one-liter Colortec C-41 kit. For details on things like how to insert the film into the reel and the reel into the tank, see section 6.3.4.

The kit consists of six bottles: three with developer, two with the bleach/fix (blix) components, and one with stabilizer. These can be mixed with water heated to the appropriate process temperature to make three basic solutions. The solutions can be used multiple times, and can be poured back into the bottles after use. The standard temperature for this process is 38° C (100.4° F), and you need to be precise about this. This is why we recommend you use a rotation processor that automatically regulates the temperature (see pages 183–184). Higher (or lower) temperatures require you to compensate by decreasing (or increasing) the time taken for each step. For more information, see the manual provided with the kit.

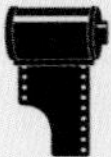
Heat the water bath to a couple degrees warmer than the process actually requires. A rotation processor has less trouble regulating the temperature than it does heating water that is too cool.

1. Insert your film(s) into the tank, and warm them up to 38° C/100.4° F for 5 minutes.

2. Pour the color developer into the tank, and agitate it for 3 minutes, 15 seconds (or, for a subsequent film, for the longer time given in the manual). You can develop up to 12 films using one liter of solution, and the time required for each film increases as the developer solution becomes weaker. Pour the developer back into its bottle once you are done.

3. Pour the blix solution into the tank and agitate it for 4 minutes. Again, take care to observe the increased time required when developing subsequent films. Pour the blix solution back into its bottle when you are done.

4. Now perform the interim wash according to the instructions in the manual (i.e., 3 minutes with a change of water every 30 seconds). The water doesn't have to be at precisely 38° C/100.4° F for this step: It can be anywhere between 30° and 40° C (86°–104° F).

5. Pour the stabilizer solution into the tank, and agitate it for 1 minute. The temperature of the stabilizer solution can be anywhere from 20° to 40° C (68°–104° F). Pour the stabilizer solution back into its bottle when you are done.

To make color and contrast consistently reproducible, the manufacturers of film development chemicals quote very narrow tolerances for the times and temperatures required when using their products. The following sections detail some useful tips for keeping things accurate when developing films by hand or using a temperature-regulated rotation processor.

By Hand

When developing films by hand, place the tank in the water bath (for example, in a wash basin or a bucket) so it doesn't float when it is full. Do the same with your bottles of chemicals. The best way to keep the temperature constant is to measure it regularly using a digital thermometer and keep a kettle of hot water on hand to add as necessary.

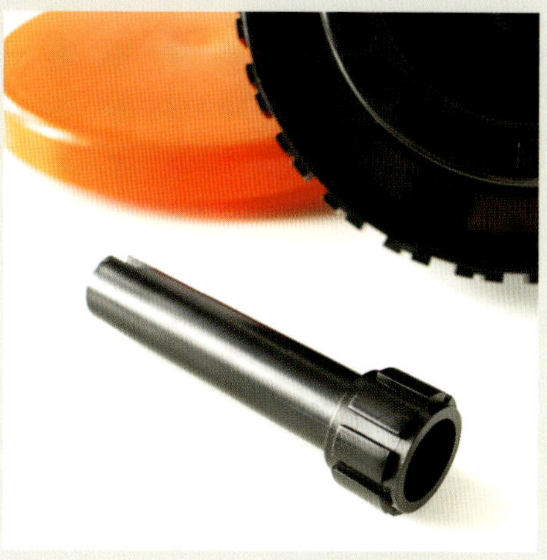

Have you ever asked yourself what this part of the developing tank is for?

$\rightarrow$

If you remove the tank from the water bath to agitate it, this can cause slight variations in temperature. (Make sure you have a supply of towels handy too.) Some tanks—for example, those made by AP and Paterson—are delivered with a special accessory that you can insert into hole in the lid and use to rotate the center column and the attached spools while the tank itself remains motionless in the water bath. The bottom of the AP center column is wave-shaped, and there is a corresponding flange at the bottom of the tank that moves the spools up and down while they rotate, thus ensuring that the films are evenly covered with chemicals.

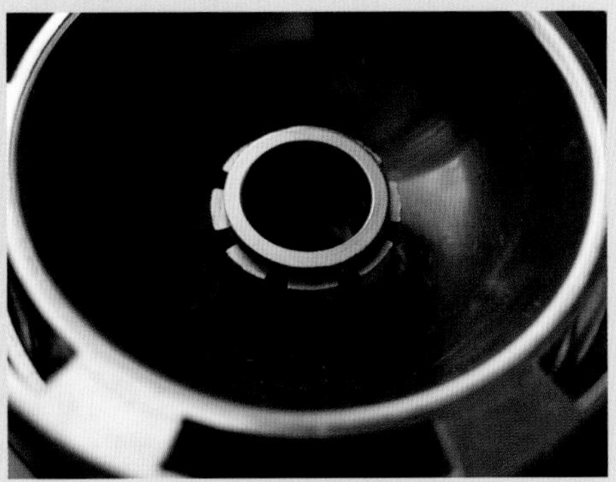

Instead of moving the entire tank, you can use the agitator to rotate the spools from the outside

Using a Rotation Processor

A rotation processor, such as those made by JOBO, simplifies the development process. This type of machine uses a thermostat to keep the temperature of the water bath constant and continually rotates the tank (which lies on its side) back and forth. The horizontally positioned tank is only slightly submerged, making it easier to access when adding and removing chemicals. This design also means you have to use less solution to keep the film covered during processing (a vertically positioned tank requires much more solution to keep the films submerged). The required amounts of solution are clearly shown on the outside of the tank.

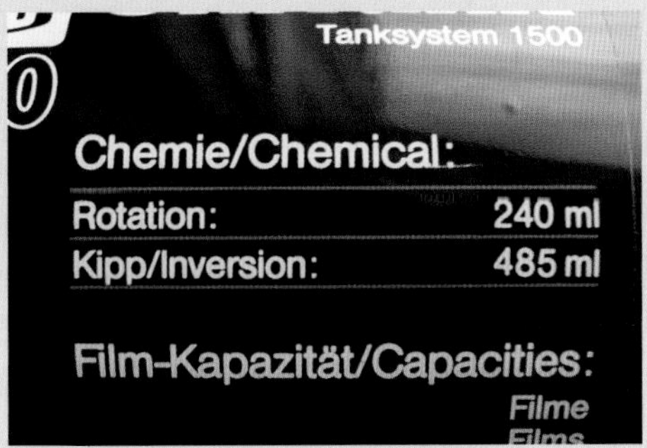

The required amounts of chemicals for inversion and rotation development are shown on the outside of the developing tank

The tank is connected to the processor using a magnetic coupling and runs on rollers that can be raised or lowered to accommodate different sized tanks. Standard ring-shaped magnets from JOBO are mounted on the four studs on the bottom of the tank and work with most JOBO models.

JOBO also sells specialized tanks for developing paper prints, so make sure you purchase the correct type. The processor can be switched between two rotation speeds. The slower speed is for developing paper prints while the faster speed is recommended for developing film.

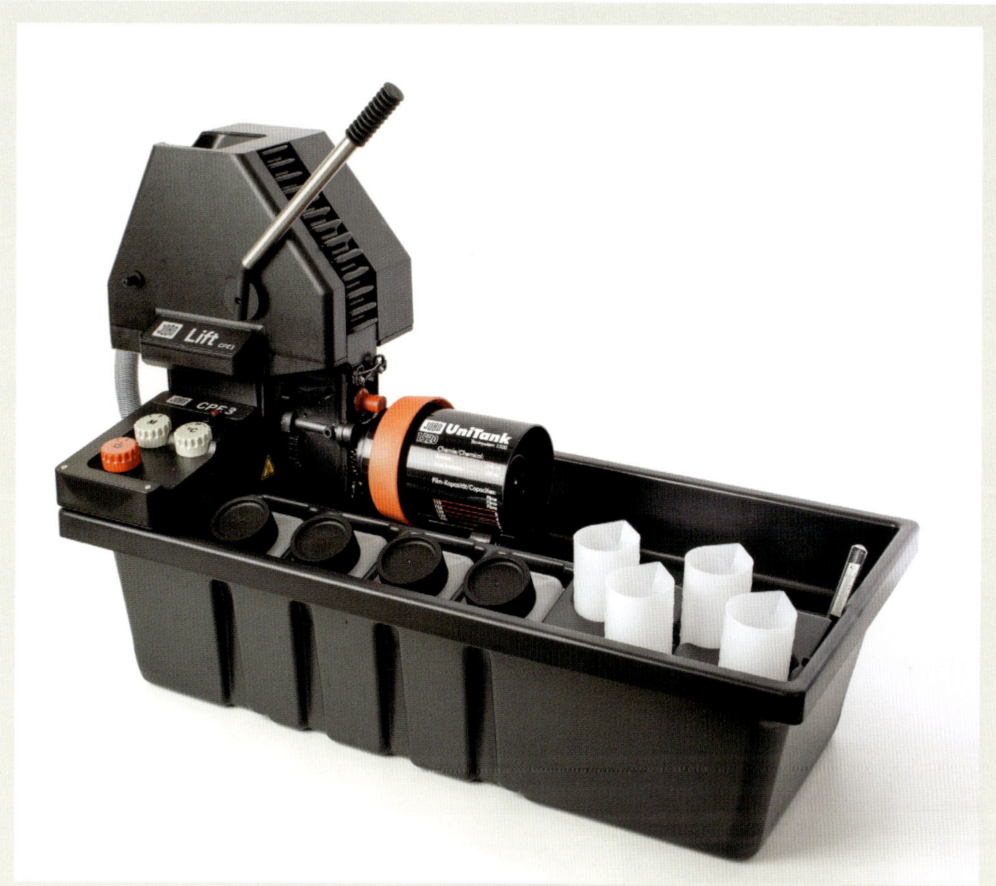

JOBO sells a lift accessory that enables you to fill and empty the tank without decoupling it from the processor. Instead of a magnet, the lift configuration uses a toothed wheel around the hole in the tank's lid to drive the rotation movement.

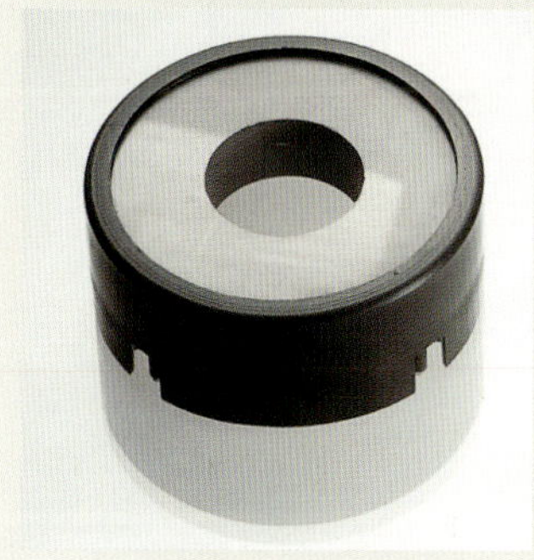

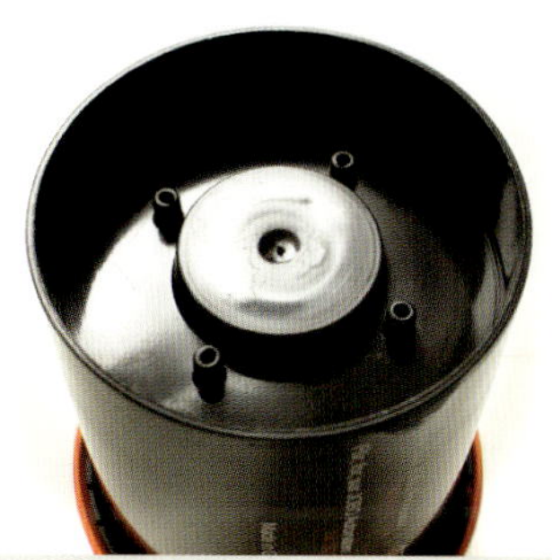

JOBO developing tanks have four studs on the bottom for mounting a ring-shaped magnet (shown on the left). This enables them to be used in an automated rotation processor.

6.4.4   Step-by-Step E-6 Developing

Slide (color positive) film can be developed using an E-6 Tetenal kit in a similar way to the C-41 color negative process described in section 6.4.3, though the chemicals and the steps involved are slightly different. Here, too, the time required for the development and blix steps increases with the number of films you develop (see the developer kit manual for details). For more details on how to insert the films into the spools and the spools into the tank, see section 6.3.4. Following are the steps, in brief, for E-6 developing:

1. Insert film(s) into the tank and heat it to 38° C/100.4° F
2. First developer (6 minutes and 16 seconds)
3. First wash (2 minutes and 30 seconds)
4. Color developer (6 minutes)
5. Blix (6 minutes)
6. Wash (4 minutes)
7. Stabilizer (1 minute)

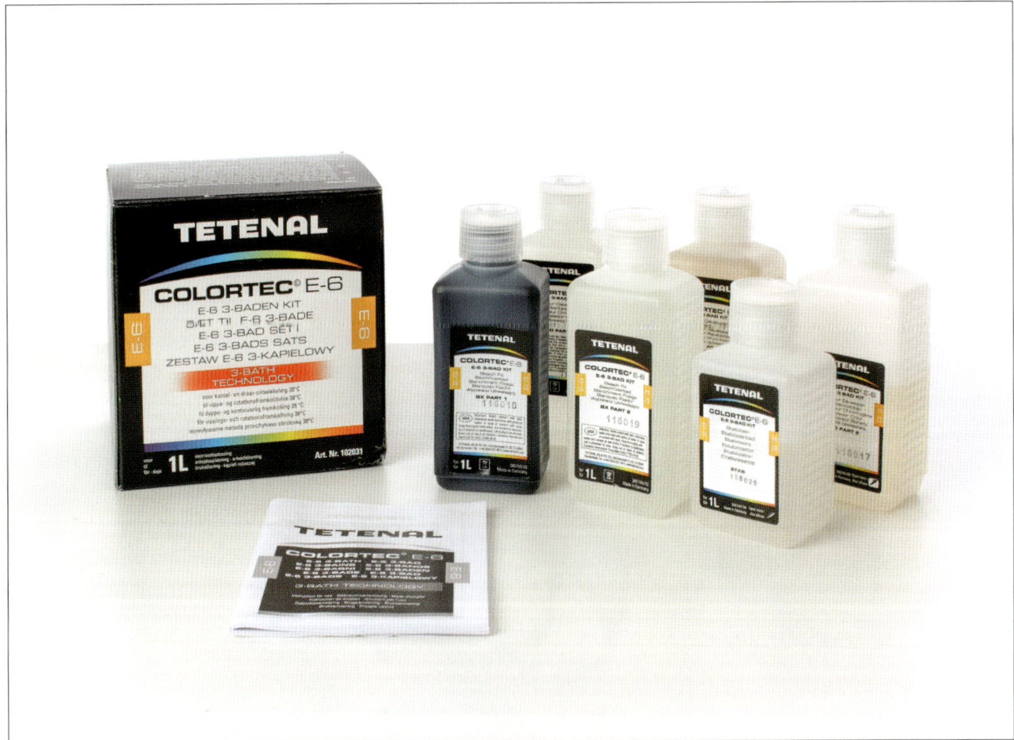

The Tetnal three-bath slide developer kit

Developer	Process	Description
CineStill CS41 Color Simplified Quart Kit	C-41	Three-part powdered developing kit for simplified two-bath development of color films.
CineStill CS41 Color C-41 Two-Bath Process	C-41	Six-piece liquid developing kit for developing color films at temperatures between 22 and 39°C.
CineStill Cn2 "Color Negative" ECN-2 Developer	ECN-2	Powder developer for the development of color films in low-contrast cinema style. For up to 16 films. (Other required components, such as bleach fixer bath, must be purchased separately).
CineStill Cs 2 "Cine Simplified" ECN-2 Bad Powder Kit	ECN-2	Three-part powdered developing set for processing all color films in low-contrast cinema style. If a remjet layer is present, it can be removed manually under running water after development. Suffices for up to 16 films.
Compard Digibase C-41 Kit	C-41	The six-part working set includes starter, color developer A, color developer B, color developer C, bleach fixing bath, and stabilizing bath. Available in Mini, Midi, Maxi, and Super packaging for 10, 20, 50, or 100 films.
Fuji C-41 Film X-Press Kit 5L	C-41	Six-piece developing kit for 60 films ISO 400 and 80 films ISO 100.
Rollei Colorchem C-41 Kit	C-41	Color development kit with six components: Color developer A, color developer B, color developer C, bleach fixer A, bleach fixer B, and stabilizer bath. Processing is possible at 25°C, 38°C, or 45°C.
Tetenal Colortec C-41 Negative Kit Rapid	C-41	Six-part development kit for standardized development at 38°C. The associated data sheet also contains times for alternative development at 30°C. The set is available in assemblies for 12-16 as well as 25-40 color films.
Tetenal Magic-Box C-41 Developer	C-41	Six-part developing kit for the preparation of 250ml, sufficient for the development of one color negative film. Develops at 30°C according to the data sheet.
CineStill D6 Daylight-Chrome First Developer	E-6	The neutral tone first developer for the three-bath process from CineStill (liquid concentrate). Optimized for a filling temperature of 40°C. For a complete process, one needs a first developer of choice (DynamicChrome, TungstenChrome, or Daylight-Chrome), the combined reverse second developer (Cr6), and the bleach fixer (Bf6).

→

Developer	Process	Description
CineStill T6 Tungsten-Chrome First Developer	E-6	Cold-tone first developer for the three-bath process from CineStill. Compensates the color cast of tungsten lamps on daylight film (powder). Optimized for a filling temperature of 40°C. For a complete process, one needs a first developer of choice (DynamicChrome, TungstenChrome, or Daylight-Chrome), the combined reverse second developer (Cr6), and the bleach fixer (Bf6)
CineStill D9 Dynamic-Chrome First Developer	E-6	Warmtone first developer for the three-bath process from CineStill (powder). Optimized for a filling temperature of 40°C. For a complete process, one needs a first developer of choice (DynamicChrome, TungstenChrome, or Daylight-Chrome), the combined reverse second developer (Cr6), and the bleach fixer (Bf6).
CineStill Cr6 Second Developer 2-in-1	E-6	Second developer for the three-bath process of CineStill (liquid concentrate), consisting of Part A and Part B. For a complete process, one needs a first developer of choice (Dynamic Chrome, Tungsten Chrome, or Daylight Chrome), the combined reverse second developer (Cr6), and the bleach fixer (Bf6).
CineStill Bf6 Bleach Bath and Fixer 3-in-1	E-6	The bleach fixer for the three-bath process from CineStill. Consisting of Part A, Part B, and Part C. (Liquid concentrate.) For a complete process, one needs a first developer of choice (Dynamic Chrome, Tungsten Chrome, or Daylight Chrome), the combined reverse second developer (Cr6), and the bleach fixer (Bf6)
Tetenal Colortec E-6 Three-Bath	E-6	Six-part set for developing all types of slide films in the three-bath process with first developer, two color developers, two bleach-fixing baths, and a stabilizing bath. Optimized for processing at 38°C.
Tetenal Magic-Box E-6 Developer Kit	E-6	Slide film chemistry in a beginner's box. Contains all the concentrates needed to mix the developing baths. For developing one roll of 135-36 film or one roll of 120 film. Optimized for processing at 38°C.

Color Developer

6.4.5   Useful Accessories

Different accessories can help you achieve color developing at home.

Water Bath

A water bath with a thermometer can help achieve a constant temperature. Put the developing tank and the bottles of developer chemicals into this water bath at least half an hour before you start developing to bring them up to the right temperature. To avoid having to lift the developing tank out of the water, some tanks come with a special device that enables you to rotate the reel inside the tank from the outside without having to lift the tank.

Circulation Pump

To achieve better temperature distribution in the water bath, use a small aquarium pump. This circulates the water and ensures the temperature remains constant. This works equally well whether you are developing your films by hand or are using a rotation processor.

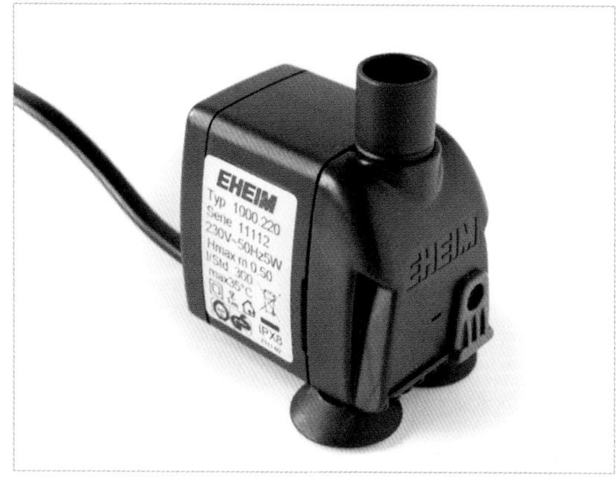

A cheap aquarium pump circulates the water in the bath and ensures even temperature distribution. This image shows the Compact 300 model from Eheim.

Sous Vide Cooker

Sous vide is a modern kitchen technique in which vacuum-sealed food is cooked slowly in a warm water bath at a constant temperature. The immersion heaters used for this not only keep the water at a precise temperature, they also ensure constant circulation and thus an even temperature distribution. This is ideal for color film development.

Please confirm that the cooker covers the desired temperature range, as some models only start at higher temperatures. Also make sure that you use it exclusively for film development, just as you would with other utensils, such as thermometers and jars. This will help you avoid contaminating food with film chemistry.

Sous vide cookers start well under $100.

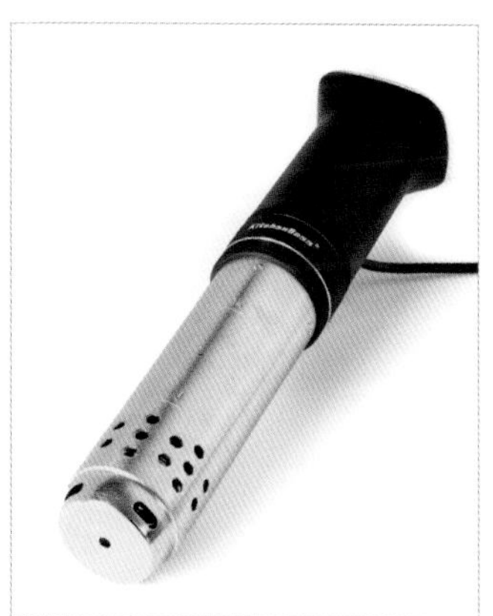

A sous vide wand is great for color development at home

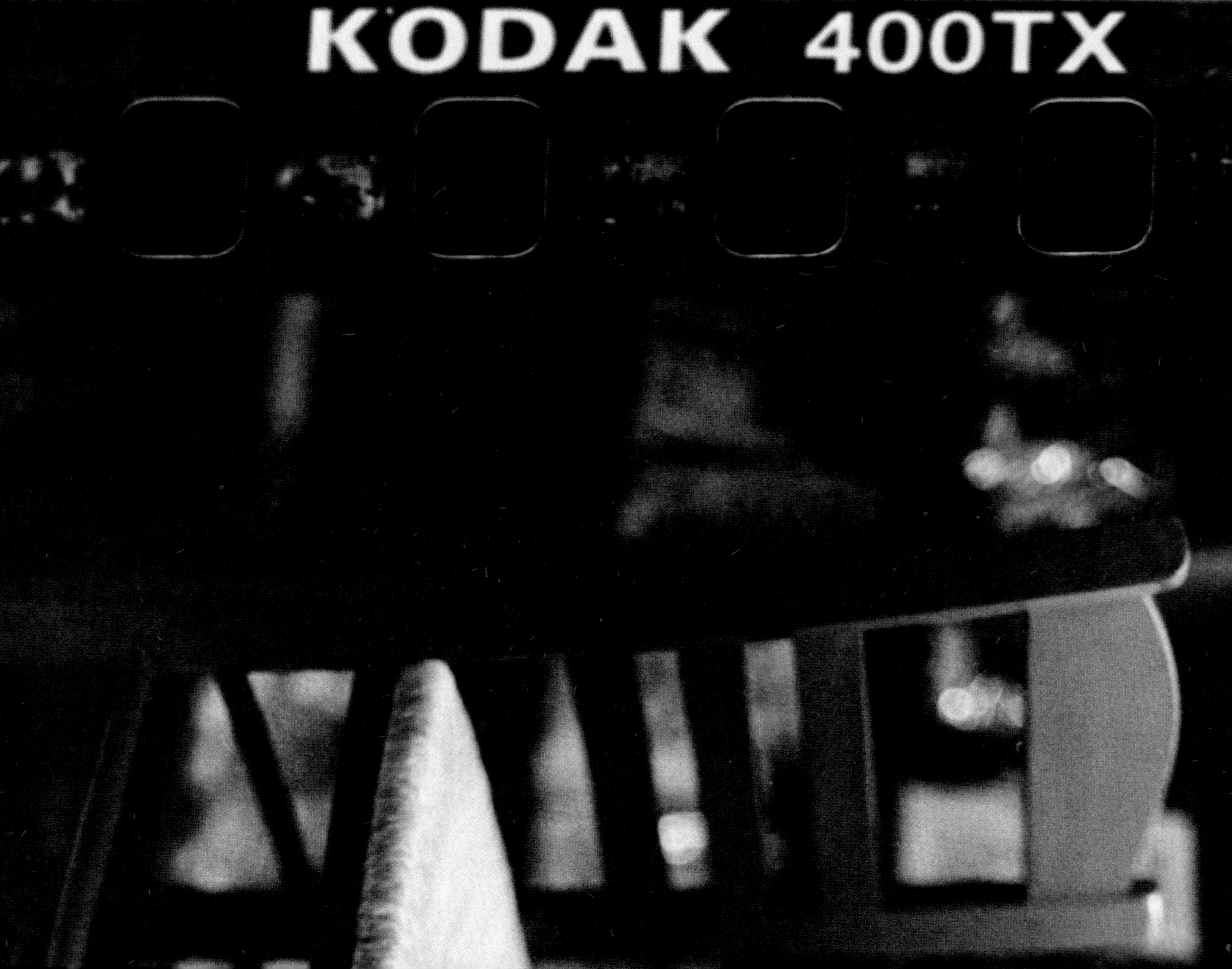
KODAK 400TX

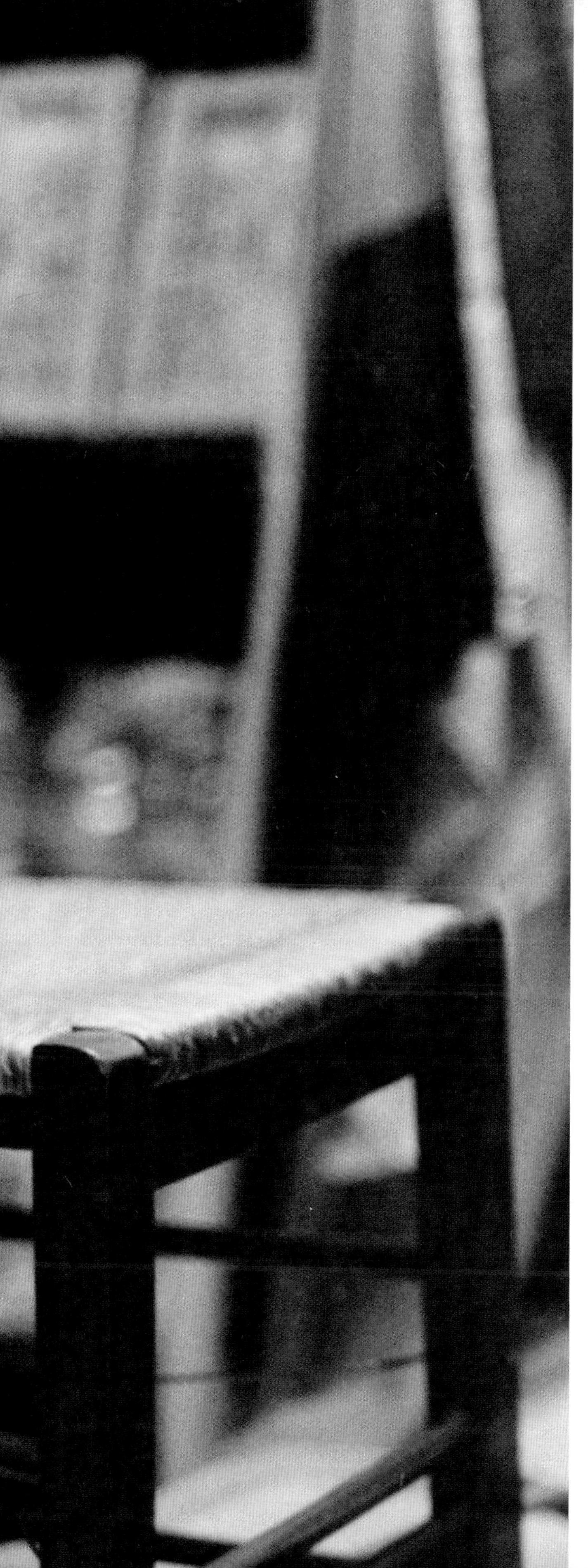

7
Post-Processing

7.1   Traditional

Darkroom work is time consuming and labor-intensive, but it's also one of the most satisfying aspects of film photography. Even though the types of paper available for printing your scanned and digitally processed pictures are excellent these days, they don't even come close to the haptic experience of a classic silver gelatin print on baryta paper.

Much of this satisfaction is due to creating a successful end result, but the interesting aspect of developing film is the process: retreating into a darkened room, working in dim, amber-colored light, and experiencing the moment when the first traces of a picture become visible on a print in the developer tray. There's something magical in this ritual.

You need certain things to produce your own prints. We are going to deliberately restrict ourselves to black-and-white prints—creating color prints is much more elaborate.

7.1.1   The Enlargement—General Principle

In the simplest case—for a black-and-white enlargement—a negative picture is projected onto a piece of photographic paper by an enlarger and exposed. Then, the exposed paper undergoes three chemical baths. The exact length of the baths will vary depending on the photo chemicals you use.

The exposed paper is placed into the tray with developer solution for about two minutes. After developing, the paper goes into the tray with a stop bath to stop the developer action. Then comes the last bath with the fixer. This takes about eight to ten minutes. In the last step, the picture is washed thoroughly to remove the last traces of fixer and other chemical remnants that could limit the storage properties of the finished print.

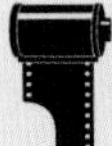 The photo chemicals used for creating photo prints are not significantly different from the ones used for negatives. Only the dilution of the chemicals is different.

7.1.2   Equipment for a Black-and-White Laboratory

The key for making good prints lies in meticulous handiwork, not automation. You can use relatively simple lab equipment, if it is good quality.

In the dry area of the lab, you will need an enlarger with a suitable lens, an exposure timer, and a masking frame. The enlarger should be sturdy and have a sufficiently large baseboard. The negative carrier, lens, and baseboard should be parallel or easy to adjust so you can make them parallel. As an additional bonus, some enlargers have a head that can be rotated to horizontal. A color-mixing head makes working with variable contrast paper easier. You can get a multitude of lenses of different qualities in specialist shops or on the secondhand market. The focal length of the lens determines the level of magnification. The quality and suitability for larger formats increases with the number of integrated lens elements. Three-element lenses are quite rare these days—they are suitable only for enlargements up to 13×18cm. Usually, you will find four- or six-element lenses being offered for sale. If you value good-quality lenses for your camera, you should apply similar standards to the darkroom, too, so the quality of the enlargement matches that of the shot.

For the wet area, you need at least four sufficiently large laboratory trays that should always be one size bigger than the paper size you are using. For each tray, you need a pair of lab tongs. You should also get enough bottles and measuring cylinders so you always have a full set for each processing step. We would advise you to use each bottle and measuring cylinder for only one of the processing steps. Otherwise you risk cross contamination and spoiled solutions.

The requirements in terms of which room you use are fairly minimal. You must be able to darken the room, and you need to have electricity and water. That's why some photo enthusiasts regularly turn their kitchen or bathroom into a darkroom. A dedicated room is perfect if it has enough space for a separate dry and wet area, plus enough storage space for photo papers and chemistry.

7.1.3   The Right Paper

As far as the emulsion carrier is concerned, there are two different types of black-and-white paper: resin-coated paper and fiber-based baryta paper.

With resin-coated paper (RC), the paper base is sealed with polyethylene on both sides, which stops water and photo chemicals from penetrating to the core. The necessary processing time, final wash, and drying time are much shorter than for fiber-based baryta paper. The longtime storage qualities of RC paper depend on the quality of the substrate. High-quality papers such as Ilford Multigrade and ADOX MCP can be stored with no loss of image quality for 60 to 80 years (or longer under optimal storage conditions).

Fiber-based (FB) baryta paper is the classic photo paper for high-quality black-and-white photos that can be archived and stored for many decades. It features a layer of barium sulfate (baryte) between the paper base and the emulsion. The paper core is not sealed, which is is the biggest disadvantage of baryta paper. Because it absorbs water and chemicals well, the final wash and drying time is much longer. The final wash can take up to an hour for optimum storage quality. The drying time is about 12 hours in open air. For making the greater processing effort, you are rewarded with the typical baryta sheen and a subjectively deeper and warmer looking picture.

The light-sensitive layer is the same for both types of paper. It consists of silver halides embedded in gelatin, just as with film. The silver halides are only sensitive to blue and violet light, which is why photo paper can be processed in safelight (yellow-green or amber light in the darkroom).

7.1.4 Grades

Black-and-white photo paper is manufactured as variable contrast paper or graded paper in different grades of hardness. Common grades are 0 (soft) to 5 (hard). By choosing the right grade, you can harmonize the contrast range of the negative and the photo paper. A negative with high contrasts needs a rather soft paper for optimal separation of tonal values. For a negative that has less pronounced contrasts, the opposite applies.

Variable contrast or multigrade papers are photo papers where the contrast behavior can be adapted. They have individual emulsions with different gradations. The silver halides in the harder grade layer are sensitized to other colors of light than those in the softer grade layer. Depending on the color with which you expose the paper, you can tease out a softer or harder grade.

Adapting the light in the corresponding spectrum can be done either with color foil filters or by setting a specific color of light in the color-mixing head.

7.1.5 The Contact Print

Especially today, when you can use hybrid processing (see page 195) to get excellent results, it makes sense to reserve working in the darkroom for those special pictures. Darkroom processing isn't about making a large number of prints as quickly as possible; instead, it's about achieving the best possible interpretation of your picture and creating a good print based on a specific negative.

The first step is creating a contact print. The contact print is your starting point for the pictures you are going to devote a lot of time to later. It helps with the decision of which picture you are going to use for printing, and which part of that picture will make it onto the print in which orientation.

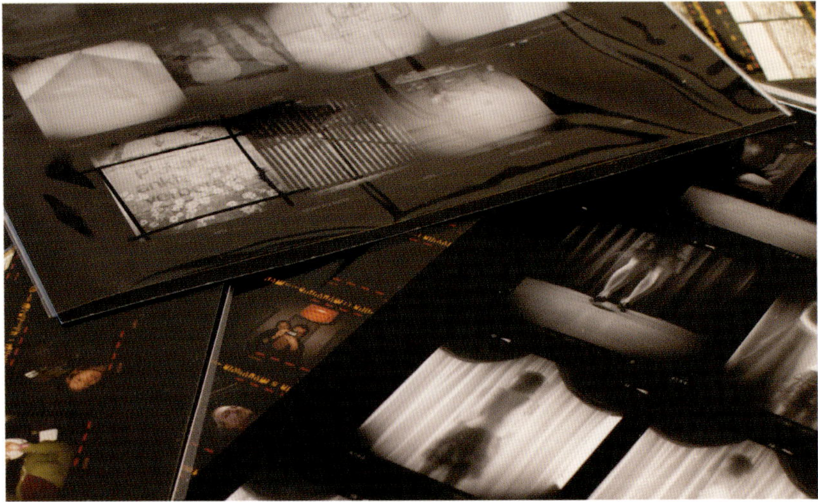

Contact prints

Under a safelight, place a sheet of photo paper under the enlarger and put the individual negative strips directly on top of the paper. Cover the negatives with a glass plate to ensure they lie flat. If you keep your film strips in a transparent pocket, you don't even have to take them out. Use softer-grade paper for the exposure so all areas of the negative show good detail. Here, it is more important to get clearly visible details in all image areas than to achieve the best exposure. To determine the exposure, you'll prepare test strips later.

As soon as the contact print is dry, you can use it to mark which picture you like and which ones you like so much that you want to enlarge them later. With a special easel or a frame made of cardboard, you can cover up all the unimportant image areas on the contact print and find the part of the picture you want to print. You can either mark the desired area directly on the contact print or put the contact print into a transparent pocket and then draw on it with transparency pens—just in case you change your mind one day.

With the finished contact print, you have a decision-making tool for later processing steps in the darkroom. You can retreat back into your photographic red room with a clear idea of how the picture should look when it's finished.

7.2   Hybrid Analog/Digital

These days, a large part of film photography is done in a hybrid process. In other words, it's a combination of analog photography and digital processing. After development, the films are digitized, and then refined in image-editing programs.

7.2.1   Scanner Types

Most scanners used for digitizing films are those that scan the image line by line. With increasingly higher-resolution camera sensors, scanning methods that take a picture of the whole image are also a good idea.

Flatbed

Flatbed scanners are the generalists among the scanners and also the cheapest option. They can cope with scanning both reflective material (such as photos on paper) and transparent originals, such as negatives and transparencies.

For transparent originals, the scanner has a backlight unit that is usually integrated into its lid. Depending on the model, this unit is narrower or wider and can then either scan 35mm or medium format, and may even be wide enough to scan negatives in 4×5-inch format.

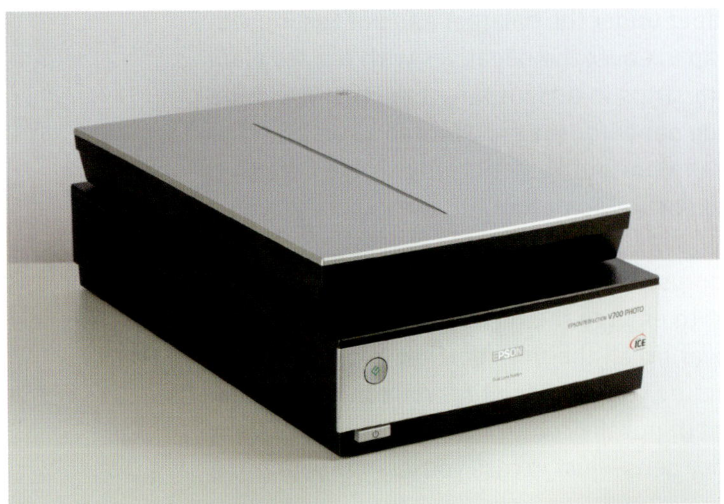

Epson V700 flatbed scanner

Generally, we would advise you to buy a scanner with a wider transparency unit. We've already met many newbies who thought 35mm was enough for them—only to learn they've branched out to a Mamiya 645 medium format camera six months later.

In addition to Epson and Reflecta devices, it is worth taking a look at the Canon CanoScan 9000 Mark II, which produces great results and can be found for as little as $200 on the used market (some are still available new for around $550).

Sheet-Feed Scanner

Sheet-feed scanners pull the negative over rubber rollers past a scan element. These devices are particularly suitable with 35mm film for batch processing whole films. Also, they usually offer a higher resolution than flatbed scanners.

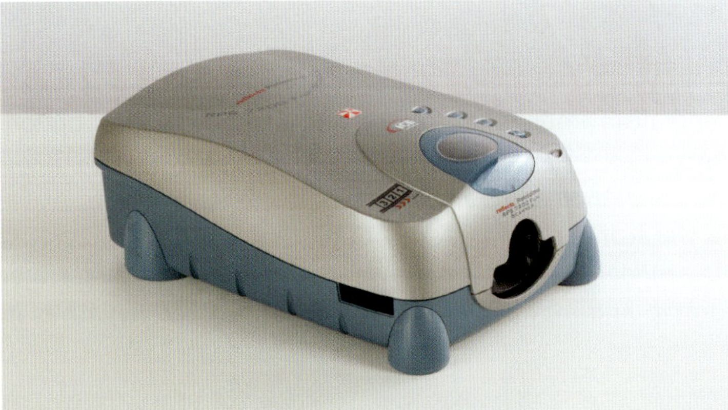

Reflecta RPS 7200

Scanners That Are Not Scanners

There is a group of negative scanners that are not really scanners. We are talking about devices that do not scan a picture line by line, but contain a backlight unit and a small digital camera that takes complete photos of the picture.

http://www.filmscanner.info/en/ FilmscannerTestberichte.html has lots of tests and information on film scanners.

This category of devices starts in a price class below \$100 and usually offers the option of saving the pictures directly to a memory card. Most of these devices are limited to 35mm format; some can also manage 120 medium format. Personally, we don't have any experience with these types of devices, but the low price suggests that you probably cannot expect an overly high dynamic range in the digital cameras or lenses used. Still, such a device can probably provide good results if you want to quickly capture negatives for a first overview, or if you're scanning snapshots.

The Professionals

In the higher price market, you can find scanners that meet considerably higher expectations. For example, there are scanners that you feed with slide magazines just like the good old slide projectors, but these machines automatically scan the pictures instead of projecting them on a wall. There are also high-end scanners by Hasselblad or drum scanners, but these are far outside the normal household budget.

Do It Yourself

You do not necessarily need to use a purchased scanner. With digital equipment, many photographers already have everything they need for digitizing negatives: a camera with corresponding resolution, a tripod, and a macro lens or a normal lens with extension tubes. The only thing you still need for a successful DIY solution is a transparency unit in the form of a light area that needs to be as even as possible. With a tripod and a diffusely backlit surface, photographers have been able to create high-quality "scans."

7.2.2 Scanner Parameters

Before buying a scanner, you are probably studying websites and data sheets. Some of the specifications you find there may be somewhat cryptic. Let's try to bring light to the darkness.

Density and Density Range

The density of a negative or positive is basically the same as its level of transparency. The less transparent it is, the higher its density. Ultimately, it's about how much light is absorbed by the dark areas in the image. The density range is the difference between the lowest density (D_{min}) and the highest density (D_{max}).

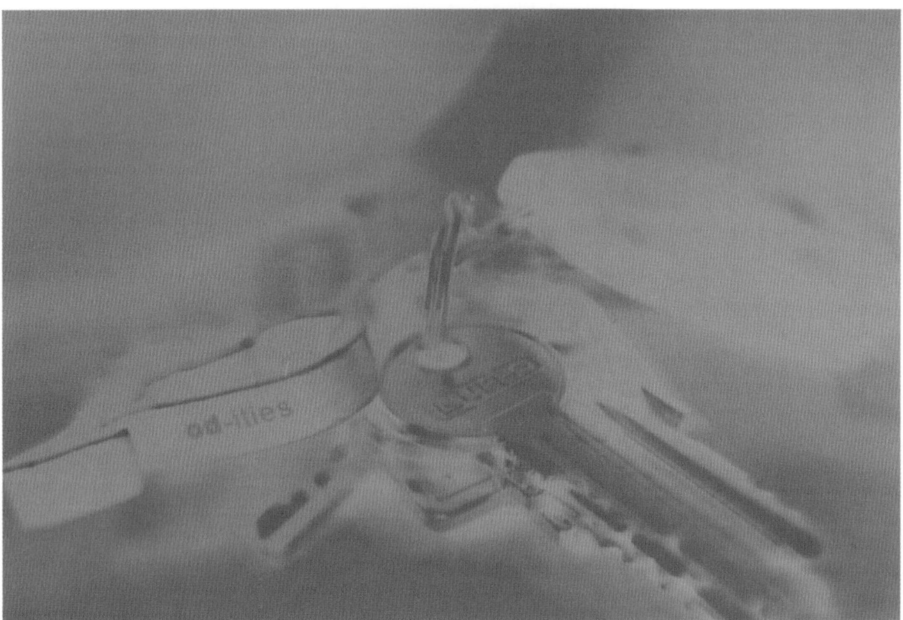

Negative with low density range

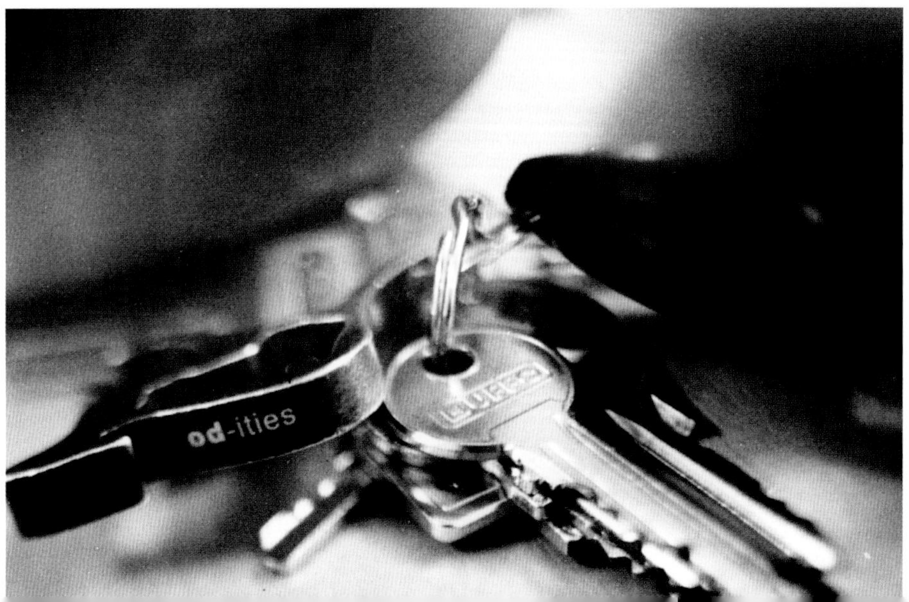

After scanning and developing

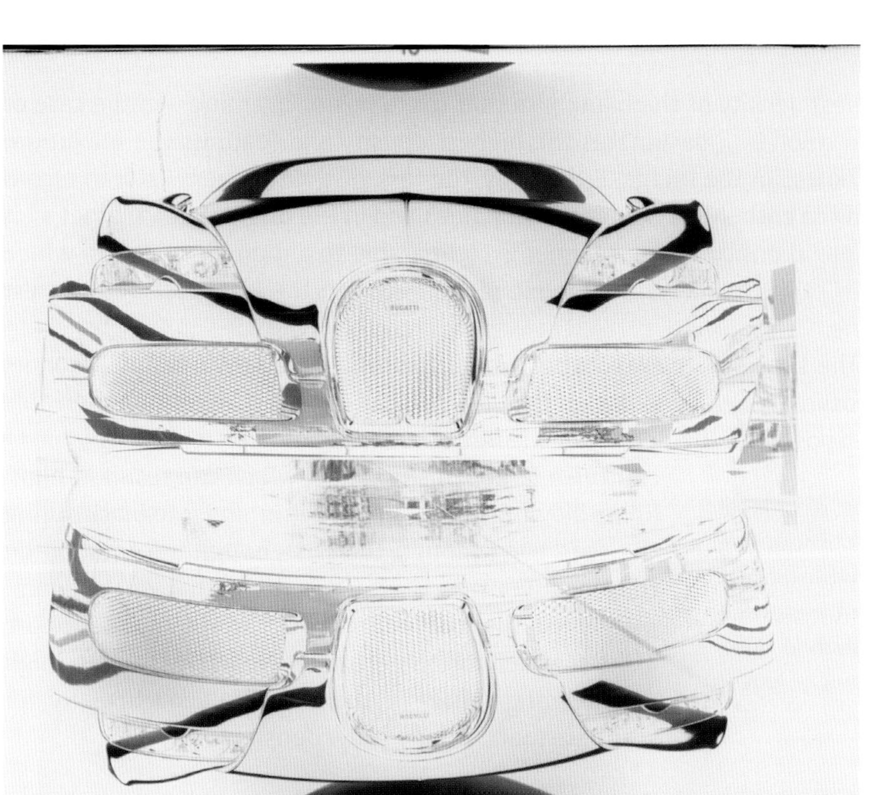

*Negative with
high density range*

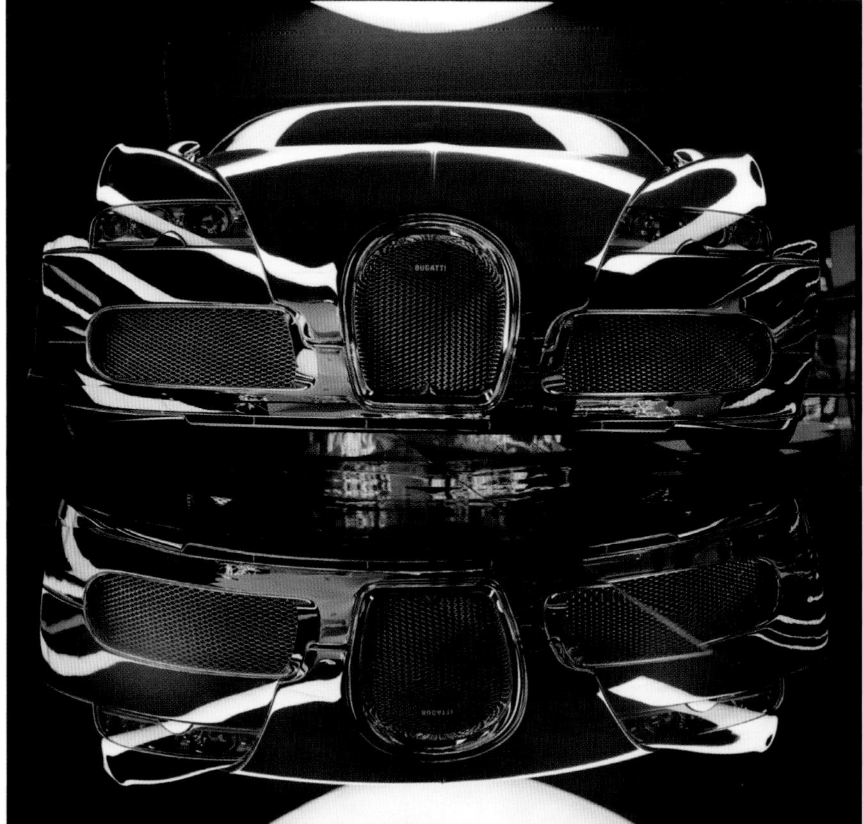

*After scanning
and developing*

D_{min} and D_{max}

D_{min} is the lowest density of the blank film that contains no silver and—in the case of color film—no color. D_{max} designates the highest density and features the maximum degree of blackness in the image. Either way, the task of the scanner is still to record details both in the entirely blackened picture areas and in the bright areas that let a lot of light through. In principle, the scanner is comparable to a digital camera, in which the sensor can capture a certain dynamic range between the brightest and darkest parts of a scene.

To achieve the best possible exposure when scanning a negative, many scanners meter for exposure (generally as part of the preview scan). Some scanners are then able to adapt the exposure to the density of the film. Cheaper scanners are often unable to capture a large density range, which can result in highlights blowing out or shadows running into black during the scan even though there is enough information on the negative. This is why negatives that do not completely use the maximum density range of the film are a little easier for the scanner. Negatives with a high density range make it more difficult, particularly for scanners that manage a low density range only.

In order to increase the recordable density range, some types of scanning software support a multi-exposure mode in which several differently exposed scans can be combined. This method does, however, require a correspondingly longer scanning time.

(True) Resolution vs. Step Size

Caution: The resolution of flatbed scanners usually comes out lower than the data on the packaging suggests. Sometimes the data sheet lists a resolution of 6400 dpi (dots per inch), but in reality, the resolution test shows only 2000 dpi. The reason for this is that the manufacturers like to use the theoretically possible resolution of a scan line for their data sheets, without taking into account the optical system of mirrors and lenses that is between the negative and the scan line.

Another problem is that in the case of scanners, resolution is two-fold. On one hand, we have the (theoretically possible) resolution of the scan line, and on the other, the stepping motor that moves the image or the scan line. Both axes contribute to the resolution, one in terms of horizontal movement, the other in vertical. This is often specified as two numbers for the resolution, e.g., AAAA × BBBB. When in doubt, go with the lower number.

35mm Scan

A small calculation will make it clearer what all this means in practical terms of resolution: A 35mm negative measures 24×36mm (0.95×1.42 inches). At 6400 dpi, that would be 6080×9088 pixels or an impressive 55 megapixels. But if we estimate 2000 dpi (a much more realistic figure for flatbed scanners), that only leaves 1900×2840 pixels, which is about 5.4 megapixels.

Medium Format Scan

Let's work it out for a medium format picture sized 6×7cm. If you convert centimeters to inches, the picture is 2.36×2.75 inches, which, at the same 2000 dpi resolution, results in 4720×5500 pixels or 25 megapixels. So with medium format and an affordable flatbed scanner, you are already within the resolution range of current digital cameras.

Large Format Scan

If we put a large format 4×5-inch negative onto the scanner at 2000 dpi, we get 8000×10,000 pixels, which equals 80 megapixels.

You can indeed select higher resolutions in the parameters of your scanning software, but in reality, this will have little effect on the sharpness of the resulting images. It just increases the time the scanner takes per picture.

The numbers quoted here are values that mainly refer to flatbed scanners, and are based on our personal experience. There are film feed scanners that can achieve higher resolutions.

7.2.3   Scanning Software

Due to the high number of different systems and manufacturers, we cannot discuss all types of scanning software in detail here; but there are currently two systems that either come with a corresponding scanner or can be used as universal program for many scanners: Silverfast and VueScan.

Silverfast

Many scanners these days come with a limited version of Silverfast. To get the full range of features, you usually have to pay for an upgrade. Silverfast is tied to a particular scanner. To use another scanner, you usually also have to purchase another version of Silverfast.

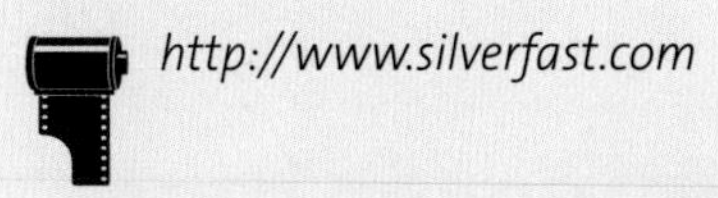

VueScan

According to the manufacturer, VueScan is compatible with more than 2500 different scanners and
offers a large range of functions. However, it does
require a bit of user know-how, especially for scan-
ning films, and beginners may find it a bit confusing to use. You do have the option of
testing the software with a free trial version.

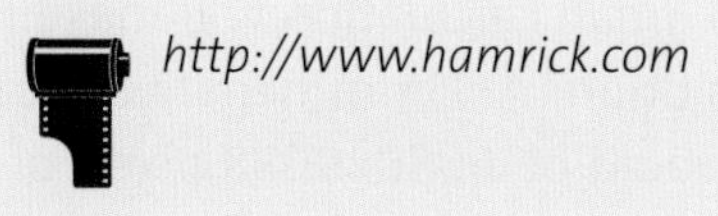

Manufacturer-Specific Software

Some scanner manufacturers now rely entirely on Silverfast or VueScan and are no
longer developing their own proprietary scanning software. But there are still manufacturers with proprietary software, such as Epson and its Epson Scan software.

7.2.4   Scanner Profiling

Just like monitors or digital cameras, scanners are subject to certain manufacturing
tolerances and aging processes. These affect the exactness of the scanned colors and
contrasts. For black-and-white scans, the process described here is sufficient. We personally do not work with special profiles for scanning black-and-white originals.

If, however, you want to balance out the tolerances even more or you want to achieve
a greater accuracy in color, you will have to deal with the process of scanner profiling
sooner or later.

7.2.5   Accessories

Certain accessories are useful for increasing the quality of your scans.

Brushes

"Lint is a film photographer's biggest enemy." —Michael Weyl

"So is cat hair." —Monika Andrae

Negatives consist of plastic and gelatin, and sometimes have the tendency to become
statically charged. That's why they attract dust and fluff. With a good brush, you can
effectively remove the dust before scanning.

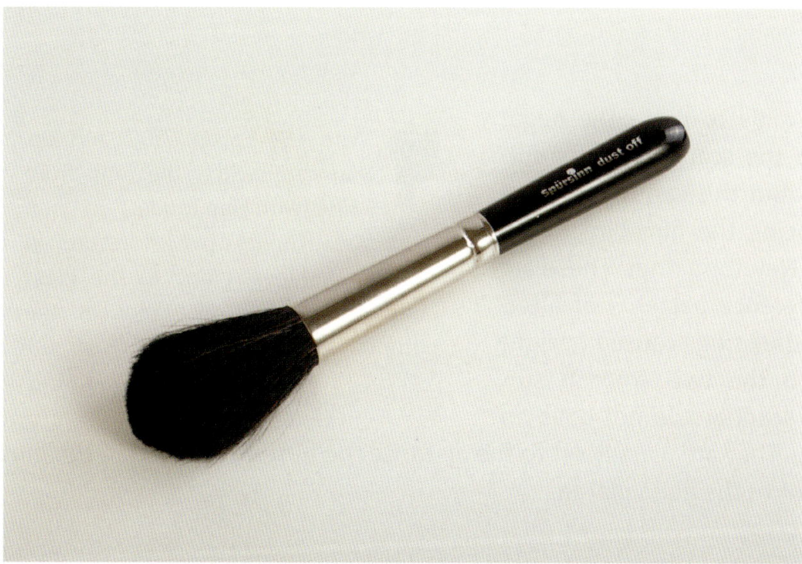

Brush

Antistatic Wipes or Gloves

Antistatic wipes or gloves can also help keep dust off. We use the wipes for cleaning the scanner's glass surface from fingerprints and dust.

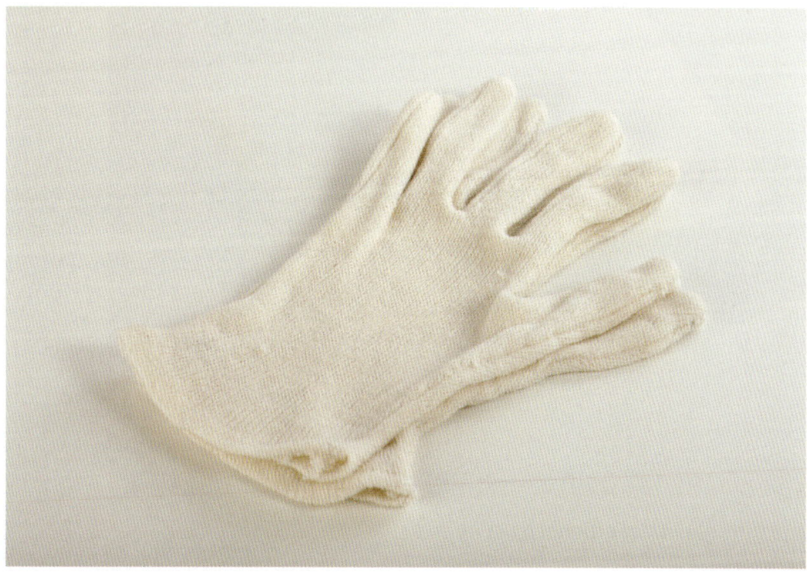

Gloves

Antistatic gloves stop negatives from getting statically charged and prevent finger-prints ending up on your valuable pictures.

Scanning on Glass

Generally it is possible to place the negatives directly onto the scanner's glass surface to scan them. But this can cause problems. For one, placing the film directly on
glass can result in Newton's rings. These are
ring-shaped interference patterns of alter-
nating bright and dark rings caused by light
reflection between the two smooth surfaces. Also, cheap scanners do not have an
autofocus function. They are usually set to the distance the film would be at in the film
holder supplied, not to the glass platen.

> With the Epson V700 and up, you can switch the lens from "Film (with Film Holder)" to "Film (with Area Guide)," which results in shifting the focal plane to the glass plate. However, it also reduces the potential resolution.

Holders Supplied

All manufacturers supply film holders for scanning film; some can even hold mounted
slides for scanning. Depending on the manufacturer, these inserts can be easy to use.

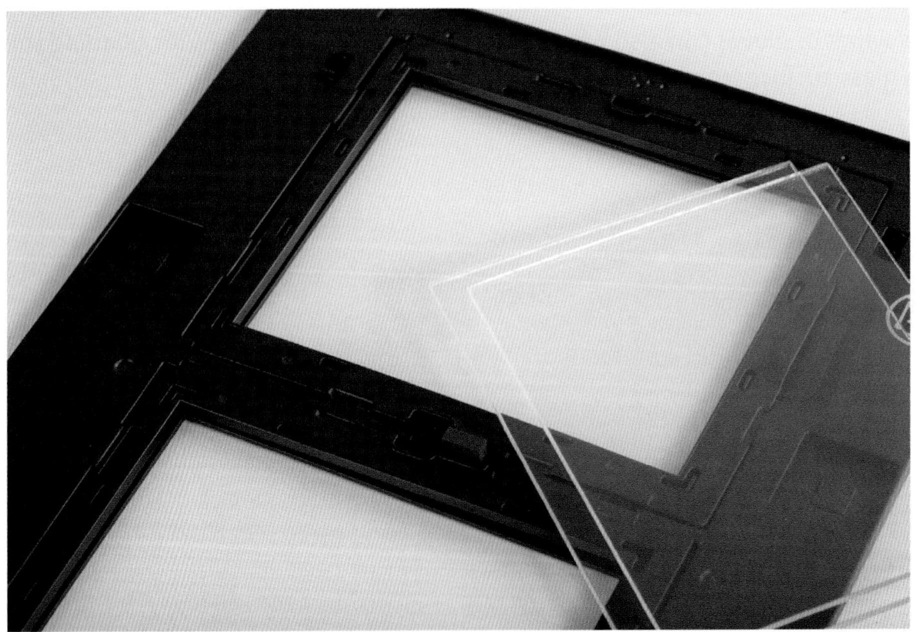

Negative holder for large format with additional glass inserts

Glass Inserts

For the flatbed scanners popular for medium and large format, an accessory market has evolved. Many products are available for making scanning easier and for improving results. For some scanner models by Epson, for example, the German company Monochrom and the website *www.betterscanning.com* offer glass inserts that keep the negatives nice and flat. Take out the upper plastic sections from the film holder, and use the glass inserts to stop the negatives from curling. The glass inserts are anti-Newton glass, i.e., they have been specially treated to prevent Newton's rings. You need to make sure the slightly rough side of the insert is resting on the film. (You can tell which side is which if you hold the glass at an angle into the light.)

Alternatives

To scan negatives including the edges, the film holder DigitaLIZA, made by the company Lomography, comes in two sizes: 35mm and medium format. The holders pinch the negatives at the outermost edges and enable you to scan them complete with perforation, including the exposed image numbers on the edge.

7.2.6   The Scanning Process

Each type of scanning software offers various automatic modes that should do a lot of the work for you. They can set the exposure automatically, remove scratches, and smooth grain. Unfortunately, these auto modes rarely produce high-quality results. Overexposure and underexposure are common, scratch removal often messes up and removes important details from our valuable photos, and the automatic grain smoothing makes the picture "digitally smooth" again.

  We can do much better. To get optimum results, we are going to show you the entire process, from inserting the negative to digital editing, using the example of a black-and-white medium format negative.

Overview of the Scanning Process

Example: Flatbed scan of a black-and-white medium format negative.

1.   Dust and clean the glass platen with an antistatic cloth.
2.   Place the negatives into the suitable film holder.
3.   If you want the negatives to stay flat, you can use a suitable glass insert accessory.
4.   Dust the negatives from both sides, with bellows or a brush, for example.
5.   Close the scanner, and start the scan preview.
6.   Set the scan area in the preview, or let the scanner determine it automatically.
7.   Set the parameters for the scan. This includes settings for resolution, bit depth, sharpening, and automatic dust removal.
8.   Use the histogram preview to set the correct exposure.
9.   Specify the file type and location for saving your scan.
10. Start the scan.

Dusting the Glass Surface

First, clean the scanner's glass thoroughly with an antistatic cloth to remove finger-prints, dust, fluff, and cat hair.

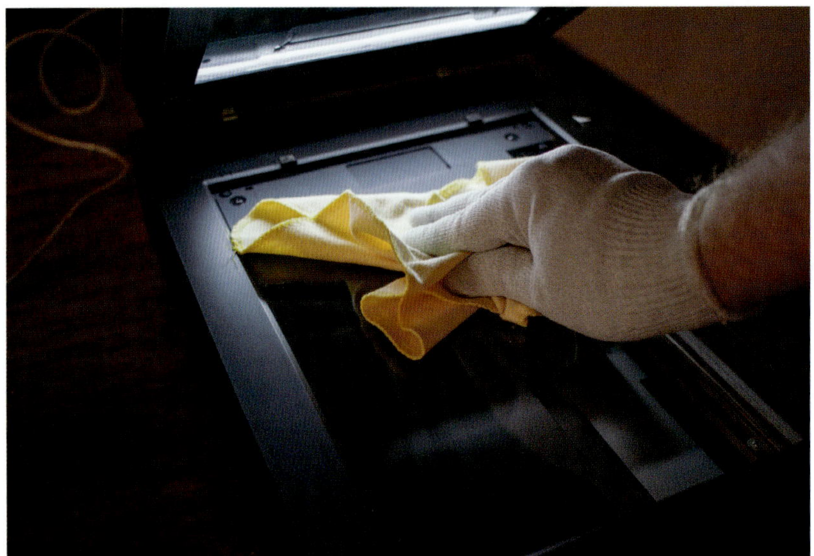

Wiping the scanner's glass with antistatic cloth

Inserting the Negative

Place the negative holder onto the scanner, and insert the negatives.

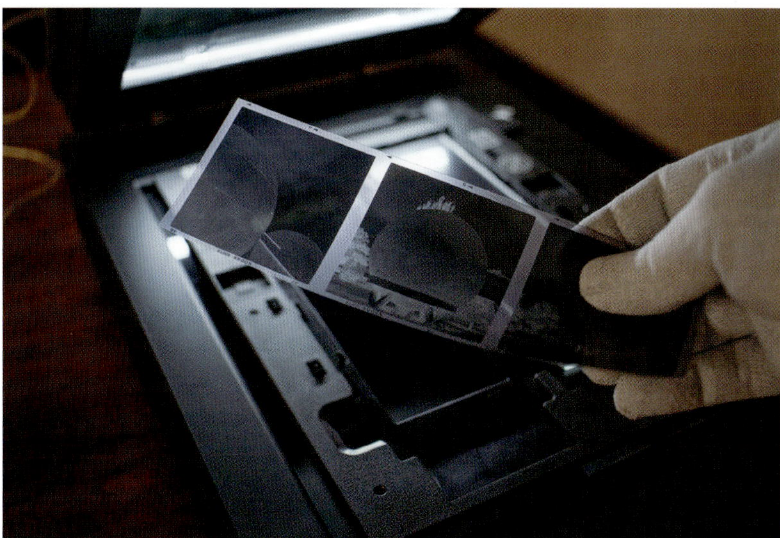

Inserting the negative

Adding the Glass Insert

We use Monochrom or *betterscanning.com* glass inserts. These are not obligatory, but they keep the negatives flat. Before you can use them, you need to remove the upper part ("lid") of the negative holders. Wipe the glass inserts with an antistatic cloth, just as you did with the scanner glass surface.

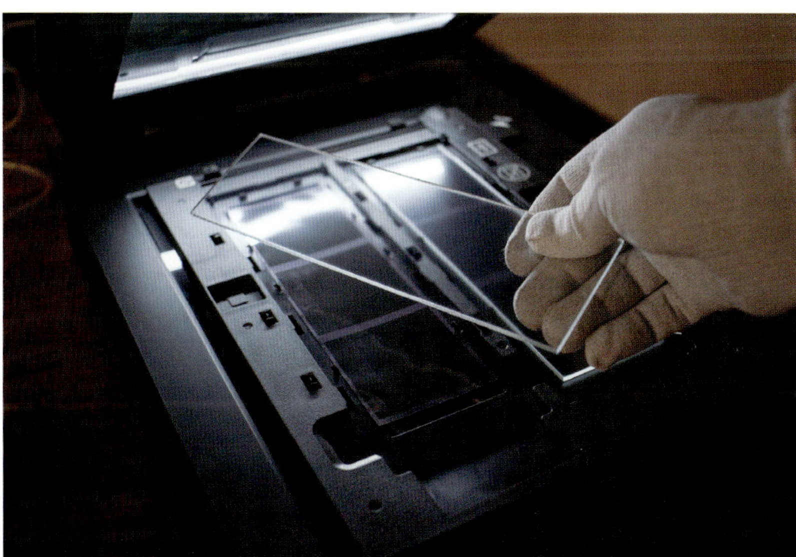

If available: Use glass inserts to keep negatives flat.

Dusting the Negative

Either use a small bellows to remove dust from the negative or use a suitable brush. We consider this step mandatory, both before adding the glass insert and after.

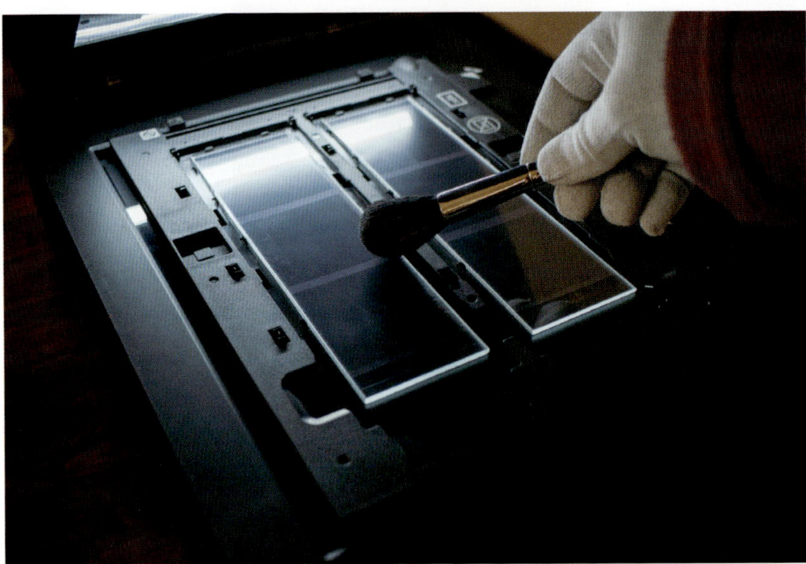

Dusting negatives with brush

Preview

Now it's time for the preview scan. After the scanner's light source has warmed up...

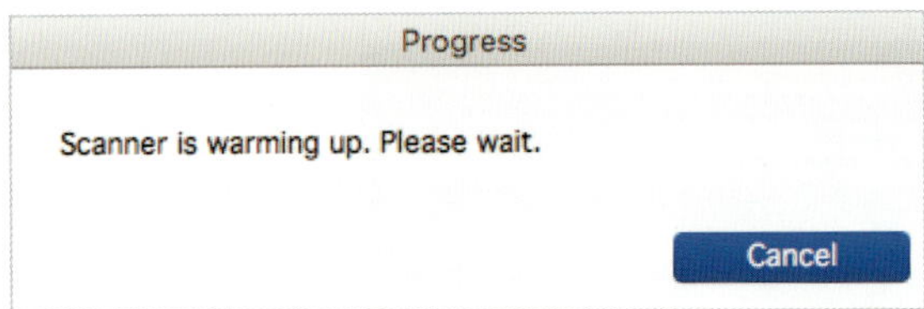

Warm-up stage

...the preview scan only takes a few seconds. Depending on the scanner settings, it will try to automatically find the image for you and crop it.

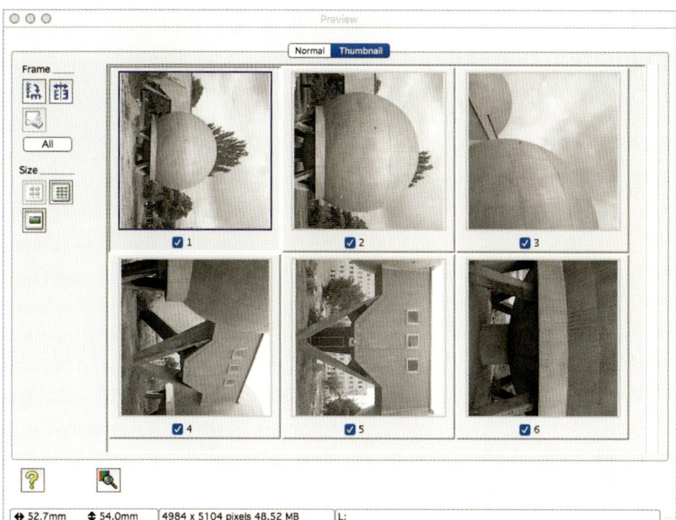

Automatic preview

Or switch to normal preview to view the entire scan area.

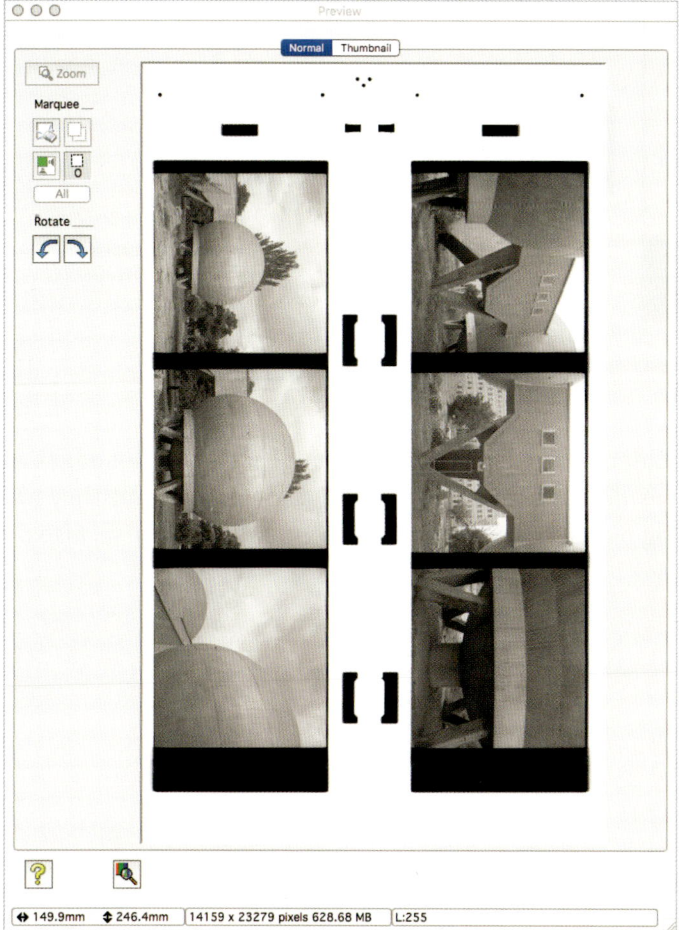

Complete preview

Letting the software crop the image automatically only works properly if you have set the right image size in the configuration beforehand.

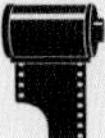 The auto crop sometimes removes too much from the image edges. That's why we prefer to use the normal preview and select the scan areas a bit bigger, to be on the safe side. Any excess material can be easily removed later on.

Setting the Scan Area

Next, select the area you want to scan in the preview. We usually select it a bit larger than the size of the negative so we still have space later for cropping the edges neatly.

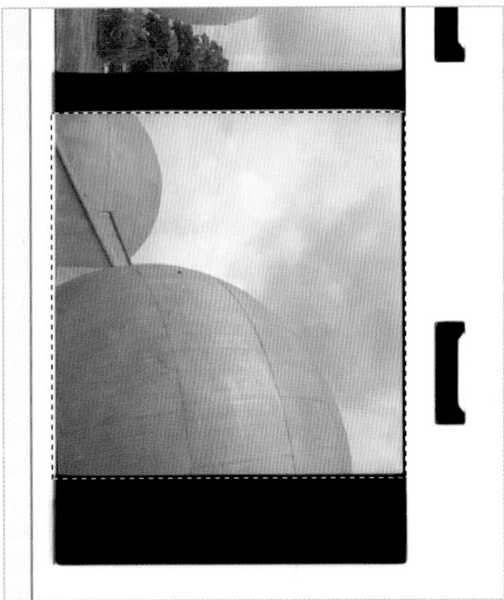

The scan area has been set manually.

Depending on the negative holder, you also have the option of scanning the edges of the negative. Sometimes this is done deliberately to show the viewers that they are looking at an uncropped analog picture. Not removing the edge can, of course, also be part of your artistic expression.

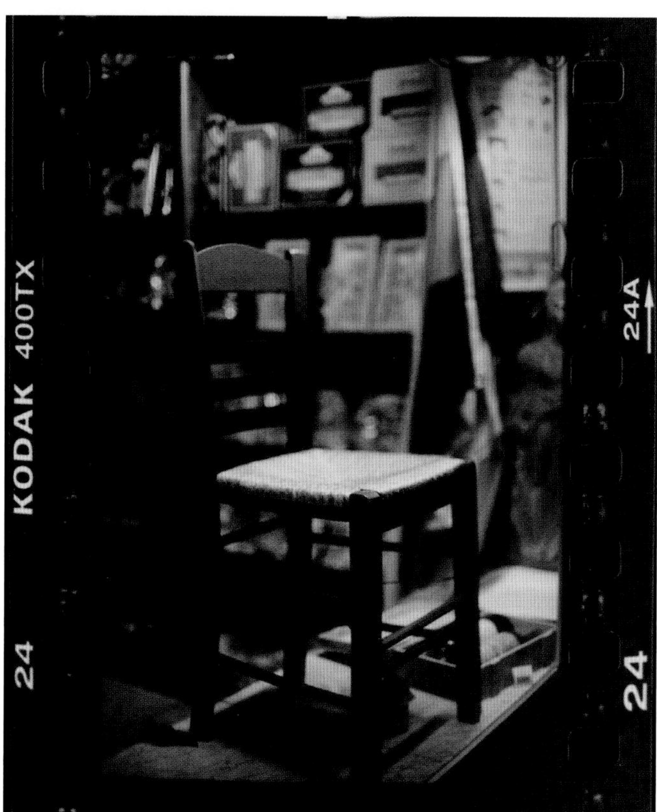

35mm scan with image edges and perforation

Selecting the scan area also has another function: For automatic exposure, it determines what is factored into the calculation and what is not. For example, if you have included many very bright areas outside of the picture, the scan may end up too dark in the end. In that case, we use manual control.

Settings

Before we start with the actual scan, let's have a look at the main window of the Epson Scan software. First, switch to *Professional Mode* so you can see all the available options.

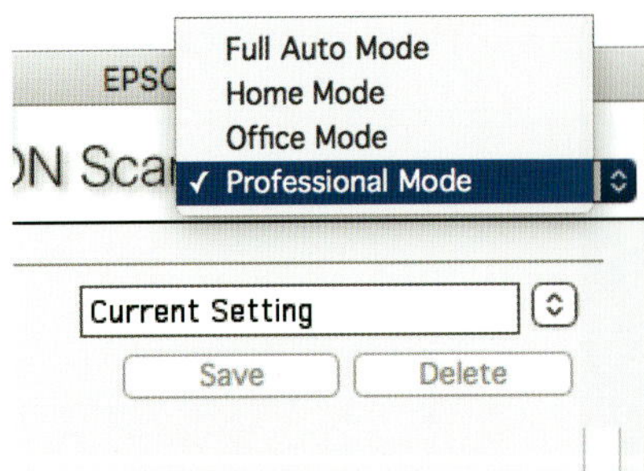

Switching to Professional Mode

Image Types

If you select *B&W Negative Film* for the *Film Type*, the software will automatically turn the negative into a positive image for you. In the *Image Type* setting, set the scan of black-and-white negatives to *16-bit Grayscale*. This ensures that the highest possible resolution in the tonal values is achieved. For color scans, use 48-bit color. Then each of the three color channels is scanned at 16 bits for the highest possible number of brightness levels.

The fewer bits you scan with, the less leeway you have later when editing the contrasts. This is particularly important for "thin" negatives, which appear low in contrast after the scan.

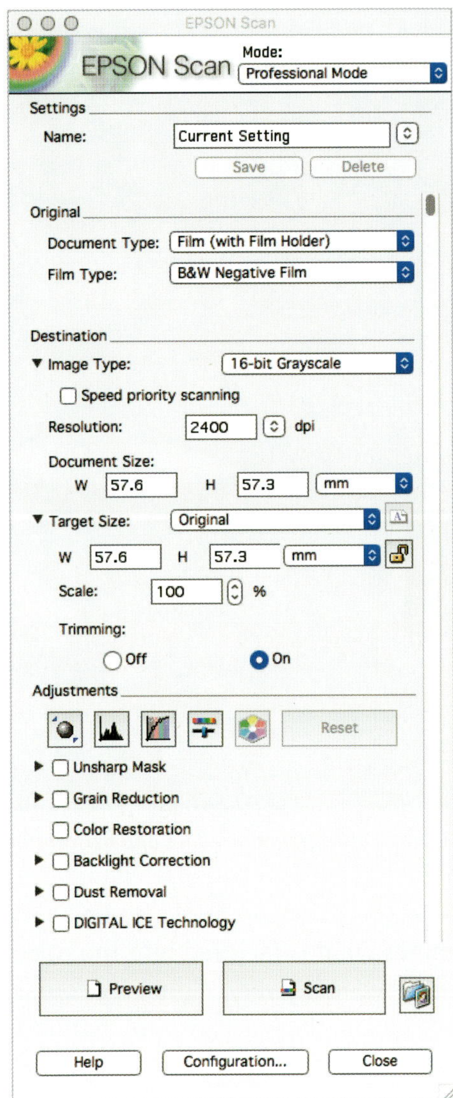

Epson Scan—main window

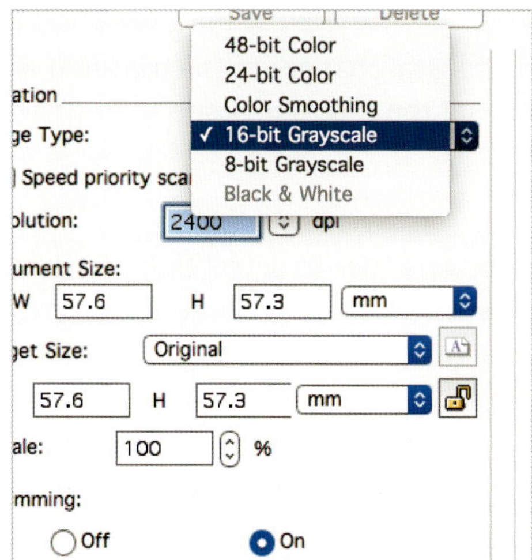

Setting the image type

Resolution

The Epson V750 has a resolution of up to 2300 dpi, according to the relevant test reports. So we usually set the scan resolution to 2400 dpi. Our experiments with higher resolutions have shown that no additional detail is achieved with a resolution of 4800 dpi or more—it only makes the files much bigger. The scan times also get longer. 6×6cm medium format negatives at 2400 dpi yield files of about 30 megapixels.

Unsharp Mask

The *Unsharp Mask* setting instructs the scan software to digitally sharpen the image after scanning. But you can do a much better job of this in digital post-processing (if it is necessary at all). Turn this setting off.

Grain Reduction

The grain is an important component of the analog picture. The digital grain reduction gives the picture an unnaturally smooth finish during scanning. Turn this setting off.

Color Restoration

For black-and-white pictures, you do not need the *Color Restoration* setting. For scanning color negatives (keyword: orange mask), this function can help create more natural-looking colors. Old, faded negatives can also benefit from this feature. Turn this setting off for black-and-white scans.

Backlight Correction

The *Backlight Correction* function results in further digital changes to the picture that tend to cause more problems, especially if you have set the exposure properly. Turn this setting off.

Dust Removal

If you enable the *Dust Removal* option, the scan software tries to detect fluff and dust and remove it via the software. This rarely works very well and tends to have side effects; it can cause important image areas to be accidentally interpreted as dust, so they are removed. Turn this setting off.

Digital ICE

ICE stands for Image Correction and Enhancement. This procedure helps remove scratches and dust on negatives. It involves a second scan (in addition to the original one) with an infrared light source that makes only dust and scratches visible. This scan is then used to correct the first scan.

This method works well for color negative and slide film. For black-and-white film, the results are almost always worse, and the scan takes considerably longer to complete. Turn the *Digital ICE* setting off for black-and-white film.

Exposure and Contrasts

After selecting the scan area, you can either let the scanner determine the exposure and set the black point, white point, and contrast curve, or you can set these yourself. We prefer a mixed approach. We first turn off the auto-exposure in the configuration (continuous auto exposure: off). Then we click the button for automatic exposure.

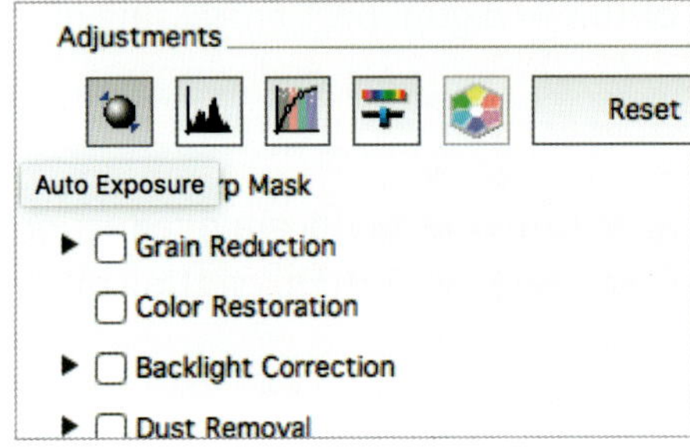

Automatic exposure

In the picture, you see the (relatively narrow or thin) histogram of the preview. The three arrows (black, gray, and white) below the histogram show how the scanner has automatically selected the black point, midtones, and white point. Now you can adapt the black and white points without clipping the histogram.

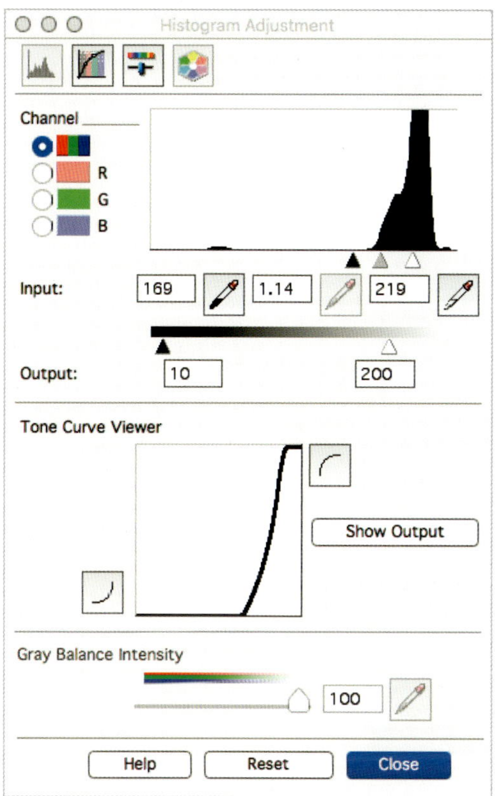

Before

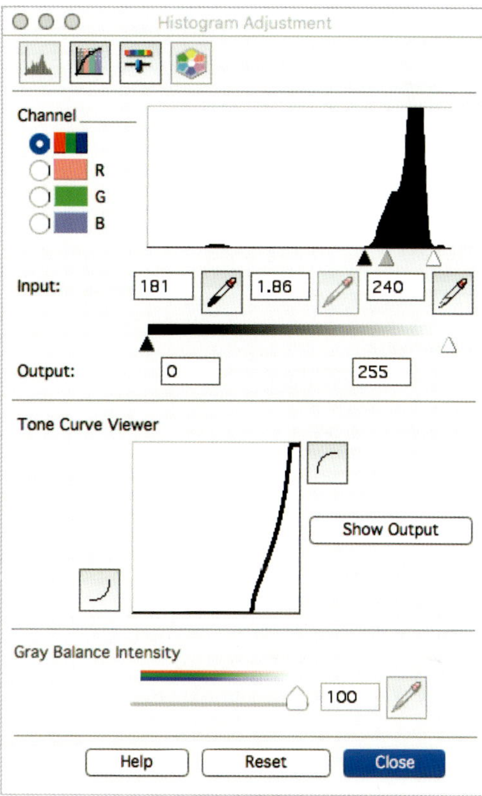

After

If in doubt, drag the arrows outward a bit further. This prevents overexposure and underexposure when scanning. The aim is to get a picture that is as complete as possible for editing, and that has as much information as possible, both in the highlights and the shadows.

You should change the sliders for *Output* from 10 and 200 to 0 and 255. This also ensures that the scan maintains the biggest possible contrast range for later editing.

Scanning

Before you click the Scan button, you should play it safe and take another look at the settings—particularly *Unsharp Mask,* which has the tendency to turn itself back on from time to time. Now you will be asked where you want to save the pictures, and in what format.

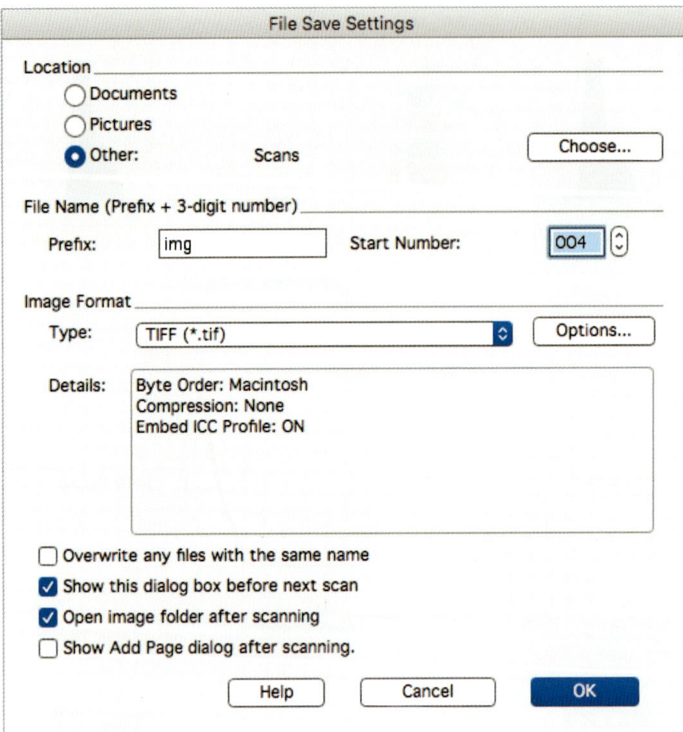

Many questions

Set the file location and file name. The file format is particularly important here. Because we are scanning with a depth of 16 bits, we need to select a format that can hold the corresponding amount of information. The most suitable is TIFF.

Now the scan process can start. Depending on the number of pictures and the resolution you chose, you have time to go stretch your legs or make a cup of coffee. The scanning process can take several minutes per individual picture. In our case, Epson Scan creates an uncompressed grayscale TIFF file from the 6×6cm medium format negative. The TIFF file has a color depth of 16 bits and an edge size of 5389×5257 pixels. This file is ideal for digital editing.

Editing

For digital editing, we use Adobe Lightroom. But you can carry out these steps with any common image-editing software that can handle 16-bit TIFF files.

Import

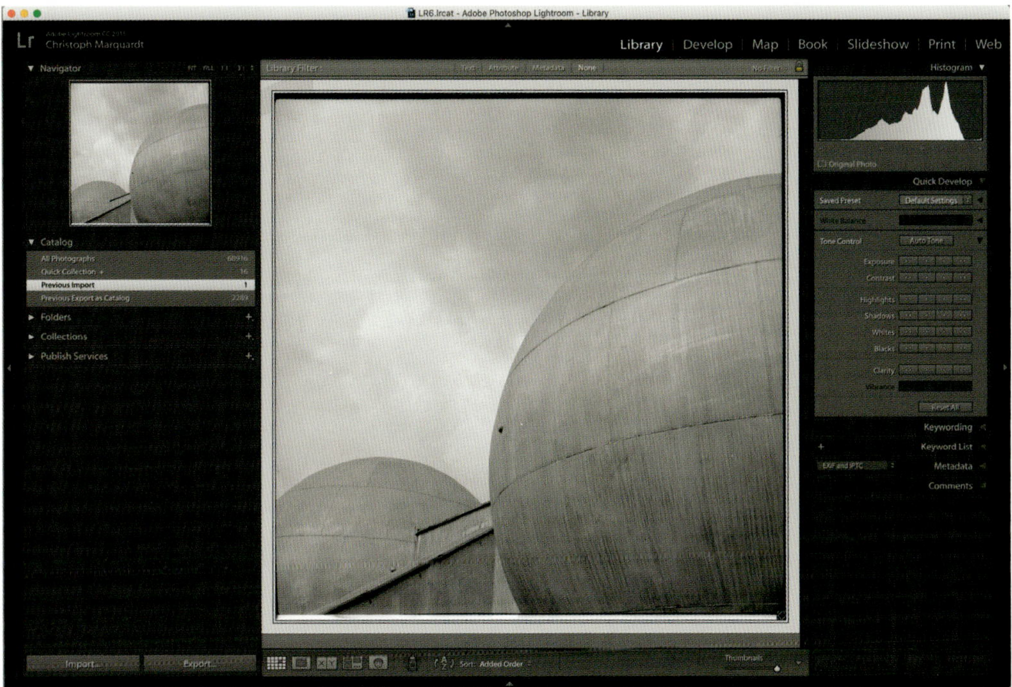

Importing

First, we import the picture into our software. There, we can see the histogram that we made wider by setting the black and white points after the scan. The picture is now considerably less "thin" than before the scan.

Crop

Cropping

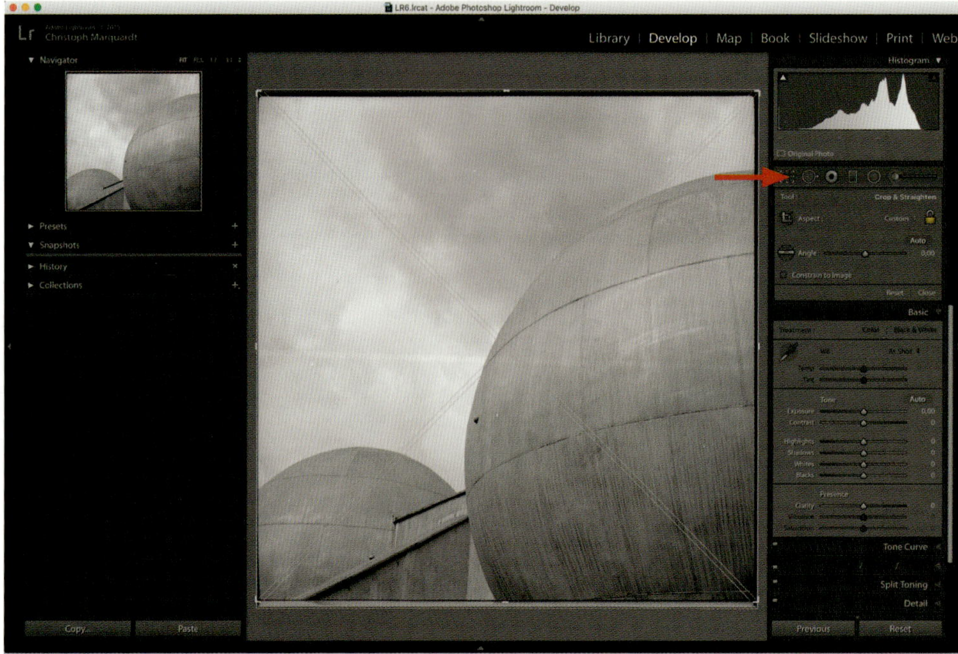

If the scan area we set in the preview was too large, we can now crop the picture to its final format.

Adapt Contrasts

Adapting contrasts

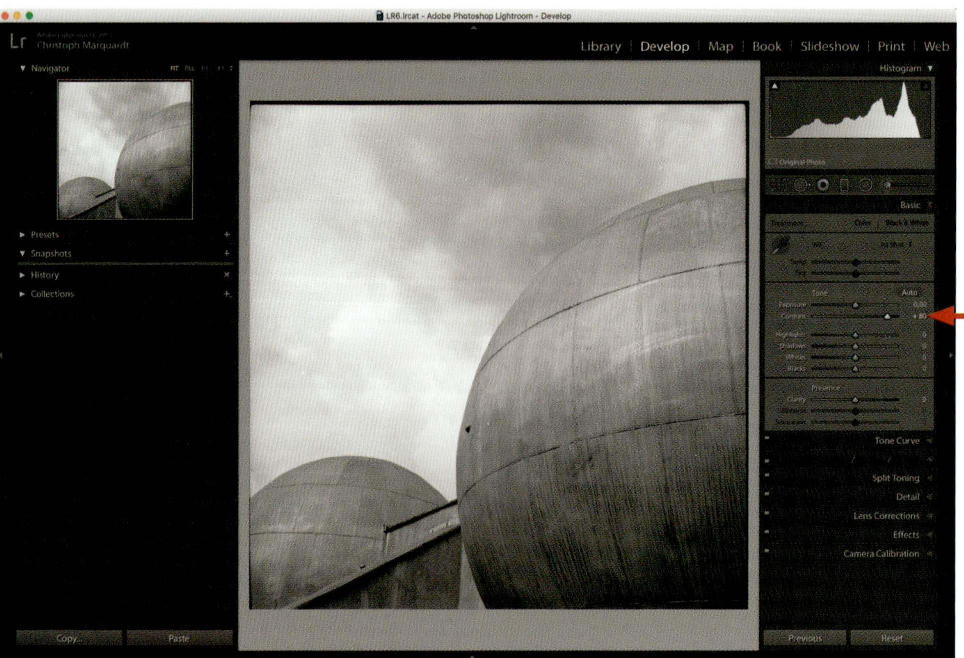

After scanning, the pictures are often a bit low in contrast, too bright or too dark, and have to be adjusted. In this case, we adapt exposure, contrast, highlights, and shadows accordingly. This process approximately corresponds to choosing the paper grade and exposure in the analog darkroom.

Retouching

Now you will see how tidy your work was. Dust and fluff might have crept in after exposing during drying and scanning. In the past, scratches on negatives and on printed pictures had to be retouched using very fine brushes and albumen. Today we can do it more quickly and digitally.

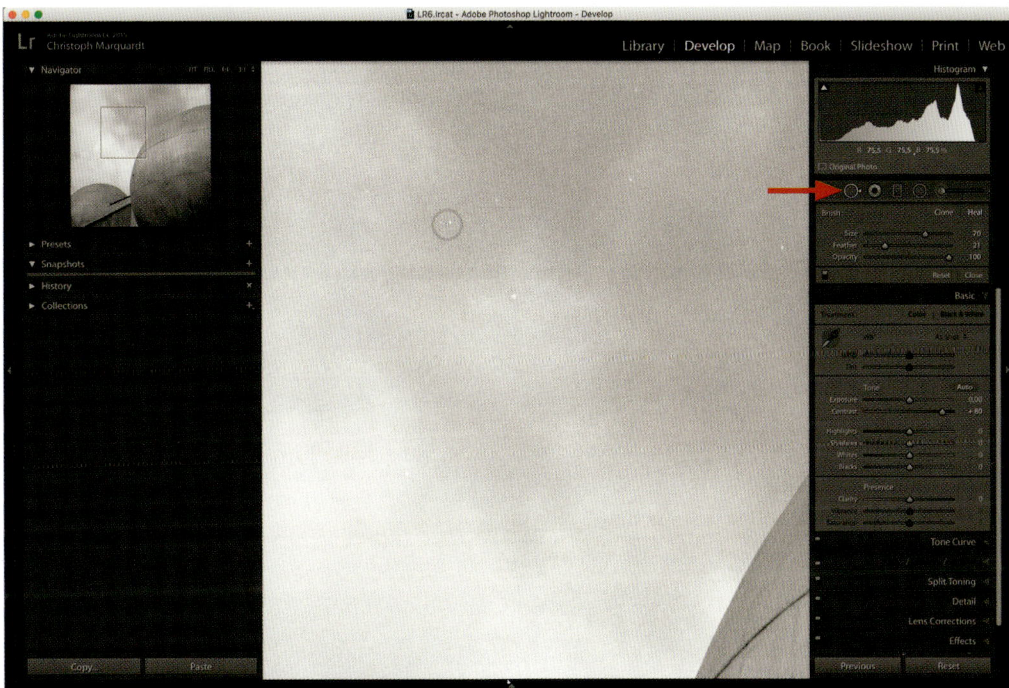

Retouching #1

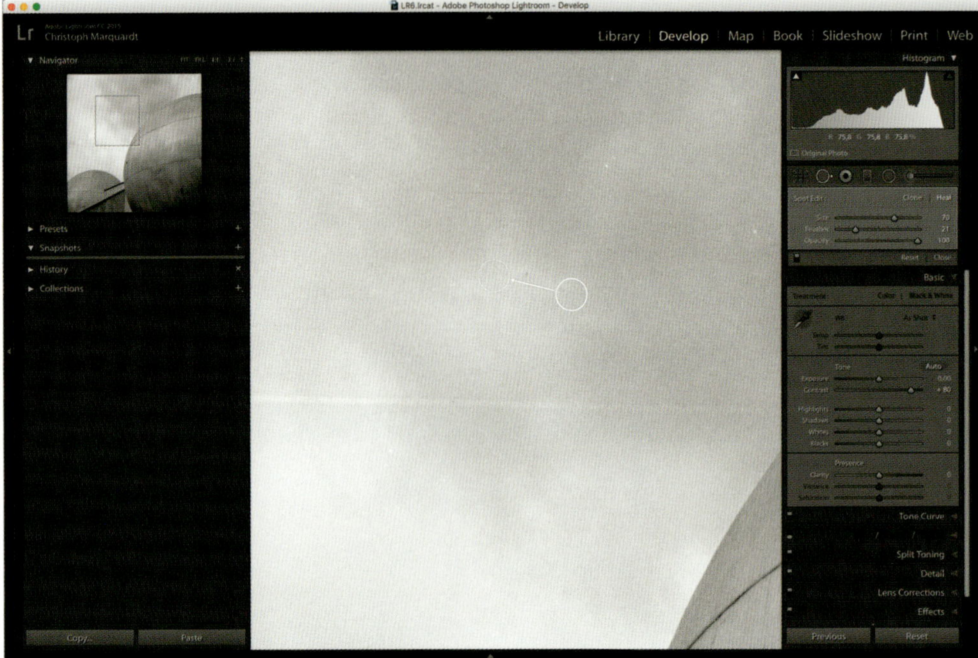

Retouching #2

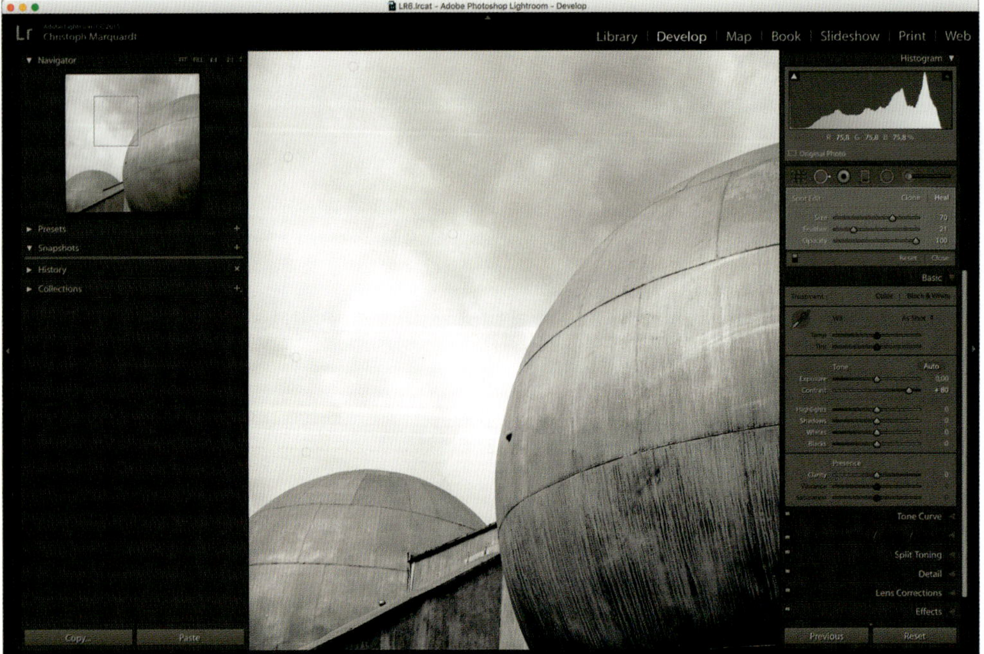

Retouching #3

About 20 areas on this picture had to be repaired.

Split Toning

This step is optional. It corresponds to another method of the analog darkroom. The printed black-and-white picture is composed of two elements.

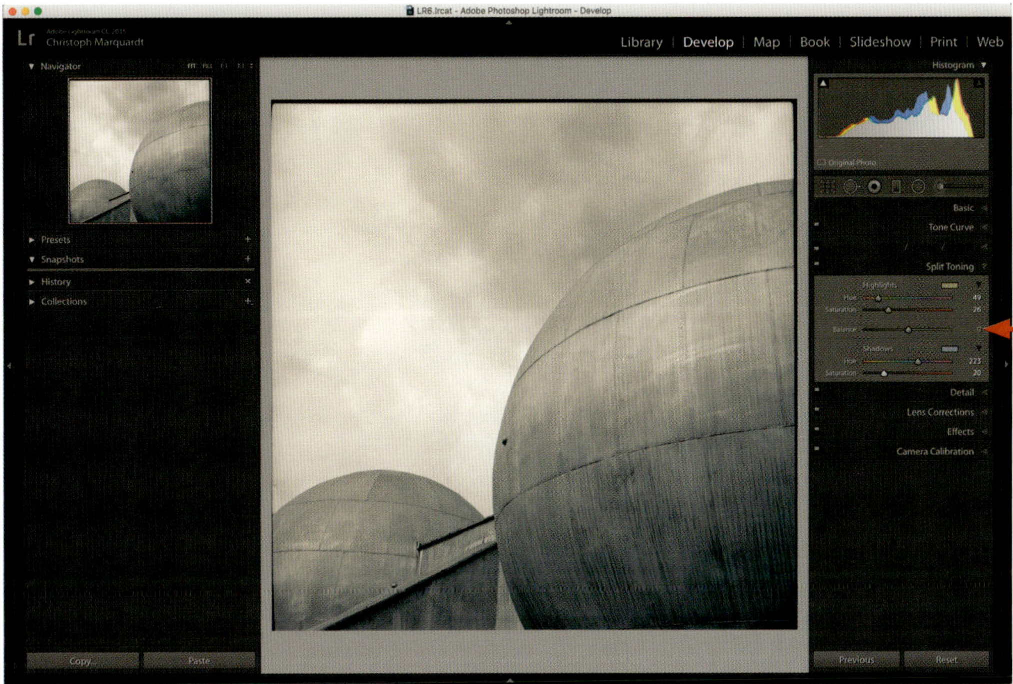

Split toning to taste

The bright photo components are the areas where the photo paper shines through. Depending on the paper tone, the highlights of the picture can take on warm, neutral, or cool tones. The shadows of the picture consist of silver. This, too, can take on a color tone during developing. The best-known example is sepia toning. But there are also toners that color the silver blue, golden, platinum, or copper.

With split toning, you can mimic this process in the digital workflow by coloring the highlights (the paper) and the shadows (silver) separately. In our case, we gave the highlights a warm tone and dipped the shadows to a light blue. The picture is now ready for sharing or printing.

7.2.7 Scanning Without a Scanner

Digital cameras offer ever-higher resolutions and the quality of current macro lenses can be phenomenal. This combination is also great for digitizing negatives and slides. Even smartphones with macro capability can be a viable option. This is not only faster than scanning, but also often provides better resolution than most flatbed scanners.

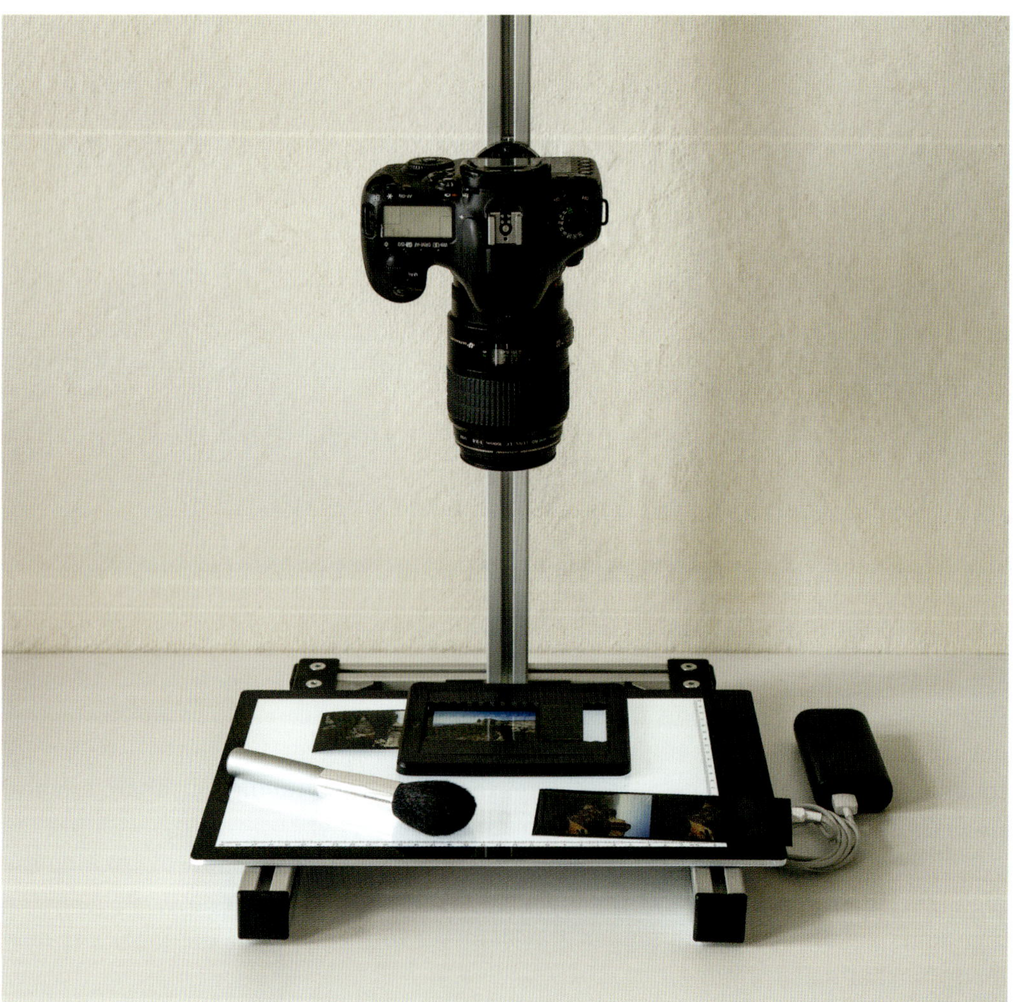

Photographing slides and negatives in good quality: Copy stand, camera with macro lens, light source, film mask, and dust brush

What You Need

- A light source. You can find USB-powered light panels in the craft/copy supplies section, but of course also at photo supply stores. For black-and-white, the light quality is secondary. For color, we have had good experiences even with relatively inexpensive lights. As an alternative to the DIY approach, there are now suppliers who offer complete solutions.

- A tripod. To get started, a normal tripod is sufficient, as long as you can align the camera to point straight down onto a table. A spirit level will be helpful with this. The more parallel you get the camera, the better the image sharpness of the "scans" will be. An alternative would be a copy stand. This consists of a base plate on which the light source is placed and a column to which the camera is attached so that it looks vertically down on the negative.

- A macro lens. The better you can fill your frame with the negative, the less you'll have to crop it later and the more resolution will be left in the end. As an alternative to a macro lens, you can also use extension tubes.

- A negative mask. In the simplest case, you can make this yourself from black cardboard. The purpose of the mask is to block the stray light that radiates from the light source around the negative toward the lens. This improves contrast. The mask also helps keep the negative as flat as possible, improving sharpness.

- A reasonably dark-ish room. Light in the room (for example, the bright ceiling) can be reflected by the negative and leave artifacts in the resulting image.

Chances are you already own a flat light source that you can use for this. It's called a tablet. Most commercial light plates intended specifically for photographing are so fine in their surface structure that they do not leave any artifacts in the digitized image. If you use a tablet or smartphone as a light source instead, then note that the display pixels can end up as artifacts in your photos. That's especially true if the negative rests directly on the glass surface. A film holder can help here. This puts some distance between the negative and the light source and moves the tablet pixels out of focus.

A macro lens reveals the pixel structure of a tablet

Commercial Film Holder Solutions

A selection:

- pixl-latr: An affordable modular film holder that handles 35mm, medium format, and large format.
- Negative Supply: Various kits and light sources for different sizes of negatives. High quality (and also somewhat high priced).
- Essential Filmholder: Well-built film holder for various formats. Very good flatness.
- Valoi 360: Another very neatly produced all-in-one solution that can be operated with its own light source.
- Lomography DigitaLIZA+ and DigitaLIZA Max: Holds film in 35mm and medium format and comes with backlight. DigitaLIZA Max covers the same formats, but adds a column to the package, to which a smartphone or other camera can be attached for taking pictures.

Sources can be found in Appendix A.3 on page [289].

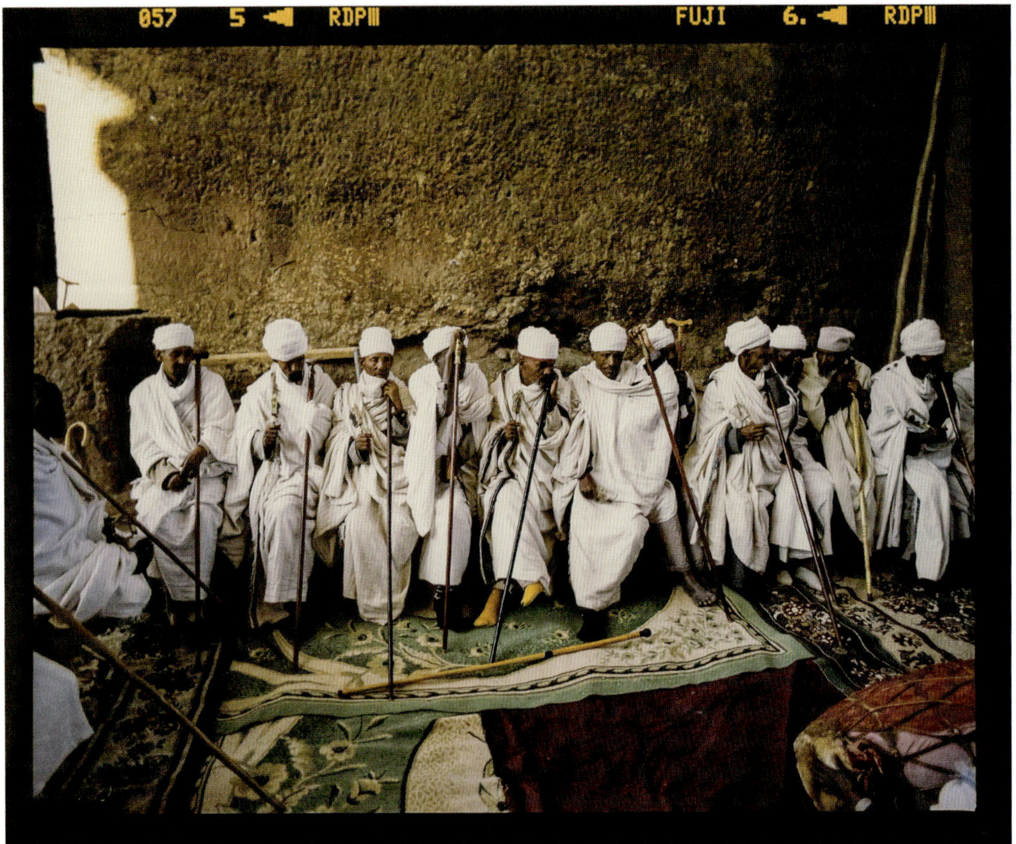

Medium format slide, photographed with DSLR and macro lens

Step by Step

1. Align the camera parallel to the light table.
2. Place the negative on the light table and cover the surroundings with the negative mask.
3. Set the camera to manual exposure mode (M).
4. Adjust the exposure on the camera so that neither underexposure nor overexposure is visible. The easiest way to do this is in Live View with the histogram and overexposure warnings turned on.
5. A medium aperture around f/8 will typically give you a good level of detail sharpness.
6. To avoid camera shake, trigger the camera wirelessly.

Post-Processing

- Slides: Crop the photos and adjust the contrasts in your post-processing software. For color correction, we will look for an area in the image that is as color neutral as possible and set white balance off of that. With some advance planning, you can of course also photograph a gray card on one of the images as a neutral reference. This works especially well if all images on the roll of film were taken under the same lighting conditions.
- Black-and-White Negatives: We manage and edit our negatives in Lightroom Classic. It's possible to invert negatives by reversing the tone curve, but that's a bit clunky as afterward the brightness and contrast controls no longer behave as usual. Instead, it has proven useful to first invert the negatives in other software (for example in Affinity Photo) before then importing them into Lightroom and adjusting them the same way we did for the slides.
- Color Negatives: Inverting color negatives is a bit tricky. Thanks to its orange mask, color film processing requires special color correction. Generally, it's easiest to do this is by using specialized software. Here are a few options:
    - Filmory: AI-supported photographing and inverting. Relatively low resolution. (iOS)
    - Film Scanner Pro: Free. (iPad)
    - FilmBox: Easy to use, good color conversion results. (iOS/Android)
    - FilmLab: One solution for all major platforms. (Windows/macOS/iOS/Android)
    - Kodak Mobile Film Scanner: Free. (iOS/Android)
    - Negative Lab Pro: A paid plug-in for Lightroom Classic. Gives you good results directly in Lightroom. Operation takes a little getting used to—the tutorial videos on their website help. (macOS/Windows)

The traditional film scan will not go away. Digitizing using the photo method requires a few more steps, while scanning software will typically offer batch processing and direct conversion of images, which makes it easy to scan multiple negatives in one go. Also, with larger negatives like medium format or even 4x5", the resolution advantage will move farther toward scanning. Our rule of thumb is to use the photo method for 35mm (almost always), for medium format (sometimes unless we need really high resolution), and almost never for 4x5".

However, flatbed scanners also have their disadvantages. For one, they usually do not exceed 2000 dpi optically, despite claiming higher resolutions on the box. Those specs refer to the stepper motors and scan line and ignore the upstream optical system, in which lenses and mirrors contribute to the final image. So realistically, you can't really expect more than 10 megapixels for a 35mm scan when done on a flatbed scanner. The camera method will basically provide you with the resolution of the camera sensor, minus some loss from cropping.

Scanners are also much slower, especially at higher resolutions. Just for fun, set your scanner to 6400 dpi and time how many minutes it takes to scan a 35mm negative. When using a camera, that gets reduced to seconds.

7.3   Digital Printing

Print your pictures! Or have them printed. Your best pictures need to be brought to light. Surround yourself with your work, and don't let them gather virtual dust like the countless digital snapshots on your hard drive or in the cloud. This does not really suit the tactile process of developing. Pictures that we are physically holding in our hands have a significantly higher value than those we just scroll through on the screen.

Of course, not all pictures need to be printed on paper. Photographers who work with film exclusively usually print only the best of their pictures. We do the same for printing digitally.

You will learn more about your own photography if you have your pictures all around you. You learn more about your own photography by keeping it near you. It's often enough to just pin a few photos to the pin board you walk past several times a day. In our house, we have professionally framed pictures hanging on the wall in the hallway, but we also have photos we've had printed via the online service taped to the kitchen door with sticky tape. In addition to high-quality prints from the Lambda printer, we also hang up photos from the cheapest postcard printer. It doesn't always have to be champagne. The important thing is for the pictures to have a presence.

7.3.1   Having Photos Printed: By a Discounter

The easiest way of getting your pictures onto paper is ordering them via one of the many online services. Just upload your photos, and a few days later you get the prints in the mail. There are some differences in terms of quality, and you will not always have the option of influencing how your photos are printed. Usually you will have to make a compromise between quality of the results, price, and convenience.

Depending on which operating system you are using on your computer, you may already have a photo service. On Macs, for example, you can order prints directly from inside the Photos app. No matter how you proceed, the result is a printed photo on paper—or, depending on your taste and provider, even on a coffee mug, mousepad, or sofa cushion. Usually, online providers want files in JPG format with a high resolution and not much compression. It's best to check first on the provider's website.

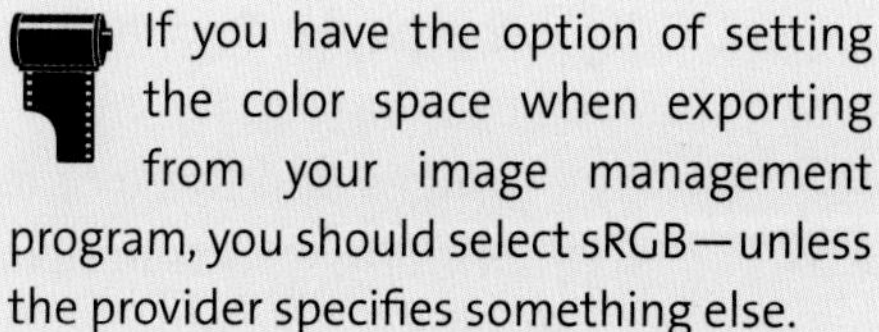

If you have the option of setting the color space when exporting from your image management program, you should select sRGB—unless the provider specifies something else.

7.3.2   Having Photos Printed: At a Professional Lab

If you want to be able to hold your best shots in your hands as professional quality prints, you have a lot of options, including inkjet printers, printing with pigment ink (referred to as Giclée prints) on high-quality paper, or printing digital data on photo paper. Good professional labs are available in many places and often give you the option of uploading the image data via Internet platforms. For photos on paper or canvas, you do not need to have a printer at home. If you pass your image files to a professional photo lab, they will be printed either with a photographic printing machine or an inkjet printer.

Printing on Photo Paper

The photographic printing machine does not really print; it is, in fact, an exposure system. The exposure on photo paper produces photochemical prints. The printing machine transforms the information of the image file into signals, which determine how the machine's red, green, and blue light gets a photographic image onto photo paper that contains silver.

These types of photographic printing machines are (very) large and expensive, and meant for professional use. You will find them in good professional laboratories.

Probably the best known photographic printer is the Durst Lambda, a machine that creates photo prints using laser light. These true photo prints are often referred to as Lambda prints. The latest generation of photographic printers work with LED light instead of lasers.

These photographic prints show a subtle, finely graded tonal reproduction. Most labs expose them onto photo paper coated with resin (RC). A disadvantage of photo prints is that a selection of different papers is not usually offered.

Inkjet Printer on Fine Art Paper

Compared to a traditional darkroom, the inkjet printer is a relatively new method for creating prints. With this method, ink is sprayed onto paper via a printer in a halftone dot pattern without the paper touching the print head. Purists think using a printer to get photos onto paper is the inferior method, but we disagree.

If you just try to lump all inkjet printers together and use your cheap inkjet printer and domestic PC as a reference point, you are comparing apples and oranges, and not doing inkjet printers justice. There are different types of inkjet printers, and a whole range of parameters is responsible for the results you get: the printer, the ink used, and the paper. To achieve high-quality, archive-standard fine-art prints, professional labs use large-scale inkjet printers that work with pigment inks in six or seven color cartridges and three or four different black levels. The large color space (gamut) of inkjet printing results in rich, intense colors and crisp contrasts.

A big advantage of these fine art prints, also referred to as Giclée prints, is that the selection of paper is greater than for photo prints. You can use the same subject and printing method to create completely different effects. Depending on whether you are using baryta-coated paper (e.g., Hahnemühle Baryta), heavy rag paper, or textured water-color paper, the contrasts and colors can come out with different intensity.

In contrast to prints from a simple inkjet printer for home-office use, archival-standard inkjet prints from a professional lab will keep for up to 200 years if the ink and paper have been matched well. As you can see, the decision whether to print your photo or have it printed as a fine-art print depends on what you want to use it for. It's usually a matter of personal preference.

Current studies on the archival longevity of modern pigment ink in combination with fine art paper are being carried out, for example, by Wilhelm Research Inc., and can be accessed via the website: *http://www.wilhelm-research.com*.

7.3.3   Printing Photos Yourself

If you want to get your hands on your pictures more quickly, you can print them yourself. Many all-in-one office printers can also print photos these days. The results are similar in quality to cheap online services, but cost a bit more. However, they have the unbeatable advantage in terms of time.

Apart from the usual paper trays in A4 or Letter size, many printers also offer an additional tray for photo paper in postcard format. The paper is usually available from the printer manufacturer and can either be ordered online or purchased in large electronics stores and stationery stores. Often you can also get two-in-one packs of paper and suitable ink cartridges. In the end you just need to select the right paper tray when printing, and the printer does the rest.

A few more words on inks and paper: For financial reasons, it seems to make sense to buy cheap refill cartridges of ink and affordable photo paper from the discount store. For office use, that's absolutely fine. But for photos, we would advise against it, because the cheaper alternatives often don't have the same color fade resistance as a branded product by the manufacturer of your printer.

7.3.4   High-End Inkjet Prints

The smaller photo and office printers take many (often technical) decisions out of the users' hands and provide results that are fine for everyday use. If you want to have full control over the print result, you will have to delve more deeply into topics such as color space, color management, printer and media profiles, and ink systems. The scope of this book does not allow us to explain all these topics in detail, but we will briefly mention a few.

Ink Systems

When it comes to printing photos, inkjet printing is the dominant system, and it uses primarily two ink systems: dye ink and pigment ink.

Dye Ink

With this ink system, the color particles are dissolved in liquid, just like the blue ink for fountain pens. The very homogenous solution is then sprayed onto the paper in fine droplets during printing. Because the ink is liquid, it soaks into the paper along the paper fibers. Depending on the paper type, this can cause fine structures to look slightly blurry. You particularly notice it with classic copier paper (20lb Bond Letter size/80gsm A4). High-quality office paper and photo paper have corresponding coatings to counteract the dye from running.

Pigment Ink

The higher-end printers use pigment ink. These types of ink do not contain dissolved colors but solid color particles. The pigment is suspended in the carrier solution, so it is floating in the liquid. During printing, the color pigments rest on top of the paper fibers, resulting in a clearer printed picture with stronger colors and higher contrasts.

> Depending on the system, pigment ink tends to clump more, so the printer nozzles can clog up more easily. This is particularly the case if the printers are not used regularly. The manufacturers try to counteract it with electrostatic systems, but it can help to take the ink cartridges out of the printer from time to time or carry out a little nozzle test where the printer head is flushed through with a tiny quantity of ink.

Thermal Printing

With thermal transfer printing and dye-sublimation printing, the picture is not created by putting ink on paper. Instead, colors on a color foil are melted or evaporated via heating elements and transfered onto the photo paper. The print results are consistently very high and comparable to color photos. However, this method creates more waste compared to the ink methods, because a piece of color foil the size of the entire photo is used for each color component (cyan, magenta, yellow, black).

Paper Types

Depending on method and budget, there are many choices of media for printing.

Photo Paper
The normal print media are the many varieties of photo papers. There is photo paper with different types of surface finish, from matte to satin to high-gloss. It comes in weight categories from thin paper to heavy card stock.

Cotton-Based Paper
Depending on subject and printer, you can also use matte cotton paper. This type of paper, also referred to as photo rag, is particularly popular for fine-art prints and almost always printed with pigment inks. Cotton rag paper has a fine, matte finish.

Canvas
Printable canvas has a canvas texture and is coated for inkjet printing. Canvas prints are usually mounted on a stretcher frame, just like a painting.

Acrylic Glass, Aluminum, and Textiles.
In addition to paper and canvas, many other materials are available for printing. For example, sheets of acrylic glass can be printed on from the back with special dyes. The pictures have a very sculptural look with strong contrasts. Other materials that can be printed on and that have their very own effects are, for example, aluminum or textiles.

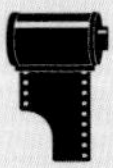

Manufacturers of high-quality print paper:
Hahnemühle: *http://www.hahnemuehle.com*
Canson: *http://www.canson-infinity.com*
Museo: *http://www.museofineart.com*
Rauch: *http://www.rauch-papiere.de*

7.3.5   Profiling

"Why don't my prints look like the picture on the screen?"

There are several answers to this question. One, printed pictures never look like photos on a computer screen because we are dealing with two different systems. The computer screen is backlit, but the paper is a reflective medium. What it looks like depends on the light source used to illuminate it. Pictures on paper can be assessed most accurately in the best-quality light source we have available: daylight. Moreover, printers and screens are not always 100% true color. This is mainly due to the fact that the devices are subject to manufacturing tolerances and aging processes. It's indeed possible for a monitor to develop a slight green cast over time, while a printer may overemphasize the color yellow.

Color profiles can help in this situation. A profile is meant to compensate for the tolerances between devices, and this applies to monitors, printers, and scanners.

Monitor Profiling

The most important profile is probably the one for the monitor. If the screen shows nonsense, such as the wrong colors and contrasts, then all corrections we make in image editing won't be any good. We will not be able to tell if our digital image corrections are accurate.

Monitor profiling is done automatically these days via a colorimeter. These devices are placed onto the computer screen and connected to the USB port. The associated software then displays a series of color charts on the screen and the colorimeter measures them. The monitor profile is generated from the difference between display and measurement. The profiling software usually saves it into the system automatically.

Under the hood, a profile is nothing more than a correction chart inside the computer between the input and output device. If the computer wants to display, for example, a specific shade of green on the screen, it uses the profile to correct the color before displaying it.

Printer Profiling

Printing involves two aspects, but luckily they can be governed via a common profile. Every printer has certain production tolerances, and each type of paper has specific qualities that can be adapted via a profile. For example, if the medium itself has a warm tone, it can help to have the printer put less yellow or red onto the paper. Printer profiles always represent a combination of printer and paper.

Luckily, integrating the profiles is not too hard—at least, not if you are using the printer manufacturer's brand of paper. You just have to select the right paper type in the printer driver, and the rest happens automatically. This gets you quite good results. If you want to use paper made by a third party, it becomes a bit more complicated. Depending on the printer, you may be able to find the suitable profile to download on the paper manufacturer's website. You then need to install the profiles in your system before you can use them. The installation often happens directly via your printer driver.

It becomes even more complicated if you want to create profiles yourself, for example, for other types of paper or even more exotic materials. In that case, print a color chart first. Then measure the color fields in the chart with a spectrophotometer and the software generates a corresponding profile from the results.

Scanner Profiling

We deliberately did not go into much detail regarding scanner profiling because our main focus was on scanning black-and-white originals, for which scanner profiling is not essential. Generally, scanner profiling works the same for any other image-capturing device. First, you scan a card or transparency with different color fields (referred to as an IT8 target). This scan is then analyzed by corresponding software that generates a profile from it.

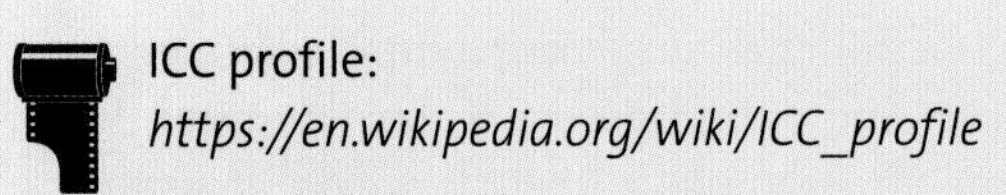

ICC profile:
https://en.wikipedia.org/wiki/ICC_profile

7.3.6   Printing Workflow

Due to the multitude of systems and manufacturers, we can only discuss a few general settings here. The possible options can differ greatly depending on the printer driver and printer. In general, high-quality devices also offer more options.

Soft Proof

This step takes place during image editing. If your editing software supports the feature *Soft Proof,* you can get a simulated preview of the result via the printer/media profile of the output device. You can, for example, see if all colors of the picture can still be suitably represented in the (smaller) color space of the printer. Then you can correct colors that are too saturated for printing and improve your print results.

Color Management

Depending on manufacturer and system, you can choose if you want the device to take care of converting the color space between monitor and printer, or if your software should do this conversion itself. The default setting is conversion by the printer or printer driver. If you do not want to leave this task up to the printer, you need to use the suitable printer profile.

Paper

After setting the page size, you can select the type of paper you are going to print on in the printer driver. If you are using the printer manufacturer's paper, the printer is automatically going to use the right profile with this setting. With the paper selection, the printer driver also sets other parameters; for example, which drying times are required between the individual passes so the corresponding medium can absorb the relevant amount of ink.

Quality

Here, you should experiment. On the lowest quality setting *(Draft),* the printer is going to use noticeably less ink and print quicker at the expense of quality. On the highest setting, printing takes longer and more ink is used. We tend to print with the *Normal* setting most of the time.

Profile

With professional printers, you can use the profile function to include profiles for third-party media.

To Scale or Not to Scale?

To avoid interpolation artifacts, purists sometimes scale their pictures exactly to the size they want to output. Printer drivers now do this scaling in very good quality, so we prefer to give the printer a high-resolution image, which is then automatically scaled to the output size in the printer driver.

To Sharpen or Not to Sharpen?

Some editing software enables you to sharpen images for the relevant output purpose, and sometimes even for the type of paper you are using (matte or glossy). Again, the printer drivers are now very good, so you do not really need to select anything here. If you are not sure, compare the results you get for different settings.

7.4   Historical Processes

There is a range of (usually) manual, photochemical reproduction processes that offer alternatives to the traditional positive prints created in the darkroom or hybrid prints from the inkjet printer. These processes usually involve a contact print where the negative is placed directly onto the paper during the exposure.

For many of these processes, you do not necessarily need analog photos nor a darkroom to experience the tactile pleasure of analog prints. You can use digital photos to create non-reproducible unique pictures that are a combination of painting and photography in one. The following sections will tell you how these work, using the examples of cyanotype and albumen print.

Although photo trays and a pair of lab tongs are quite useful, you can usually do the methods introduced here with household items—for example with scrapped kitchen utensils—and commercially available sets with chemicals and paper. If you do not have the right tools, a quick trip to the DIY store can help. Make sure you never use items you are still going to use for eating or cooking!

7.4.1   Cyanotype

The cyanotype process, invented in 1842 by astronomer Sir John Herschel, was the first photographic printing method that did not use silver. In this method, iron compounds are used to create the picture. The images in the book *British Algae: Cyanotype Impressions* (often referred to as the world's first photo book) were created with this method in 1843 by British biologist and botanist Anna Atkins.

Because the procedure for cyanotype images was simple, relatively cheap, and produced sufficiently fast results, one version of this method was commercially successful for a while. The "blueprint method" was used for reproducing construction plans. Special, coated papers were commercially available starting in 1870. Later, this process was replaced by other, dry-copying methods, but the term blueprint is still used today.

Today, the cyanotype process is still a way of creating relatively inexpensive prints of selected photographs. The chemicals you need are available individually or as cyanotype sets—with or without suitable paper—in specialist photo shops. Pre-coated cyanotype paper is also available, for example, for greeting cards. The formula used to create cyanotypes has basically not changed since Herschel's time, but the concentration of the solution you prepare will vary depending on your preferences.

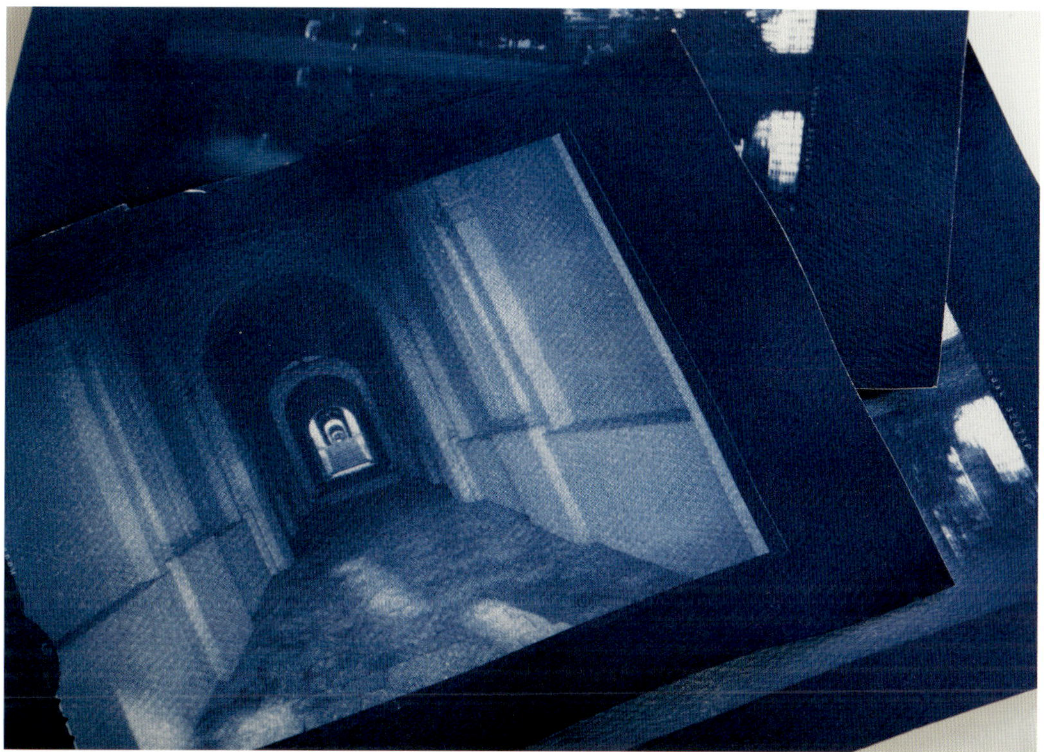

Cyanotype, contact prints of 4×5" large format negatives

Chemistry, Sample Recipe

- 25 g ammonium iron (III) citrate
- 16 g potassium ferricyanide ("prussian red," "red prussiate of potash")
- (distilled) water

Both ingredients are dissolved separately in 100 ml of distilled water. The easiest way to prepare the solutions in in brown glass bottles, because then you can shake the bottles to mix the chemicals and also store the solution in them later. As long as the two separate solutions have not been mixed together, you can store them for a long time. You can prepare the solutions in daylight.

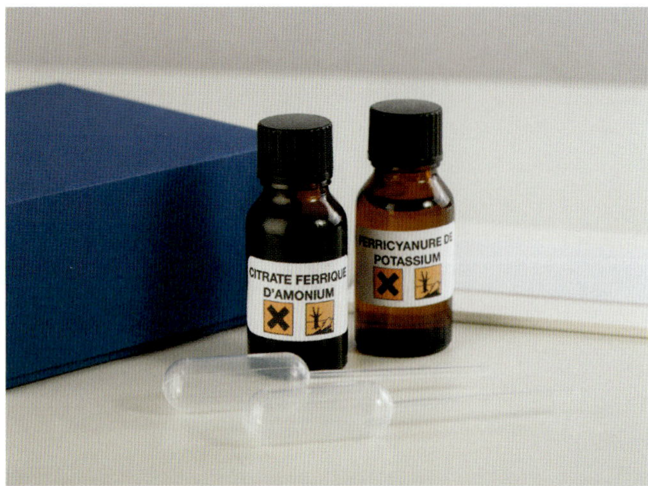

Cyanotype set by Monochrom

To sensitize the image medium—usually paper—mix small amounts of the individual solutions together in a ratio of 1:1. Because the finished mixture keeps for only a few hours or, at most, days, you should ideally use it immediately.

Paper

The picture is usually printed onto paper—but by experimenting a little, you can also print on wood or fabric (for example T-shirts or cotton bags). The paper is wet-coated, and the print is fixed under running water later, so you should use paper that can withstand rinsing and that dries without losing its shape. A heavy watercolor paper or handmade paper with a weight of about 250 gsm is usually quite good.

To sensitize the paper, coat it evenly in dim light with the mixture of the two solutions and then leave it to dry in a dark place. A large cardboard box with a lid is quite handy and protects the paper from light until it has dried completely. To apply the solution as evenly as possible, a wide brush or foam roller without a metal fitting is ideal. Depending on the thickness of the paper and how much mixture you have applied to it, air drying can take over an hour. If you use a hair dryer to speed things up a bit, you can get the paper dry in a few minutes.

Although you can coat the paper in dim light, the solution becomes sensitive to ultraviolet light while it dries. So, once you have sensitized the substrate material, you need to keep it in the dark until you are ready to expose it.

Preparing a Negative

You can expose a cyanotype either as a photogram using objects (parts of plants, feathers, etc.) as positive or the classic way via a negative. Because the cyanotype involves a contact exposure, the size of the negative also determines the size of the finished picture. It is not possible to enlarge during the exposure process. For this reason, large sheet film negatives are particularly well suited for this printing process. If you do not (yet) have any, digital technology is your ally in this instance. As long as you have editing software and a printer, you can manage entirely without analog negatives.

Pick one of your favorite pictures, and use your image-editing program to convert it to a high-contrast black-and-white picture. Then invert it and print the file onto a suitable transparency. Now you have a digital negative, so to speak.

Exposure

For the exposure, place the negative directly onto the sensitized substrate and cover it with a glass plate to keep it flat. A standard clear-glass, clip-type picture frame is handy, because it can serve as both base and cover. Then expose this "sandwich" to UV light. On a sunny day, just put it on the garden table in full sun. On cloudy days, you can use a facial tanner for UV rays. Depending on the light source and/or time of year, the exposure time is between 10 minutes and several hours. Time to experiment—cyanotype is no exact science. The good news is that real overexposures rarely happen. If the coated paper changes color in the shadows of the subject from greenish to dark grayish, and the highlights start turning pale blue, then the exposure process is complete.

Washing and Simultaneously Fixing

The next step is very easy. The paper is developed in water—in other words, washed thoroughly until the highlights look pure white. This is best done with the exposed side downwards in a large basin. In a room that is not too bright, you can also rinse under running water.

This step of the process has two purposes: one, it washes the iron salts out of the unexposed areas (which still look yellowy-green). Two, the washing starts the oxidization process of the coating in the areas that have been exposed to UV light, and the characteristic blue color forms. The development is finished once no more blue color runs off.

You must avoid damaging the sensitive coated side, so try not to touch it. If you want to increase the oxidization and blue coloring, you can give your cyanotype an acid bath in 2% citric acid or 0.3% hydrogen peroxide. After another wash, your print is ready for drying.

Drying

There are different ways to dry a finished cyanotype. First, remove surface water with blotting paper or several layers of newspaper. Then, you can hang up the print to dry, and press it flat afterwards.

Tip for keeping it flat: Let the paper dry by sticking it onto a sheet of glass, with the coated side up, held in place with wet-adhesive tape.

7.4.2   Albumen Print

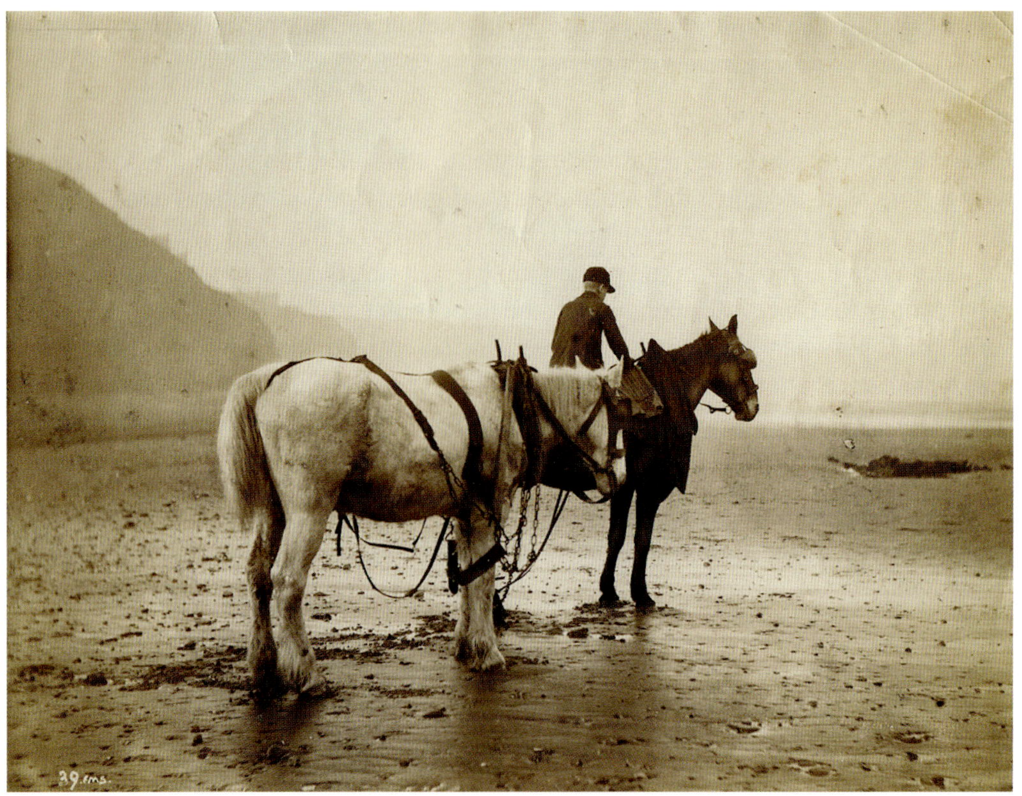

Example albumen print: Photograph by Frank Meadow Sutcliffe, England. Courtesy of Preus Museum, Norway.

Until 1900, albumen prints were one of the most popular photographic reproduction methods. The technique was created around 1850 by Louis Désiré Blanquart-Evrard. It made very detailed reproductions possible and was more cost-effective than previously used methods, such as ambrotype or daguerreotype. Warm, usually brown-black tones are typical of an albumen print.

The question of what came first, the chicken or the egg, can be answered (at least as far as albumen prints are concerned). The traditional process of coating the paper used for this process starts almost like preparing a good meringue—with plenty of egg white (albumen). The egg white is mixed with salt and used for preparing a liquid to coat the paper with a glue-like layer. This seals the surface and ensures that the silver nitrate solution applied later does not penetrate into the paper. The hardened egg white layer also provides a glossy sheen and the rich detail and high contrasts.

You can create your own albumen liquid. The procedure is not difficult, but it takes a long time. The easier way, if not as inexpensive, is using albumen powder or complete albumen printing kits. Both are available in specialist retail shops.

A typical kit contains: silver nitrate in a brown glass bottle, albumen solution, powdered fixer for preparing your own working solution, eyedropper, flat brush, and sometimes a few sheets of special paper for printing. The most important steps are:

1. Preparing or selecting a suitable negative
2. Coating the paper with albumen
3. Sensitizing the paper
4. Contact exposure in sunlight or UV light
5. Washing and fixing

Preparing or Selecting a Suitable Negative
As with cyanotypes, you use contact exposure, so you need a negative in the same size as the finished picture you want to create. You can create a foil negative as described for cyanotypes. Pictures with a high contrast range are best for albumen printing.

Coating the Paper with Albumen
Prepare the albumen solution according to the packaging instructions, and pour it into a large, shallow bowl. Place a sheet of your selected paper onto the liquid so the paper is evenly wet. Try to avoid getting albumen onto the back of the paper—this will cause uneven density in the finished print. Let the paper float for about three minutes. You can also apply the liquid with a surface brush.

If you have coated the paper using the floating method, wait three minutes, then lift one corner of the paper carefully with a toothpick and pull the paper from the albumen liquid quickly and evenly. Hang it up to dry, and carefully remove large quantities from around the edges with a paper towel. This prevents uneven, thicker areas around the edges of your paper.

Albumen-coated paper has good storage stability. You can prepare it in advance and build up a supply.

Sensitizing the Paper

You can sensitize the paper immediately prior to the exposure only, because the combination of silver nitrate solution and the salts present in the albumen layer will only keep for a few hours.

Caution: Make sure you are working with chemical-resistant gloves (for example nitrile) and protective goggles. Splashes of silver nitrate can permanently damage your eyes!

The actual coating can be done under the light of a weak lightbulb, but ideally in safelight. Mix 37.5 g of silver nitrate with 250 ml of distilled water to create a 15% silver nitrate solution. The prepared solution becomes light-sensitive as soon as it comes into contact with organic materials—for example your skin or the albumen coating on the paper. Pour the liquid into a shallow bowl, for example a photo tray, and proceed with coating as described for applying the albumen. After three minutes, you can again lift off the paper and hang it up to dry.

Exposure

Expose as soon as the paper is fully dry. The longer you wait, the less sensitive the paper will become. The best way to expose is in direct sunlight on a warm day. If you want to work indoors, you need a strong UV light source such as a facial tanner.

Place the (transparency) negative onto the sensitized paper with the coated side down and weigh it down with a glass plate. If you do not have a frame for contact prints, you can use a clear-glass clip-frame. Place the sandwich you have created in the sun. Expose it until the highlights are starting to turn slightly violet, and the shadows look a bit bronze. Bear in mind that the print gets lighter during further processing.

Washing and Fixing

Wash the print thoroughly to remove surplus silver nitrate. As long as silver nitrate remains, the water that runs off will look milky. Once it runs clear—probably after about 15 minutes—you can fix the print.

Prepare a fixer bath. Pour it into the tray, and fix your print for usually no more than 60 seconds. The final wash of the finished print should take about an hour. After the final rinse, you can carefully remove surplus water with blotting paper or newspaper before hanging the print up to dry.

A Comment on Suitable Papers

The effect of an albumen print is strongly determined by the paper quality. Lightweight paper is usually more suitable because it absorbs less of the albumen solution, but the material needs to be stable enough to survive prolonged washing and long wet stages without falling apart. For an impression with the best sharpness, the albumen coating has to rest on top of the paper and should not soak in too much. Extremely pure watercolor papers made of rag are very suitable because they have a smooth, finely grained, closed surface.

In the mid-19th century, Dresden, Germany, was the main producer of albumen paper worldwide. Allegedly, the paper manufacturers used around 70,000 chicken eggs per day for making albumen paper.

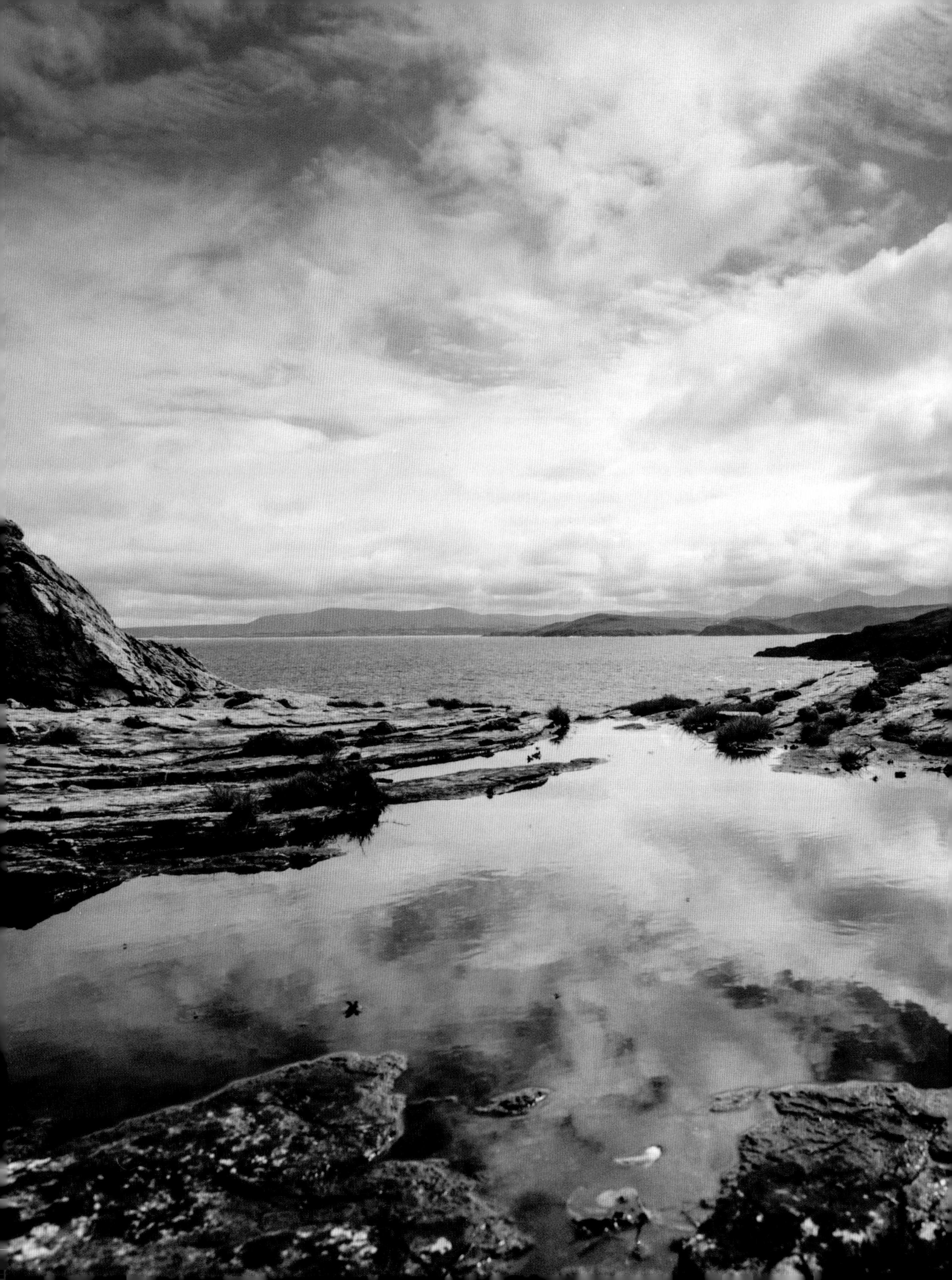

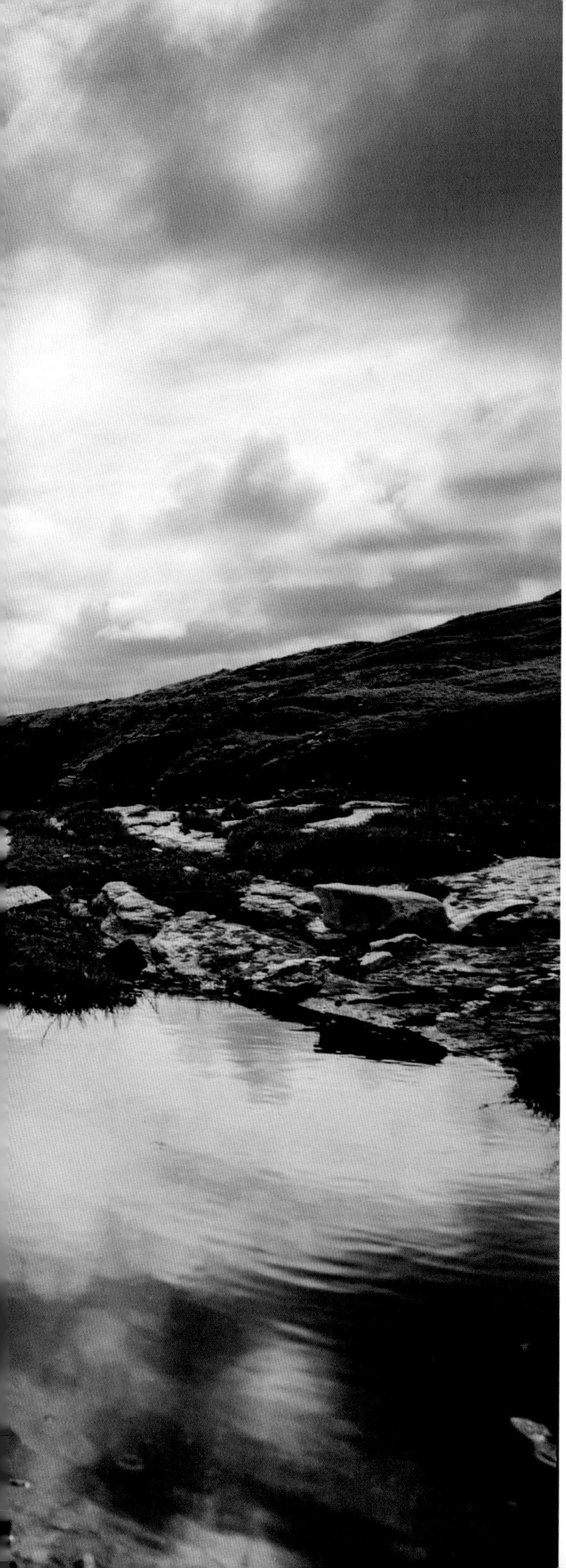

8
Presentation

Traditionally, negatives are enlarged in the darkroom and exposed onto photo paper. Today, the hybrid process is more dominant. In other words, negatives are scanned and brought to paper via various methods. If you have scanned your photos and now have them in digital form, you will be happy to see how great they look on the screen and how easy it is to upload pictures to platforms such as Flickr or 500px for discussion and ratings.

Although it is indeed great fun to exchange views with other enthusiasts (and it can give you great feedback for your own development as a photographer), it is also a very special experience to grasp the results of photo excursions and subsequent developing sessions in a tactile way. We have to remind ourselves constantly to not just share our photos in digital form, but also print them in large format. Once the finished photo is in front of us, it is all the more satisfying.

8.1   Mats

A mat or passe-partout (from French *passer* [pass through] and *partout* [anywhere]) is a piece of card with a cutout opening through which you can see the picture or object behind it. This piece of cardboard has several purposes. It acts as a spacer between the picture and the glass of the frame, protecting the photo from damage and adding an additional impression of depth. Thanks to a special cutter, the edges of the cutout are at an angle of 45°, so your picture is enclosed by an additional, fine border.

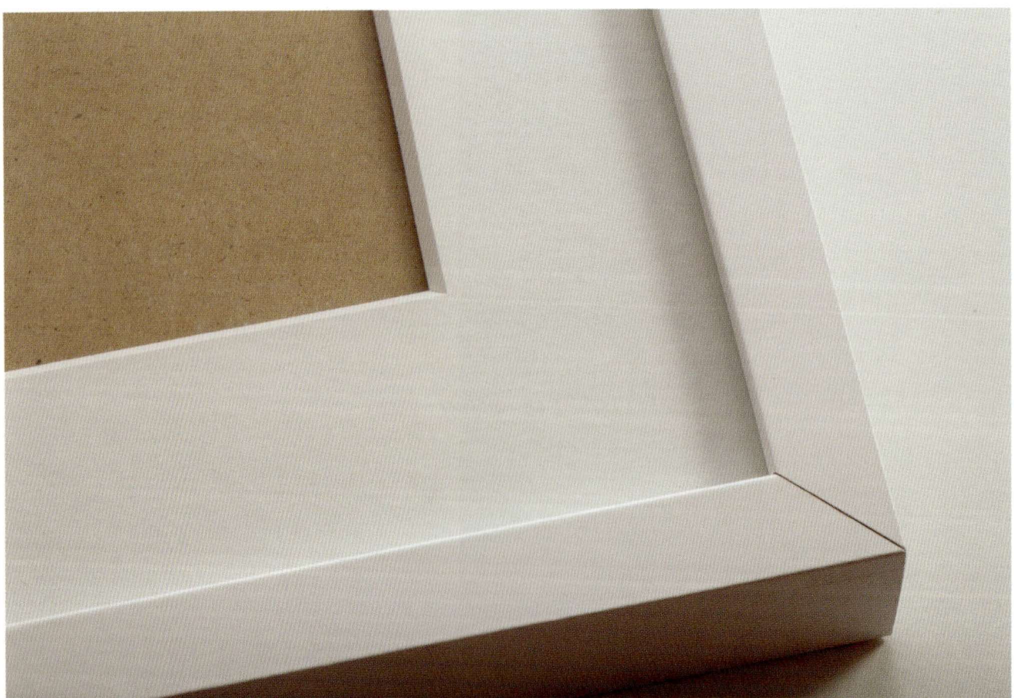

Ready-made mat in frame

Mats also create a visual transition between your picture and the generally larger picture frame. They are an important design tool that you can use to influence how the viewer sees your picture. Mats are available in different versions: ready-made for standard frame or picture sizes, or custom-made for different aspect ratios and cutout shapes. You also have the choice between different thickness levels of cardboard and a large range of different types of paper.

It is entirely up to you if you prefer working with bright or dark mats, subdued or vivid colors. We suggest using unobtrusive colors so they don't detract from the picture. We tend to use warm-white, neutral gray, or black mats. Use samples in different colors and brightness levels to see the effect they have on the impact of the picture. Ideally, select a suitable background for each individual picture. Sometimes you have to adapt the contrast curve of individual prints to the selected background, especially if you have a whole group of pictures you want to present as a unit.

Museum-quality mat card is not only available in art supply stores; you can also find it in some craft or do-it-yourself stores. In both cases, you can also ask the store to cut the mat or cutout to the right size for your print. Some stores even offer a complete service to mat, mount, and frame your photo.

Valuable photos and artwork must not be left in permanent contact with acidic paper. If you want to ensure your pictures will last a long time, only use mats made of acid-free card.

8.1.1   It's All About the Right Size

Adapt the picture size and the mat cutout according to the expected viewing distance. As a rough guide, the image diagonal should correspond to the viewing distance. For the mat, the rule of thumb is that there should be at least two inches (five centimeters) between cutout and frame. If you make this distance bigger, you should move the cut-out window slightly upwards. Due to an optical illusion, it can otherwise look like centered pictures are too low in the frame.

If you are planning an exhibition, have a look at the venue first to work out the viewing distance to your work ahead of time. There will be a considerable difference in picture size for images exhibited in a café versus images displayed in the foyer of a bank.

8.2   Frames

You can buy frames in different materials, sizes, and colors. If you want something very affordable, you can use clip-on photo frames without edges. That's probably the most inexpensive solution, but hardly the best or prettiest. The most common way of presenting your photos is behind glass, in a frame with edges. If you decide to use this form of presentation, there are certain elements you should consider.

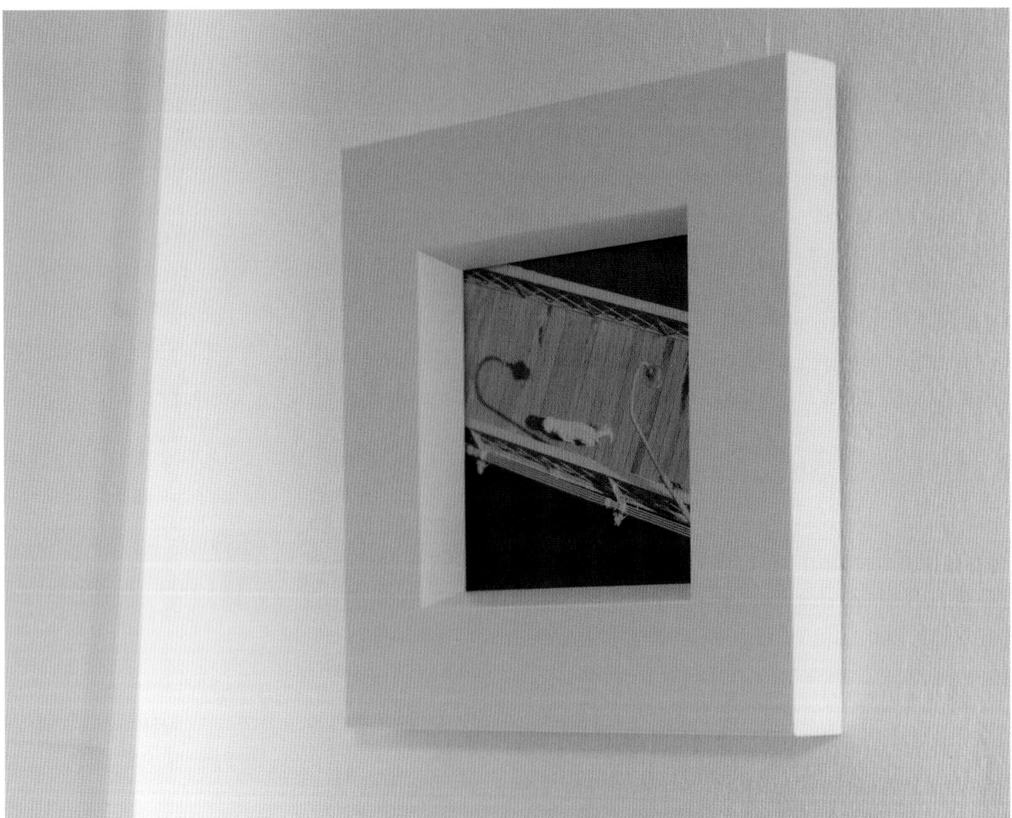

Picture frame

The color of the frame should be determined by whether you want the picture to "float" in front of the wall or if you want to add emphasis to the photo via an additional frame edge. In the first case, we like to use a frame that is the same color as the wall. It works well for more subtle pictures that you don't want to overwhelm with additional accents. The deeper the frame profile, the more you can have the picture contrast with the wall without having to choose a frame in a strong color. High-contrast and expressive subjects or pictures in dark mats combine well with colored or very dark frame profiles.

For most pictures, it's a good idea to present them in a frame that is significantly bigger than the displayed picture. Make sure you choose a frame with clear glass for a high-contrast, brilliant appearance. Anti-reflective glass makes photos look dull and lackluster. If you cannot find a place to display the photo without reflections, think about leaving the glass off altogether. This removes an additional layer of protection from your photo, but it enables direct access to the picture. The tactile effect of the photo paper you choose will also be more noticeable this way.

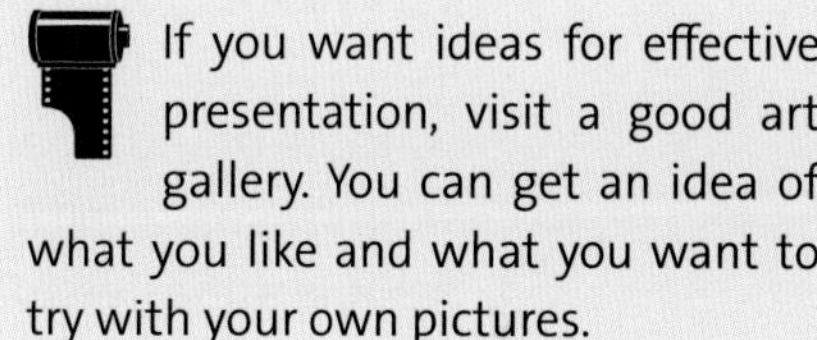

You can usually find particularly deep picture frames with and without glass if you search online for "box frame."

A particularly nice way of presenting your photo is framing with a shadow gap. This approach is suitable for pictures that have the best effect when displayed in full size without a mat. The term *shadow gap* refers to the 5–7mm-wide gap between the frame and the canvas with the photo on it. This gap creates a visual break between picture and frame, which gives greater visual depth. As a result, it looks as if the picture is floating inside the frame.

If you want ideas for effective presentation, visit a good art gallery. You can get an idea of what you like and what you want to try with your own pictures.

8.3   Mounting Techniques

Whether you mount a photo temporarily with photo corners or hinges, or you intend to attach it permanently to a backing board, depends on the way you want to present it—but it also depends on the value of your work. For valuable, unique pictures, we would advise against non-reversible mounting.

8.3.1   Matting

Heavy, handmade paper and watercolor paper (for traditional processes), or baryta paper and other fibrous papers, change over time. They tend to swell or warp with changing climate conditions. In a museum, this downside is often accepted, as mounting would diminish the value of the artwork.

For presenting photos, you have to fix together the photo and the matting in such a way that they do not slip out of place. The problems that arise when fixing together photo paper and cardboard are that both materials contract in dry air and expand in high humidity. Depending on the type of material used, they do not contract or expand at the same rate, which must be taken into consideration when you attach your picture to the matting.

If you want to fix your picture in place with photo corners, you need to make sure that they do not fit snugly onto the corners of your picture. You need to leave a bit of space at the top and bottom corners. The same goes for fixing the photo down with sticky tape. You should stick the photo down on one side only, so it can expand freely in all directions. If you use sticky tape for fixing your picture down, make sure you use a suitable brand. There are special one-sided, self-adhesive papers available in art supply shops (usually in the section for frames and mats). These have a solvent-free, acid-free, flexible adhesive coating for long-term archival.

8.3.2 Mounting

Especially large pictures may need to be mounted on a solid material in order to keep them nice and flat. There is a great variety of different materials, such as cardboard, wood, and special plastics, but also metals, that are suitable for this process. For example, Kapa (light-weight foam boards), PVC-Forex (hardened foam), or Alu-Dibond (an aluminum composite panel) are appropriate mounting options.

If you want to mount the picture yourself, you can find different adhesives and adhesive films for this purpose in art or photo supply shops. Spray adhesives or special types of glue are suitable for *wet mounting;* double-sided adhesive foils are suitable for *dry, cold mounting.* This is not the place for economy: You should spend the money to use materials that are intended for photos, or you may find that the glue shines through after a while and causes ugly brown stains or bubbles on the front of your image. Good, wrinkle-free mounting requires lots of practice and a steady hand. We always have it done by a reliable professional laboratory or frame shop. High-quality prints are best entrusted to the hands of an expert.

For *hot mounting* you need special double-sided, self-adhesive foil that melts when heated and a press, which is quite expensive and bulky. The press bonds the materials together under heat: the photo on one side, the foil in the middle, and a final sheet in the same thickness as the photo on the outside. This counter-mount prevents the final product from warping.

As always, remember to use only acid-free and lignin-free materials for archival quality.

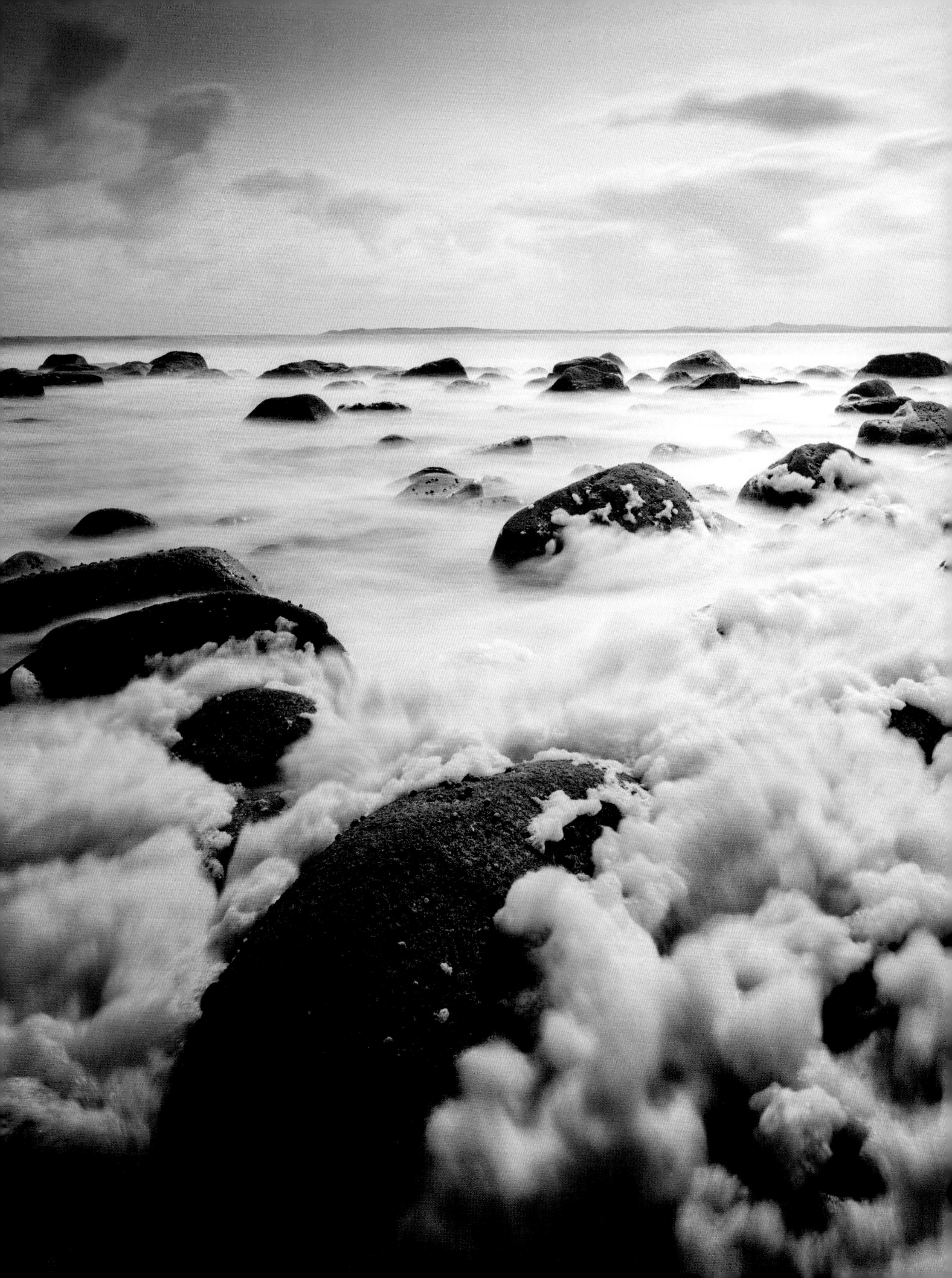

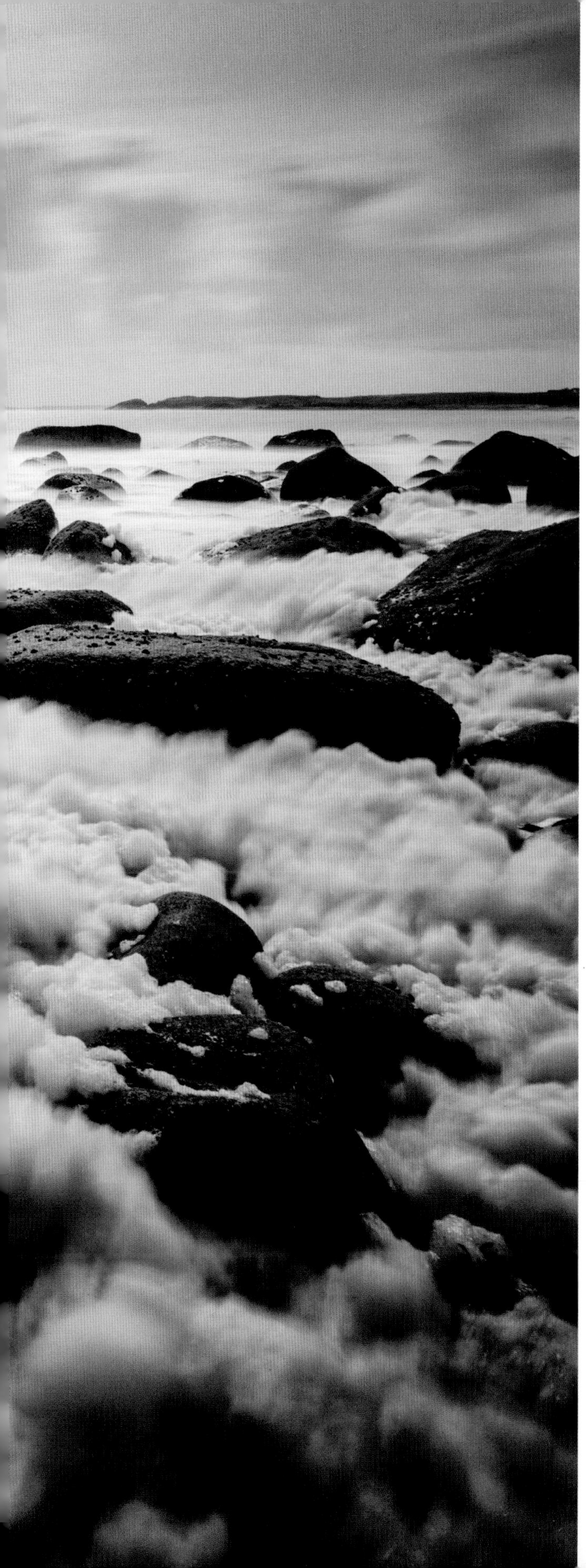

9
Storage and Archiving

Data safety plays an important role in both film and digital photography. It's a good idea to consider how you are going to store your negatives and prints. Truly professional-level archival storage is only possible in a closed archive, one that is potentially even subdivided into several rooms. Storing at home and occasional handling or exhibiting pictures is not really archiving in its strictest sense.

9.1   General Considerations

The following comments relate mainly to storing and safe-keeping black-and-white material. Color materials stored in the same conditions are not as storage-proof, let alone archive-proof, as black-and-white materials. With color prints, the latent silver particles are replaced with organic color particles during the developing process. These are much less stable than silver crystals, and are subject to a decay process that can be slowed by storing these materials in appropriate conditions and handling them carefully. To slow down the aging process of color materials in the long-term, you need to deep-freeze them.

9.2   Storing Negatives

You can already safely store negatives when you develop the films: Make sure you fix the films sufficiently and rinse them well. If you want to protect them even more, you can add selenium toning to protect the silver in your picture from airborne pollutants.

The finished negatives need to be stored in a dark, cool, dry place and in a climate that remains as constant as possible. Ideally, the temperature should be no higher than 21°C (69.8°F), and the humidity should stay below 50%. You may not have the perfect archiving room at home, but these values at least make it clear that photos should not be stored in the attic or the cellar.

To keep the film safe from dust, fingerprints, and scratches, it's a good idea to put it in negative sleeves as soon as possible after processing, once the film is fully dry. Most commonly available negative sleeves are suitable for arranging several negative strips above or beside one another. Then label them and store them in folders.

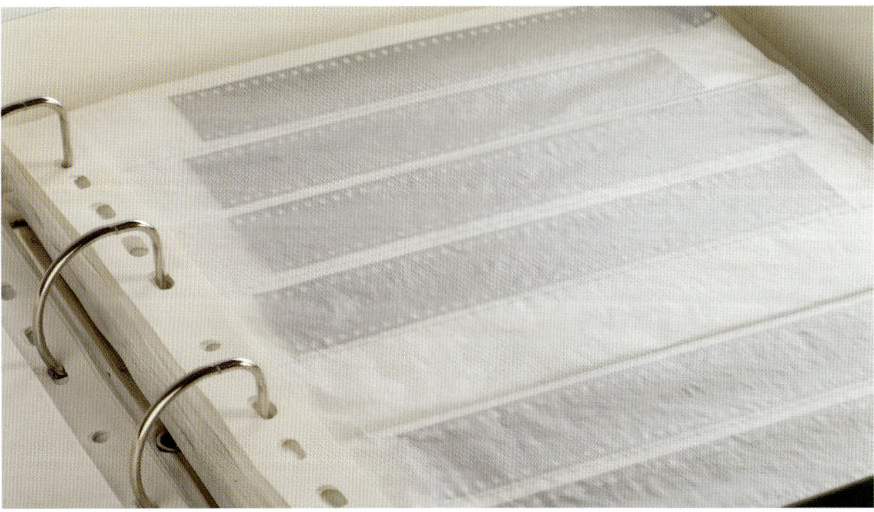

Glassine negative pockets

Negative sleeves are available in different versions. They can be made of photo glassine paper, acetate, polyethylene, polypropylene, or polyester with a polyethylene coating. Above all else, you should ensure the material is pH-neutral and free of lignin, bleaching agents (e.g., peroxide), and softening agents.

The most affordable option is glassine. Photo glassine is made of 100% pure, undyed cellulose, and is free of chlorine, acid, lignin, metal, and softening agents. Its satin surface is transparent enough to see the subject on the negative. If you want to assess the image density or make a contact print, you will have to take the negative out of the sleeve.

Up to a point, glassine is able to adapt to slow fluctuations in climate conditions. It absorbs moisture present in the negative or the surrounding air and lets the moisture evaporate again. Because glassine does not become statically charged, it presents fewer problems with dust particles than plastic pockets. However, when inserting the negatives, you need to ensure that you do not scratch them on the rather sharp edge of the glassine paper.

As for archival longevity, polyester pockets (available, for example, from the brand *Mylar*) or polypropylene pockets perform better than glassine. They also have the advantage of being so transparent that you don't need to take the negatives out of the sleeves for assessing the pictures or making a contact print. This way, the negatives are less likely to suffer mechanical damage.

Storing negatives in polypropylene or polyester pockets is only recommended if the negative is free of residual moisture and can be stored in a dry room. In rooms with fluctuating or continuous high humidity, an unfavorable microclimate can develop inside the air-impermeable plastic pockets, and in the worst case, your negatives may mold.

Large format polyester sleeves

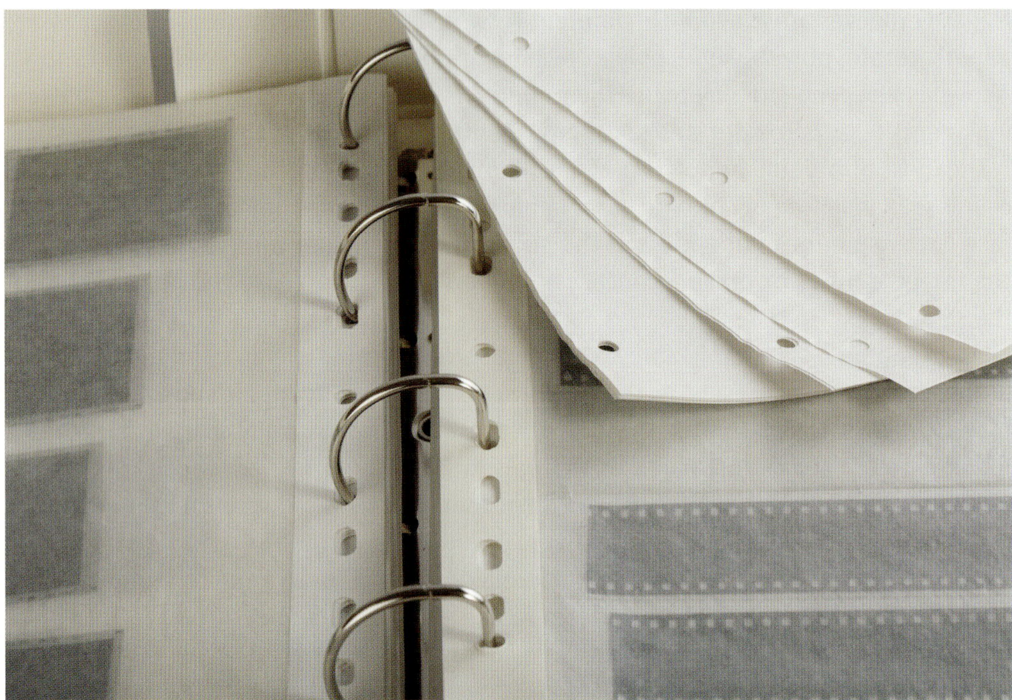

Archive binder with glassine pockets

The pockets with film sleeves are best stored by clipping them into archive binders. To make sure the negatives do not curl, you should store the archive boxes lying down. You can use inserts of archive-proof cardboard to gently persuade particularly stubborn film strips to lie flat. Never store 35mm film or roll film by rolling it up. Sooner or later, films that are stored in a roll can get too curly to scan or use to make prints. In the worst case, not even a heavy book or weights will ever make them flat again.

Many manufacturers now label their materials as "archival" or "acid-free." If you want to be on the safe side, check if the material has a PAT certificate. Materials that have successfully passed the *Photo Activity Test* (PAT), created by the famous Image Permanence Institute in Rochester, are suitable for storing and archiving photographic materials.

Almost all chemical fumes and vapors are dangerous for photo materials. This can also include vapors seeping out of wood fibers, solvents of paints and adhesives, and many other substances. Metal cupboards are better suited for storing photos and film than wooden or plastic ones, which can release volatile substances.

9.3   Prints

For storing prints, the same rules for storing developed film apply. Plus, paper absorbs ambient moisture from the air and releases it again when the humidity decreases. You need to take this breathing process into account when storing photos printed on paper or photo prints. You can either store the prints lying down in glassine pockets, or push them into clear polyester or polypropylene pockets with a 1–2mm-thick strip of archival cardboard. The pockets need to be open on at least two sides. The archival cardboard inside the plastic pockets has a climate-regulating effect, and behaves similar to the prints. Together with the cardboard, you can store the photos vertically in a drawer, similar to index cards in an old card catalog.

Photos that are not stabilized with cardboard need to be stored lying down in archive boxes. To reduce the pressure on the material—particularly if you handle them occasionally—you should avoid stacking more than 25 sheets.

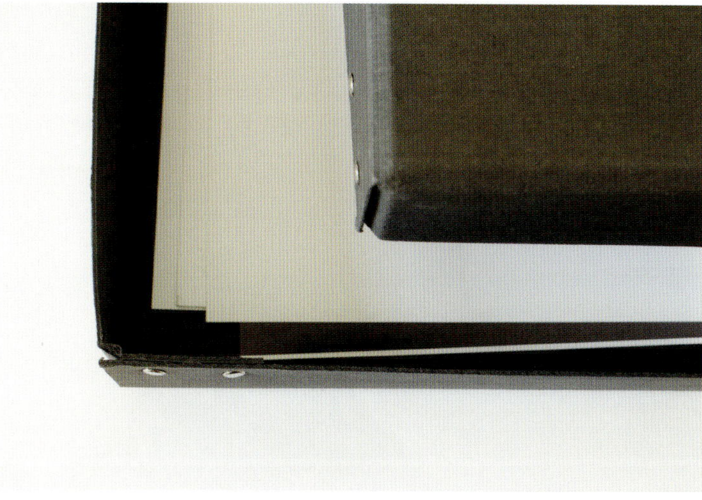

Archive box

9.4   A Tidy House, A Tidy Mind

If you are working on film, you are likely to accumulate a considerable number of photos and films. Work out a good filing system that keeps the originals and associated scanned files in order. You should be able to find important pictures at any time. If you want to revisit projects later on and continue them, it is important to know not just the film type you were using, but also the recipe for development.

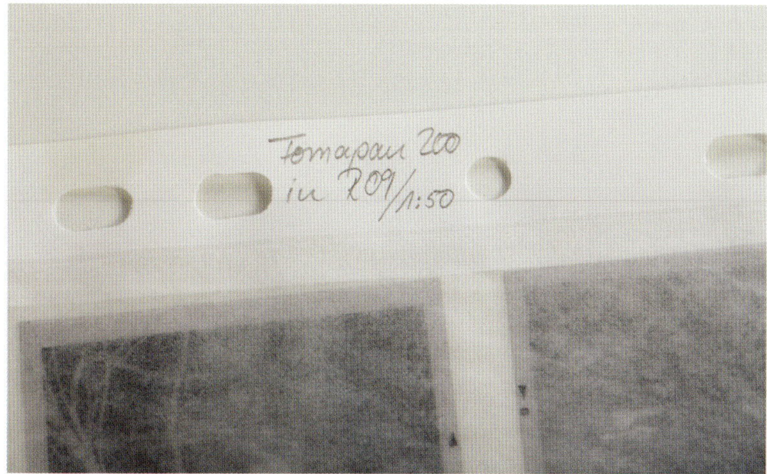

Glassine pocket, labeled in the margin

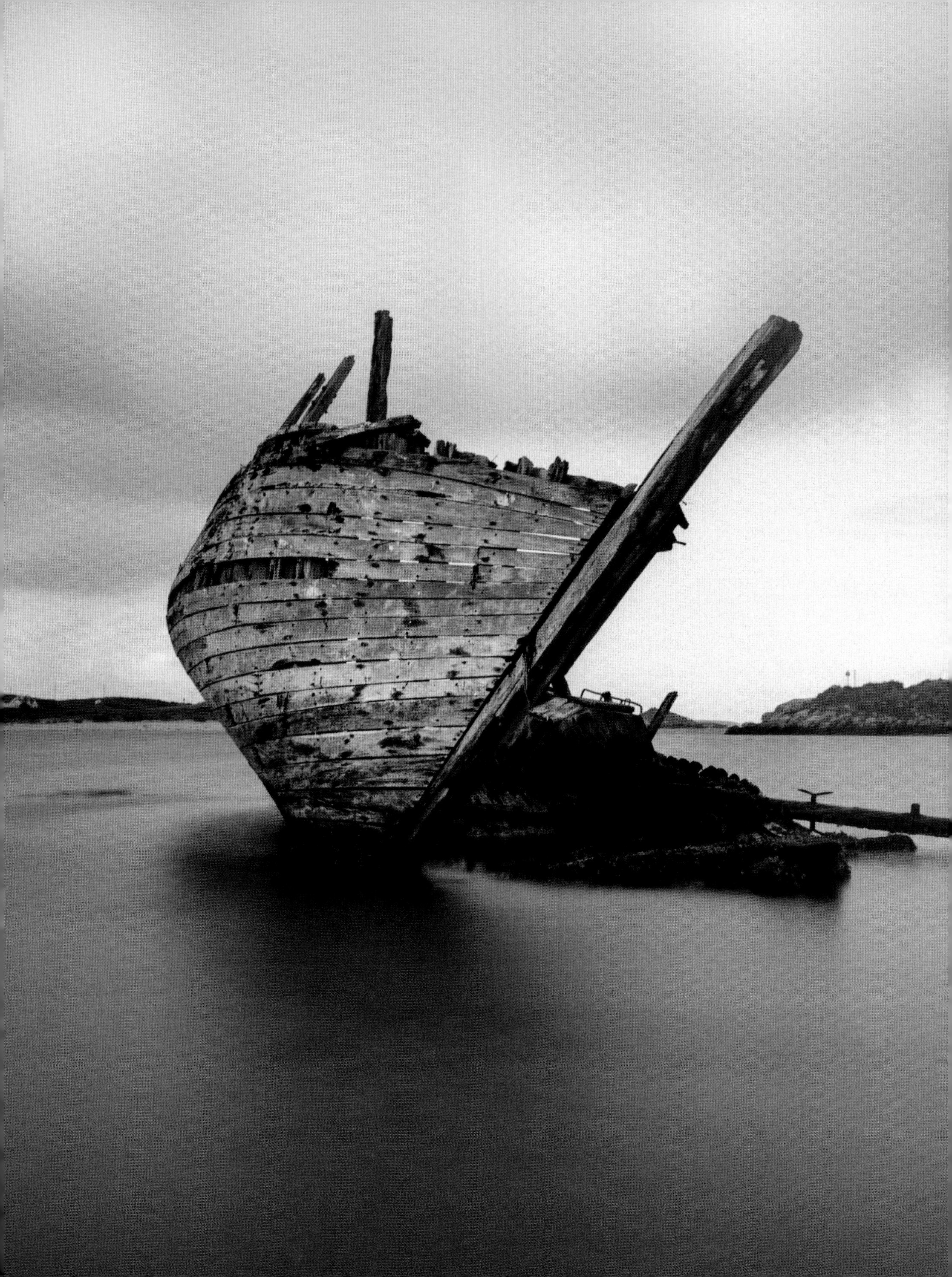

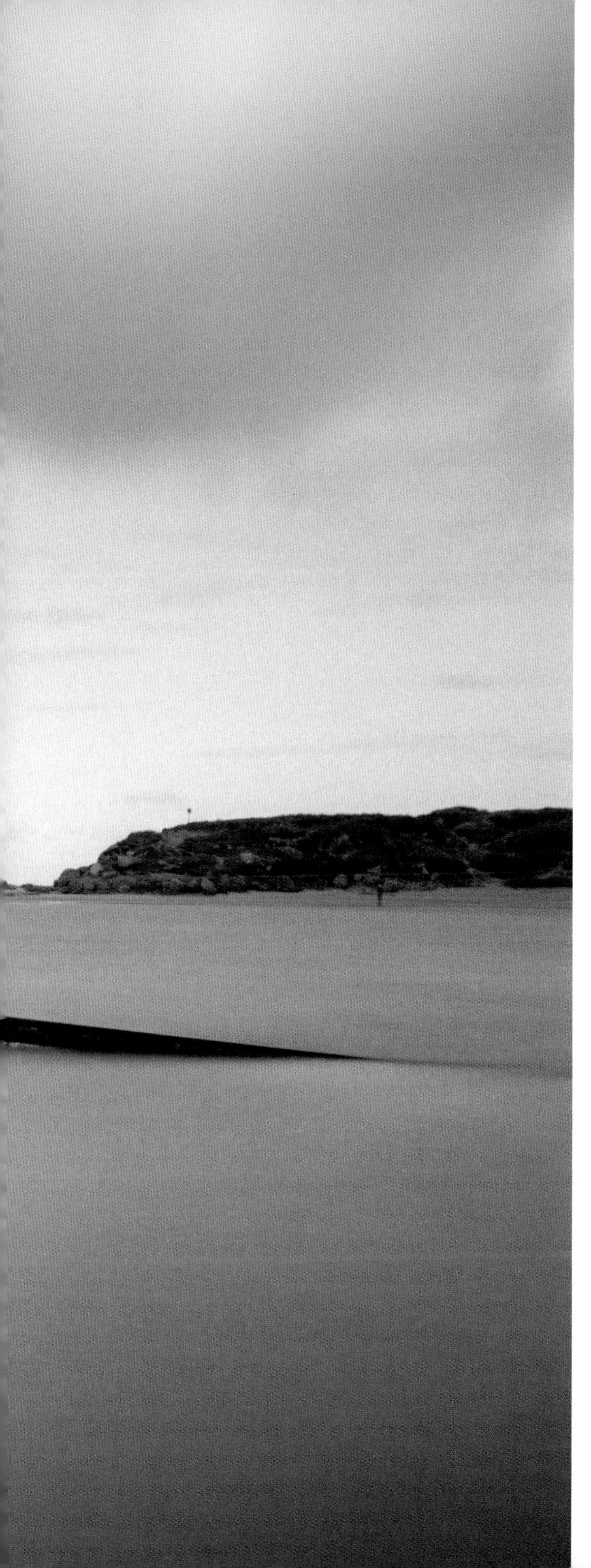

10
Fun with "Planned Accidents"

10.1   Cameras and Optics

If you consider how complicated our modern digital cameras are, it can be helpful and refreshing to remember that a camera is basically nothing more than a dark box with a hole in it and a shutter, with a piece of film or photo paper inside.

There are many cameras and optics nowadays that can let you experience the joy of low-tech photography. The less there is for you to adjust, the quicker you can shoot pictures instead of battling with buttons and wheels. See subject, point camera, shoot. That's how easy photography can be.

10.1.1   The Box Camera

The box camera is one of the dinosaurs among the simple cameras on the market. It has been available for more than a hundred years. Provided you don't try to get a collector's item, it's also generally one of the cheapest options if you want to take up low-tech photography. At flea markets or on Internet auction sites, you can get a working model for less than $12.

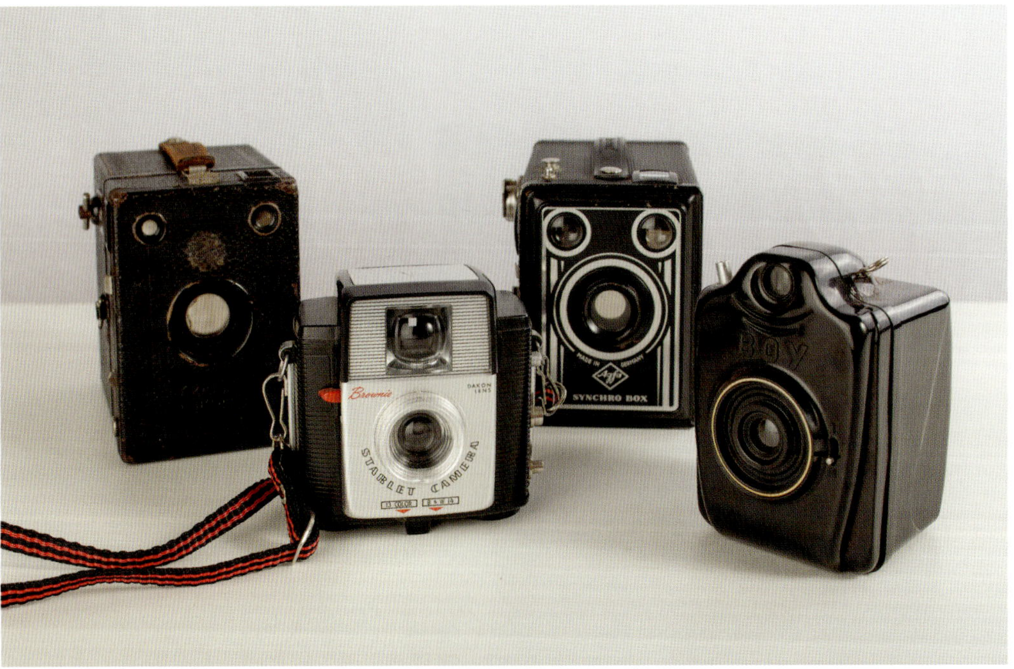

From left to right: Zeiss Ikon Box Tengor, Kodak Brownie Starlet, Agfa Synchro Box, Bilora Boy

A box camera is exactly what its name suggests — a box. This box has an opening at the front to let the light in and a film at the back. There are very few things you can adjust. Sometimes there are one or two different sliding apertures behind the lens element, and even more rare is a small yellow filter that can swivel in front of the lens.

Most of these box cameras manage with a simple lens element, referred to as *meniscus lens*, which resembles the lens in a pair of spectacles. This lens has no or very little coating. This gives the results of using this type of lens their special charm by adding "dreamy" unsharp effects or circular lens reflections to the pictures.

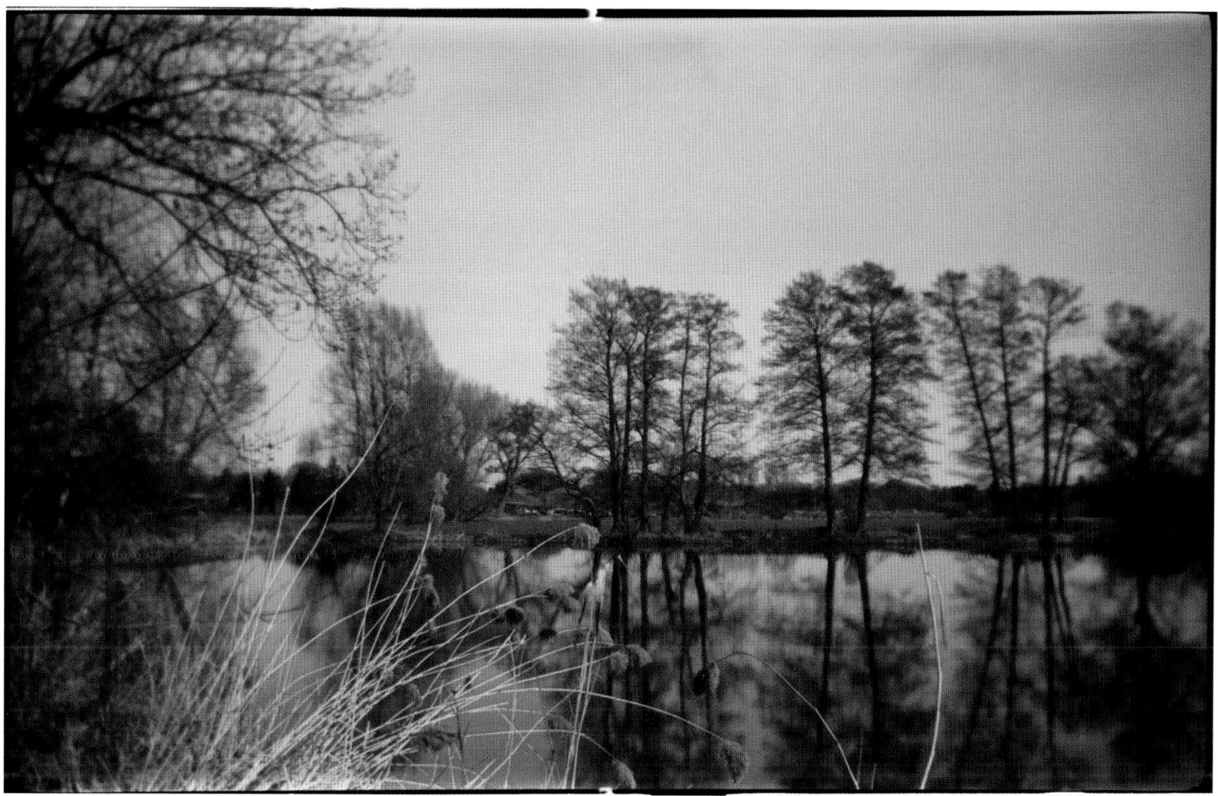

Landscape shot on Efke 50, taken with Agfa Synchro Box

In terms of film type, the box camera is inseparably linked to roll film. Most box photographers use either type 120 or type 127. Depending on the model, the image formats are 6×9cm, 6×6cm and 6×4.5cm (film type 120), or 4.5×4.5cm (film type 127).

Although all box cameras are slow (they shoot at around 1/25 sec. and their small lens aperture doesn't let in much light), we have not yet had a completely misexposed picture, even with medium-sensitive or low-sensitive films. You can safely leave your light meter at home when going on a photo excursion with the box camera. Being overly precise when composing your shot is also not recommended with most box cameras. The viewfinder crystals are often not positioned above the lens, so image elements you deliberately arranged at the edge of the shot may be cut off. The good old bull's-eye perspective can help: If you put your subject right into the center of the shot, or at least leave a bit of a safety margin around the edges, you'll usually keep the subject in the frame.

Most of these cameras are held at belly height for shooting, so you shoot from the hip. Take this as an incentive to listen to your gut rather than your head when taking snapshots with the box.

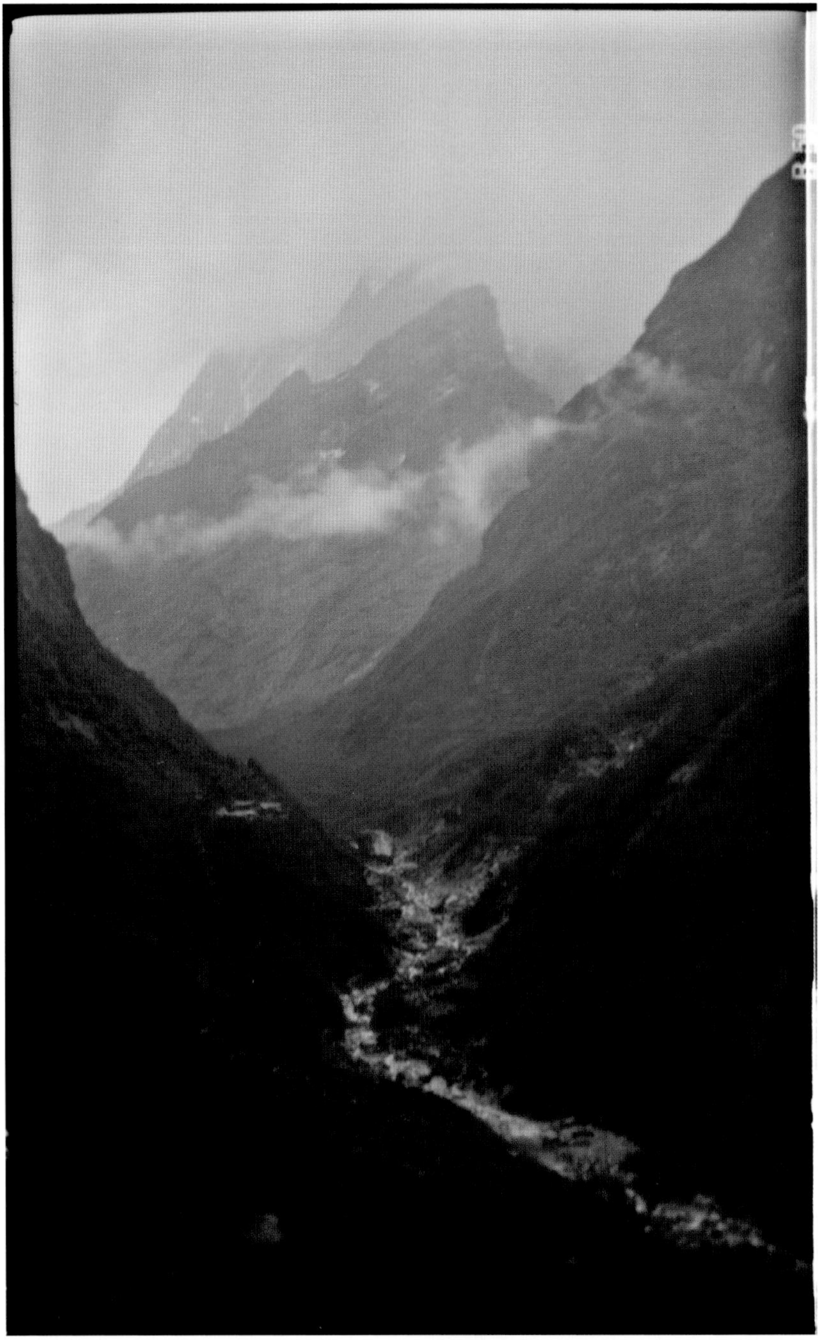

Landscape shot along Annapurna Circuit on Efke 50, shot with Agfa Synchro Box

10.1.2   Diana, Holga, and Other Toy Cameras

It all started with the Lomo LC-A, a viewfinder camera with fully automatic exposure control. It was mass-produced in St. Petersburg, Russia, in the 1980s and had one thing, above all: faults. Due to the great number of its weaknesses, this camera was not very popular in its domestic market. Serious photographers who were able to afford alternatives chose to steer clear of it.

In 1991, some students from Vienna (Austria) came across the LOMO Compact Automat in a photography shop in Prague and started experimenting with it. They were delighted by the creative potential of its flaws and founded a photo initiative in 1992: the Lomographic Society International. They laid the foundations for a trend in which light leaks, strange contrasts, and a shifted color representation were no longer regarded as flaws, but deliberately used as creative design tools. In the wake of this trend, simple cameras, such as the Lomo LC-A (35mm) as well as the plastic Diana and Holga (both medium format cameras), experienced a renaissance.

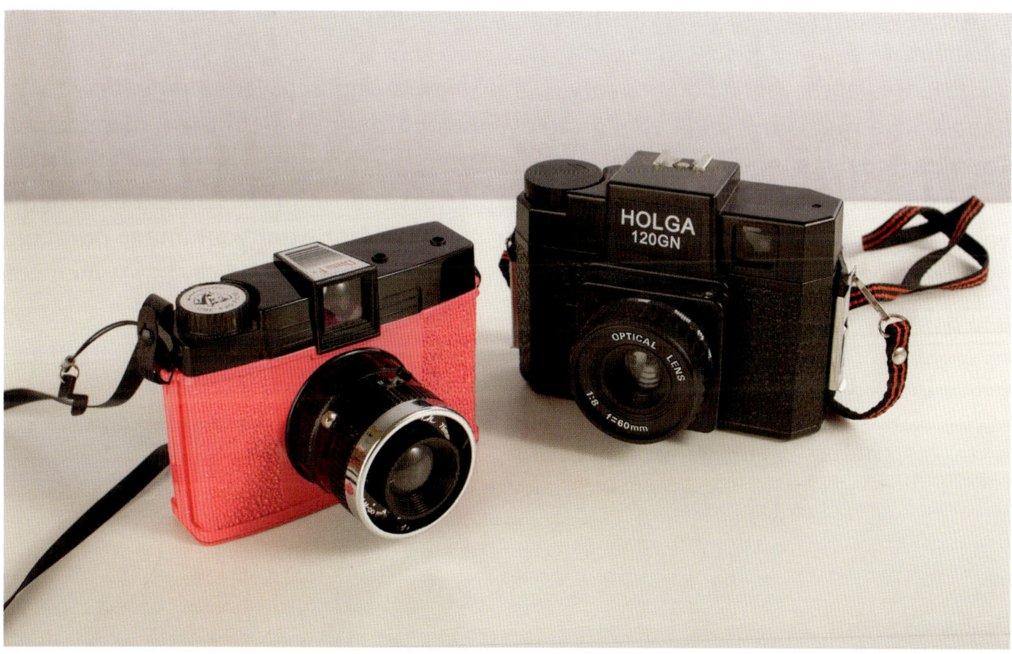

Diana F+ and Holga 120GN

The Diana

The original Diana is a camera classic. It was produced en masse in the 1960s by the Great Wall Plastic Company in Hong Kong and sold on the American and European markets. The manufacturers originally specialized in toys and promotional gifts, which is exactly what the Diana was. The original price for a Diana was less than $10. The Dianas that are made nowadays for and sold by the Lomographic Society are much more expensive copies (although still very affordable by comparison to other cameras).

Just like back in the 1960s, the Diana is a simple medium format camera for roll film format 120, with one shutter time and three available aperture openings. The camera has three distance settings of moderate precision. So far, we have been unable to determine if it makes any difference whatsoever to the resulting picture where the arrow on the focus ring is pointing.

The Diana has always been made entirely out of plastic and manufactured so cheaply that it should really be classified as a disposable camera in terms of the material value, even though many modern disposable cameras have clearly superior optics. In contrast to the Diana, modern disposable cameras are also light tight. As if that was what it's all about.

The lenses of the Hong Kong beauty contain simple meniscus lens elements with an image circle that is not wide enough to evenly light the picture in the 6×6cm frame. The viewfinder is simple, but sufficient for pointing the camera in the desired direction. There is no exposure counter. Instead, a red plastic window on the camera back helps you wind the film forward to the right place. If you do not want your image numbers exposed onto the film, you should cover this window with a bit of sticky tape when not using it to check the film transport.

Double Dresden. *Diana on expired Fuji Astia, cross processed using C-41 process*

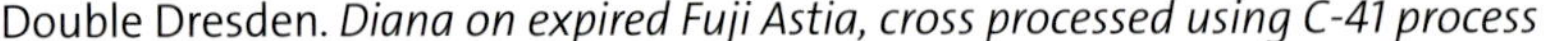

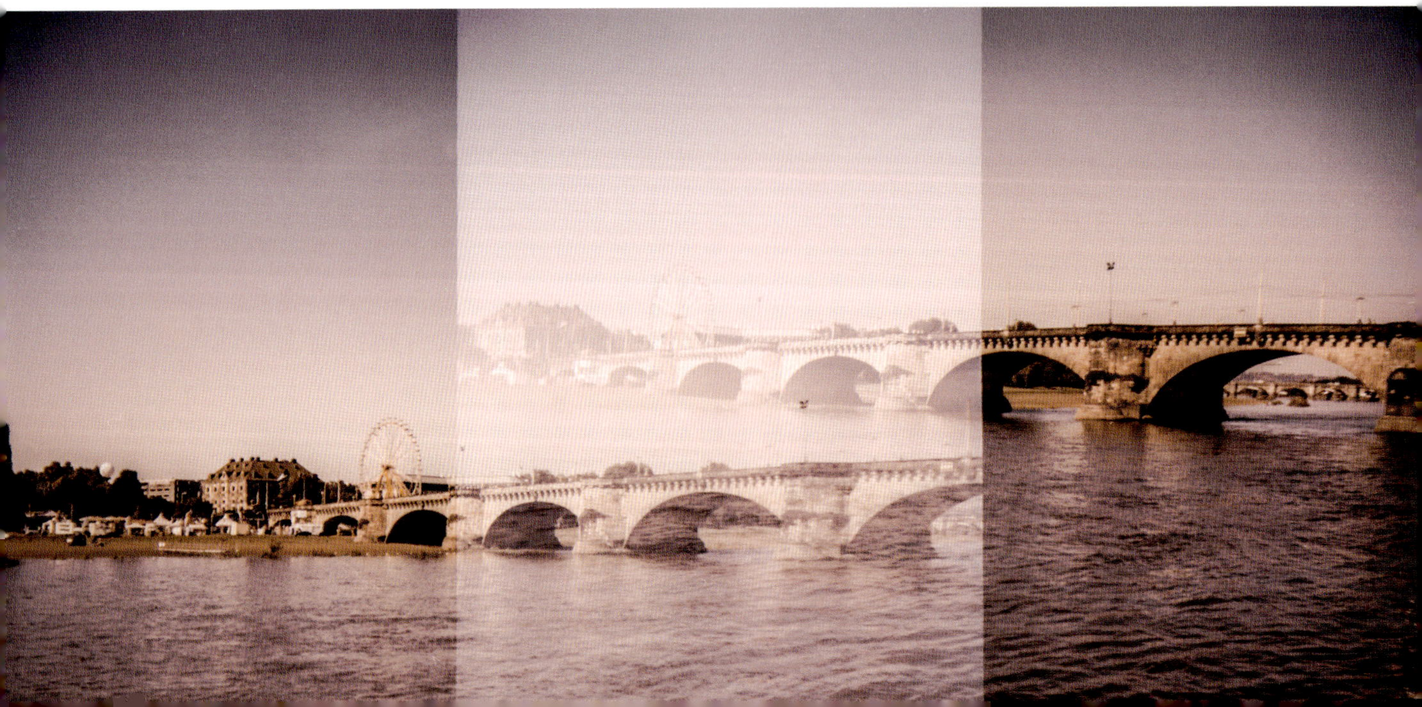

Sounds dreadful, doesn't it? Yet despite, or rather *because* of its flaws, the Diana is very charming. The pictures have a soft, slightly dreamy quality that you can hardly achieve via digital means. The too-small image circle of the lens causes natural vignetting, rather than the kind you add via image-editing software. If you deliberately or accidentally fail to wind the film-advance wheel far enough, this can result in double exposures, producing an interesting panorama picture of overlapping images.

The Diana is now sold as a "system camera." In addition to five lenses, there is a flash unit, different film masks, and other accessories, all made of plastic. Plus you can also use it entirely without a lens—with shutter lock—as a pinhole camera.

The Holga

The Holga, launched in 1982 by Hong Kong company Universal Electronics Industries, follows a camera principle very similar to the Diana. The Holga designer, Lee Ting-mo, created a camera that features partial unsharpness, possible color distortions, and dramatic shadows in the image corners. The case is also prone to light-leak. Holga fans know (just like fans of the Diana) that there is one thing they definitely will not get with their camera: technically flawless photos. But the Holga is still one of the most popular toy cameras and, by now, has become an object with a cult following.

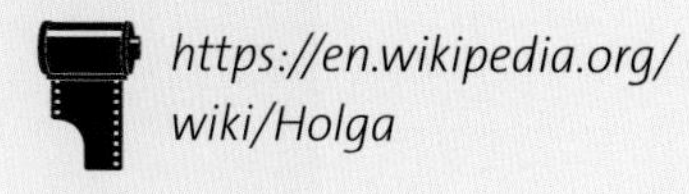

The Holga is slightly more robust, but even more basic, than the Diana. The different aperture settings, which appear as sun, sun with clouds, and cloud icons next to a lever on the lens, work in only the later models (from about 2009), and you can basically only shoot at 1/100 of a second with one single aperture (around f/13). Vignetting and edge unsharpness are comparable to those produced by the Diana. Some Holga models offer one single luxury: They feature an integrated flash.

All toy cameras have one thing in common: In terms of photography, they are great levelers. Because there is practically no technology to master, photographers can concentrate fully on the imagery of the picture. The popularity of Holga and Diana extended beyond the Lomography movement. These cameras were used at universities and photography schools because they gave students an uncomplicated means for training their creative eye.

Both cameras are also great gateway drugs for getting into medium format.

10.1.3   The Pinhole Camera

Whether for hobbyists, experienced photographers or absolute beginners, pinhole camera photography is always an interesting exercise and an experience that sticks in your mind. Compared to pinhole cameras, even Holga, Diana, and box cameras seem to have extravagant features. Taking pictures with a pinhole camera means getting right down to the mere essence of photography and omitting pretty much anything except the laws of optics. You'll experience how the basics of photography work: how a camera functions and how an exposure takes place.

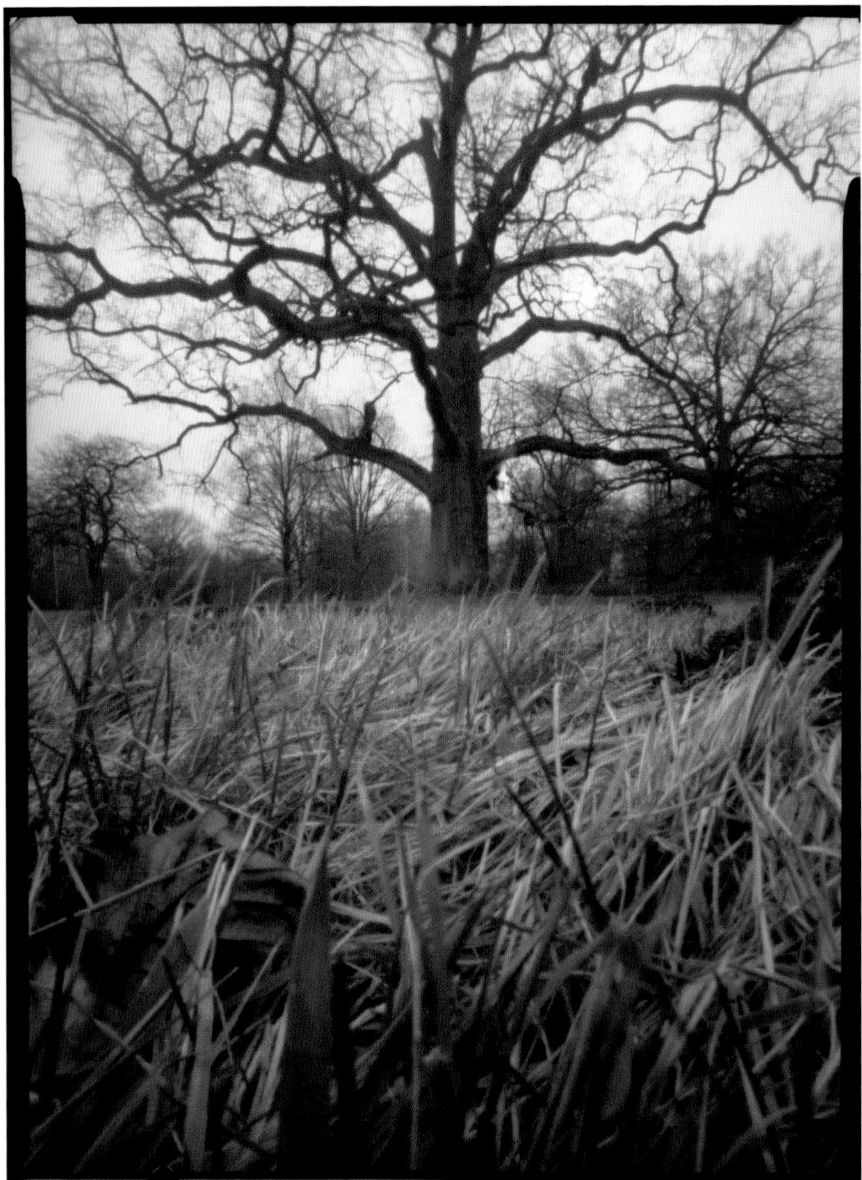

Hanover, Marquardt International Pinhole (MIP)

Pictures from a pinhole camera are truly unique. They look ethereal and atmospheric, because unlike with most modern cameras, the pictures captured are not just a moment, but a considerably longer period of time. Pinhole camera photography reduces the camera to its absolute minimum. Even the simplest lens is omitted. Instead, the camera uses only a very small hole, a pinhole, to bundle the light. The resulting pictures show an infinite depth of field. All non-moving elements in the picture, regardless of their distance to the camera, are always represented with the same level of sharpness.

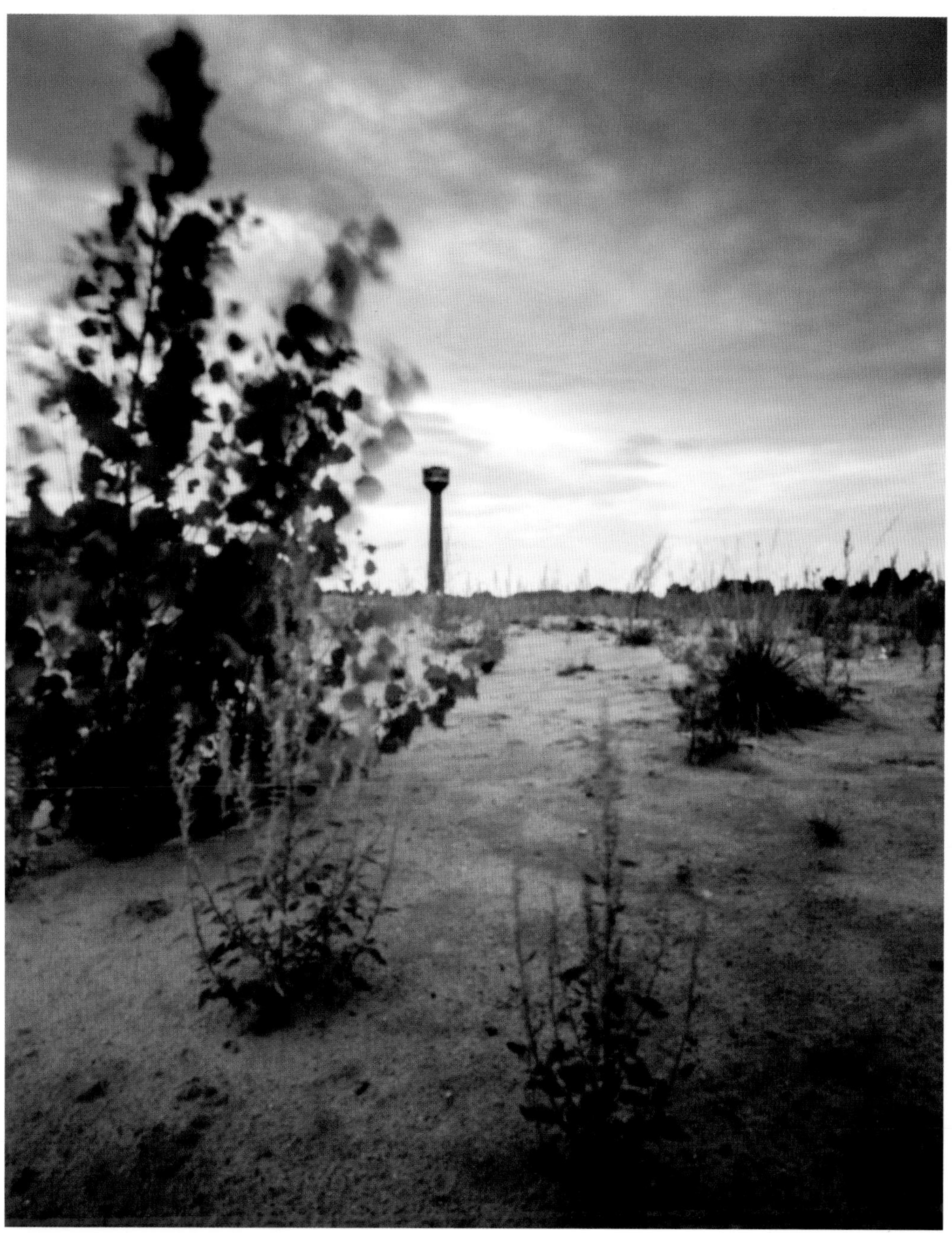

Old Continental Tire Company, Hannover, Germany.
Marquardt International Pinhole on Neopan Acros 100.

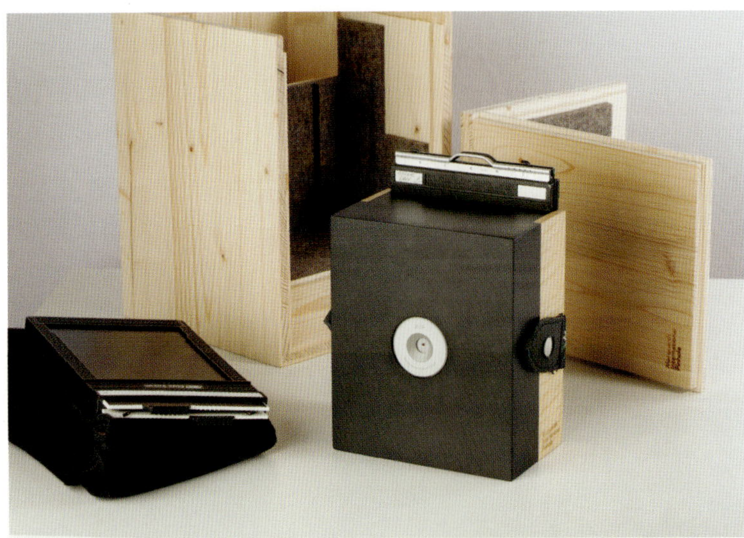

4×5" large format pinhole camera: MIP

Shots taken with pinhole cameras are long-time exposures. Depending on the size of the hole, the exposure time can be a few seconds, several hours, or even days. Because the tiny hole represents a very small aperture and lets in little light, pinhole photography is best suited for outdoor shots.

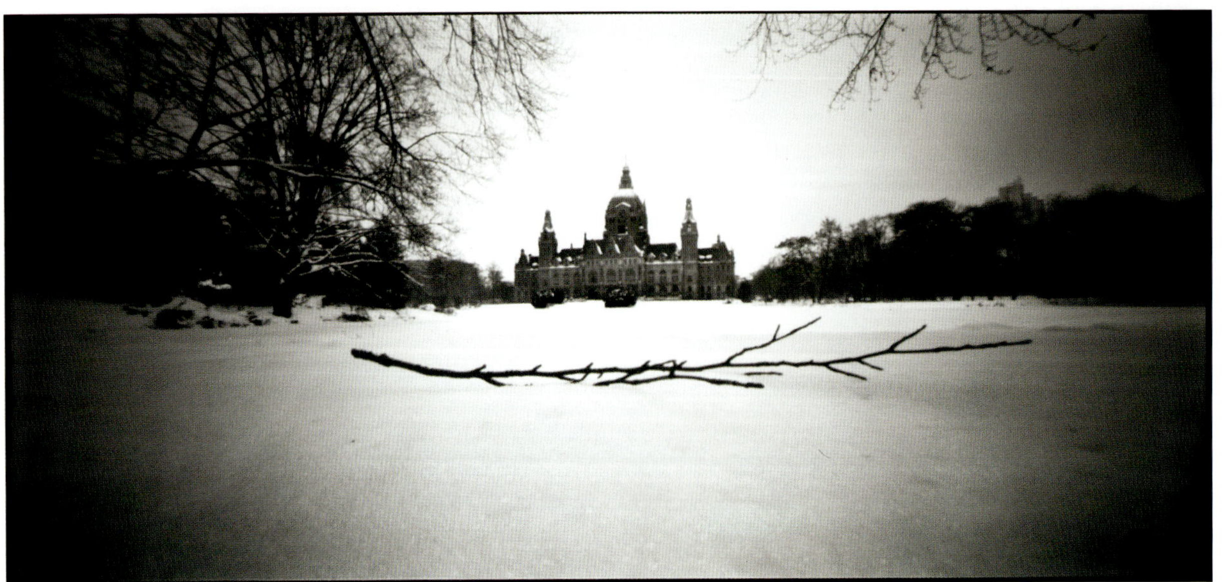

Hanover, town hall. Developed in Caffenol-C-H

If you buy a standard pinhole camera, the camera's f-number is usually known. A smart-phone app can help you work out the suitable exposure time. This type of minimal camera is available in many versions—from very basic and cheap (in the plastic universe of toy cameras) to noble wooden cameras with or without brass fittings. You can find something to suit every taste. Even digital photographers will get their money's worth. Specialist camera shops offer camera body caps with a built-in pinhole (some even offer sophisticated vignetting) for many common system cameras.

You can easily build pinhole cameras yourself out of a tea caddy, beer can, bin, matchbox, pumpkin, and more. Sometimes all it takes is a rainy afternoon, a suitable camera/container, a pin, some black cardboard, sticky tape, and spray paint.

10.1.4   The Subjektiv

You can have fun with "planned accidents," and not just with camera models. You can also go crazy with various lenses and adapters.

Certainly one of the more luxury models of pinhole camera is the Subjektiv, developed by Monochrom in collaboration with Novoflex. This modular lens has a focal length of 65mm and is an optical system with four interchangeable optical modules. It gives you the option of capturing light in many different ways, and each module has its own characteristic imagery. You get a pinhole aperture, a zone plate, an acrylic lens element, and a meniscus glass lens. There are also pinhole aperture sieves and photon sieves available. All models have something in common: They are not suitable for technological precision and optically perfect photography. They are used because their optical flaws, faults, and quirks contribute to a creative image composition.

10.1.5   Zone Plate

A zone plate is a plastic disk or foil with a printed pattern of concentric circles. It has similar properties to a lens, but the mechanism of the pattern is light diffraction instead of light refraction. A zone plate shows more pronounced irradiation than a pinhole aperture, which can create a creamy, impressionist-style image.

10.1.6   Lensbaby

Although the name Lensbaby now refers to a whole product range of different lenses or lens-type optical attachments (some of which show resemblance to the Subjektiv), we still associate this term with the original version: a flexible, bellows-like tube with a simple lens and interchangeable aperture inserts.

Our favorite Lensbaby, marketed in various versions as Lensbaby 2.0, Muse, or now Spark, is a selective-focus lens. You focus it by compressing the flexible tube and then bending it upward, downward, left, or right, until the small area of focus is where you want it. As you can see, the Lensbaby is also not for perfectionists. Precision is not its strength.

The size of the focus sweet spot can be adapted for the Muse model via differently sized aperture inserts. The Spark has a fixed aperture f 1/5.6.

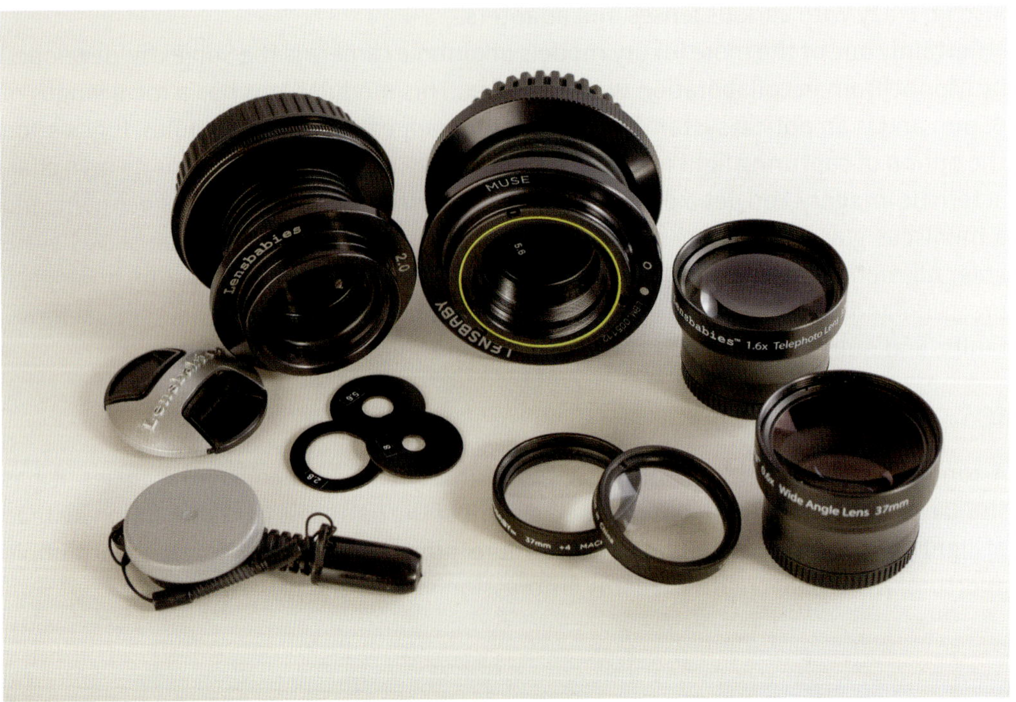

Lensbaby 2.0 with accessories and Lensbaby Muse

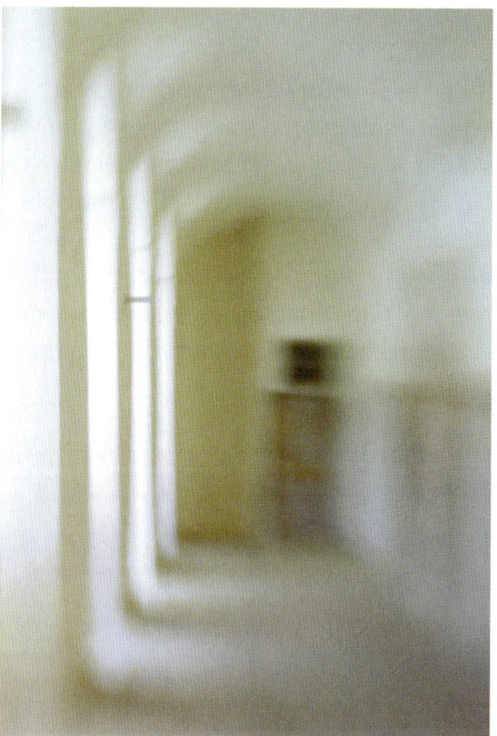

Cloisters, *Inzigkofen, Germany. Lensbaby Muse at fully open aperture on expired Kodak Portra 160 NC*

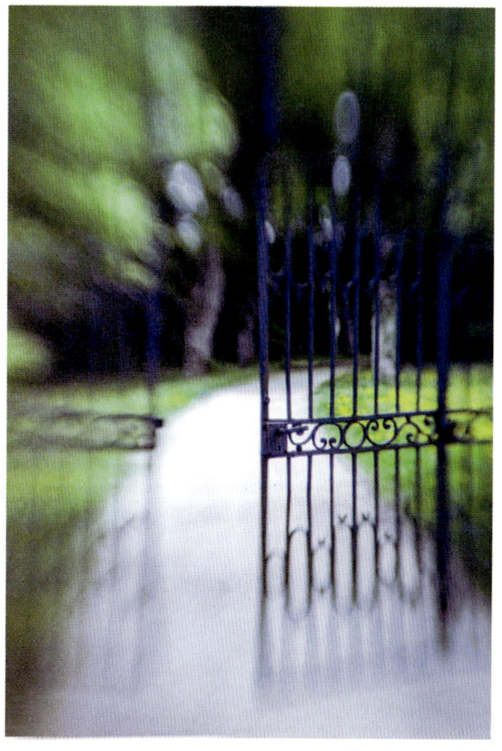

Gateway to the Cloisters, *Inzigkofen, Germany. Lensbaby Muse at fully open aperture on expired Kodak Portra 160 NC*

Squeezerlens: The Squeezerlens (http://squeezerlens.com) follows a similar concept to the Lensbaby.

Using lenses that were predominantly not intended for use on a camera—for example lenses from old projectors or enlargers—Frank Baeseler, who died in 2021, created optics that produce a very special image impression. His son Sven has continued the business ever since. The usually very high-quality glass is mounted in a bellows, which has a bayonet on the other side to match the respective camera. Focusing is usually done by compressing or expanding the bellows.

Monika owns a Squeezerlens for her Pentax 67. This special lens is now available not only for medium format, but also for many SLRs and mirrorless system cameras.

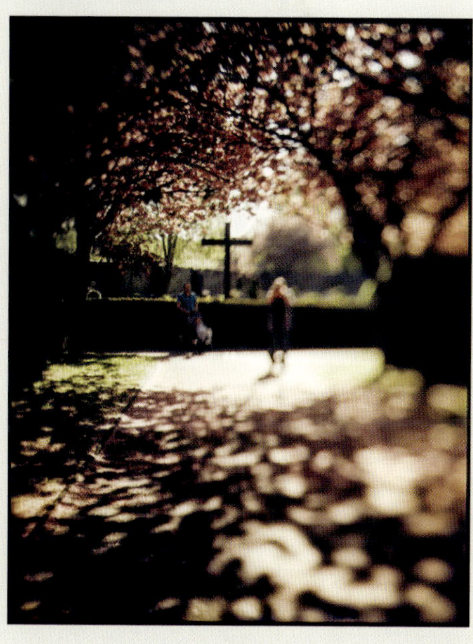

Cherry blossoms. *Squeezerlens on Pentax 67 on Lomography Slide / X-Pro 200*

10.2   Expired Film

Expired films are those in which the recommended best-before date has been exceeded (by quite some time). Unlike with old food, your films won't start smelling musty, curdle, or go moldy, but for a photographer who wants predictable and consistent results, expired film is unusable. For photographers who like experimenting, however, expired films can be just the thing.

When films age, their properties change. With some films, the changes are subtle; with others, changes are more dramatic. There are films that are so stable they can still yield normal and first-class results beyond their best years. Provided you keep them protected from heat and radiation, you can enjoy regular results well past the best-before date.

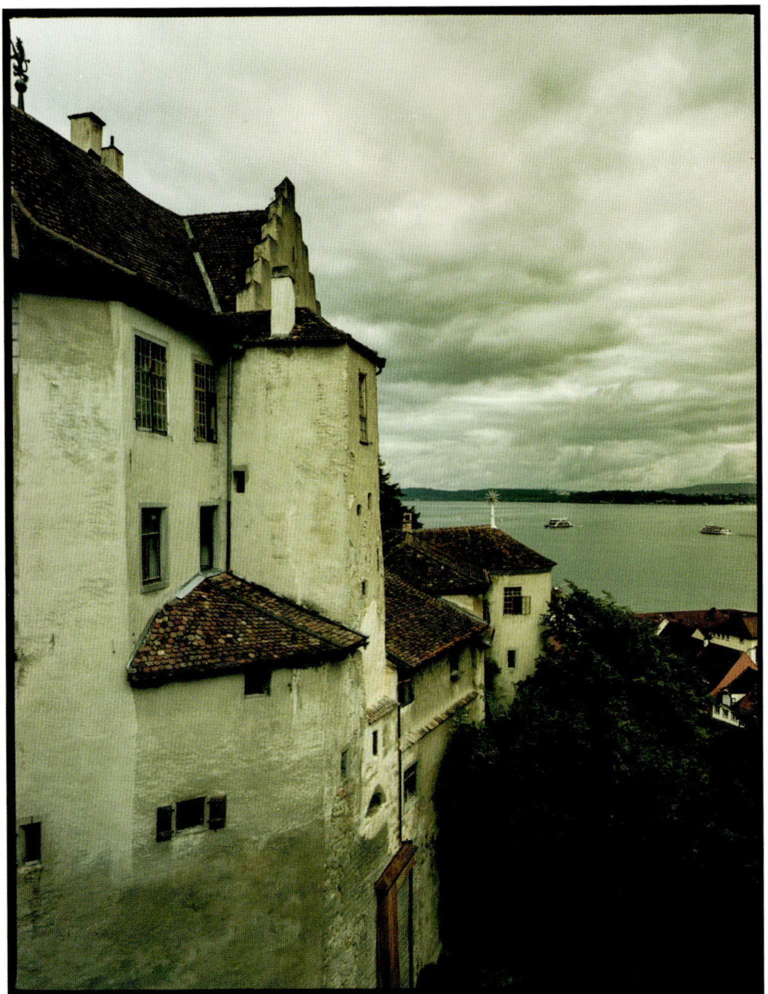

Pentax 67 on expired Kodak Portra 160 VC

But most old rolls of film have an eventful past (many journeys, a few days spent on the parcel shelf of a car, and so on). You'll often observe that the film grain is inconsistent with your expectations; the color particles in the emulsion appear rougher or more enlarged than they should, so the sensitivity decreases. Rule of thumb: The higher the nominal film speed, the more it degrades over time when stored. You should also always expect color shift because not all of the pigments in the emulsion share equal stability. For example, you will notice that films lose their reds first, and the color effect changes to look yellow-green or blue. Some films show a desaturation of colors, some don't. Expired films are like a grab bag: You never know what you're going to get.

> Black-and-white film has better storage stability than color film.
> We have used black-and-white film successfully (without any exposure time adjustments) even when it was 10 or more years past its expiration date. Films you discover in cellars are particularly interesting in this respect, because they've been stored at stable temperatures.

If you want to preserve the qualities of your favorite old film for longer, it's best to store it in a cold place. Storing film in the fridge or freezer can postpone its slow decay.

10.2.1   Experimenting Is Fun

You can have hours of fun rooting around on photo platforms such as Flickr and 500px for pictures taken on expired film. You can admire the effects, but please do not make the mistake of assuming that the same film in your camera will behave in exactly the same way. Too much depends on how long the film has been past the expiration date, how it has been stored, which camera you are using, and the light conditions in which your photo is taken. The composition, age, and temperature of the developer chemicals also play a role in the result you eventually get. In the end, you can only do one thing: experiment, experiment, and experiment some more.

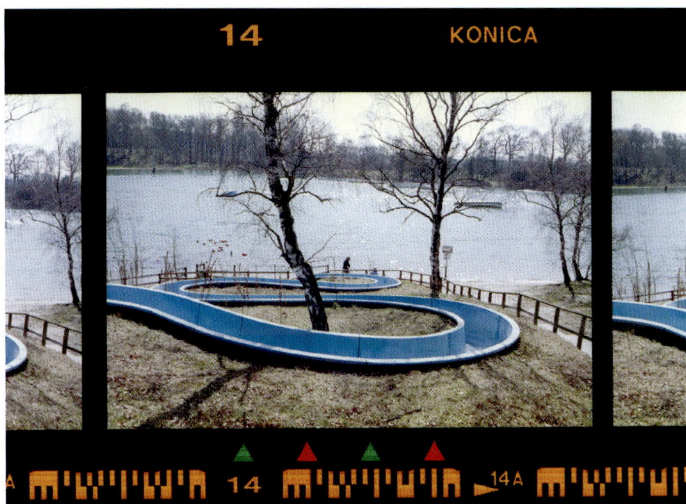

Konica Centuria 100, expired 05/2005. The color shift from the long storage period fit well for this design.

Take the time and have fun checking out different makes and different film speeds at different times of the year in varying conditions. Feel out how overexposure or underexposure can affect the result, and figure out which camera works best with a certain film and its quirks. Be open to the wide range of results you'll achieve, and let yourself be surprised and enchanted by them.

Due to the color shifts, it is not necessarily a good idea to test out unfamiliar expired film in a portrait session, unless you and your model are specifically after unusual skin tones. Generally, landscape shots or architecture shots are better suited for testing expired films. If you come across a particular film that you like in its expired version, go ahead and get a few extra rolls. Most likely, they will behave consistently to each other, so you have plenty of spare material to accomplish even larger projects.

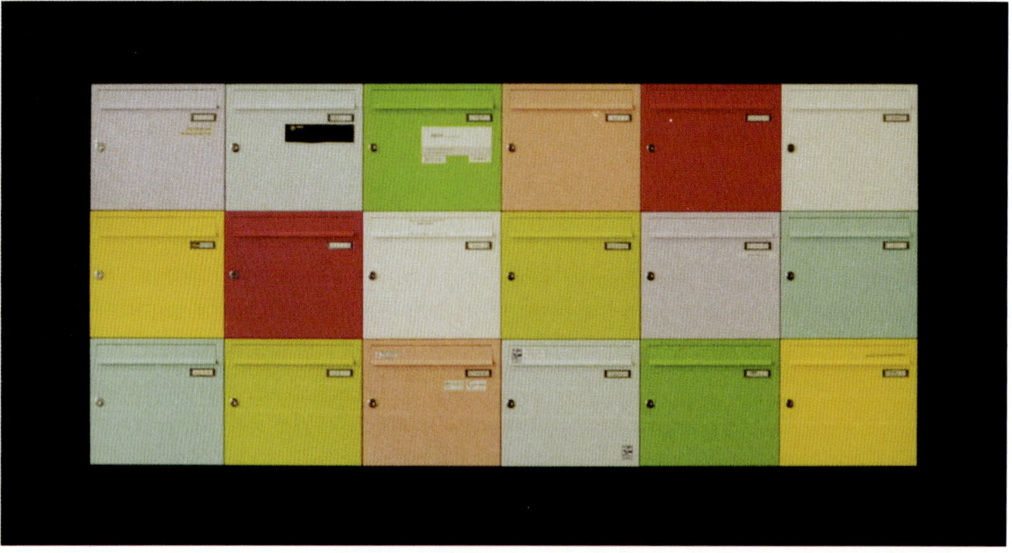

Konica Centuria 100, expired May 2005. An image of the same subject shown on page 69 displays a color shift due to the long storage period of the film.

10.2.2   Film Speed and Light Conditions

If you search for tips on how to use expired film, you'll often hear that it should be used in plenty of light, for example outdoors or in the studio, due to its decreased sensitivity. The general advice is to expose one stop brighter for every five years the film has been expired. Indeed, you can minimize the risk of completely failed shots if you follow this rule, but it does not always allow you to check out the interesting limits of old film. Some of our most impressively atmospheric shots on expired film came about by exposing it at nominal speed in indoor scenes with low light, and then developing the film normally. For our willingness to embrace risk, we were rewarded with an almost monochrome effect and very pronounced results in vibrant colors. If you want to be on the safe side, you can take a sequence of shots at different exposures.

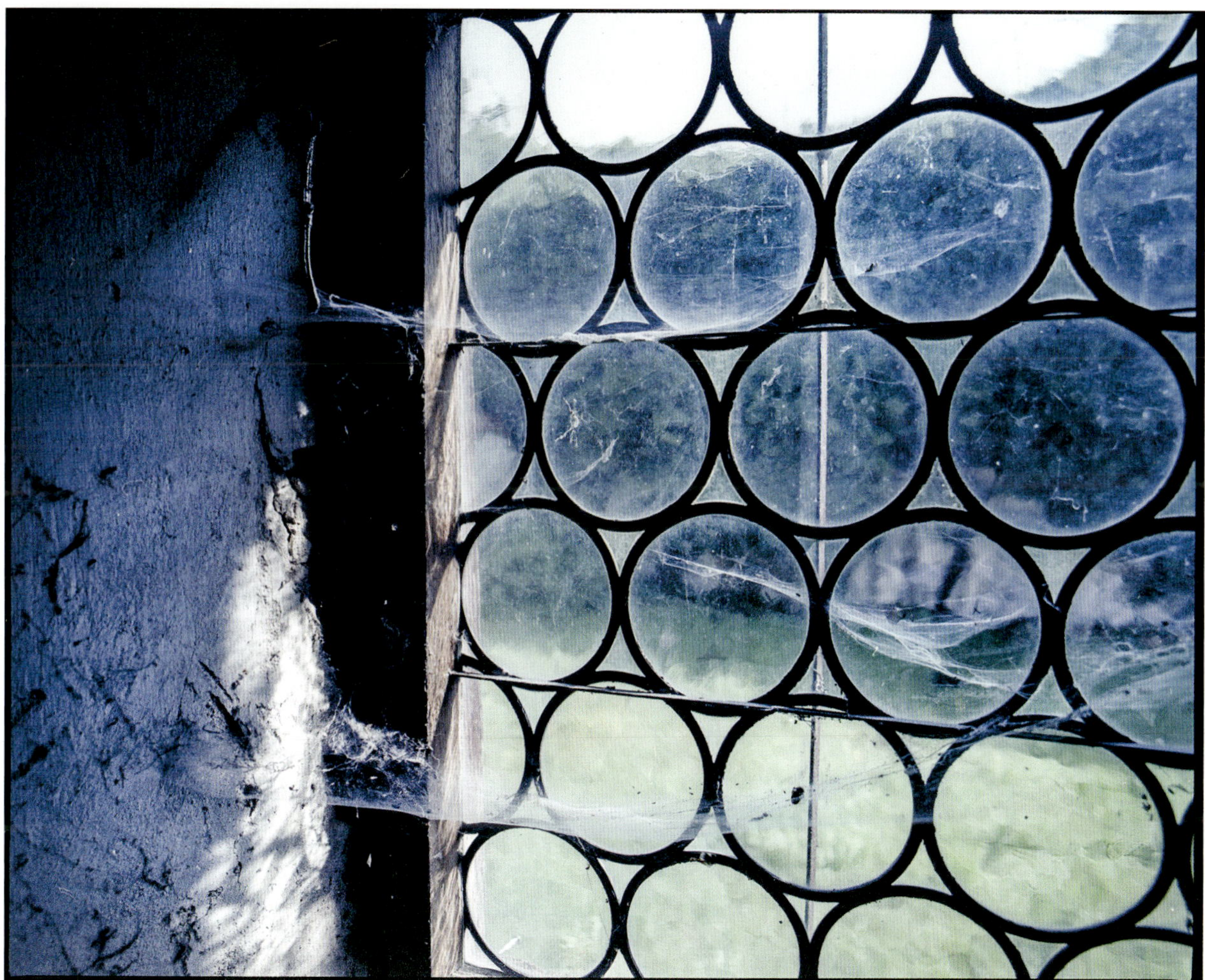

Silence. *Inzigkofen Monastery on expired Kodak Portra 400 VC, MHD 2004*

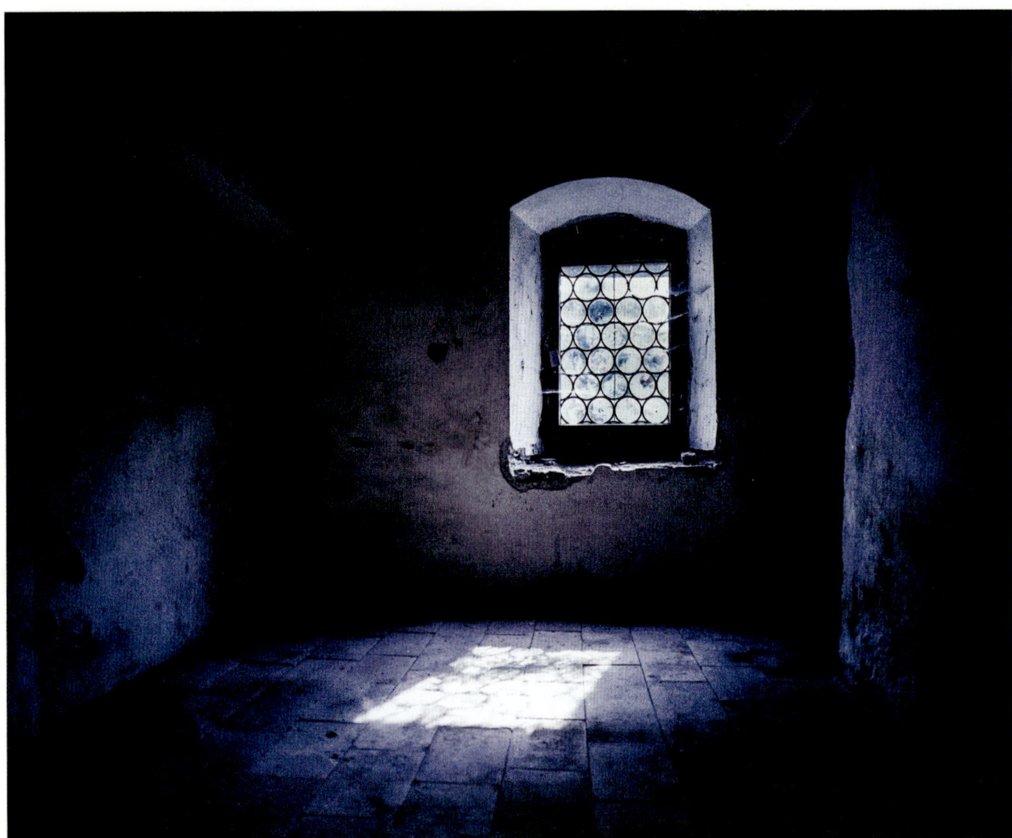

Total Silence. *Inzigkofen Monastery on expired Kodak Portra 400 VC, MHD 2004*

10.2.3   The Special Joys of Cross Processing

Cross processing, or developing slide film in C-41 process or color negative film in E-6 process, offers plenty of room for creative experiments, even with fresh film. In this case, you can achieve many different and unpredictable results just by varying exposure settings or using different makes of film.

Slide film that you're going to cross process often benefits from overexposing the film by up to two stops. On the other hand, it can sometimes pay off to starve the film of light. Many cross-processed films show an entirely different color temperature when you underexpose them than when you overexpose them. Pictures tend to have a warm color climate when overexposed, and dark image areas often look very cool. If you cross process expired film, the film's rougher structure and already present color shifts will be emphasized for a more surreal effect.

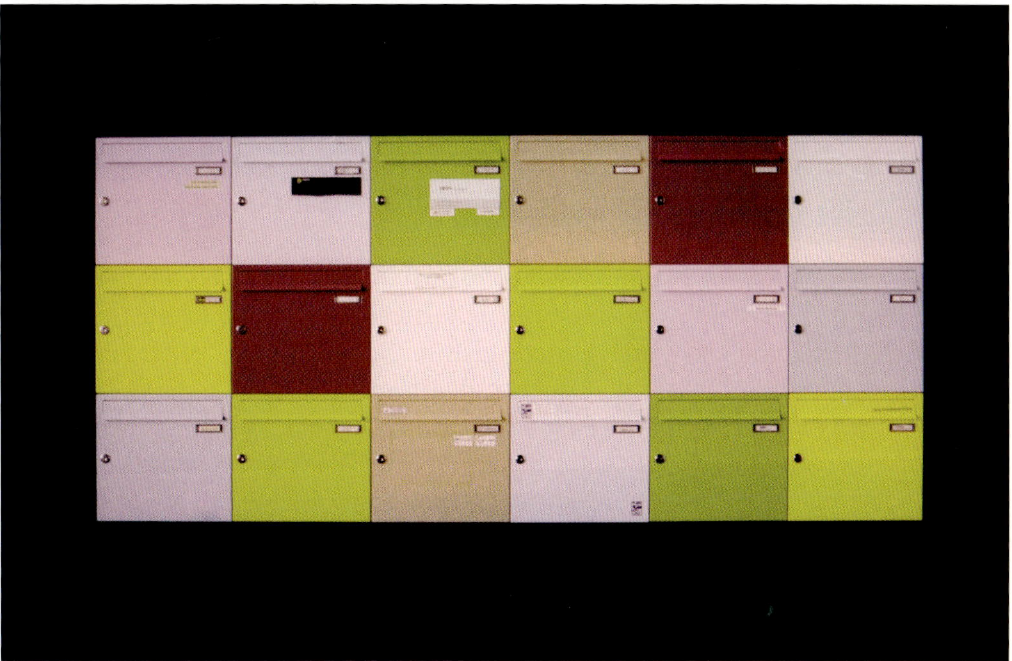

Fuji Sensia in cross development. Here, too, the colors of the Mailboxes have significantly shifted, especially the blue tones.

10.2.4   A Residual Risk Always Remains

The many wonderful and often dreamlike pictures on exposed film that you can marvel at online are certainly only a fraction of the number of shots that were actually taken. You can assume that there are also many unsightly results that are not being displayed online. That's the risk you have to accept: There is no guarantee that your pictures will be successful.

10.2.5   Treated Film

Are experimental optics, expired films, and multiple exposures still too tame for you? If so, taking a trip into the realm of pretreated or post-treated film may be for you. Not so very long ago, you were able to go to small online shops to buy film material that had been manipulated in various ways. While we were working on this book, these online shops seem to have disappeared. Perhaps the market for ready-made experimental films is not a very profitable niche. However, those who treasure complete surprise derived from utterly unpredictable results might like to go hands-on themselves. This does require a bit of time, but is much cheaper and also more fun. For some effects, all you need are a few DIY tools and a changing bag. For others, you need white goods and a darkroom.

If you search online for "film photography hacks" you will quickly find tips. The number of possible tortures you can submit your film material to is enormous. You can bend or scratch your film before or after exposure to get more texture into the picture. You can wash the film in the washing machine or dishwasher, spray it with salt water or soak it in fizzy drinks or vinegar, followed by a long bath in cold water and a hair-dryer session in the darkroom. Often these experiments are done with slide film, which is then cross developed in C-41 process.

Photo emulsions that have been subjected to such treatment react in a totally unpredictable way, and it's hardly possible to match the subject to the effect. Depending on your approach, you can observe more texture on the surface, color shifts, color clouds, and/or partial tearing of the light sensitive layer.

Warning: We found many interesting and beautiful pictures online. But we did not try any of these experiments ourselves. If you want to experiment, you are doing so at your own risk—and maybe it's best not to use the most valuable camera you own for these experiments.

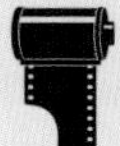

Dr. Lab Experiment One: Do the Dishwasher
http://www.lomography.com/magazine/47053-dr-lab-experiment-one-do-the-dishwasher

30 Ways to Hack Your Next Roll of Film
http://www.gizmodo.co.uk/2011/12/30-ways-to-hack-your-next-roll-of-film

10.3   Double and Multiple Exposure

Double exposures are among the great creative playgrounds in photography. They are rather unpredictable and use up a lot of film, but they are great fun and always good for unexpected results. They offer the option of combining many small stories into one, or presenting them side by side in one picture. You can correlate things that are foreign or combine different perspectives of a subject into one picture. When using color film, the colors of the individual exposures also overlap and mix under the principles of additive color. If you combine all of this, you can create surreal image worlds that can be interpreted very differently by each viewer.

Although unplanned or even unintentional double exposures can often have appealing results, you can get more success if you do more than just press the button more than once. You are trying to overlap the exposure of two (or more) pictures in such a way that you get the different levels to interact, not just blend together.

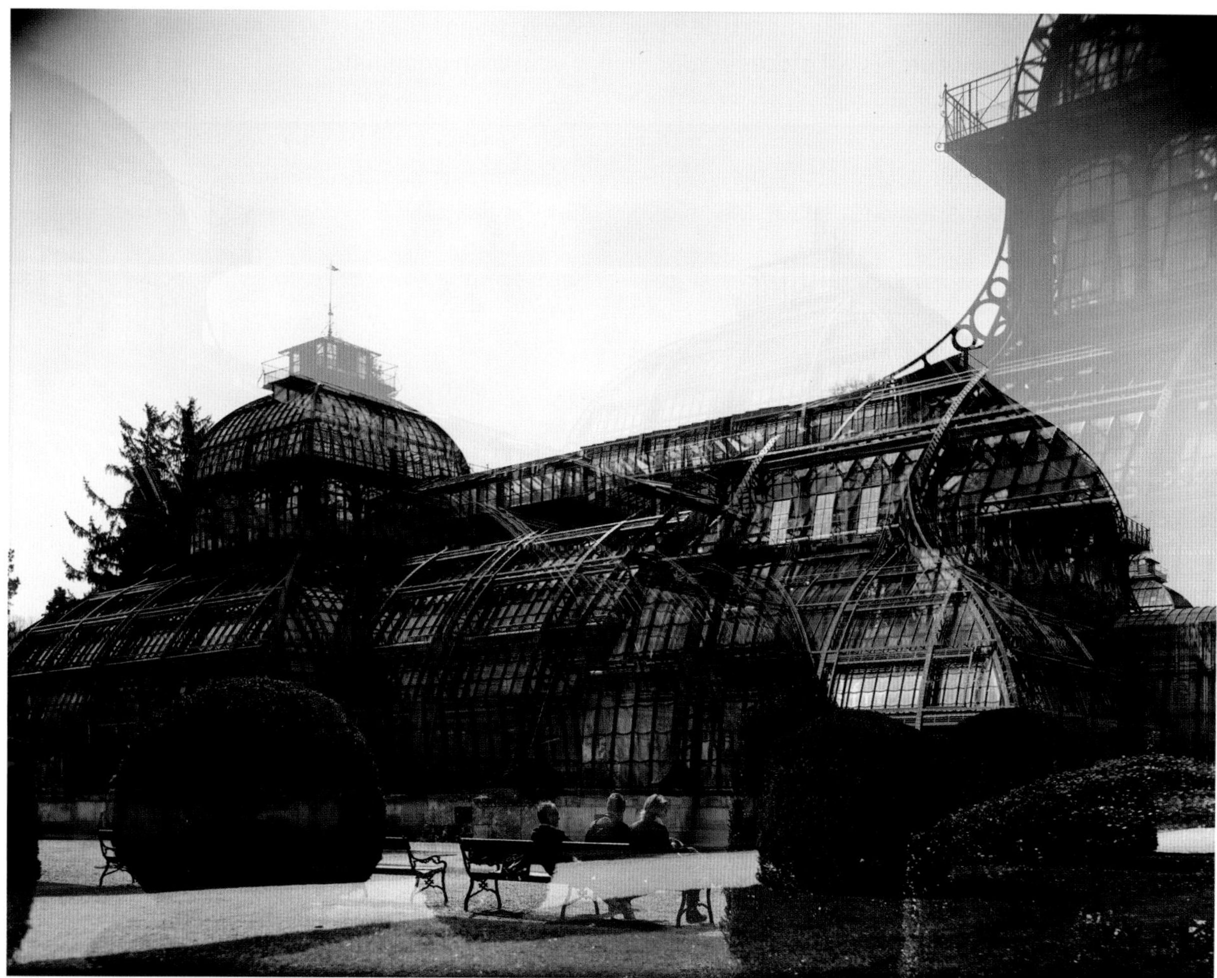

Accidental double exposure: Greenhouse in Schönbrunn Palace park, Vienna. Graflex Crown Graphic on wephota ortho 25.

If you want to control your multiple exposures, you can draw up a sketch of the envisaged effect and think carefully about how to arrange the central image elements in the viewfinder. But often, it's enough to visualize where the darker areas of the shot will be, because that's where a second exposure will be the most obvious. High-contrast shots with larger bright and dark areas are best for practicing. Combine patterns and textures with portraits or architecture, close-ups with things that are far away, water with desert, or silhouettes with plants: Your limit is your own imagination!

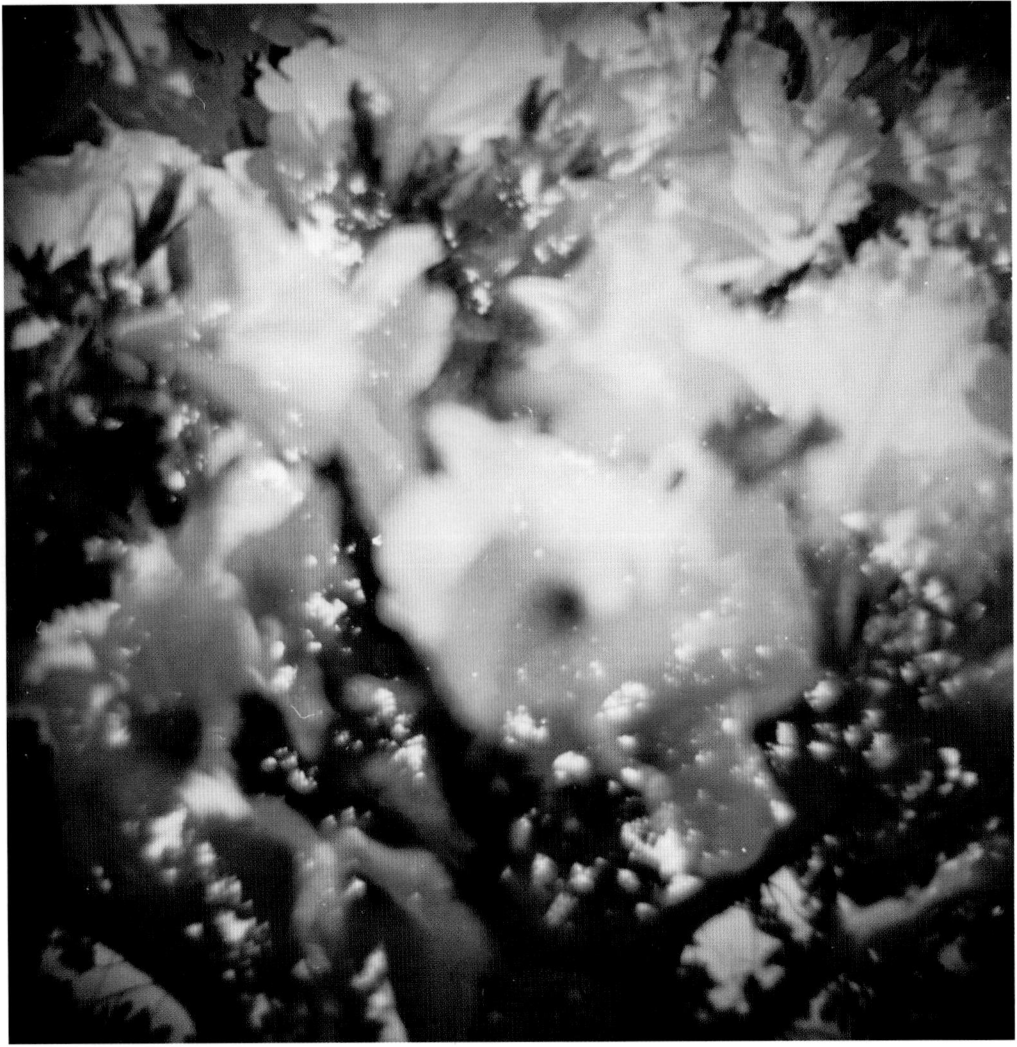

Double exposure with Diana F+ on expired Ilford XP2

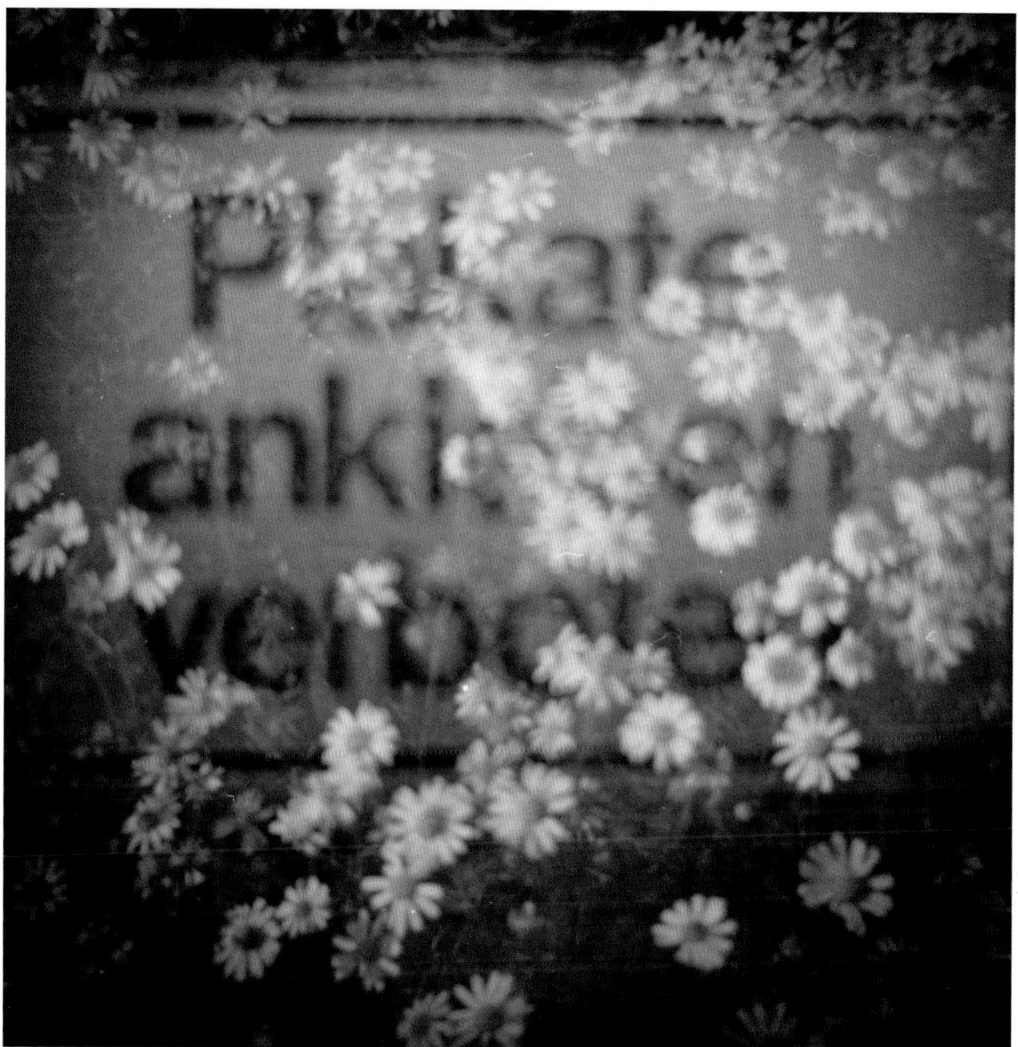

Double exposure on Diana F+ on expired Ilford XP2

The Exposure

Negative film is very forgiving when it comes to overexposure, but you should try to adapt the exposure of individual shots so it adds up to the correct exposure for the composite. Otherwise, you may find that you end up with overly washed out or poor-contrast pictures. You have the option of controlling this via the ISO value—for example, if you are using a film with ISO 100, do each exposure at the setting for ISO 200. Or, you can adapt the time and/or aperture value.

If you want to give both exposures the same amount of space in the finished picture, stick with halving the amount of light per shot. But you can also emphasize one of the two exposures more than the other by splitting the exposure in a different ratio, such as 1:3 to 2:3.

There are cameras where precise exposure control is hardly possible, or not possible at all. This includes simple cameras such as the box camera or the Diana. If you want to use these for multiple exposures, just use a lower speed film. As a basic rule: Negative film is better suited than slide film because it has a greater exposure latitude. Black-and-white film is more forgiving than color film.

Which Cameras Are Suitable?

Multiple exposures are easiest to achieve with cameras where the film simply has to be wound manually via a rotary control. As soon as you "forget" to wind it on, double exposure is possible. That's how it works with the classic box camera or with a Diana or Holga.

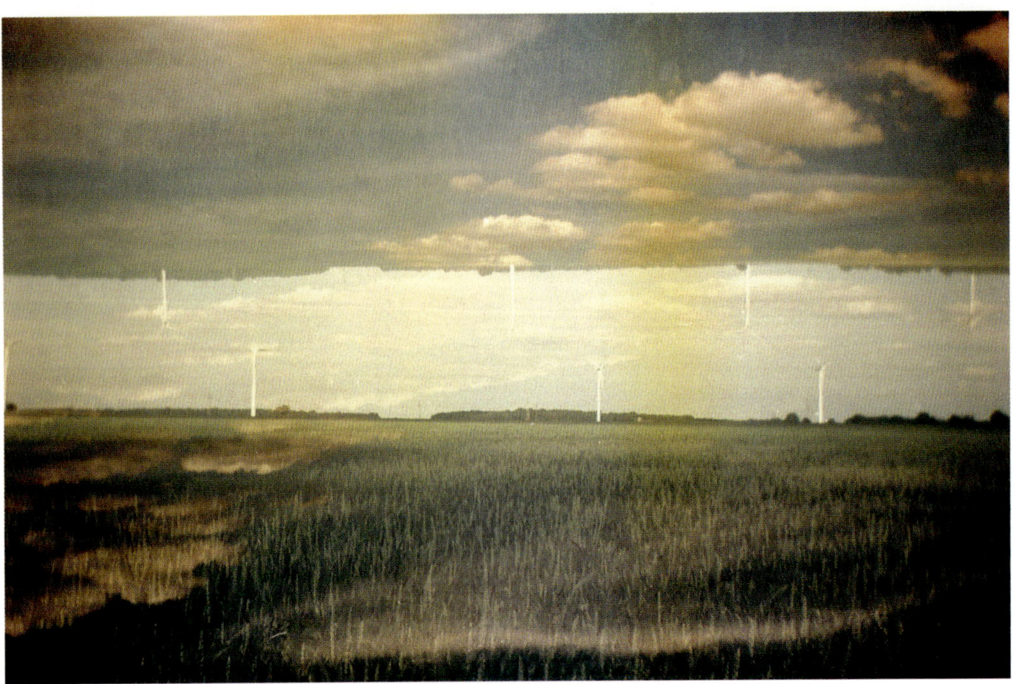

Double exposure with Agfa Synchro Box on expired Kodak Portra 160 VC

With many camera models, the shutter cocking mechanism is linked to the film advance. There are cameras that have a button for disabling this mechanism, so you can cock the shutter without advancing the film. This button is often referred to as the double exposure switch or the MX switch (MX = Multiple Exposure). Some cameras can also be tricked by pressing the rewind button while cocking the lever. But this method does not always work and is not very accurate because you cannot tell how much of the film advanced, and your shots can overlap around the edges.

If your favorite camera does not like double exposures or refuses to be tricked, you can just put the film into the camera twice. With 35mm cartridges, this is quite straightforward. Make sure you do not completely rewind the film at the end of the first sequence of shots to prevent the film leader from vanishing into the cartridge. (If that happens by accident, a film leader retriever can help.) Then you can put the film back into the camera a second time and expose it again. To make sure the new pictures are exposed in the same places as the first, you should mark the film with a foil pen at the point where the film was pulled out of the cartridge for the first exposures. Then wind the film to the same place before threading it back into the camera so the result will be accurate.

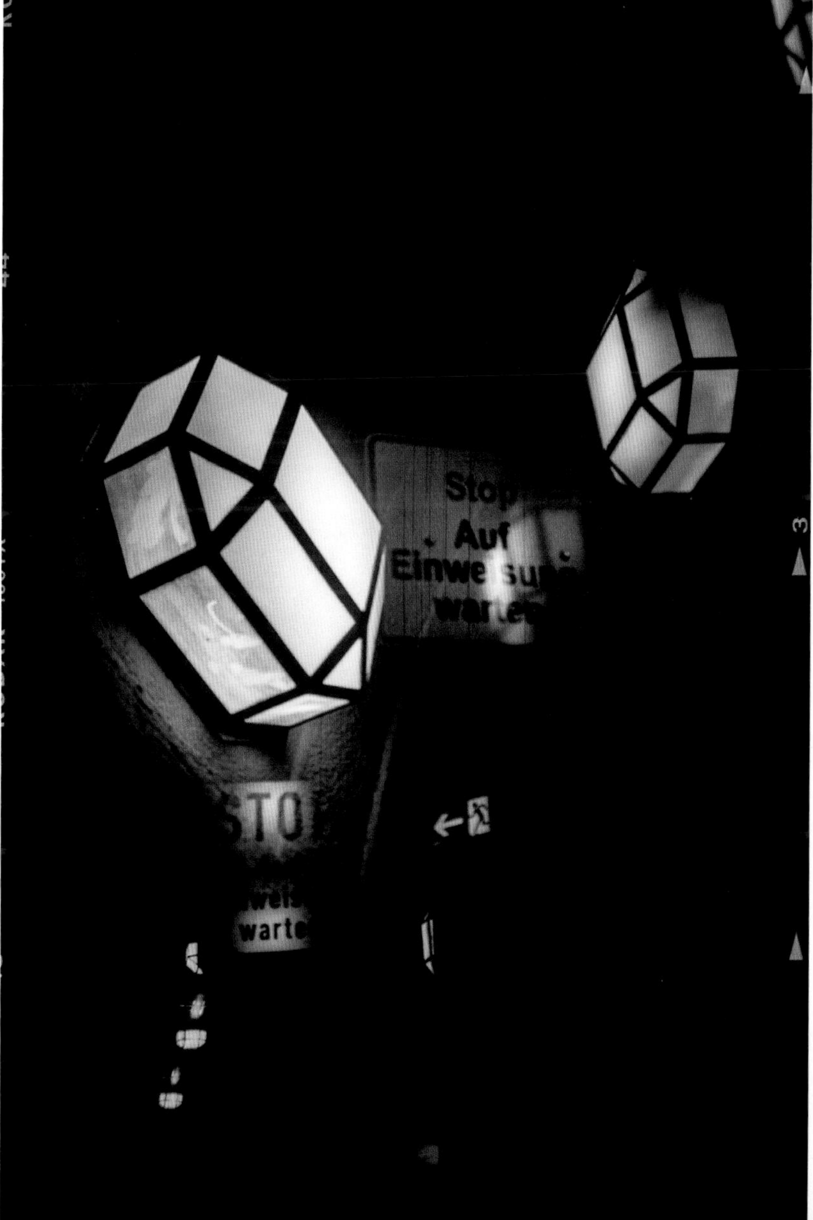

Multiple exposure in old Elbe Tunnel, Hamburg, Germany

Fans of unplanned double exposures pass an exposed film on to a photographer friend for the second set of exposures. Let yourself be surprised by the results and see what can happen if two different views of the world mix together.

Roll film is not rewound at the end of the film, but advanced fully onto the take-up reel and held down with sticky tape. If you want to put roll film back into the camera a second time, you have to wind it onto an empty reel in the changing bag, first.

Fake Double Exposures

Another option of working with different levels in one picture—creating a kind of fake double-exposure effect all at once—is playing around with simultaneous reflections and views through other objects. This enables you to combine different perspectives. For the viewer, this forms a kind of picture puzzle that will hold the eye for more than just a few seconds.

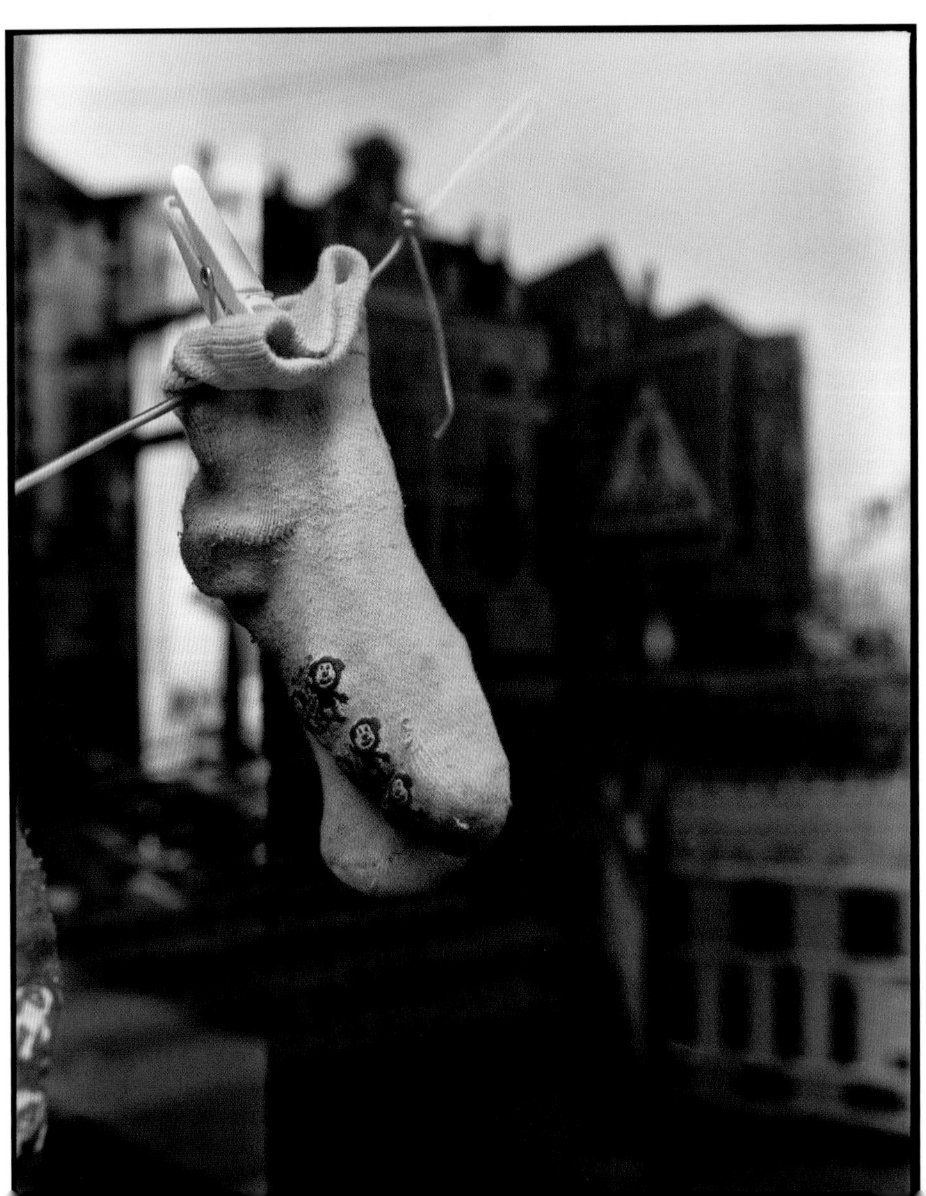

Waiting.
*Pentax 67 on
Kodak Tri-X 400*

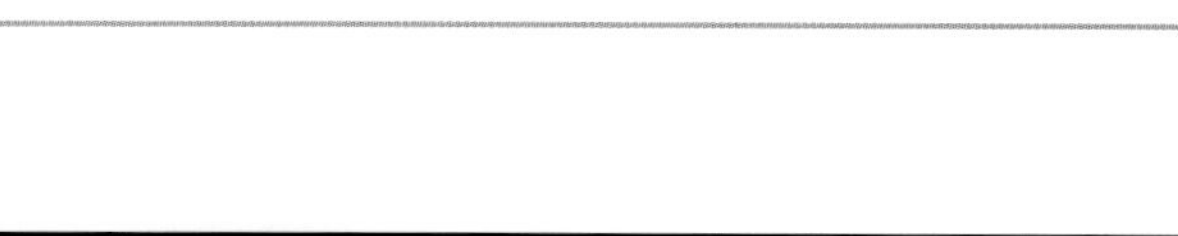

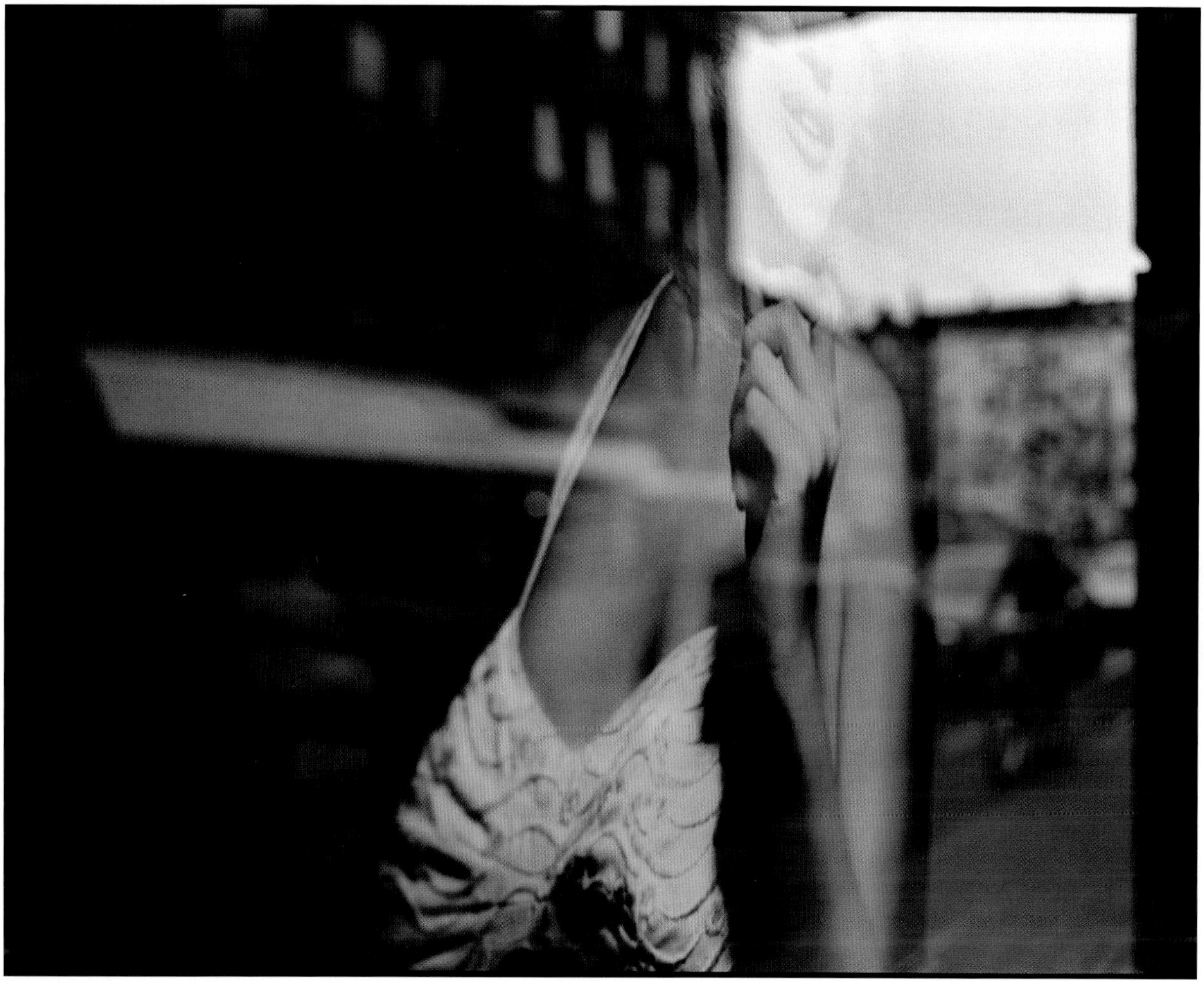

Oh, Marylin. *Pentax 67 on Kodak Tri-X 400*

Long Exposures

In the early days of photography, when the photo material was not very sensitive and the lenses were not very long, exposure times of 5 seconds or more were a necessity. If you sat for a photo portrait, your smile may well have frozen on your face. Sitting still for so long was incredibly tiring, which is perhaps why the people in the old photos always look so serious.

Today, the situations in which you *have* to use long exposure times are getting rare, but situations in which you can have fun with long exposure times are still a-plenty. The long exposure time has become a creative tool. If you use it during bright daylight instead of at night, it has the potential of producing a photograph that can turn the viewer's way of looking at things on its head.

Visible or Invisible?

You can use long exposure times to turn people who are walking through the picture invisible. If the people only appear in the viewfinder for a short time in comparison to the shutter time, they will not leave any visible traces on the emulsion. An absence of people where you would expect to see people can create a very special atmosphere in architectural shots. On the other hand, you can also emphasize how lively a city is by not freezing ambient movement, and instead making it visible through blurriness.

In contrast to exposures that happen in the blink of an eye, shots with long exposure times do not just capture a moment. They show the subject in time. They visually shrink down the time of the shot to a single moment for us as viewers. Movements of things or people are blurred, and seem to flow through time. Depending on whether you expose for a few seconds or several days, you can capture moving clouds, flowing water, or the wilting of a flower. For the human eye, this suddenly reveals connections that were hidden before.

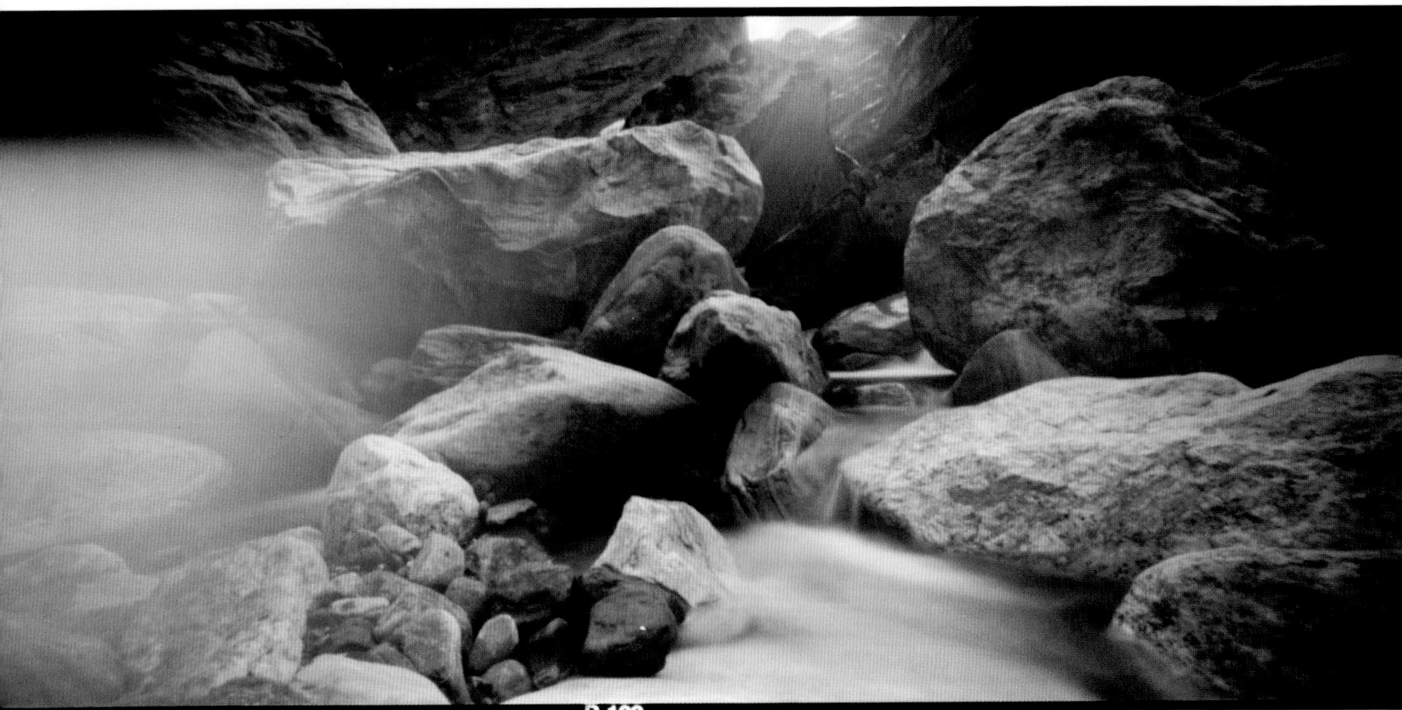

Long exposure time along Annapurna Circuit on Efke 50, shot with Holga-120WPC

Accessories

To be able to play around with long exposure times in daylight, you often need a bit of help. Even with low-speed film of ISO 25 or 50, and depending on the weather, you may only achieve exposure times of a second at the most, even with the aperture closed. This is often not enough to really make movement visible. ND (Neutral Density) filters or gray filters can help. With these, you can reduce the light getting in through the lens as much as is required to achieve the desired exposure time.

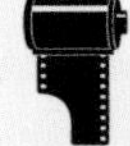 You should also definitely arm yourself with a sturdy tripod.

Depending on the camera type or model, you have different modes to choose from for setting long exposure times. Only a few analog treasures feature an automatic system that covers exposure times beyond one second. Most cameras have either a bulb mode (B), where the shutter is kept open for as long as you hold down the button, or a (T) mode where the shutter opens when you press the button the first time and closes with the second press. In both cases, you should use a (lockable) cable release or a remote release for more modern cameras, for shake-free triggering.

Reciprocity Law Failure

Every film—but also other analog materials, such as photo paper—has a typical sensitivity to light. Within certain limits, you can assume that the ratio of incident light to optical density is linear and yields comparable results in constant lighting (light intensity multiplied by exposure time). This is referred to as the Bunsen-Roscoe law or reciprocity law. With long exposure times (and with particularly low light), a photographic emulsion often no longer behaves in a linear way. Doubling the exposure time does not necessarily produce twice as much density on the film. In this case, the exposure time determined by the light meter needs to be extended by a certain factor for each specific material. This effect is referred to as reciprocity law failure, reciprocity failure, or Schwarzschild effect (after the person who discovered it, astronomer Karl Schwarzschild). Depending on the material, reciprocity failure can occur with exposure times of more than about one second (with color film, it can even happen at about 1/30 second).

Check the packaging of the film you are using or the included data sheet: The curve shown there will show you exactly which value you'll need to correct the measured exposure time.

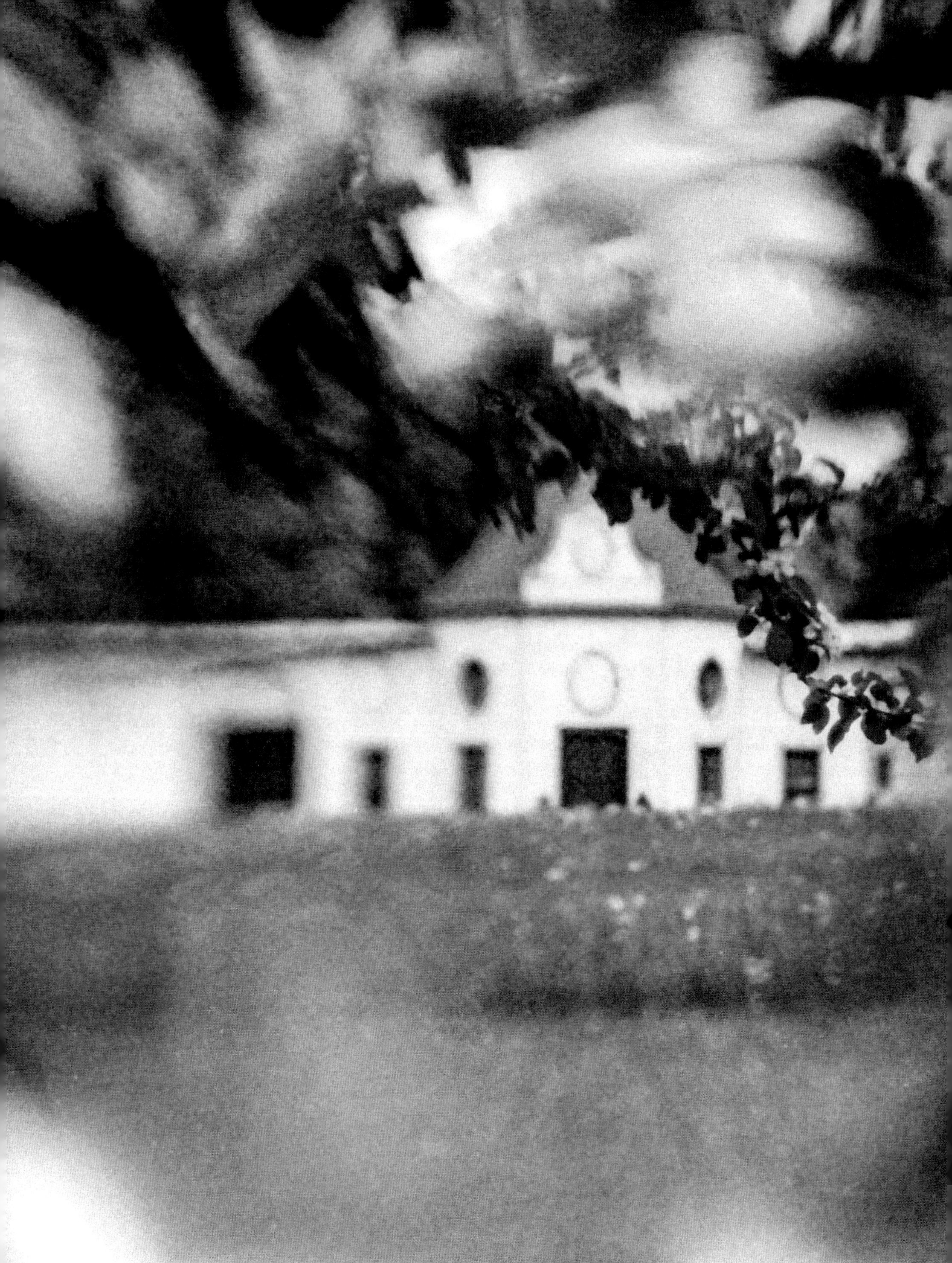

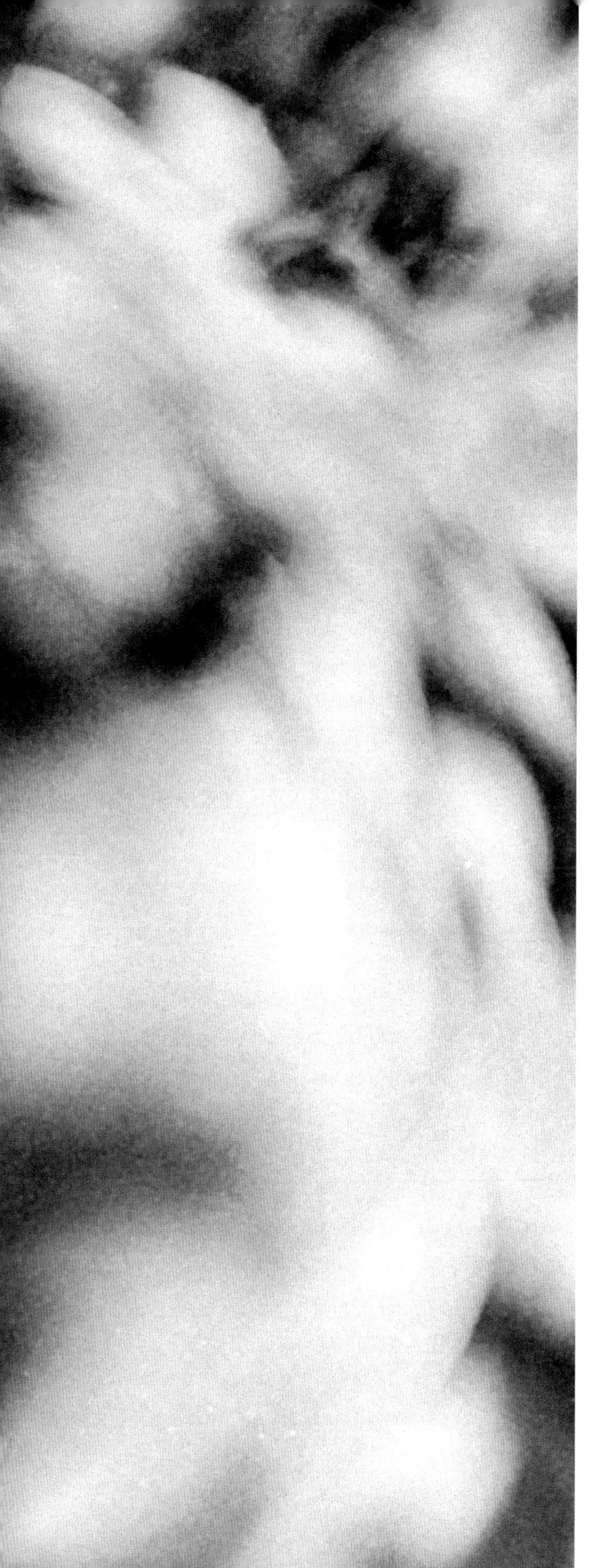

Appendix

A.1   Film, Chemicals, Accessories

B&H

Film, accessories
http://www.bhphotovideo.com

Film Photography Project

Film, instant film and cameras, darkroom supplies
http://filmphotographyproject.com

Freestyle Photographic Supplies

Film, paper, chemicals, alternative processes
http://www.freestylephoto.biz

Frugal Photographer

Film at unusual sizes (including 110 and 127), inexpensive 120 film, flash cubes and bulbs, film processing
http://www.frugalphotographer.com

Lomography

DigitaLIZA scanning accessory, film, cameras and lenses, positive paper
http://www.lomography.com

The Impossible Project

Instant film, cameras, accessories
http://impossible.supersense.com

A.2   Apps

Develop! Film Development Timer (iOS)

Film development timer, imports recipes from *filmdev.org*
https://apps.apple.com/us/app/develop/id568421864

Film Developer Pro (Android)

Development recipe database, development timer
https://play.google.com/store/apps/details?id=photography.darkroom.pro

Massive Dev Chart Timer (iOS & Android)

Development recipe database, development timer
iOS: *https://apps.apple.com/app/massive-dev-chart-timer/id402405770*
Android: *https://play.google.com/store/apps/details?id=com.digitaltruth.mdc&hl=us*

Shutter-Speed (iOS)

Determine camera shutter speeds
https://www.apple.com/us/search/shutter-speed?src=globalnav

A.3   Commercial Film Holders

pixl-latr

https://pixl-latr.com

Negative Supply

https://www.negative.supply/

Essential Filmholder

https://clifforth.co.uk

Valoi 360

https://www.valoi.co

Lomography DigitaLIZA+

https://shop.lomography.com/de/digitaliza

Lomography DigitaLIZA Max

https://shop.lomography.com/de/digitaliza-max

A.4 Other

Foma

Fomapan 100 R Black-and-White Reversal Film
http://www.foma.cz/en/fomapan-R-100

Gossen

Lunasix 3 Battery Adapter
http://www.gossen-photo.de/english/foto_s_batterie.php

A.5 Further Reading

Making Kodak Film, Expanded Second Edition

Robert L. Shanebrook
A behind-the-scenes look at how film is made
Shanebrook 2016
http://www.makingkodakfilm.com

The Film Developing Cookbook

Steve Anchel, BIll Troop
An in-depth look at film development chemistry
Focal Press 1999

The Chemistry of Photography

Roger K. Bunting
Photoglass Press 1982

The Albumen & Salted Paper Book: History and Practice of Photographic Printing 1840-1895

James M. Reilly
Cary Graphic Arts Press 2012
http://albumen.conservation-us.org/library/monographs/reilly/albumen-reilly_delivery.pdf

Alternative Photography

Mike Ware
http://www.mikeware.co.uk

Index